ORTHODOXY AND THE COURTS IN LATE ANTIQUITY

Orthodoxy and the Courts in Late Antiquity

CAROLINE HUMFRESS

OXFORD
UNIVERSITY PRESS

OXFORD
UNIVERSITY PRESS

Great Clarendon Street, Oxford, OX2 6DP,
United Kingdom

Oxford University Press is a department of the University of Oxford.
It furthers the University's objective of excellence in research, scholarship,
and education by publishing worldwide. Oxford is a registered trade mark of
Oxford University Press in the UK and in certain other countries

First Edition published in 2007

Published in the United States of America by Oxford University Press
198 Madison Avenue, New York, NY 10016, United States of America

British Library Cataloguing in Publication Data
Data available

Library of Congress Cataloging in Publication Data
Data available

ISBN 978–0–19–820841–9

For Mac Samuel Bradley and Edward Jack Hayden, in memory of their much loved Grandad.

Preface

It is the aim of this book to explore the remarkable culture of forensic argumentation that flourished during late antiquity, rather than the intellectual system of Roman law *per se*. Whilst my research has focused primarily on the later Roman Empire, I hope that legal historians, theologians, and medievalists alike might find the arguments in this book of interest. The project began its formal life as a doctoral thesis at St John's College, Cambridge, supervised by Peter Stein in its first year, and then by Peter Garnsey; submitted under the literal, rather than chic, designation: 'Forensic Practice in the Development of Roman and Ecclesiastical Law in Late Antiquity, with Special Reference to the Prosecution of Heresy.' I owe the incomparably more elegant title of the monograph to Jill Harries, with gratitude. The germ of the idea for the doctoral thesis in fact took hold during a supervision on St Augustine with George Garnett, held during the Lent term of my first year as an undergraduate, under an apple (as opposed to a fig) tree. The present book has preserved essentially the same structure and line of argument as the doctoral thesis, but the text itself has been rewritten extensively, partly in order to make certain revisions and modifications in the light of important recent scholarship (as noted in the Introduction below), but also because my own intellectual perspectives have, or so it seems to me at least, broadened considerably over the last six years.

First I would like to thank Peter Garnsey for his wisdom, guidance, and unfailing conviction that this research would finally see the light of day as a published volume; he also valiantly read and critiqued drafts at all stages of the project. My Ph.D. examiners, Henry Chadwick and David Johnston, made many insightful and constructive comments that have helped to shape my ideas; my thanks also to the former for gently enquiring, whenever we met, 'and the book, Caroline?'. Professor John Crook generously read my doctoral thesis and I am indebted to his razor-sharp observations and constructive criticisms, which on certain occasions caused me to entirely rethink the direction of my argument. Jill Harries kindly identified herself to me as an initial reader of my manuscript for OUP, and my thanks to her also for her subsequent encouragement and intellectual stimulation. The unstinting generosity of Professor Luigi Capogrossi Colognesi made repeated research trips to

Rome a joy. I am also indebted to Pasquale Rosafio for his intellectual insight and warm friendship, shared in Rome and Cambridge alike.

I would also like to express my gratitude to the fellows of Queens' College, Cambridge, St John's College, Cambridge, St Catherine's College, Oxford, and the British Academy for their support, alongside the electors and committee of the Carlyle Fellowship in the History of Political Thought at the University of Oxford. I also owe a deep debt of gratitude to my former colleagues and students in the Department of Rhetoric and Film Studies, University of Berkeley at California, and in particular to David Cohen. To my colleagues and students at Birkbeck, my sincere thanks for providing such a warm and intellectually stimulating research environment. Sincere thanks also to the staff of the Edoardo Volterra Collection, housed by L'École Française de Rome, where I had the good fortune to find much of the continental research that has formed my intellectual approach here, and in addition to the staff of Cambridge University Library, the Bodleian Library, Oxford, and the Robbins Collection at the Law School in Berkeley. Thanks are due to so many others for discussion, help and support, gratefully received, including: John Arnold, Mark Bevir, Daniel Boyarin, Brendan Bradshaw, Averil Cameron, Gillian Clark, Simon Corcoran, David D'Avray, Catharine Edwards, Karen Gray, Jose Harris, Matthew Innes, Neil McLynn, Fergus Millar, Lance Millar, Magnus Ryan, Paul Stephenson, and Shannon Stimson. I have explored a number of arguments relating to this book in conferences, seminars, and lectures at Cambridge, Oxford, London, Leeds, Bristol, Sydney, Berkeley, Princeton, Washington, DC, Vancouver, Paris, and Rome—my ideas have, as a result, benefited enormously. I am also grateful to Ruth Parr, who commissioned this book as an editor at OUP, and to Rupert Cousens and Seth Cayley who guided the manuscript through its final stages. I hope it goes without saying that remaining errors and oversights are all my own.

Finally, I wish to take this opportunity to record my profound debt of gratitude to my husband and all my family, in particular to my dearly loved Mum and sister, and to those who are no longer with us: Enid Humfress, William Fullerton Humfress, Carole Hurst, Bridget Hurst, James William Hurst, and my Father, Eric Humfress. Their love and encouragement is still felt, every day.

Contents

Abbreviations

AARC	*Atti dell'accademia romanistica costantiniana*
ACII	*Acta Congressus Iuridici Internationalis* (Rome)
ACO	E. Schwartz, *Acta conciliorum oecumenicum*, 4 vols. (Berlin and Leipzig: de Gruyter, 1914–74)
ANRW	*Aufstieg und Niedergang der römischen Welt: Geschichte und Kultur Roms im Spiegel der neueren Forschung*
BA	*Bibliothèque Augustinienne*
BASP	*Bulletin of the American Society of Papyrologists*
BGU	*Aegyptische Urkunden aus den Königlichen* (later *Staatlichen*) *Museen zu Berlin, Griechische Urkunden* (Berlin, 1895–)
BICS	*Bulletin of the Institute of Classical Studies of the University of London*
BIDR	*Bullettino dell'istituto di diritto romano*
BLE	*Bulletin de littérature ecclésiastique*
BMCR	*Bryn-Mawr Classical Review* (http://ccat.sas.upenn.edu/bmcr/)
BSNAF	*Bulletin de la Société Nationale des Antiquaires de France*
CAH	*Cambridge Ancient History*, NS (Cambridge University Press)
CCSL	*Corpus Christianorum: Series Latina*
Chiron	*Chiron: Mitteilungen der Kommission für alte Geschichte und Epigraphik des Deutschen Archäologischen Instituts*
CI	*Codex Justinianus*, ed. Paul Krüger, *Corpus Iuris Civilis*, ii. *Editio Minor* (Berlin, 1877)
CIL	*Corpus Inscriptionum Latinarum*
CJ	*Classical Journal*
Const. Cordi	*Constitution Cordi* (third preface to the 534 *Codex*, announcing its promulgation)
Const. Deo Auctore	*Constitution Deo Auctore* (first preface to Justinian's *Digest*)
Const. Haec	*Constitution Haec* (first preface to the 534 *Codex*, originally ordered the compilation of the first *Codex* in 528)
Const. Omnem	*Constitution Omnem* (second preface to Justinian's *Digest*)

Const. Summa	*Constitution Summa* (second preface to the 534 *Codex*, originally promulgated the first *Codex* in 529)
Const. Tanta	*Constitution Tanta* (third preface to Justinian's *Digest*)
CPR	*Corpus Papyrorum Raineri* (Vienna, 1895–1915)
CSCO	*Corpus Scriptorum Christianorum Orientalium*
CSEL	*Corpus Scriptorum Ecclesiasticorum Latinorum*
C.Th.	T. Mommsen and P. M. Meyer, *Theodosiani libri XVI cum Constitutionibus Sirmondianis: et leges novellae ad Theodosianum pertinentes*, 2 vols. (Berlin, 1905, publ. 1904)
C.Th. Kreuger	P. Krueger, *Codicis Theodosiani fragmenta Taurinensia* (Berlin: Duemmler, 1880)
D.	*Digesta Iustiniani*, T. Mommsen (ed.), *Corpus Iuris Civilis*, i (Berlin 1872). Tr. (unless specified), follow Alan Watson *et al.* (Philadelphia, 1985)
FIRA	S. Riccobono *et al.*, *Fontes Iuris Romani Anteiustiniani*, 2nd edn., 3 vols. (Florence: Barbèra, 1940–3)
GCS	*Die griechischen christlichen Schriftsteller der ersten drei Jahrhunderte*
ILS	H. Dessau, *Inscriptiones Latinae Selectae*, 3 vols. (Berlin: Weidmann, 1892–1916)
IURA	*Iura: rivista internazionale di diritto romano e antico*
JAC	*Jahrbuch für Antike und Christentum*
JRS	*Journal of Roman Studies*
JTS	*Journal of Theological Studies*
LABEO	*Labeo: rassegna di diritto romano*
Mandouze, *Prospopographie Chrétienne*	A. Mandouze, *Prosopographie Chrétienne du Bas-Empire*, i. *Prosopographie de l'Afrique Chrétienne (305–533)* (Paris: CNRS, 1982)
Mansi	*Sacrorum Conciliorum nova et amplissima collectio*, ed. J. D. Mansi
MEFR	*Mélanges d'archéologie et d'histoire de l'École Française, Rome*
MSNAF	*Memoires de la Société Nationale des Antiquitaires de France*
N. Marc.	Marcian, *Novellae*, in *C.Th.* ii
Nov. Iust.	*Novellae* (Justiniani), ed. Rudolf Schöll and Wilhelm Kroll, *Corpus Iuris Civilis*, iii (Berlin, 1895)
NPNF	*Nicene and Post-Nicene Fathers of the Church*

NRHDFE	*Nouvelle Revue Historique du Droit Français et Étranger*
N.Th.	Theodosius II, *Novellae*, in *C. Th.* ii
N. Val.	Valentinian III, *Novellae*, in *C. Th.* ii
NTS	*New Testament Studies*
P. Abin	*The Abinnaeus Archive: Papers of a Roman Officer in the Reign of Constantius II*, ed. H. I. Bell, V. Martin, E. G. Turner, and D. van Berchem (Oxford: Clarendon Press, 1962)
P. Ammon	*The Archive of Ammon Scholasticus of Panopolis*, i. *The Legacy of Harpocration*, ed. W. H. Willis and K. Maresch (Opladen: *Pap.Colon.* XXVI/1, 1997)
P. Berl. Zill	*Vierzehn Berliner griechische Papyri*, ed. H. Zilliacus (Helsingfors, 1941)
P. Cairo Maspero	*Papyrus grecs d'époque byzantine, Catalogue génèeral des antiquités égyptiennes du Musée du Caire*, 3 vols, ed. J. Maspero (Cairo, 1911–16)
P. Col.	*Columbia Papyri* (New York, 1929–)
P. Fam. Tebt.	*A Family Archive from Tebtunis*, ed. B. A. van Groningen (Leiden, 1950)
PG	*Patrologia Graeca*, ed. J. P. Migne
PL	*Patrologia Latina*, ed. J. P. Migne
P. Lips.	*Griechische Urkunden der Papyrussammlung zu Leipzig* (Leipzig 1906–)
P. Lond.	*Greek Papyri in the British Museum* (London, 1893–)
PLRE i	*Prosopography of the Later Roman Empire*, i, ed. A. H. M. Jones, J. Morris, and J. Martindale
PLRE ii	*Prosopography of the Later Roman Empire*, ii, ed. J. Martindale
P. Mert.	*A Descriptive Catalogue of the Greek Papyri in the Collection of Wilfred Merton*, ii, ed. B. R. Rees *et al.* (Dublin: Hodges, Figgis, 1959)
P. Mich.	*Michigan Papyri*
P. Oxy.	*Oxyrhynchus Papyri*
P. Princ.	*Papyri in the Princeton University Collections*
Projet Volterra I databases	Description of project and link to database at: http://www.ucl.ac.uk/history/volterra/perl/volterra.htm
P. Sakaon	G. M. Parássoglou (tr.), *The Archive of Aurelius Sakaon* (Bonn: Habelt, 1978)

P. Strass	*Griechische Papyrus der Kaiserlichen Universitäts- und Landes-bibliothek zu Strassburg*, ed. F. Preisigke (Leipzig, 1912–89)
PSI	*Papiri greci e latini* (Florence, 1912–79)
P. Thead	*Papyrus de Théadelphie*, ed. P. Jouguet (Paris: Cisalpino-La Goliardic, 1911)
RE Aug.	*Revue des Études Augustiniennes*
Rech. Aug.	*Recherches Augustiniennes*
RE	*Real-Encyclopädie der klassischen Altertumswissenschaft*, Pauly-Wissowa (-Kroll)
Rev. SR	*Revue des Sciences Religieuses*
RHD	*Revue d'Histoire du Droit* (*Tijdschrift voor Rechtsgeschiedenis*)
RHDFE	*Revue Historique de Droit Français et Étranger*
RIDA	*Revue Internationale des Droits de l'Antiquité*
RLM	*Rhetorici Latini Minores*, ed. K. F.Halm
SC	*Sources Chrétiennes*
SDHI	*Studia et Documenta Historiae et Iuris*
VC	*Vigiliae Christianae: A Review of Early Christian Life and Language*
ZKG	*Zeitschrift für Kirchengeschichte*
ZNW	*Zeitschrift für die Neutestamentliche Wissenschaft und die Kunde des Urchristentums*
ZPE	*Zeitschrift für Papyrologie und Epigraphik*
ZSS, Rom. Abt.	*Zeitschrift der Savigny-Stiftung für Rechtsgeschichte* (*Romanistische Abteilung*)
ZSS, Kan. Abt.	*Zeitschrift der Savigny-Stiftung für Rechtsgeschichte* (*Kanonistische Abteilung*)

Introduction

'Why do the Christians not worship the Emperor? Because he is not a god, but a man, appointed by God, not to receive homage, but to give judgment rightly.'[1] Late second-century 'Christians', such as Theophilus, bishop of Antioch, and non-Christians alike, could agree that the divine function of the Emperor included deciding the disputes of Roman citizens—even if some 'Christian' communities chose instead to follow the Gospel precepts and avoided the 'gentile' courts. With the advent of a 'Christian' Emperor in the early fourth century, Christianity itself became part of the structure, as well as the fabric, of Empire—the legal system was now accessible to 'Christians', as 'Christians'.

This book does not seek, however, to give an account of the gradual establishment of an imperial Christian church in late antiquity, nor does it set out, primarily at least, to analyse the extent to which Roman law must play a part in any narrative account of the 'rise of Christendom'. Nor have I attempted to write the story of a 'gradual fusing of two traditions':[2] the blending of a 'Roman' tradition of civil law, that by the fourth century focused almost exclusively on the relations between the inhabitants of Empire (rather than their relations with the gods), and a 'Christian' tradition of a divine law, focused on the precepts and rules laid down by the Christian God himself. The idea of a 'fusing' of Roman and Christian laws can certainly be found in certain texts from late antiquity, such as the so-called *Syro-Romano Lawbook*, possibly written in the mid-fifth century, within a Syriac tradition: 'But all laws became as nothing because of the Messiah's coming, and the one law of the Messiah was given for all people by the Christian kings, of whom the first was the chosen, saintly and victorious

[1] Theophilus of Antioch, *Ad Autolycum*, 1. 11, quoted from F. Millar, 'Paul of Samosata, Zenobia and Aurelian: The Church, Local Culture and Political Allegiance in Third-Century Syria', *Journal of Roman Studies*, 61 (1971), 1–17.

[2] T. Honoré, *Law in the Crisis of Empire* (Oxford: Clarendon Press, 1998), 122.

king Constantine.'[3] Nonetheless, as far as the Imperial bureaux were concerned, and indeed the ecclesiastical hierarchy itself, things divine, including the law of the Christian God, remained primarily the remit of priests, in this case Christian clerics.[4] Nor does this book include any extended discussion of the 'Christianization' of Roman law *per se*.[5] What this book does set out to explore is the vibrant and creative culture of late Roman forensic ('courtroom') argumentation—a culture in which some leading Christian ecclesiastics and polemicists were themselves thoroughly immersed.

A decade or two ago, this book would have begun with a chapter on why the dominant paradigm of the 'decline and fall' of Late Roman law should be resisted. The idea of the 'decline', 'decadence', or even 'barbarity' of late Roman law and its practitioners still persists in some contexts; however, both continental and Anglo-American scholars in the field now agree that late Roman law is worthy of study in its own right. Post-classical law should not simply be approached as a coda to 'classical' Roman law, or as a prelude to the Emperor Justinian and his *Corpus Iuris Civilis*.[6] As John Crook has noted, however, value judgements concerning the standard of legal practice under the Late Empire still tend to be less than complimentary.[7] In any event, I have found little convincing evidence for a sudden lapse in the quality or sophistication

[3] *Syro-Romano Lawbook*, quoted from W. Turpin, 'The Law-Codes and Late Roman Law', *RIDA*, 3rd ser., 32 (1985), 339–53, at 345.

[4] Compare e.g. the 'apostate' Emperor Julian's 'Fragment of a letter to a priest', 288C: 'Though just conduct in accordance with the laws of the state will evidently be the concern of governors of cities, you in your turn will properly take care to exhort men not to transgress the laws of the gods, since those are sacred' (tr. W. Cave Wright, Loeb Julian II, 298), with the 5th-cent. Imperial constitution translated in full from the *Acts of the Council of Chalcedon* by F. Millar, *A Greek Roman Empire. Power and Belief under Theodosius II (408–450)* (Berkeley and Los Angeles: University of California Press, 2006), 143.

[5] For this perspective, see the astute comments of A. D. Lee, 'Decoding Late Roman Law', *JRS*, 92 (2002), 192–3, with references to further literature.

[6] See Ch. 1 below. On the technical concept of 'post-classical' law as 'Vulgar' law see D. Simon, 'Marginalien zur Vulgarismusdiskussion', in O. Behrends *et al.* (eds.), *Festschrift für Franz Wieacker zum 70. Geburtstag* (Gottingen: Vandenhoeck & Ruprecht, 1978), 154–74.

[7] Extended discussion in Ch. 4. For continental scholarship the work of Edoardo Volterra, Jean Gaudemet, and Detlef Liebs, amongst others discussed below, are important exceptions. In Anglo-American scholarship, four books in particular have pointed the way forward: J. Crook, *Legal Advocacy in the Roman World* (London: Duckworth, 1995), J. Harries, *Law and Empire* (Cambridge, CUP, 1999), J. Matthews, *Laying Down the Law: A Study of the Theodosian Code* (New Haven and London: Yale University Press, 2000), and Honoré, *Law in Crisis*.

of forensic argumentation in the late third or fourth century. In fact, when viewed from the perspective of law forged in practice, and not just written down in texts, there is a remarkable continuity from Early to Late Empire—which is not the same as arguing, of course, that nothing changed at all.

The history of Roman law can, and indeed has, been written as a story of the 'separateness of law as a discipline, with its own assumptions and intellectual tradition'.[8] Whilst acknowledging the importance of this perspective, particularly in terms of the development of later Western legal traditions, I have chosen to focus rather on law as a process, and in particular on the ability of individuals to work any given (legal) system, and to create new 'law', albeit not in a 'formal' sense, through concrete legal practice on the ground. In this sense, I approach the Roman courts as 'venues for finding out how far one can go in practice'.[9] Much recent and valuable scholarly work has focused on the late Roman Emperor as an authoritative (or even authoritarian) legislator, in both symbolic and practical terms. However, as Marie-Therese Fögen has argued, non-professionals such as historians, philosophers, and orators also participate in the foundation of a system of laws.[10] I have set out, in this book, to widen the parameters systematically: I argue that forensic practice, what happened in the courtrooms, alongside other broader socio-legal norms and practices should be approached as essential components in understanding how 'law' functioned in the later Roman Empire. It is perhaps worth noting here that, in arguing for this perspective, I do not intend to reopen the early twentieth-century debate surrounding the ideas of Stroux and Lanfranchi on the 'rhetoricization of Roman law'; nonetheless, it seems that analysing law from the perspective of forensic rhetoric does open up avenues of research in late antiquity that would otherwise remain closed to the historian.[11] As the ancient Athenian orator Demosthenes implied, 'laws' do not interpret themselves—one of the most remarkable achievements of the Graeco-Roman world,

[8] Harries, *Law and Empire*, 4.

[9] C. Wickham, 'Conclusion', in P. Coss (ed.), *The Moral World of the Law* (Cambridge: CUP, 2000), 240–9, at 247.

[10] M.-T. Fögen, *Die Enteignung der Wahrsager: Studien zum kaiserlichen Wissensmonopol in der Spätantike* (Frankfurt/Main: Suhrkamp, 1993).

[11] J. Stroux, *Summum ius summa iniuria* (Freiburg: Himmelschein Symb. Friburgenses, 1926) and F. Lanfranchi, *Il diritto nei retori romani* (Milan: Giuffrè, 1938). On both, see the astute review of Lanfranchi's *Il diritto* by P. W. Duff in *JRS* (1950), 154–6. For further discussion see Ch. 1 below, with particular reference to the ideas of the great 20th-cent. Romanist, Salvatore Riccobono.

then, was to develop an entire system of practical rhetoric to aid in that 'interpretative' process.[12]

In Part I I explore the contribution of forensic practitioners, especially (but not only) 'judges', legal experts (*iurisperiti* or *iurisconsulti*), and advocates, to the development of late Roman law. This analysis rests on two fundamental premisses: first, that legal experts (*iurisperiti*) were still active in late antiquity, in particular advising private clients who had the necessary means to access their services on jurisprudential questions (i.e. queries about the substantive principles of Roman law), as and when they arose. A fundamental change had taken place by at least the early fourth-century, however, in that 'jurists', in the sense of 'independent' classical jurists, had been increasingly absorbed into the imperial bureaucracy itself.[13]

The second fundamental premise of Part I argues that forensic rhetoric, the branch of rhetorical practice associated with pleading in the courts, remained the domain of the advocate, even in those cases where a late Roman advocate had received additional 'legal'/juristic training.[14] Pleading in court was the advocate's area of expertise, in the classical and post-classical Roman legal systems alike. Moreover, I shall argue that the connection between rhetorical training and forensic practice, noted for the rhetorical schools under the Early Empire, also continued into late antiquity—in the Eastern and Western Empires alike (although, as we shall see, with some regional and local variations). In other words, the late antique 'rhetorical schools' continued to provide an essentially practical training, focused on how to plead a case persuasively and convincingly within any given ('legal') context. Pleading a case might not involve any particular issue of substantive legal principle, a case could turn for example on a plausible reconstruction of 'facts', motives, or opportunity, amongst other issues (including, perhaps more realistically, how much a judge or court official had been bribed or the patronage network of the individual(s) instituting or defending the case). When issues of legal interpretation did arise in court, however, the business of both the advocate and the privately hired *iurisperitus* was

[12] Demosthenes, Oration 21 *Against Meidias*, 224: 'And what is the strength of the laws? If one of you is wronged and cries aloud, will the laws run up and be at his side to assist him? No; they are only written texts and incapable of such action. Wherein then resides their power? In yourselves, if only you support them and make them all-powerful to help him who needs them. So the laws are strong through you and you through the laws' (tr. A. T. Murray, 1939).

[13] Ch. 3 below. [14] See esp. Chs. 1 and 4 below.

to interpret the law, not for the greater coherence of imperial legislation, but for the good of the client.

The activity of forensic practitioners not only contributed to the sentencing of individual cases, it was also capable of inspiring imperial legislation.[15] As argued throughout Part I of this book, and beyond into Parts II and III, a constant dialectic operated between law 'in practice' and 'law' as issued in imperial constitutions. In fact, to view the imperial constitutions themselves as simply 'Laying down the Law' (with a capital 'L') sidelines the essentially responsive nature of late Roman legislation—even as it adequately mirrors the emperors' own self-advertisement of their 'sole' law-making authority.

Part II of the book suggests that an education in forensic rhetoric was also part of the educational formation of leading figures in the late antique Christian church. An education in forensic rhetoric, learnt as a practical skill within 'secular' contexts and then applied in the service of the Church, could be compatible with being a 'Christian', despite those late Roman individuals (such as Jerome) who eloquently expressed their doubts. The idea that an antithesis might exist between a 'pagan' rhetorical education and a 'Christian' formation was expressed in late Roman sources, especially perhaps from the early fifth century onwards; however, leading Christian ecclesiastics could and did make extensive use of skills and techniques learnt at the Late Roman rhetorical schools. Some leading ecclesiastics and polemicists had even practised as advocates, or taught future ones, and some had been active as legal experts and judges/arbitrators. This is not to suggest, of course, that all late Roman bishops, in particular, had received this kind of educational formation and Chapter 6 below discusses a variety of other episcopal social origins. Moreover, as Claudia Rapp has argued, the concept of 'charismatic' and spiritual authority is an integral part of episcopal power.[16] In fact, the figure of the uneducated, unlettered bishop became itself a celebrated late antique literary topos. Nonetheless, the particular forensic backgrounds of some leading bishops, monks, and Christian polemicists has been relatively neglected in modern scholarship (or at least in later twentieth-century accounts).[17]

[15] See in particular Ch. 2 below, but this argument is also stressed in Part III.

[16] C. Rapp, *Holy Bishops in Late Antiquity: The Nature of Christian Leadership in an Age of Transition* (Berkeley and Los Angeles: University of California Press, 2005).

[17] Ch. 5 below.

The life of the late Roman church, at least as far as disputes were concerned, was dominated by a culture of forensic argumentation. Individuals within the church applied their forensic and legal skills in a variety of different contexts, including dispute resolution, as well as on occasion scriptural exegesis. They also contributed to the early development of a system of 'ecclesiastical' or 'canon' law peculiar to the church itself (Chapter 7).

Forensic expertise also, however, contributed to the exacerbation of 'internal' Christian disputes. Between the fourth and sixth centuries a vast body of legislation against specific named Christian 'heretics' was issued by the imperial authorities. Theology interacted with Roman law case-by-case, defining and categorizing heretical groups and establishing penalties that covered both this life and the next.[18] Part III analyses the role that forensic practitioners played in the development of anti-heresy legislation, and also explores the way in which 'heresy' itself became a lived reality in a number of different late antique contexts, stretching from the age of Constantine to Justinian. Legal decisions by Roman Emperors were an important mechanism by which issues of authority could be resolved within the church; however, modern scholars have tended to privilege the authoritative position of these imperial constitutions by concentrating on what they prescribed, rather than the way in which they were generated and used in practice.

Virtually no historical studies have sought to investigate how individual prosecutions were undertaken on the basis of accusations involving charges of heresy, nor how defence strategies were developed by those who stood accused. The case study of the prosecution of heretics in Chapter 9 thus acts as a culmination to the ideas contained in Parts I and II. In the particular case of heresy, new legal categories were developed case by case; advocates, *iurisconsulti*, and *iudices* (both secular and ecclesiastical) played an important role in the development of these new theological/legal classifications. The prosecution of heretics also had important implications for the interaction between law and theology in a crucial area of Christian self-definition: the creation of 'orthodox' Christian belief itself.

[18] Ch. 8 below.

I

FORENSIC PRACTITIONERS AND THE DEVELOPMENT OF LATE ROMAN LAW

1

Introduction and Background

FROM LATE REPUBLIC TO LATE EMPIRE

In September 91 BC, as Cicero presents it, a debate took place at the Tusculan villa of L. Licinius Crassus on the question of whether legal studies ought to form part of an advocate's education. The augur Q. Mucius Scaevola, erudite in Roman legal science, declared it was a desirable ideal, but rarely in his experience had he seen it realized in practice. Crassus, an advocate with renowned legal expertise and Cicero's boyhood tutor in rhetoric, likewise argued that a grasp of civil law was essential to the advocate in court and proceeded to recount a long list of forensic orators who had lost their cases because they blundered in the most trifling and insignificant legal technicalities (*De Oratore* 1. 166–70). According to Cicero's characterization, both Scaevola (an orator and jurist) and Crassus (a legally skilled orator) were agreed that advocates ought to be educated in the *ius civile.* Cicero, however, has M. Antonius—himself a distinguished advocate and former consul but with no formal training in Roman law—object to Scaevola's and Crassus' line of reasoning:

For if you were claiming that anyone who is a jurisconsult is also an orator and, likewise, that anyone who is an orator is at the same time a jurisconsult, then you would be setting up two noble arts, equal to each other and partners in dignity. As it is, you admit that there can be, and indeed have been, numerous jurisconsults who did not possess the kind of eloquence that we are examining, while you deny that one can be an orator without also acquiring this knowledge of the law. Thus, from your point of view, the jurisconsult in his own right is nothing but a cautious and clever legal technician, a crier of prescribed phrases, a chanter of formulas, a snatcher of syllables. But just because the orator often enlists the support of the law when pleading his cases, you have attached legal knowledge to eloquence as a sort of slave girl, an attendant.[1]

[1] *De Oratore* 1. 236: 'Nam, si ita diceres, qui iurisconsultus esset, esse eum oratorem, itemque qui esset orator, iuris eumdem esse consultum: praeclaras duas artes constitueres,

Antonius' objection is then reinforced by a list of practical arguments against the acquisition of legal knowledge by the forensic orator: there is dissent as to the law even amongst the most juristically skilled of men (1. 238); even if there are disagreements amongst legal experts the role of the advocate is simply to find some authority in favour of whichever side he is supporting and to hurl these javelins with all the might of his orator's arm (1. 242); and in any case the ancient statutes have either sunk into the decrepitude of their old age, or have been repealed by new laws (1.247). Antonius' coup de grâce is that the study of civil law may even be harmful to the orator, as it drives out the essential lessons on eloquence learnt in the rhetorical schools.

In the later Roman Empire learned men were still debating the relative merits of rhetoric and law in the training of the forensic orator, despite the fact that the social and political context for the practice of both advocacy and jurisprudence had changed fundamentally since the time of Cicero.[2] In an oration probably delivered in AD 382, the renowned Antiochene rhetorician, Libanius, attempted to defend himself from potentially ruinous accusations that he was a useless educator by laying the blame at law's door:

> Always before this, you could see youngsters from the factories whose concern was for their daily bread, going off to Phoenicia to gain a knowledge of law, while those of well-to-do houses, with illustrious family, property, and fathers who had performed civic services, stayed at school here. And it was thought that to learn law was a mark of lower status, while not to need it indicated a higher standing, but now there is a mass stampede towards it, and lads who know how to speak and are able to move an audience race to Berytus [Beirut] with the idea of getting some advantage.[3]

atque inter se pares, et eiusdem socias dignitatis. Nunc vero, iurisconsultum sine hac eloquentia, de qua quaerimus, fateris esse posse, fuisseque plurimos, oratorem negas, nisi illam scientiam assumpserit, esse posse. Ita est tibi iurisconsultus ipse per se nihil, nisi leguleius quidam cautus et acutus, praeco actionum, cantor formularum auceps syllabarum; sed quia saepe utitur orator subsidio iuris in causis, idcirco istam iuris scientiam eloquentiae, tanquam ancillulam pedisequamque, adiunxisti.' Tr. J. M. May and J. Wisse, Cicero *On the Ideal Orator* (New York and Oxford: OUP, 2001), 116.

2 On the practice of advocacy and jurisprudence in the 1st cent BC see E. Fantham, *The Roman World of Cicero's* De Oratore (Oxford: OUP, 2004), 102–30, and A. Lewis, 'The Autonomy of Roman Law', in P. Coss (ed.), *The Moral World of the Law* (Cambridge: CUP, 2000), 37–47.

3 Libanius, *Oration* 62. 21, ed. Foerster (Leipzig: Teubner, 1963 repr.), iv. 357, tr. A. F. Norman, *Antioch as a Centre of Hellenic Culture as Observed by Libanius* (Liverpool: Liverpool University Press, 2000), 95.

According to Libanius, ill-bred boys had always studied law at Beirut whilst the well-bred remained at Antioch—content to master the art of rhetoric from him. What had changed, therefore, was that the well-bred now thought it a career advantage to seek out teachers of law.[4] As John Matthews has stated: 'Most modern writers see in such passages the recognition of a real and significant shift from the old literary to the new professional studies'—those in question being shorthand-writing and law as taught in late Roman law schools (such as the famous school of Beirut).[5] Leaving the notaries and their technical practice to one side for the moment, should we accept that the law schools flourished at the expense of the schools of rhetoric in the late fourth-century East? Writing in 1946, Schulz argued on the basis of Libanius' *Oration* 62. 21 that 'by the fourth century things had changed in the Eastern Empire: advocates were now really lawyers'.[6] Honoré's 1998 discussion of the evidence from Libanius links the apparent rise in the status and numbers of 'lawyers' (professional legal experts) with a growing imperial concern for 'fostering the rule of law' in the East. Honoré suggests that the Emperors Constantius II and Theodosius II attempted to make their governments 'more professional' by recruiting lawyers and short-hand writers, 'often of humble extraction'. In addition to the issue of social status, Honoré comments that 'Professionals are not popular with the amateurs whom they displace, and Libanius expressed the shock of those to whom good family and a command of rhetoric were obviously sufficient for high office'.[7] Note that the 'amateur' referred to here by Honoré is the advocate or bureaucrat who has been trained in rhetoric. So, on the basis of Libanius' evidence, we have an argument where the prestige of law was on the ascendancy in the late fourth century and advocates (or bureaucrats in general) could no longer rely on rhetorical

[4] On trained rhetoricians who subsequently studied law see also Libanius, *Oration* 50. 6–7, *Ep.* 339, and *Ep.* 1013; P. Petit, *Les Étudiants de Libanius* (Paris: CNRS, 1957), 181.

[5] Matthews, *Laying Down the Law*, 23 and n. 43 citing Jones, *Later Roman Empire*, 512, 753, 989–90; J. H. W. G. Liebeschuetz, *Antioch: City and Imperial Administration in the Later Roman Empire* (Oxford: OUP, 1971), 242–55, and Honoré, *Law in Crisis*, 9–10. See also the discussion of Libanius' passage in B. Sirks, 'Instruction in Late Antiquity: The Law and Theology', *AARC* 15 (2005), 493–513, at 493–6.

[6] F. Schulz, *History of Roman Legal Science* (Oxford: Clarendon Press, 1946; repr. with addenda 1963), 268–9. For the Western Empire Schulz clarifies that 'the advocate was still in the first place a rhetorician' (ibid. 270).

[7] Honoré, *Law in Crisis*, 10.

training as an adequate preparation for practice. In the Eastern Empire at least, late antiquity was the age of the 'lawyer', trained in established schools of law—yet, as we shall see, few modern historians would agree that is was also the age of the 'true' jurisprudential expert.[8] All of which suggests a late Roman culture in which 'lawyers' (in the East at least) were expected to display legal learning, but not to the standards set by the classical period of Roman law.

What, then, was the fate of the rhetorically trained advocate—as championed by Cicero's Antonius—in late antiquity? Let us return to Libanius' argument in *Oration* 62. Having noted the stampede to study law at Beirut by the well-born young men of the day, Libanius continues:

> But what they haven't noticed is that, instead of getting some advantage, they are getting an exchange . . . So as to whether they behave so with the idea that their pursuit of law is the pursuit of a more useful acquisition, I believe that it is no matter of inquiry, for there is no question today of acquiring leave to bring a lawsuit between law and rhetoric. But it is enough for me to demonstrate that the skills instilled by earlier studies must inevitably be ruined by the effects of the later, and these must prevail, while the former vanishes, in some cases completely, in others, to no inconsiderable degree.[9]

In echoing the words of Antonius' coup de grâce in Cicero's *De Oratore*, Libanius is (self-consciously) entering into a debate on the merits of the legally skilled advocate that was almost as old as the Roman profession itself.[10] Libanius' remarks on legal study also need to be read in the context of his oration as a whole.[11] In *Oration* 62 Libanius is defending himself against 'slanderous' accusations that he is a bad educator whose ex-pupils have not prospered in their careers. Libanius is not complaining that the law school at Beirut has stolen pupils who would otherwise

[8] Matthews, *Laying Down the Law*, 23–9, discusses the 'prevalence of Roman law in the cities of the East', the rise of the legally trained 'lawyer' and the modern perception of 'a serious decline in the quality of late Roman jurisprudence'. See also T. Honoré, 'Roman Law AD 200–400', in S. Swain and M. Edwards (eds.), *Approaching Late Antiquity* (Oxford: OUP, 2004), 111, and J. Crook, *Legal Advocacy in the Roman World* (London: Duckworth, 1995), 175–8 and 188–92.

[9] Libanius, *Oration* 62. 22–3, ed. Foerster iv. 357, tr. Norman, *Antioch*, 95 (with slight modification).

[10] Also Cicero, *De Legibus* 1. 12 and Quintilian, *Inst.* 12. 3. 9–11. Tacitus (or Ps-Tacitus, *pace* Crook, *Legal Advocacy*, 10) has Messala argue that a forensic orator must have knowledge of the civil law in the *Dialogus de oratoribus* (late 1st cent AD)

[11] As briefly noted by M. Heath, *Menander: A Rhetor in Context* (Oxford: OUP, 2004), 282–3.

have come to him for rhetorical instruction; he is implying that good students from good families have raced off to law school after their rhetorical education with him. These ex-students believed that formal legal instruction would give them an edge in the careers that Libanius' rhetorical training had already equipped them for—but in fact their formal legal study undid all Libanius' good work. Hence, the audience is expected to conclude, it is not Libanius' fault if those same ex-students subsequently turn out to be deficient pleaders whom nobody wishes to employ in lawsuits.[12] Libanius' stress on the attractions of the law school at Beirut is thus part of an elaborate self-defence strategy, which in turn relies on an argument that formal legal instruction is harmful to the trained rhetorician. *Oration* 62. 21–3 thus cannot be read simply as literal evidence for a 'real and significant shift' from rhetorical to legal studies in the late fourth-century East.

In the Late Empire proficiency in rhetoric signalled membership in a cultural and political elite. As Peter Brown has (persuasively) argued, powerful men knew the art of persuasion.[13] An education in rhetoric demanded the mastery of complex and sophisticated rules of spoken and written communication. It could take up to six years to complete. Rhetorical instruction thus functioned as a way of 'making men'; it necessitated a disciplining of the self so that the student could successfully negotiate the elite social code that they aspired to operate within.[14] Whilst this cultural and political dimension to rhetorical education is crucially important in understanding the functioning of elite networks in late antique society, we must also remember that rhetoric continued to operate as a specific career-orientated training for forensic advocacy. Between the fourth and sixth centuries AD, the skills acquired through an education in rhetoric were still acknowledged as the proper training for a forensic advocate. Of course, not everyone who

[12] In an *Oration* composed in AD 388–9 Libanius states that the consul of Syria, Eutropius, had formally studied rhetoric, then law, as a youth; however, 'when he was inscribed onto the roll of advocates he never pleaded for anyone, neither for strangers nor citizens, not for men nor women, not for the poor nor the rich' (Libanius, *Oration* 4, ed. Foerster (Leipzig: Teubner, 1963 repr.), i. 279–300). Here Libanius uses the topos that law drives out eloquence to attack Eutropius' social and professional reputation.

[13] P. Brown, *Power and Persuasion in Late Antiquity. Towards a Christian Empire* (Madison: University of Wisconsin Press, 1992), 35–70. Also P. Brown, *Authority and the Sacred: Aspects of the Christianisation of the Roman World* (Cambridge: CUP, 1995), 38–40.

[14] For discussion see M. Gleason, *Making Men: Sophists and Self-Presentation in Ancient Rome* (Princeton: Princeton University Press, 1994).

had mastered the art of rhetoric decided to practise advocacy—and not everyone who practised advocacy had been trained for the job.[15] The important point to note is that those who did move straight from rhetoric to the law courts were not thought of as 'amateur' lawyers, but rather skilled 'professional' pleaders. Just as Cicero's Antonius had been.

The evidence from Libanius does suggest, however, that certain individuals from propertied 'well-to-do' houses hoped that a period of formal legal study might advance their careers as advocates. Libanius' 'well-to-do' individuals belonged to the Eastern civic elite, the curial class; we meet with a similar argument that advocates from high-status families should be formally educated in law in the Late Roman Republic.[16] In the Late Republic the venues that could demand the highest level of forensic expertise, where a personal reputation could be lost through lack of formal legal knowledge in complex high-status cases, were the centumviral courts; in the Late Empire it was the imperial bureaucratic courts of the Praetorian Prefects. Those whose expectations (and patronage connections) stretched to being enrolled as pleaders in the Praetorian courts may well have seen formal legal study as an essential preparation for their forensic practice. High-ranking imperial officials, who may have had the ear of the Emperor, frequented the Praetorian courts; as did high-status elite litigants and spectators. The courts of the Praetorian Prefects also functioned as the highest courts of appeal where—by definition—the most complex cases were heard. An ambitious advocate, with the necessary social standing, money, and patronage connections, stood the best chance of consolidating his reputation here. Accordingly, the Praetorian courts were the only venues where formal legal instruction came to be prescribed for advocates in late antiquity.[17] Formal legal study was thus in general viewed as an optional 'extra' for advocates in the Late Empire; it was thought essential

[15] Libanius, *Oration* 62. 46 (ed. Foerster, iv. 369–70): Heliodorus, a 'hawker of fish-pickle', 'divided his interests between the sale of fish-pickle and *listening to lawsuits*, and in a short time, [he] suddenly made his appearance as an orator'. According to Libanius, Heliodorus was extremely successful but never managed to live down jokes about fish-pickle—this story should also be understood as another strand in Libanius' self-defence strategy in *Oration* 62.

[16] *D.* 1. 2. 2. 43 (Pomponius): Quintus Mucius declared that 'it was disgraceful for a Patrician of noble family who regularly appeared as an advocate in the courts to be ignorant of the law on which his cases turned'.

[17] Libanius, *Ep.* 916, *Ep.* 172, and *Oration* 58. 26 implies that Tatianus, Praetorian Prefect of the East, required legal study for admission to his bar in AD 388. Honoré, *Law in Crisis*, 7, doubts Libanius' accuracy; Petit, *Les Étudiants*, 182, notes Libanius' statement that Tatianus' 'law' was in any case repealed in 390. It was not until 460 that

at only the highest levels of the bureaucratic courts. In the Late Empire, as in the Late Republic, there were advocates whose only training was in rhetoric, as well as some advocates who in addition undertook a formal legal training.[18] As we shall see, especially in papyrological reports of 'lower level' court proceedings, pleading a case successfully did not necessarily demand a familiarity with the complex subtleties of juristic reasoning.

Teachers of late Roman rhetoric (including Libanius) were well aware that advocates needed a basic legal framework to operate within—as did any Roman citizen who owned property, made gifts, swore oaths or contracts, or had any kinds of dealings that touched upon the civil law. As the late Roman rhetorical handbooks demonstrate, some knowledge of Roman law, and legal procedure in particular, was thus provided within formal rhetorical instruction.[19] With an echo once again of the Ciceronian debate, a fifth-century Latin handbook on the art of rhetoric advises future advocates that: 'The study of the civil law is not to be passed over; nor however should it be pursued in any depth. For the orator should not be ignorant [on the subject]. However, if he gives a great deal of attention to legal science the style and force of his oratory will suffer considerable consequences.'[20] In the Late Western Empire, as in the East, forensic advocates were expected to be trained in rhetoric, whether or not they ignored the advice of teachers such as Julius Severianus and took legal study (too) seriously. On the other hand, as already noted above, advocates who were attached to the top-level Praetorian courts could be expected to display a professional standard of legal knowledge. Even an advocate who had been formally trained in law, however, did not deploy this knowledge 'neutrally' in the interests of greater legal coherence; his legal expertise was deployed tactically in order to win the client's case through persuasive argument.

Ammianus Marcellinus' *History of the Late Roman Empire* (completed at Rome in the 390s) offers us four types of rapacious advocates whom he

the Eastern Emperor Leo made legal study a prerequisite for being enrolled on the list of advocates at the Eastern Praetorian court (*CI* 2. 7. 11).

[18] As noted by Honoré, 'Roman Law AD 200–400', 121, *contra* Jones, *Later Roman Empire*, i. 499–501.

[19] See Ch. 4 below.

[20] Julius Severianus, *Praecepta artis rhetoricae* 2 = *RLM* 356, 1. 2–5: 'Iuris vero civilis neque omittendum studium est nec penitus adpetendum; nam nec rudis esse debeat orator, et si se multum iuris scientiae dederit, plurimum de cultu orationis adque impetu amittet.'

apparently had the misfortune to come across during his residence in the East. Ammianus' famous excursus at 30. 4. 3–22 is, as he himself styles it, a discussion of 'the profession of forensic orators'. It is Ammianus' second type of forensic orator, however, that has attracted the attention of modern scholars ever since Gothofredus, writing in 1665, referred to it in order to illustrate the decline of jurisprudence in the Late Empire.[21] This second type is characterized by modern scholarship as, once again, the 'lawyer' with a formal legal education:

> The second class comprises those who profess a knowledge of law, which, however the self-contradictory statutes have destroyed, and reticent as if they were muzzled, in never-ending silence they are like their own shadows. These men, as though revealing destinies by nativities or interpreting a Sibyl's oracles, assume a solemn expression of severe bearing and try to make even their yawning saleable. In order to seem to have a deeper knowledge of the law they quote Trebatius and Cascellius and Alfenus and laws of the Aurunci and Sicani which have long been obsolete, buried centuries ago with the mother of Evander. And if you pretend that you have purposely murdered your mother, they promise, if they have observed that you are rich, that their many recondite studies will secure an acquittal for you.[22]

According to Matthews, Ammianus' second class of 'lawyer' is the only 'professional' type mentioned in the excursus: 'The one category that is to some extent recognisable in professional terms is the second, that of the jurisconsults. Here Ammianus does offer some points of legal interest.'[23] Honoré, on the other hand, acknowledges that Ammianus'

[21] Gothofredus, *Comm. C.Th.* i, pp. ccxxiii–ccxxiv. J. Matthews, 'Ammianus on Roman Law and Lawyers', in J. den Boeft *et al.* (eds.), *Cognitio Gestorum: The Historiographical Art of Ammianus Marcellinus* (Amsterdam: Royal Netherlands Academy of Arts and Sciences, 1992), 47–57, and Matthews, *Laying Down the Law*, 19, focus on Ammianus' 'attitude to the civil law' and his moral judgements on 'lawyers'; as do G. Sabbah (ed.), *Ammianus Marcellinus* (Paris: Budé, 1999), vi. 220–1 at n. 257, and D. Liebs, *Die Jurisprudenz im spätantiken Italien (260–640 n. Chr)* (Berlin: Duncker & Humblot, 1987), 98.

[22] Ammianus Marcellinus, 30. 4. 11–12, ed. Sabbah vi. 69–70: 'Secundum est genus eorum, qui iuris professi scientiam, quam repugnantium sibi legum aboleuere discidia, velut vinculis ori inpositis, reticentes, iugi silentio umbrarum sunt similes propriarum. Hi, velut fata natalicia praemonstrantes aut Sibyllae oraculorum interpretes, vultus grauitate ad habitum conposita tristiorem, ipsum quoque venditant quod oscitantur. Hi ut altius videantur iura callere, Trebatium loquuntur et Cascellium et Alfenum, Auruncorum Sicanorumque iam diu leges ignotas, cum Euandri matre abhinc saeculis obrutas multis. Et si voluntate matrem tuam finxeris occidisse, multas tibi suffragari absolutionem lectiones reconditas pollicentur, si te senserint esse nummatum' (tr. W. Hamilton, *The Later Roman Empire AD 354–378* (London: Penguin Classics, 1986).

[23] Matthews, 'Ammianus on Roman Law', 49

second type refers to advocates with legal training, but stresses their overall incompetence: their 'knowledge of classical law was not combined with a proper grasp of the imperial constitutions. Their advice could be dangerously misleading.'[24] Legal incompetence is a charge frequently laid against late Roman advocates in modern secondary scholarship.[25]

Ammianus Marcellinus' satirical comments on 'legally trained' advocates have been linked by modern historians to section 21 of an almost contemporary text: *De Rebus Bellicis*.[26] The anonymous author of this text (like Ammianus, writing at Rome) addressed a plea to the Emperors to remedy the contradictions and confusion of the laws with their 'divine medicine'—and by implication, through a process of codification.[27] On the basis of this passage from the *De Rebus Bellicis* Falchi argues that, in the late fourth century: 'There was full recognition of the state of uncertainty of law, deriving either from the contradictory opinions of jurisprudence, or from the abundance and fragmentation of Imperial constitutions.'[28] Yet, as we have already seen, this charge was laid against legal science in the first century BC in Cicero's *De Oratore*. It is included in Antonius' practical objections to the orator being compelled to study law.

A perceived need for systematic codification did not suddenly arise in the Late Empire; already in 45 BC Julius Caesar had proposed a scheme for the codification of existing statutes with the force of law, to be prepared by C. Ofilius.[29] This plan, however, was never realized. Most of the work of compiling authoritative legal texts into a referable system took place from the late third century AD onwards. For this reason the post-classical period is often described as the 'age of compilation', usually with reference to the *Codex Gregorianus* (*c*.292), the *Codex Hermogenianus* (*c*.295, with later additions), the *Codex Theodosianus* (promulgated in 438), the so-called 'barbarian codes' (including the

[24] T. Honoré, 'The Making of the Theodosian Code', *ZSS, Rom. Abt.* 103 (1986), 174, and Honoré, *Law in Crisis*, 196.

[25] See Ch. 4 below.

[26] Matthews, 'Ammianus on Roman Law', 49, and *Laying Down the Law*, 19–20; also Sabbah, *Ammianus Marcellinus*, vi. 221 at n. 258.

[27] On the plea for 'codification' see the discussion of D. Nörr, 'Zu den geistigen und sozialen Grundlagen der spätantiken Kodifikationsbewegung (Anon. *de rebus bellicis* xxi)', *ZSS, Rom. Abt.* 80 (1963), 109–40. Matthews, 'Ammianus on Roman Law', 49, and Harries, *Law and Empire*, 9, also place the *De Rebus Bellicis* passage in the context of the codification of the *Theodosian Code*.

[28] F. L. Falchi, *Sulla codificazione del diritto romano nel v e vi secolo* (Rome: Pontificia universitas lateranensis, 1989), 9.

[29] Suetonius, *Div. Jul.* 1. 44.

Breviarium of the Visigothic King Alaric, issued *c.*506), and the *Corpus Iuris Civilis* of Justinian (completed in 534). Whereas these codes are often viewed as compilations of Imperial constitutions alone, the original AD 429 plan for the compilation of the *Codex Theodosianus* signalled a concern with systematizing the vast juristic elaboration of legal principles between the first and early third centuries;[30] as did the sixth-century *Breviarium* of Alaric and Justinian's *Digest*. Whilst acknowledging the particular concrete political circumstances that gave the impetus to each of these very different late Roman codes, the post-classical activity of compilation should be viewed, in general, as an evolutionary stage of legal development.[31] As Honoré phrases it, there is a new emergent view of late Roman legal history which 'rejects the straightforward model of decline. It seeks to strike a balance between elements of decline and elements of progress, elements of continuity and elements of change.'[32]

Whether we view codification as a symptom of legal evolution or decline, however, it is still understood by most historians as an attempt to 'fix' or 'stabilize' law. Late Roman codification is thus still viewed as an inherently uncreative activity—contrasting unfavourably with the creative reasoning of the classical jurists themselves. This tone was set by the great twentieth-century textbooks of Roman law: for example, Schulz, writing in 1946, stated that post-classical law's 'tendency to convert all law into statute law' was 'quite alien to earlier Roman jurisprudence. . . The tendency of the jurists had been rather the contrary, namely to prevent the law from being petrified and stabilised.' In 1952 Jolowicz stated unequivocally that the post-classical period had never produced 'constructive work' comparable to that of classical

[30] Gesta Senatus 4 = *C.Th.* 1. 1. 5, brilliantly discussed in the context of the later 435 text (itself excerpted at *C.Th.* 1. 1. 6) by Matthews, *Laying Down the Law*, 55–71.

[31] On the particular circumstances that prompted the compilation of the Diocletianic *Codex Gregorianus* and *Codex Hermogenianus*, see S. Corcoran, 'The Publication of Law in the Era of the Tetrarchs: Diocletian, Galerius, Gregorius, Hermogenian', in A. Demandt *et al.* (eds.), *Diokletian und die Tetrarchie, Aspekte einer Zeitenwende* (Berlin and New York: de Gruyter, 2004), 56–73; for the *Codex Theodosianus*, Matthews, *Laying Down the Law*, 1–54; for the 'barbarian' codes, T. Charles-Edwards, 'Law in the Western Kingdoms between the Fifth and the Seventh Century', *Cambridge Ancient History*, xiv, ed. A. Cameron *et al.* (Cambridge: CUP, 2001), 260–87; on Justinian's compilation, C. Humfress, 'Law and Legal Practice in the Age of Justinian', in M. Maas (ed.), *Cambridge Companion to the Age of Justinian* (Cambridge and New York: CUP, 2005), 161–84.

[32] Honoré, 'Roman Law AD 200–400', 109. For 'positive' general assessments see Matthews, *Laying Down the Law*; also Honoré, *Law in Crisis*, 127–8, and Harries, *Law and Empire*, 59–60, as noted by A. D. Lee, 'Decoding Late Roman Law', *Journal of Roman Studies*, 92 (2002), 187.

times.[33] John Matthews, whose recent monograph, *Laying Down the Law: A Study of the Theodosian Code*, has gone further than any previous study towards understanding the complexity of late Roman legal texts, still sounds a cautionary note: 'The fourth century was as much a time of litigation and lawyers as any other period of the Roman Empire; how should it be otherwise? A question still attaches to the quality of the product, and some observers have perceived a serious decline in the quality of late Roman jurisprudence.'[34] Detlef Liebs, on the other hand, has challenged this assessment of a serious decline in late Roman jurisprudence, through a systematic analysis of late Roman juristic literature and the identification of named *iurisconsulti* who practised as such between the third and sixth centuries.[35] A fundamental argument of Part I of this book is that *iurisconsulti*, working together with forensic advocates on the pleading of concrete cases could—and did—contribute to the development of late Roman law. The profession of forensic advocacy was a crucial part of legal practice and legal development between the early fourth and early sixth centuries AD.

To return to Ammianus' polemic against forensic orators, there is good reason to look a little closer before accepting it as a straight condemnation on the practices of fourth-century advocates.[36] For example, Ammianus' amusing pastiche of advocates citing the recherché jurists Trebatius, Cascellius, and Alfenus was no doubt written with a historical and literary context in mind. The Republican jurists were the object of satirical wit long before Ammianus used them. Horace's literary satire on the jurist Trebatius still circulated in late antiquity: it was glossed by Pomponius Porphyrion in his *Commentarii in Q. Horatium Flaccum*

33 H. F. Jolowicz, *Historical Introduction to the Study of Roman Law* (Cambridge: CUP, 1952), 471; F. Schulz, *History of Roman Legal Science* (Oxford: Blackwell Publishing, 1967, corr. edn.), 285–6.

34 Matthews, *Laying Down the Law*, 24.

35 D. Liebs, 'Römische Provinzialjurisprudenz', *ANRW* ii/15 (1976), 288–362; Liebs, *Die Jurisprudenz im spätantiken Italien;* Liebs, 'Römische Jurisprudenz in Africa im 4. Jh. n. chr', *ZSS, Rom. Abt.* 106 (1989), 201–17; Liebs, (ed.), *Das Gesetz in Spätantike und frühem Mittelalter* (Göttingen: Abhandlungen der Academie der Wissenschaften, 1992); Liebs, 'Die pseudopaulinischen Sentenzen', *ZSS, Rom. Abt.* 112 (1995), 151–71; and Liebs, *Römische Jurisprudenz in Gallien (2 bis 8 Jahrhundert)* (Berlin: Duncker & Humboldt, 2002). See also Ch. 3 below.

36 T. D. Barnes, *Ammianus Marcellinus and the Representation of Historical Reality* (New York: Cornell University Press, 1998), 8, questions Matthews's reading of 30. 4. 3–22: 'Thus although Matthews concedes the force of Ammianus' rhetoric, he consistently emphasizes the "precisely observed detail" over the possibility that such details may be subservient to rhetoric and prejudice.' I shall return to the question of rhetoric and representation below.

(early third century AD).[37] Moreover, jurists and advocates appear as the subject of dinner-party conversation in Macrobius' *Saturnalia*, written in Rome only a generation after Ammianus had himself resided there. In the *Saturnalia*, however, anecdotal knowledge about the jurist Cascellius is deployed in order to showcase the high culture and classicizing *paideia* of the assembled literati;

> Let me turn back now from stories of women to stories of men and from risqué jests to seemly humour. The *iurisconsultus* Cascellius had a reputation for a remarkably outspoken wit, and here is one of his best known quips. Vatinius had been stoned by the populace at a gladiatorial show which he was giving, and so he prevailed upon the aediles to make a proclamation forbidding the throwing of anything but fruit into the arena. Now it so happened that Cascellius at that time was asked by a client to advise whether a fir cone was a fruit or not, and his reply was: 'If you propose to throw one at Vatinius, it is.'[38]

More jokes on ancient jurists and orators follow. The *Historia Augusta*, also with a Roman context and written about a generation before Macrobius' *Saturnalia*, likewise plays with clever puzzles and learned stories about classical jurists.[39] Were the targets of Ammianus' polemic the same elite Roman *litterati* who were expected to get the recondite legal jokes in Macrobius' *Saturnalia* and the *Historia Augusta* (and to be seen to be laughing at them)? In any event, Ammianus Marcellinus' damning excursus cannot be taken as a straight comment on the legal expertise (or otherwise) of late fourth-century advocates in the Eastern Empire.

Few modern scholars go on to analyse Ammianus' three remaining types of forensic orators, none of whom he credits with any specific training in law. In fact, Ammianus states that some of the fourth

37 Porph. *ad Hor. Sat.* 1. 3. 30 and 2. 1. 81. Horace's text itself is discussed by J.-H. Michel, 'La Satire 2, 1 à Trébatius ou la consultation du juriste', *RIDA* 46 (1999), 369–91. The jurist Trebatius is also attacked by Cicero at *Ad Fam.* 7. 12. 1: according to Cicero, Trebatius' Epicureanism was incompatible with being a jurist. Trebatius and Cascellius are mentioned at *D.* 1. 2. 2. 45 (Pomponius, *Enchiridion*).

38 Macrobius, *Saturnalia* 2. 6. 1: 'ed, ut a feminis ad viros et a lascivis iocis ad honestos revertar, Cascellius iuris consultus urbanitatis mirae libertatisque habebatur, praecipue tamen is iocus eius innotuit. Lapidatus a populo Vatinius, cum gladiatorium munus ederet, optinuerat ut aediles edicerent, ne quis in arenam nisi pomum misisse vellet. Forte his diebus Cascellius consultus a quodam, an nux pinea pomum esset, respondit: Si in Vatinium missurus es, pomum est', tr. P. V. Davies, *The Saturnalia of Macrobius* (New York and London: Columbia University Press, 1969). The passage is also discussed by David Daube, 'Ne quis fecisse velit', in D. Cohen and D. Simon (eds.), *Collected Studies in Roman Law*, ii (Frankfurt: Klostermann, 1991) 1057–8.

39 Honoré, *Law in Crisis*, 190–211, discusses law and 'lawyers' in the *Historia Augusta*.

group are 'so totally uneducated that they cannot remember ever having possessed a law book, and if the name of an early writer is mentioned in cultivated company they think it is a foreign name for a fish or some other foodstuff'. John Crook concludes that Ammianus' categorization of the Eastern advocates is a 'piece of polemic rather than analysis'.[40] Even audiences who listen to polemic, however, have expectations. Ammianus' invective paints a picture that he expected his intended audience to recognize, whether from contemporary practice or classical topoi or most probably both. Hence Ammianus' exaggerated 'piece of polemic'—designed to entertain as much as inform—is nonetheless constructed around a list of forensic skills and practices which would have rung true for his contemporaries: for example, advocates use their talent like a dagger, making cunning speeches to sway the judge in their party's favour (30. 4. 9); they produce legal complications and raise difficult questions in order to further their case (13); they compose speeches before entering into court, but they may also learn their client's name and business once they are before the judge (15); they might make citations of legal authorities (19); they often work in groups, hierarchically arranged, and the most skilled advocate may be mandated by his colleagues to conduct the summing up of the case in court (20). In sum, what emerges is a rhetorical picture of forensic practice that would not be out of place in Juvenal or Cicero, albeit wrapped up in Ammianus' own late fourth-century witty satire.[41]

TAKING LEGAL PRACTICE SERIOUSLY

In an article published in 1934 the great Romanist Salvatore Riccobono stated that what was missing from the accounts of both classical and post-classical Roman law given by the Romanists of his day was 'a knowledge of legal practice'.[42] With this statement Riccobono was

40 Crook, *Legal Advocacy*, 189.

41 Sabbah, *Ammianus Marcellinus*, 217, 218, and 220 at nn. 246, 247, and 256 respectively, detects textual echoes of Aulus Gellius, *Attic Nights*, Quintilian 1. 12, Juvenal, *Satire* 7. 105–49, Plato, *Gorgias* 463b, and possibly Cicero, *De Republica* in the 'excursus on advocates'. Ammianus had also undoubtedly read Cicero's *De Oratore*.

42 S. Riccobono, 'La prassi nel periodo post-classico', *Atti del Congresso internazionale di diritto romano*, 1 (1934), 317–50, at 321. See also S. Riccobono, 'Fasi e fattori dell'evoluzione del diritto romano', *Mélanges de droit Romain dédiés George Cornil*, ii (Vanderpoorten, Gand, and Paris: Sirey, 1926), 238–381.

entering (once again) into the great debate over 'interpolation-hunting': the hunt to identify post-classical revisions in classical juristic texts, with the aim of restoring the latter to their original state. Riccobono was not questioning his colleagues' method of detecting interpolations, but rather their conclusions. In his opinion the interpolations that had been identified in the classical juristic texts excerpted in Justinian's *Digest* were not solely 'Tribonianisms' as humanist scholars such as Cujas and Favre had proposed, nor were they attributable to pre-Justinianic revisionists working in the academic atmosphere of the Eastern law school at Beirut.[43] They were rather the products of Western forensic practitioners.[44] Those practitioners were namely the advocates, *iurisconsulti*, and *iudices* who, through their courtroom activity, worked with the principles established by classical law, reasoning out from them and attempting thereby to create new practical solutions. Riccobono's thesis attracted criticism on the charge that it almost entirely discounted the influence of the professors in the Eastern schools. Jolowicz's objections to Riccobono's thesis were based almost entirely on proofs 'that Byzantium contributed much that was of permanent value for the clarification of legal thought'—moreover, Jolowicz dismissed the contribution of Western forensic practitioners on the basis that they 'were men of poor intellectual attainments'.[45] Riccobono's views on the creativity of practitioners in the lawcourts were thus lost amidst the debate that raged amongst the scholars of his time on the possibility of a thorough 'Byzantine' reworking of classical legal texts in the era before Justinian. Current scholarly debates remain predominantly focused on the changes made (or not) to classical texts by either Justinian's legal compilers, or the professors of post-classical law schools in the East.[46]

Leaving 'the great interpolation hunt' to one side, two important lines of enquiry open up as a result of Riccobono's insistence that

[43] Riccobono's earlier work was challenged by P. Collinet, 'Le Rôle de la doctrine et de la pratique dans le développement de droit privé romain au bas-empire', *RHDFE* 7 (1928), 551–83 and 8: 5–35, who, with a single exception (the *interdicti actio,* in *Sent. Paul.* 5. 6. 10), attributed all the post-classical interpolations to Eastern 'academics'.

[44] L. Wenger, *Der heutige Stand der römischen Rechtwissenschaft* (Munich, Beck, 1927) [= Münch. Beitr], 105–20, concludes that certain 4th-cent scholia/glosses on classical texts were made by forensic practitioners.

[45] Jolowicz, *Historical Introduction*, 534–8. Also M. Bohácek, 'Un esempio dell' insegnamento di Berito ai compilatori: *Cod.Just.* 2,4,18', *Studi Riccobono*, 1 (1936), 337–96 at 337.

[46] D. Johnston, *Roman Law in Context*, 17–22, gives a balanced overview of current scholarly debates in this area.

'practice appears as the living force that animates and transforms legal institutions'.[47] The first relates to the creation of new law by forensic practitioners under the so-called 'formulary procedure' of classical Roman civil law.[48] The second relates to the continuance of this forensic creativity in the courts of the Late Empire, under the various *cognitio* procedures. Modern scholars are still more accustomed to emphasizing the differences between the civil procedures of the 'classical' and 'post-classical' periods: however, if we focus on the actual activities of advocates, *iurisperiti*, and *iudices*, a picture of substantial forensic continuity emerges. In the case of the advocates in particular, the techniques that they deployed in the courts of the Late Empire were still based on a structure of rhetorical argumentation that had originally developed in step with the 'formulary' proceedings.

Only a brief outline will be given here of the classical formulary procedure, in so far as it bears upon our view of the later developments. The purpose of the following sketch is to show the interaction of forensic practitioners in court under the classical formulary procedure—at the same time as highlighting their contribution to the development of new substantive law when the instant case demanded it. At Rome, these forensic practitioners were the praetor, *iurisconsulti*, and advocates in the first phase of the case and the *iudex privatus*, *iurisconsulti*, and advocates in the second phase. A formal 'two-stage' formulary procedure does not seem to have been standard in the provinces: the provincial governor (or an appointed deputy) took responsibility for the whole case. Aside from the unitary hearing, however, provincial civil procedure under the Late Republic and Early Empire seems, on balance, to have been modelled on the practice of Rome.[49]

The role of the praetor, or magistrate with *iurisdictio*, under formulary procedure was to establish whether the case could proceed to *litis contestatio* (joinder of issue). This was achieved through the agreement of a written *formula* in which authorization was given to find against

[47] Riccobono, 'La prassi nel periodo post-classico', 349.

[48] The formulary procedure was officially sanctioned as available to Roman citizens by a *Lex Aebutia* in the first half of the 2nd cent BC, and the procedure *per legis actiones* was abolished (almost completely) by the Emperor Augustus in 17 BC (Gaius, *Inst.* 4. 103–5). Johnston, *Roman Law in Context*, 112–21, gives an overview of both the Roman and provincial 'formulary procedure'; also Matthews, *Laying Down the Law*, 106–8.

[49] See M. Kaser, and K. Hackl, *Das römische Zivilprozessrecht*, 2nd edn. (Munich: C. H. Beck, 1996), 163–71. Also E. Metzger, *Litigation in Roman Law* (Oxford: OUP, 2005) and P. Birks, 'New Light on the Roman Legal System: The Appointment of Judges', *Cambridge Law Journal*, 47/1 (1998), 36–60.

the defendant if certain factual or legal circumstances appeared proved, or to absolve him if this was not the case. A formula was first proposed by the plaintiff, most likely having agreed its contents in consultation with a *iurisconsultus.* The defendant was entitled to ask for the insertion of 'exceptions' and for other modifications of the formula, again having privately consulted a *iurisconsultus.* Further modifications were possible: a plaintiff's *replicatio,* answered by a defendant's *triplicatio* for example. Advocates also had their place, as their forensic expertise was available to plaintiffs or defendants in presenting the juridical and/or factual reasons for accepting the proposed formula or exception.[50] The praetor's edict set up the models of procedural *formulae* upon which the parties would normally have to base their suits, if they expected to be heard.[51] The praetor also had the right to grant a formula not promulgated in his edict; *iurisconsulti* (*iurisperiti* or 'jurists') played an important role in the creation of these innovatory 'non-standard' *formulae,* through their advice both to the parties and to the praetor himself. In fact, classical jurists cooperated case by case in the continual correcting and enlarging of the branch of Roman civil law that came to be known as the *ius honorarium.* The classical jurists' casuistic involvement in actual court cases militates against viewing them exclusively as a closed body of academic legal scholars, creating law exclusively through argumentation amongst themselves. If we view the classical jurists as contributing to the decision of actual cases in court then it necessarily affects our value judgements of *iurisconsulti* in the Late Empire who, I will argue, acted in the same capacity.

The final written formula gave the 'programme for litigation' that would be followed if the case proceeded to the next phase. Under the two-stage procedure at Rome the *iudex* (or *iudices*: *recuperatores*) was usually a private citizen whose name was included in the annual *album*

[50] Crook, *Legal Advocacy,* 159–60, and O. E. Tellegen-Couperus, 'The Role of the Judge in the Formulary Procedure', *Journal of Legal History,* 22/2, (2001), 1–13, at 2.

[51] Provincial governors also had the *ius edicendi,* and issued provincial edicts. A revision and codification of the praetorian edicts was made by the jurist Salvius Julianus at the initiative of the Emperor Hadrian, *c.*132 (reconstructed by O. Lenel, *Das Edictum Perpetuum,* 3rd edn. (Leipzig: Tauchnitz, 1927)). This effectively froze the edictal activity of the praetors, but the codification itself became the subject of commentaries by other jurists: particularly extensive were those of Ulpian and Paul in the first decades of the 3rd cent. Evidence for the use of the 'perpetual edict' as a source of law in the Late Empire is discussed by P. De Francisci, 'Ancora dell'editto nel periodo postclassico', *BIDR* 11 (1960), 39–46, and Corcoran, 'Publication of Law', 59–60.

iudicum. His role was to investigate fully the facts of the case, to take the proofs, and to render sentence. The *iudex* was bound by the formula, in that he had to decide only the questions of law and of fact that were presented in it. Despite the technicality of the wording of the formula, however, questions of substantive law could still arise.[52] The *iudex*—as the praetor or any magistrate with *iurisdictio*—might accordingly retain legal advisers who formed part of a *consilium*. Under the Principate *iurisperiti* received compensation for their role as *adsessores* in judicial proceedings at Rome and in the provinces alike.[53] In the early third century the jurist Paul wrote a monograph *de officio adsessorum*, and the extract from this work preserved at *D*. 1. 22. 1 specifies that the duties of the *adsessor* were performed by *iuris studiosi*.

The second phase of the case, however, was the principal field of activity for the advocates; their aim was persuasive eloquence and their skill lay in the rhetorical handling of their client's case before the court.[54] The Latin rhetorical treatises of Cicero, the *auctor ad Herennium*, and Quintilian, as well as the extant corpus of Greek technical writing on rhetoric, all devote extensive treatment to complex rules for the artistic development of an argument in forensic speeches. As Malcolm Heath has stated, the 'primary concentration of rhetorical teaching' was on 'judicial oratory'.[55] The technical discovery of (seemingly) valid arguments to render a case plausible was the first section of any formal treatise on rhetoric; this 'discovery' or *inventio* enabled an advocate to elaborate on the factual or legal circumstances contained in the words of the given formula, thus potentially introducing new information for the consideration of the judge.

52 Tellegen-Couperus, 'Role of the Judge', 2–3, and E. Metzger, 'Roman Judges, Case Law, and Principles of Procedure', *Law and History Review*, 22 (2004), 243–75.

53 On *adsessores/assessores* see H. F. Hitzig, *Die Assessoren der römischen Magistrate und Richter* (Munich, Ackermann, 1893), with a useful review by B. Kübler, in *ZSS, Rom. Abt.* 14 (1880), 285–95. O. Behrends, 'Der assessor zur Zeit der klassischen Rechtswissenschaft', *ZSS, Rom. Abt.* 86 (1969), 192–226, also discusses assessors under the Early Empire.

54 A. Steinwenter, 'Rhetorik und römische Zivilprozess', *ZSS, Rom. Abt.* 64 (1947), 69–120, gives a detailed analysis of the influence of rhetorical training on the development of classical procedure. J. Stroux, *Summum ius summa iniuria: Ein Kapitel aus der Geschichte der 'Interpretatio Iuris'* (Freiburg: Himmelschein Symb. Friburgenses, 1926), on the other hand, claimed that rhetoric had also influenced the development of substantive legal principles. In his preface to the Italian translation of Stroux's article Riccobono stated that he had found his 'spiritual peace' in its arguments; Levy's review of Stroux's 'Summum ius' in *ZSS, Rom. Abt.* 48 (1928), 668–78, was distinctly less enthusiastic.

55 Heath, *Menander: A Rhetor in Context*, 4.

The first matter to be decided by the advocate was the determination of the 'issue' on which any given case depended (*constitutio causae*). In this respect both the classical and post-classical rhetorical treatises function effectively as pleaders' handbooks; they lay out classificatory schemes for the application of *inventio* (developed in the post-classical rhetorical handbooks via Hermogenean 'issue-theory' from the second or early third century AD onwards) to each type or subtype of issue that could arise under the *genus iudicale*—thus providing strategies for both prosecuting and defending advocates. Again, as Heath notes: 'Superficially similar situations may have an utterly different underlying logical structure. A dispute that turns on a question of fact will require a different treatment from one in which the facts are admitted, but not their categorization or evaluation.'[56] That 'categorization or evaluation' might involve a point of legal interpretation, but not necessarily, and book 2 of the *Ad Herennium* provides advocates with detailed instructions on how to proceed when the 'issue' of a concrete case is discovered to turn on a point of written law. The advocate could, as the occasion demands, plead that the intention of the framer appears to be at variance with the letter of the text, and so urge the principle of equity (2. 13–14).[57] He could state that two statutes conflict (2. 15), or establish that the text is regarded as ambiguous by *iurisconsulti* (2. 16). He could also redefine a legal offence in order to decide whether an admitted defence comes within the definition (2. 17), or argue by analogy that a matter not provided for by any special law comes within the spirit of existing laws (2. 18). Cicero, *De Inventione* 2. 116, provides a concrete example of ambiguity in a written text of private law and gives a detailed treatment of how the advocate for the prosecution should handle it (116–21). Thus new questions of legal interpretation could arise in the second phase of the formulary procedure, and the rhetorical skills of advocates included being able to exploit such interpretations in their client's favour (as necessary), whether they had legal expertise themselves or accessed it through advice from others.

A further strategy of persuasion open to the advocate was to provide the *iudex* (either the judge in the second phase of the hearing, or a provincial magistrate) with examples of previous *sententiae* issued by

[56] Heath, *Menander: A Rhetor in Context*, 5.

[57] As the Urban Prefect Symmachus archly noted in AD 384: 'There may be a reason for it, or it may be chance incidental to lawsuits, that often one party to the case bases himself on equity, the other on law' (*Relatio* 39). See D. Vera, *Commento Storico alle Relationes di Quinto Aurelio Simmaco* (Pisa: Giardini editori, 1984), 293.

judges for analogous cases.[58] Cicero includes *res iudicatae* amongst the advocate's modes of extrinsic proofs in the *De Oratore* (2. 27. 116), relying on Aristotle's division between 'artistic' (intrinsic) and 'non-artistic' (extrinsic) arguments. According to Aristotle, 'artistic' arguments are those created through reasoning, non-artistic arguments are those that are 'found' by the orator (*Rhet.* 1355^b35). *Res iudicatae,* included in the latter category, can only function in court as 'evidence' for how analogous cases should be decided. Thus it was open to an advocate to make skilled use of *res iudicatae* to persuasive ends. Whether the judge chose to be influenced by previous judgements depended on the advocate's skill in deploying them in forensic argumentation—a skill in which, as we shall see, the advocates of the Late Empire were equally well practised.

TAKING LATE ROMAN LEGAL PRACTICE SERIOUSLY

The classical formulary procedure offered a number of opportunities for casuistically developing legal principles (frequently via 'procedural' innovations, as discussed above). The creative role of the praetor and the *iurisconsulti* under formulary procedure is frequently stressed in modern scholarship. It is thus easy to understand why, when we reach the Late Empire—with the formulary procedure no longer in use—the tendency should be to assume that law was no longer developed on this case-by-case basis through forensic practice, but rather advanced via imperial legislation alone. The recognition, however, that contributions to the development of Roman law could also be made under the second phase of the formulary procedure should alert us to the fact that, even where the legal issue is technically prescribed in a formula tailor-made for the instant case, it still requires interpretation and 'handling' by forensic practitioners. What are forensic arguments in a given case today could influence the judgement of cases in court tomorrow. I will argue that the

58 See A. Lewis, 'The Autonomy of Roman Law', in P. Coss (ed.), *The Moral World of the Law* (Cambridge: CUP, 2000), 37–47, at 45: 'The *commentarii* and other records from provincial courts reveal arguments from precedent: the principle that a case should be decided in accordance with the way previous such cases were decided.' B. Frier, *The Rise of the Roman Jurists* (Princeton: Princeton University Press, 1985), 129 and 229, and Tellegen-Couperus, 'Role of the Judge', both discuss *res iudicatae* in the context of the 'two-stage' formulary procedure at Rome.

gradual development of the *cognitio (extra ordinem)* procedure actually increased the opportunities for advocates and *iurisperiti* to influence the development of law on a case-by-case basis through their activities in court.[59] In Part II, moreover, I shall suggest that the creativity of forensic practitioners was a crucial mechanism behind the evolution and expansion of an entirely new body of law relating to the Christian church, from the early fourth century AD onwards.

If we leave the *notarii* to one side for the moment, there were three main types of professional forensic practitioners who functioned (to differing levels) in the various formal courts of the later Roman Empire: the late Roman magistrate or *iudex*; the *iurisconsultus* (*iurisperitus*, *iuris prudens*, *iuris auctor*, *iuris conditor*); and the *advocatus* (*causidicus*, *patronus causarum*, *togatus*, *scholasticus*, *defensor*). In the three chapters that follow we shall examine each of these forensic professionals in turn, over a period stretching from the late third to the early sixth century AD. Not all late Roman concrete cases, of course, resulted in creative interpretations that stretched or developed existing legal categories; nonetheless late Roman legal practice merits being taken seriously as a source for the development of post-classical legal principles. As we shall see, there was a lot more to the late Roman legal system than the letter of imperial laws. In highlighting the creativity of post-classical advocates in particular, we shall also be laying the ground work for Part III: an exploration of the role of forensic practitioners in the creation and 'handling' of innovative imperial constitutions against Christian heresy.

[59] On the so-called 'cognitio extra-ordinem' and Roman legal procedure see W. Turpin, 'Formula, *Cognitio*, and Proceedings *Extra Ordinem*', *RIDA* 46 (1999), 499–574.

2

Litigation and Late Roman Judges

JUDGING LATE ROMAN DISPUTES

Look, the first thing that happens in this affair is a quarrel over property. While each side feeds their cupidity by verbal abuse, momentum builds up for a battle. Then indeed the argument does grow into a contest. If only cupidity could be satisfied with that! Worse is to follow—while no one wants to lose out on a charge of false accusation, they come to blows. The slaves are given weapons, the neighbours are stirred into action, and one man's life is traded for the sake of another man's profit. Wine-induced madness gets to work and blood is poured out as the price for possession. Then at last a court is convened for the operation of the laws; an opportunity is sought for settling scores with a charge of homicide now added on.[1]

According to the mid-fifth-century Gallic bishop Valerian of Cimiez, late Roman lawcourts functioned as arenas for the expression of social, rather than individual, conflict. Valerian's comments (quoted above) were not made in a juristic treatise or textbook, but rather in the midst of a sermon against the sin of cupidity. Valerian sought to persuade his audience that Christian ethics could be practised in the context of their everyday life; hence he used the (common) homiletic technique of grounding his moralizing in vivid, realistic scenarios that his audience could imagine finding themselves in. Situations such as the following: a quarrel arises over property, verbal insults are traded, and the entire neighbourhood becomes involved. Those individuals who covet the property do not go to court to obtain it legally, but enter and

[1] Valerian of Cimiez, *Homily* 20. 3 (on 1 Tim 6: 3–10), *PL* 52. 752–3: 'Ecce fit primum in hoc loco de proprietate contentio: et dum suam quisque cupiditatem verbis fovet, stimulum litis accendit. Crescit postmodum de contentione causatio: atque utinam hoc solum sufficeret cupiditati! Illud gravius est, quod dum nemo vult inchoatae calumniae facere iacturam, pervenitur ad rixam. Armantur servi, incitantur propinqui, et in alterius lucrum pectus opponitur alienum. Animatur vino furor conductus, et effusus sanguis fit pretium possessionis. Aperitur postmodum legibus forum; et dum ultionis locus quaeritur, congeminatur homicidium.'

seize possession through violence—possession being nine-tenths of the (Roman) law. Such a series of events—unlawful seizure and occupation of land followed by a lawsuit initiated by the dispossessed—appears in fourth-century Egyptian papyri such as *P.Oxy.* I. 67 (AD 338).[2] In the case imagined by Valerian, the dispute only reaches a law court after the charge-sheet has been expanded beyond the original disagreement over property to embrace a criminal accusation of homicide. Thus, Valerian implies, the concrete case that the judge eventually presides over is as much about the hatred and enmities that have arisen within a face-to-face community as about 'applying' the Roman law of property.

Valerian's example is typical of late Roman legal disputes in several different ways. First, as Chris Wickham has argued with respect to later Lombard–Carolingian Italy: 'Cases did not happen in a void; they happened between people who had lived together before and would live together again . . . They were part of the continuous processes of social interaction.'[3] An analysis of how late Roman judges handled concrete cases and imperial 'laws' demands that we constantly look beyond the courtroom. Second, within the 'continuous processes of social interaction', individuals manipulate normative categories in order to achieve particular effects in particular situations.[4] In other words individuals do not simply obey or break 'the rules'; they also strategically choose between and manipulate sets of normative practices.[5]

A letter of Basil of Cappadocia gives us some sense of the range of normative socio-legal practices available for settling a typical grievance in the mid-fourth century.[6] Basil writes from a small town not far from Neocaesarea, seeking the help of the then governor of Cappadocia,

[2] Different scenarios arising from the same series of events are envisaged in *C.Th.* 4. 22, with the rubric *unde vi* . . . ('when by violence . . .'), referring to the opening words of the relevant Praetorian interdict. See also *C.Th.* 11. 39. 12 (given at Constantinople, AD 396, to Aeternalis, Proconsul of Asia).

[3] C. Wickham, 'Land Disputes and their Social Framework in Lombard–Carolingian Italy, 700–900', in W. Davies and P. Fouracre (eds.), *The Settlement of Disputes in Early Medieval Europe* (Cambridge: CUP, 1986), 105–24, at 122.

[4] D. Cohen, *Law, Sexuality and Society: The Enforcement of Morals in Classical Athens* (Cambridge: CUP, 1991), 32.

[5] For the late Roman period, these sets of normative practices should also include those that seek access to 'supernatural' justice, e.g. through cursing tablets and judicial binding curses. See C. Humfress, 'Law in Practice', in P. Rousseau (ed.), *The Blackwell Guide to Late Antiquity* (Oxford: Blackwell Press, forthcoming), and B. Shaw, 'Judicial Nightmares and Christian Memory', *Journal of Early Christian Studies*, 11/4 (2003), 533–63, at 537.

[6] Basil, *Ep.* 3, ed. and tr. Y. Courtonne, *Saint Basile Lettres*, i (Paris: Les Belles Lettres, 1957), 13–15.

Candidianus. A servant of Basil, probably to be understood as a slave, had apparently died whilst in debt. With no warning, the slave's creditor (described by Basil as a 'rustic') had attacked Basil's house, assaulting the women and stealing property over and above the amount owed. This act of summary justice was, of course, 'illegal', and Basil lists a number of legitimate strategies which the creditor could have alternatively chosen to pursue: he could have lodged a formal legal complaint with the authorities, or he could have approached Basil and negotiated a voluntary payment, or finally he could have *threatened* Basil with physical violence. Any of these three courses of action, Basil informs the governor, would have been acceptable. Basil is no doubt here exaggerating his 'reasonableness' in order to win the support of Candidianus—nonetheless the scenarios that he envisages gives us a concrete idea of the expected range of dispute settlement strategies: formal legal process (including formal arbitration procedures), private negotiation, and threats with menaces. Tellingly, the conclusion to the letter does not ask the provincial governor to institute a formal legal process against the 'rustic' attacker; rather Basil states that he would be happy if Candidianus would arrange for the assailant to be arrested by the local officials and locked up for a short period of time. Summary justice, without formal process, was 'legally' available to individuals such as Basil who had the right social and political connections.

A dispute may thus have had the potential to reach a court of law (i.e. the formal legal system offered a redress or 'remedy' that would cover the concrete situation) but it does not necessarily follow that a given individual would choose to initiate a legal process. Amongst other factors, the choice of whether to initiate a court case might be decided on the basis of expense—the high costs associated with late Roman litigation are well documented—or on the basis of patronage relationships.[7] The decision could also be governed by less immediately obvious considerations. In *De Moribus Manichaeorum* 72 (written AD 388) Augustine claims that a member of the Manichaean elect, whom he himself had heard speaking 'in the street of the fig-sellers', slept with a dedicated virgin and the crime was discovered because she became pregnant. The virgin's brother chose not to lodge a public accusation

[7] Harries, *Law and Empire*, 100, and C. Kelly, *Ruling the Later Roman Empire* (Cambridge, Mass., and London: Harvard University Press, 2004), 67, 107–8, and 139–42, discuss the fees and expenses associated with late Roman litigation. See also C. Humfress, 'Poverty and Roman Law', in M. Atkins and R. Osborne (eds.), *Poverty in the Roman World* (Cambridge: CUP, 2006), 183–203.

against the elect manichee 'out of regard for religion'; but succeeded in getting the man expelled from the Manichaean church. In order that the crime might not be entirely unpunished, however, the brother made an agreement with some friends to have the offender beaten up.[8] In other words, in Augustine's account, the religious sentiments of the virgin's brother did not prevent him from exacting his own revenge on the guilty party. Augustine is here seeking to score a polemical point against the Manichaean *religio* itself, by framing its adherents as both morally lax (the elect manichee) and hypocritical (the virgin's brother); for our purposes, however, it is enough to note that in Augustine's story the virgin's brother had a potential case at Roman law, but he chose rather to exact justice through a mixture of religious sanction and summary violence.

Extra-legal considerations concerning dispute settlement are also apparent in a *dialytike homologia* (an agreement concerning a settlement) from Oxyrhynchus, dated 17 March 545.[9] This papyrus records a complicated dispute between a monastery and a Constantinopolitan senator with landholdings in the Oxyrhynchite nome. The dispute never reached the courts and there is no 'judge' or 'arbitrator' involved in the case, nonetheless it was settled privately in full knowledge of the relevant civil law principles. In lines 140–76 of the papyrus, the monks who are acting on behalf of the monastery promise the senator's heirs that they will abide by the agreement that had been reached:

> for security of the matters acknowledged by them they call upon God as a witness and acknowledge that they abide by these terms, keep them, consider them binding for ever, and do not oppose them or any part or section of them, not at this time, not hereafter, not in a local court or one beyond the frontier, nor out of court, nor by petition directed to our victorious master [i.e. Justinian] . . .

The monks then go on to swear 'that they will not make accusations among friends, nor impugn them [the terms of the agreement] or part of them, either at law or in holy churches, nor say that they have suffered

[8] *PL* 32. 1375. On consecrated virginity in general see S. Elm, *'Virgins of God': The Making of Asceticism in Late Antiquity* (Oxford: Clarendon Press, 1994).

[9] *P.Oxy.* LXIII. 4397, ed. and tr. B. P. Grenfell. Compare the 6th-cent. settlement, *P. Mich.* 6922, ed. and tr., with introduction and commentary by T. Gagos and P. Van Minnen, *Settling a Dispute: Toward a Legal Anthropology of Late Antique Egypt* (Ann Arbor: University of Michigan Press, 1994) and the mid-4th-cent. settlement, *P. Mich.* 4008, ed. and tr., with commentary by T. Gagos and P. J. Sijpesteijn, 'Settling a Dispute in Fourth Century Small Oasis', *ZPE* 105 (1995), 245–52.

any fraud or neglect'.[10] Both sides in this dispute knew the power that could be gained by threatening an individual's social reputation, whether the aspersions were cast in a lawcourt, amongst friends, or 'in holy Churches'. *P.Mich.* XIII. 659 (AD 527–38) records the details of another lengthy and complicated dispute, during which one of the parties had apparently 'often used loud complaints in the Holy Church' against the other, as well as making frequent approaches to the provincial governor. As Weber argued, 'law embodies only one mode of social regulation'.[11]

In arranging private transactions, such as loans, sales, inheritances, contracts, or pacts, many Romans, and not just the social elite, observed the legal procedures and conventions which they believed would make their actions efficacious and binding. Even when a private agreement made no reference to any substantive principles of Roman law, its contents could still become subject to legal dispute, according to the long-standing rule that 'agreements made against the laws and constitutions, or against good *mores* (morals, custom), have no *vis* (force)' (*CI* 2. 3. 6, Emperor Antoninus to the private petitioner Basilla, AD 214). To this end (as we shall see) individuals might consult notaries, advocates, or *iurisconsulti* for advice and help in conducting their transactions, and they might seek to formalize both verbal and written agreements with acts of oath-swearing and formal witnessing. One aim of this activity was, of course, to lessen the chances of any subsequent litigation—or as the parties to one early sixth-century dispute put it, to destroy 'every seed of a lawsuit'.[12] This concern was nothing new: the terms of a Late Republican agreement conclude with the stipulation that, 'Both fraud *and the Civil law* shall be remote from all this'.[13] Agreements to stay away from the subtleties of the *ius civile* are also a relatively common feature of surviving late Roman contracts and private dispute

[10] For further discussion see C. Humfress, 'Law and Legal Practice', 179–83. Gagos and Van Minnen, *Settling a Dispute,* 121–7, give a list of forty-one papyri recording late antique dispute settlements in Greek between AD 276 and 647.

[11] Cited from Cohen, *Law, Sexuality and Society*, 6. The use of public outbursts in church as a means of 'legal redress' also occurs in *P. Lond.* I. 77.

[12] *P.Mich.* XIII. 659, ed. P. J. Sijpesteijn, 1977. For discussion of this case see J. Gascou and L. S. B. MacCoull, 'Le Cadastre d'Aphroditô', *Travaux et mémoires du Centre de recherche d'histoire et civilisation de Byzance*, 10 (1987), 103—58, with 10 plates, reprinted as *SB* XX 14669.

[13] *CIL* vi/2. 8862, discussed by D. Daube, 'A Corrupt Judge Sets the Pace', in D. Nörr and D. Simon (eds.), *Gedächtnisschrift für Wolfgang Kunkel* (Frankfurt: Klostermann, 1984), 37–52 at 47; compare the elaborate stipulations in *P. Mich.* XIII. 663, an early 6th-cent. deed of sale for part of a house.

settlements. Column 1 of *P.Oxy.* I. 71 (AD 303) refers to a contract for loan between a certain creditor Aurelius Demetrius and a debtor Aurelius Sotas, with the specific stipulation that repayment would be made 'without an action at law, or any delay or quibble'. Sotas, however, had apparently defaulted on these terms: *P.Oxy.* I. 71 is in fact a petition addressed to the Prefect Clodius Culcianus, in which Demetrius seeks to initiate a formal legal process—alleging amongst other things that Sotas has taken advantage of his illiteracy. The petition also explains that Demetrius had threatened prosecution before the prefect when the 'fraud' was first detected, and Sotas had in turn pleaded that he might be given time to settle the debt 'without the trouble of an action'. The notary or advocate who drafted the petition for Demetrius thus skilfully implies both that the plaintiff is a reasonable man, and that the prefect's court offers his last hope of obtaining the justice that is his due. Petitioners could, of course, threaten their adversaries with 'the trouble of an action' at each stage of the initial court proceedings, right up until the moment at which the issue was formally joined (*litis contestatio*) before a *iudex*.[14]

Formal arbitration offered a further avenue of dispute resolution, without litigation in court. The procedures for formal arbitration, unlike 'informal mediation', were governed by Roman civil law.[15] Both parties were required to swear mutual oaths (*pactum compromissi*) before the hearing began, thereby agreeing to be bound by their choice of arbiter(s) and the outcome of the arbitration. Penalties could also be agreed upon, in the event of any settlement being later broken. A private rescript issued in AD 293 clearly states that an 'agreed compromise' (*transactio*) is no less authoritative than a judgement (*CI* 2. 4. 20). The petitioner (a woman) had apparently originally asked whether it was possible to rescind an agreement 'by stating that it was made in the second hour of the night' (the Emperors' answer is no!). In AD 539 Justinian confirmed all existing laws on formal

[14] See Ch. 2 below. *P.Oxy.* XVI. 1876, details the preliminary stages for a proceeding for debt, before a provincial governor (*c.* AD 480). The creditor's petition is formally read into the court's records, followed by the magistrate's order that the creditor and debtor should either arrange terms or come into court. See also *P.Oxy.* XVI. 1877 (AD 488), where one of the named debtors is a Christian priest.

[15] On formal arbitration see Harries, *Law and Empire*, 172–84 and J. Harries, 'Resolving Disputes: The Frontiers of Law in Late Antiquity', in R. E. Mathisen (ed.), *Law, Society and Authority in Late Antiquity* (Oxford: OUP, 2001), 68–82. We will return to formal arbitration procedures in Part II, in the context of the so-called *episcopalis audientia*.

arbitration, in response to an apparent 'multitude of petitions' received by his imperial bureau; according to the drafter of Justinian's *Novel*, individuals were acting in 'complete ignorance of laws and forensic convention', by swearing 'to accept arbitrators in whom no one should entrust anything without thinking more than twice about it' and then refusing to agree to the outcome of the dispute (*Novel* 82. 11, Justinian to John of Cappadocia PP). The decision of an arbitrator who is completely ignorant of the law—but acts without deliberate fraud and in accordance with good *mores*—is valid according to the civil law, if the correct procedural formalities were observed in setting up the arbitration. As we shall see in Part II, those individuals who knew the inside of a courtroom were in high demand as 'extra-judicial' arbitrators.

When it came to settling disputes, *not* appearing as a litigant before a magistrate was thus a primary goal for many, if not perhaps most, inhabitants of the later Roman Empire. Late Roman bishops were keen to support this common-sense attitude with 'Christian' ethics based on scriptural precepts.[16] Whilst expounding a homily based around Romans 12: 20, John Chrysostom reminds his late fourth-century audience that:

> Many men, when they have a dispute with one another, save themselves loss, and alarm, and many risks if they come to a friendly understanding together outside the law court, the issue of the case turning out in accordance with the sentiment of each party; but if they severally entrust the affair to the judge the only result to them will be loss of money, and in many cases a penalty, and the permanent endurance of their hatred.

At this point those listening to the homily—baptized Christians, catechumens, and non-Christians alike—would no doubt have found themselves nodding in agreement. John's specific moral lesson, however, is fully unveiled in the lines that follow: the Christian God 'of peace and love' urges us to be reconciled with our adversaries and banish all anger and bitterness from our souls. If, on the other hand, we 'depart to that terrible tribunal in the other world' whilst still embroiled in ongoing litigation, then 'we shall ultimately pay the highest penalty at the sentence of the judge there'. Better to settle disputes quickly and privately in this life, than suffer inexorable punishment from the

[16] e.g. Matt. 18: 15–17: disputes should be settled privately between individuals or within the (religious) community.

supreme judge in the next.[17] John Chrysostom does not specifically allude to the delays that were a familiar characteristic of the judicial system, nonetheless his implication that a late Roman might die with a legal case still making its way through the bureaucratic courts is telling. Some even drew up their wills with the expectation that litigation would be necessary after their death: an Alexandrian's will from January or February 325 included instructions for a child's guardian to 'go to law' against a certain named individual (*P. Oxy.* LIV. 3756). Notwithstanding the preaching of bishops such as John Chrysostom in the imperial capital of Constantinople or Valerian in small-town Cimiez in Gaul, legal cases did, of course, reach late Roman courtrooms. It is to the subject of litigation and judicial practice that we shall now turn.

The system of courts in the later Roman Empire was tied to the administrative structure of the imperial bureaucracy; it grew up piece-meal and embodied practices and customs that could vary across place and time. It was an accepted fact that individual lawcourts, especially those of the Praetorian Prefects and the Emperor himself, had their own 'forensic conventions' with which the court's permanent officials (the office staff and advocates, if not necessarily the *iudex* himself) would have been familiar.[18] This 'local knowledge' of courtroom procedure, custom, and etiquette is difficult to access in the extant sources, yet it is crucial to our understanding of both late Roman forensic (rather than 'legal') culture and how law operated in practice. The question, in turn, of how the higher level of the bureaucratic system interacted with judicial venues in the localities is a complex one, which we shall also explore below and return to in Part II.

A further challenge lies, as ever, in the nature of the surviving sources. With respect to classical Roman law, Andrew Lewis has noted that the writings of the jurists transmitted via the Justinianic codification 'limit our understanding of the role of the judge'.[19] The same is true for the imperial constitutions of the Theodosian Code, albeit for different reasons. When assembling the mass of post-Constantinian

[17] John Chrysostom, *Homily* ('Adversus eos qui ad collectam non occorrerunt, et in dictum illud apostoli, si esurierit inimicus tuus, cibi illum (Rom 12.20), et deinimicitiarum memori'), *PG* 51. 185–6 (tr. Blackburn *NPNF* ix. 232 with slight revision).

[18] A detailed account of the structure of the late imperial courts, including those of special jurisdiction, is given by Jones, *Later Roman Empire*, 479–94. See also Harries, *Law and Empire*, 53–5.

[19] A. Lewis, 'The Autonomy of Roman Law', in P. Coss, (ed.), *The Moral World of the Law* (Cambridge: CUP, 2000), 37–47, at 39.

material, compilers of the Code tended to select imperial constitutions addressed to Praetorian Prefects, whether by choice or necessity.[20] The process of the Code's compilation involved the excision of the individual executive formula that gave instructions for the further copying and transmission of the text. It is thus frequently difficult, if not impossible, to know who finally received versions of any given imperial constitution in the fourth and early fifth centuries—and hence to work out the intended scope of a given text's original application. Eusebius reports an early fourth-century edict issued by an Eastern Praetorian Prefect, in which provincial governors were instructed to send 'letters' (i.e. convey imperial constitutions in an epistolary form) to *curatores*, *duoviri* (city magistrates), and *praepositi pagorum* (the heads of the districts or *pagi* into which a city territory was divided).[21] However, we can be sure that this apparently neat chain of command was not followed in every case. Moreover, the wording of a constitution would have reflected the status, function, and/or locality of the recipient.[22] In other words, its 'original' wording would not have remained intact, but would have been adapted (both the introductory section bearing the address and perhaps also the various operative parts of the letter) to suit the intended recipient. Anyone acquainted with the conventions of late antique rhetoric would have been aware that the epistolary form and content suited to a Praetorian Prefect on the one hand, and to (say) a *praepositus pagi*, on the other, were not the same. The surviving evidence from the Theodosian Code (which I have said comprised in the main 'letters' addressed to Praetorian Prefects) can thus mask the vitality and also the mode of operation of local judicial venues. This point will become clearer from an analysis of the Egyptian papyri in this chapter, alongside the discussion of prosecutions against 'heretics' and 'heresy' in Part III.

[20] D. Feissel, 'Un rescrit de Justinien découvert à Didymes (1er avril 533)', *Chiron*, 34 (2004), 285–365, provides a rare insight into the transmission of a text (in this case a Justinianic 'pragmatic sanction') from the imperial court, to the bureau of the Praetorian Prefect and onto the relevant provincial governor and the original petitioners themselves.

[21] Eusebius, *Hist Eccl.* 9. 1, ed. and tr. Loeb vol. ii. 328–32. See Jones, *Later Roman Empire*, 726. For 5th-cent. examples of imperial constitutions published via (extant) prefectural edicts see Millar, *Greek Roman Empire*, 177–8 and 185–8.

[22] Matthews, *Laying Down the Law*, 163: laws existed in many versions, 'as published in different places by different imperial officials'. See in general W. E. Voss, *Recht und Rhetorik in den Kaisergesetzen der Spätantike: Eine Untersuchung zum nachklassischen Kauf- und Übereignungsrecht* (Frankfurt/Main: Forschungen zur Byzantinischen Rechtsgeschichte 9, 1982).

Finally, the constitutions collected in the Theodosian and Justinianic Codes, as well as a number of literary sources, represent judges as corrupt and venal—as at best, to borrow A. H. M Jones's phrase, 'scamping on their judicial duties'.[23] In fact, we cannot know on the basis of the sources available to us whether judges were more corrupt in late antiquity than in other periods, or whether, on the other hand (as Harries has suggested) 'emperors, provincials and the ever-critical Christian church were more often prepared to say so'.[24] In any event, as we shall see, the normative idea of how a 'good' judge ought to comport himself remained substantively unchanged from the days of the early Principate.

'LOCAL' JUSTICE AND THE IMPERIAL BUREAUCRACY

The Egyptian papyri provide a valuable source for the workings of a variety of 'lower-level' judicial hearings and their interaction with the higher-level courts of the provincial governors and the Augustal Prefect in Alexandria.[25] The provenance of the papyri, however, is limited almost entirely to two late Roman provinces: the Thebaid (with major papyrological finds in Antinoopolis, Hermopolis, and Aphrodito) and Arcadia (created in the late fourth century, possibly with Oxyrhynchus as the new province's *metropolis*). The extant papyri also cluster around particular private archives. Juristic papyrologists have thus debated the extent to which this evidence is 'typical', both within Egypt and in terms of the Empire as a whole. As John Crook wryly notes, the right to use the papyri in an empire-wide context 'has to be argued for against the objection that "this is Egypt"'.[26] Alan Bowman and Dominic Rathbone have persuasively suggested that 'Egypt's main oddity' in the late Ptolemaic and early imperial periods may simply lie in its

[23] Jones, *Later Roman Empire*, 496. On 'corruption' and venality see P. Veyne, 'Clientèle et corruption au service de l'état: La Vénalité des offices dans le Bas-Empire romain', *Annales (ESC)*, 36 (1981), 339–60, and Harries, *Law and Empire*, 153–71.

[24] Ibid. 171.

[25] From *c.*AD 381, Egypt's various provinces were officially grouped together as a 'diocese', each subject to the Augustal Prefect at Alexandria (with a dignity equivalent to a vicar) and hence to the Praetorian Prefect of the East—at least until Justinianic reforms in 539.

[26] Crook, *Legal Advocacy*, 8.

'unique wealth of detailed documentary evidence'.[27] With respect to the later Empire, the kinds of judicial relationships envisaged in the papyri can certainly be supported by documentary and literary evidence from elsewhere.

Late Roman villagers in Egypt tended to appeal to both local officials and military *praepositi* (commanders) for the resolution of their disputes. Pleading a dispute before an officer stationed in a nearby military unit offered the possibility of quick and local justice, and having armed forces execute the judicial sentence must have had its attractions.[28] Libanius (writing in the East, *c.*386) mentions the fact that military officers retained *assessors* (legal experts) to advise them on cases; his further claim that these assessors needed no legal experience—as military commanders preside over corporal punishments and not judicial enquiries—is part of a satirical diatribe against the governor of Syria, Tisamenus, who had once acted as an assessor in a military court (having previously, according to Libanius, abandoned a career in 'theatre productions'!).[29] In fact, Roman law forbade civil litigants from lodging suits in military courts: military officials only had authority over soldiers (with some limited exceptions).[30] *P.Oxy.* VIII. 1101 records an edict issued *c.*AD 367–70 by Flavius Tatianus, the prefect of Egypt: the edict states that private individuals, whether from malice or ignorance, have been presenting petitions to the local military *praepositi* concerning civil judgments, something that is clearly forbidden 'by the law'. Interestingly, the prefect states that he learnt of this abuse from private petitions submitted

[27] A. K. Bowman and D. Rathbone, 'Cities and Administration in Roman Egypt', *JRS* 82 (1992), 107–27, at 108. The late antique papyri from Petra (= *P. Petra*), Ravenna (= *P. Ital.*), and the recently published cache of (Visigothic) slate slabs from Iberia, I. Velázquez Soriano, *Documentos de época visigoda escritos en pizarra (siglos VI–VIII)*, 2 vols. (Turnhout: Monumenta Palaeographica Medii Aevi series hispanica, 2000), offer further comparative perspectives.

[28] See *C.Th.* 1. 21. 1 (Constantinople, AD 393, to counts and masters of both branches of the military service); and *C.Th.* 1. 6. 11 (Ravenna, AD 423, to consuls, praetors, tribunes of Plebs and the Senate). Also *P. Abin.* 44–57 (mid-4th cent.). For a mid-5th-century example see J. Gascou, 'Décision de Caesarius, gouverneur militaire de Thébaïde', *Travaux et mémoires*, Centre de recherche d'histoire et civilisation de Byzance, 14 (2002), 269–77.

[29] Libanius, *Oration* 33. 3–4, tr. A. F. Norman, *Libanius, Selected Works*, ii (Cambridge, Mass.: Harvard University Press, 1977), 196.

[30] *P. Mich.* XIII. 660, records the proceedings of a trial presided over by a *comes militum* involving, amongst other individuals, a soldier suspected of murdering a priest. Under Roman law, cases usually followed the forum of the defendant. For military jurisdiction under Justinian see F. Goria, 'Giudici civili e giudici militari nell'età giustinianea', *Studia et Documenta Historiae et Iuris*, 61 (1995), 447–61.

directly to him. An imperial constitution issued at Constantinople in AD 397 and addressed to Archelaus, the then Augustal Prefect of Egypt, testifies to the fact that the Emperors' ears had also been bent on the same subject. In addition to punishing the civilian who took his case before a military judge, the AD 397 imperial constitution also orders a fine of ten pounds of gold to be levied against his advocate for helping to get the civil case lodged before a military court (*C.Th.* 2. 1. 9). The involvement of an advocate implies planning and a wilful attempt to manipulate the jurisdiction under which a given case might be heard. As the mid-fifth-century drafter of the Emperor Marcian's *Novel* 1 explains:

> Through falsified speeches and ornate words they [the plaintiffs] sometimes confuse the laws by means of their trickery and often drag their adversaries to alien courts. Thus it happens too often that a soldier goes as a 'foreigner' into a civil court and a private citizen goes as a 'foreigner' into a military court, each of which is unsuitable for them.[31]

Marcian's edict condemns such practices as showing 'contempt of the law and the statutes', but the litigants had obviously been employing strategies that worked for them on the ground.

Most inhabitants of the Empire's provinces could expect to appear before local officials such as the *curator* (a city magistrate, although technically an imperial appointment), the *duoviri* (municipal magistrates and their equivalent), or, in Egypt and the East, the *praepositi pagorum* (see above). As well as having a wide range of functions in entering 'legal' acts onto municipal registers, these city magistrates apparently had a clear idea of what types of cases could be pleaded before them. *P.Oxy.* LIV. 3758 records at least seven different proceedings heard before the *curator* (*logistes*) of Oxyrhynchus, probably in the months of February and March 325. The fact that these separate hearings were copied together by a scribe and then attached to the record of a concrete case demonstrates both the availability of the municipal courts' records and (as we shall see in Chapter 4) their potential interest to future litigants. The disputes in *P.Oxy.* LIV. 3758 concern inheritance law, the financing of a compulsory purchase of military clothing, conflicting claims over property and the lease of a house, and the guardianship of an orphan minor—as well as two instances of the straightforward reading of a will (*apertura testamenti*). Lines 39–77 of the papyrus

[31] *N. Marc.* 1. 1. 5 (Constantinople, AD 450). Compare *N.Th.* 4. 1 (Constantinople, AD 438 to Florentius PP).

record a complicated case between a husband and wife, involving golden jewellery given on deposit to various family members at different times; the plaintiff's advocate begins with the statement that his client had initially petitioned the office of the *praeses* (provincial governor), but the advocate is abruptly interrupted by the curator's statement that this was a superfluous act, 'since the law is clear that local judges are to hear such (?) cases'.[32] The curator at least knew which cases fell automatically under his jurisdiction. Later fourth-century emperors expected *defensores civitatum* to hear similar types of cases, albeit with the specific ideological slant of protecting 'defenceless' provincials from rapacious officials.[33] Late Roman bishops offered a further empire-wide, yet city-based, legal venue.[34]

Most disputants outside the major cities probably never saw the court of a provincial governor or prefect in action, but this does not necessarily imply that they failed to invoke those 'higher' authorities in their disputes. *P.Sakaon* 48 (6 April 343) records a petition to a *praepositus pagi* from the son of a deacon of the 'catholic' church; it asks that those guilty of assaults and thefts are either brought before the *praepositus pagi* himself to make restitution, or else are escorted to the 'great court' of the *praeses* of Augustopotamia, 'so that the appropriate severity may be prescribed against them'.[35] If the case made it as far as a formal criminal accusation (discussed further below), then it would normally automatically fall under the 'ordinary' *iurisdictio* of the provincial governor.[36] Criminal suits involving high-status litigants could be transferred to the jurisdiction of the top-level bureaucratic courts.

In civil cases it was an established practice for potential plaintiffs to send a petition to their provincial governor, or in some cases a prefect or emperor, outlining the nature of their case and requesting justice.

[32] *P.Oxy.* LIV. 3758, ll. 45–6.

[33] See R. M. Frakes, *Contra Potentium Iniurias: The Defensor Civitatis and Late Roman Justice* (Munich: Verlag C. H. Beck, 2001). At 130–1 Frakes suggests that the relationship between the *defensor civitatis* and the local elite may have shifted as a result of *C.Th.* 1. 29. 6 (387 to PP Eusignius): *defensores civitatum* are to be appointed by municipal decree, rather than by the PP and the Emperor (as was formerly the case).

[34] Discussed further in Part II below.

[35] *P. Sakaon* 48, ed. and tr. Parássoglou, *The Archive of Aurelius Sakaon*, 119–23. See *C.Th.* 9. 2. 3 (AD 380, given at Constantinople to Eutropius PP) and *C.Th.* 9. 2. 5 (AD 409/405, given at Ravenna to Caecilianus PP).

[36] See, however, the exception granted to *defensores* in 'lawless' provinces at *C.Th.* 1. 29. 8 (AD 392, given at Constantinople to Tatianus PP).

If successful, the petition could be returned to the applicant with an official subscription ordering them to approach an appropriate local judge.[37] The imperial authorities could also respond to private petitions by writing directly to a relevant local official, rather than ordering the petitioners themselves to seek him out: 'Flavius Philagrius to the *strategus* of the Oxyrhynchite nome, greetings. Eudaemon approached (me) claiming that he has debtors acknowledged as such, as you will learn from the copy of the petition he submitted. Take care, if you find that he is telling the truth, to protect him from loss.'[38] The instruction to the judge to investigate whether the facts alleged by the plaintiff are 'true' is standard in earlier imperial subscriptions (as collected in the Diocletianic Hermogenian and Gregorian Codes); establishing the 'truth' of a petition is also the subject of a late fifth-century constitution concerning all rescripts issued by the Palatine bureaux on behalf of the emperor—whether they have been sent to the petitioners themselves or to a judge (*CI* 1. 23. 7, Emperor Zeno to Sebastian PP).[39] Subscriptions continued to be issued by provincial governors and prefects throughout late antiquity. It thus seems plausible that, despite the lack of any collection comparable to the Tetrarchic Codes of Hermogenianus and Gregorianus, late antique emperors also continued to issue responses to petitions; these could be either addressed directly to the petitioner or to a relevant official.[40] When Bishop Appion, for example, petitioned Theodosius II, he received a rescript *ad iudicem* (a response via a judge).[41] In any event, we should note that officials in the central Palatine bureaux did not hold a monopoly on the issuing of official responses to petitions in late antiquity.

The possession of an official response from a provincial governor—or a higher magistrate right up to the Emperor himself—could act as a persuasive bargaining chip in the preliminary stages of litigation, as well

[37] e.g. *P.Mert.* II. 91 (AD 316). D. Feissel and J. Gascou (eds.), *La Pétition à Byzance* (Paris: Centre de Recherche d'Histoire et Civilisation de Byzance, 2004), 141–97, list 118 5th- to 7th-cent. petitions known from papyrological evidence.

[38] *P.Oxy.* XXXXIII. 3129 (AD 335).

[39] The clause 'si preces veritate nituntur' is discussed by Kaser and Hackl, *Das römische Zivilprozessrecht*, 636.

[40] U. Wilcken, 'Zu den Kaiserreskripten', *Hermes*, 55 (1920),1–42, discusses the distinction *rescriptum/subscriptio*, as does D. Nörr, 'Zur Reskriptenpraxis in der Hohen Prinzipatzeit', *ZSS, Röm. Abt.* 98 (1981), 1–46.

[41] D. Feissel, and K. Worp, 'La Requête d'Appion, évêque de syene, à Theodose II: P. Leid. Z revisé', *Oudheidkundige mededelingen uit het Rijksmuseum van Oudheden te Leiden*, 68 (1988), 97–11; see in general D. Feissel, 'Pétitions aux empereurs et formes du rescrit', in Feissel and Gascou, *La Pétition à Byzance*, 33–52, at p. 36.

as providing a means of opening the initial stages of a hearing. However, obtaining a subscription could be a lengthy and time-consuming business—especially if the opposing side in a dispute was busy lodging counter-petitions as in *P.Oxy.* XXXI. 2597: 'I have presented applications to our Lord the prefect, and no decision has been subscribed for me so far. Your opponent is tireless in making petitions, and so am I in making counter-petitions . . .'[42] The letter's sender also states that he is heeding the advice of the person with whom he is corresponding and 'staying close' to the office of the prefect.

P.Oxy. I. 67 (AD 338) records a further, perhaps typical, sequence of events with respect to the preliminary judicial stages in a property dispute. The plaintiff first addresses a petition to the prefect at Alexandria, outlining his case with special reference to two legal principles and requesting the appointment of a certain Aëtius, formerly a city magistrate of the Oxyrhynchite nome, as judge; the prefect in turn sends the following letter:

> Flavius Antonius Theodorus to Aëtius, ex-magistrate of the Oxyrhynchite nome, greeting. If the accused persons protest against the restoration of the estates of which they are said to be in occupation and of which, as at least the accompanying document testifies, the rightful owner is the accuser, take care to enforce the precepts of the law and to have the preliminary proceedings of the court conducted under legal forms.[43]

The petitioner then writes directly to Aëtius, including copies of both his original petition to the prefect and the prefect's letter quoted above. It was at this point that all three documents were collated together. Hence the petitioner had either been sent a copy of the prefect's letter to Aëtius by the prefect's office staff, or he had copied it himself from the prefectural records in Alexandria. In any event, in this case it was the petitioner himself who named his judge, and the prefect authorized the request through direct contact with the former city magistrate.

The early fourth-century papyri thus reveal at least three procedural scenarios that served to link the imperial bureaucratic courts with city officials in the localities: first, a petitioner might seek and receive a subscription that instructed them to approach a 'competent' local judge themselves; second, a petitioner might receive a subscription that was sent directly from the provincial governor or prefect to a relevant local

[42] See Bagnall, *Egypt in Late Antiquity*, 162.

[43] *P.Oxy.* I. 67, ll. 8–11. Compare *P.Lips.*, no. 38 (Hermopolis, AD 390).

official; or third, the petitioner might request the appointment of a named judge for a specific case from the governor or prefect (as in *P.Oxy.* I. 67). It is notable in each of these three scenarios that the 'higher level' bureaucrat communicated the subject of the petitioner's case to the 'lower level' judge using a relatively straightforward formula specific to the individual petition. The 'lower level' judge was, in turn, expected to use this formula in any subsequent proceedings. It is worth noting in this context that an AD 342 constitution of the Emperor Constantius does not prohibit the use of any formula *per se*, but is specifically targeted against anyone 'who lurks in readiness to *quibble over the minute details* of a legal formula'.[44] Nor should we assume that a 'higher' magistrate decided points of law and the 'lower' judge decided on facts alone. For example, lines 1–13 of *P.Oxy.* LIV. 3764 record a case heard *c.*AD 325 before a city magistrate (probably a *curator*). At the opening of the hearing the magistrate notes that the (Augustal) Prefect had already pronounced conditionally in favour of the plaintiff, if the facts alleged were proved. Both the plaintiff's and the defendant's advocates then proceed to plead *new* claims to ownership of the disputed property before the city magistrate—hence the latter is forced to re-examine the legal basis of the case as well as ascertaining the 'facts' of the dispute. Finally, mid-fourth-century imperial constitutions confirm that litigants who were not satisfied with the sentences delivered by city magistrates could appeal to their provincial governor.[45]

The bureaucratic practice of appointing *iudices pedanei*—'petty judges' with a general authority to judge certain types of delegated cases rather than a specific instruction to hear a particular suit—began under the Principate and continued in the Late Empire. Diocletian was apparently concerned that provincial governors were delegating cases too freely, and issued an edict to restrict the delegation to governors who were otherwise unable to judge all their cases, 'because they are occupied in public affairs or because of the sheer volume of judicial business'.[46] A constitution of the Emperor Julian confirms that *iudices pedanei*

[44] *CI* 2. 57. 1 (to Marcellinus, *praeses* of Phoenicia): 'Iuris formulae aucupatione syllabarum insidiantes cunctorum actibus radictius amputentur.' *Contra* Harries, *Law and Empire*, 102.

[45] *C.Th.* 11. 31. 1 (AD 363, given at Verona to the PP Mamertinus) and *C.Th.* 11. 31. 3 (AD 368/370, given at Trier to the Prefect of the City, Olybrius; given its addressee, *C.Th.* 11. 31. 3 may originally have only applied to Rome and/or possibly Constantinople. See the Tetrarchic rescript included at *CI* 3. 3. 3 (AD 297).

[46] *CI* 3. 3. 2, see also *CI* 3. 3. 3–5.

continued to be appointed by provincial governors: Julian's text survives in a number of different forms. As Denis Feissel has argued, it would be unwise to pretend that any of these forms give us a single 'original' text.[47] *C.Th.* 1. 16. 8 and *CI* 3. 3. 5 are extracts from the operative part of an *epistula* sent by Julian to the Praetorian Prefect Secundus. The specific context of Julian's measure, however, is only revealed in a number of inscriptions so far discovered in two Aegean cities. In piecing the epigraphic dossier together, Feissel plausibly suggests that Julian's letter to his Praetorian Prefect was copied and sent as a prefectural edict to the *praeses* of the Aegean Islands, whose office staff then copied a version of it to (all or perhaps just a number) of the *metropoleis* under his jurisdiction. Given the localities where the inscriptions have been found, it is thus not certain whether Julian intended his measure to apply beyond the province of the Aegean Islands. The Latin inscription referred to by Feissel as 'Plaque I' from Amorgos reads:

> Copy of the imperial letter—Some disputes are wont to arise which demand examination and investigation by a higher judge. Then again, however, there are certain affairs for which it is unnecessary to wait on the governor of a province. After weighing up the two kinds of cases, we have decided to grant governors the responsibility of appointing *iudices pedanei* to deal with those cases that are of lesser significance.[48]

In other words, provincial governors could delegate judges for run-of-the-mill cases, including those relating to petty crimes. Julian's aim, like Diocletian's, was undoubtedly to reduce the heavy traffic of business through the governor's court; both measures may well have been initially provoked by specific pleas from harassed provincial governors. In 370 the practice also seems to have been in operation in Rome.[49] Moreover, a few years later we find an imperial grant exempting *picturae professores* (painting teachers) from the jurisdiction of *iudices pedanei* in North Africa.[50] The practice of provincial governors delegating cases 'of

[47] D. Feissel, 'Une constitution de l'empereur Julien entre text épigraphique et codification (*CIL* III, 459 et *CTh* 1,16,8)', in E. Lévy (ed.) *La Codification des lois dans l'antiquité* (Paris: De Boccard, 2000), 315–37, at 336. On the wider context of imperial 'letters' and the Theodosian Code see Millar, *Greek Roman Empire*, 7.

[48] Tr. from Feissel's emended text, 'Une constitution', 21–5.

[49] *C.Th.* 11. 31. 3 (given at Trier, addressed to Olybrius, Prefect of the City): appeals from *iudices pedanei*—and city magistrates—should be heard by provincial governors. On the dating of this constitution see F. Pergami, *La legislazione di Valentiniano e Valente (364–375)*, *AARC* ii/4, (Milan: Guiffrè editore, 1993), 492.

[50] *C.Th* 13. 4. 4 (AD 374, given at Trier, addressed to the vicar of Africa) = *CI* 12. 20. 48.

lesser significance' to delegated judges thus appears to have been fairly widespread in the later fourth century—as presumably was the desire to secure imperial grants of exemption from having to appear before them. There is, however, little discussion of this in the Theodosian or Justinianic Codes.

In April 539 the Emperor Justinian entrusted John of Cappadocia with the overhaul of a particular system for appointing *iudices pedanei* that had been established by the Emperor Zeno, in the late fifth century (*Nov. Iust.* 82). The preamble to *Novel* 82 states that Zeno had 'introduced many changes', but his law 'gradually fell into almost complete desuetude'; the immediate problem being that Zeno had inscribed the names of *iudices pedanei* into a 'register of judges', but they had all died with no new names being added. According to Justinian, new petty judges had grown up by 'convention', but they had no legal knowledge and lacked any courtroom experience: they had 'to beg and borrow from other sources the honest abilities of a judge'. Justinian abolished Zeno's law, and instead appointed twelve named *pedanei iudices* for the city of Constantinople, all of them individuals who had practised either as advocates or high-ranking imperial officials (*Nov. Iust.* 82. 1–3). Delegating cases to practising advocates was an established custom, as we shall see below. Justinian's chosen twelve were to sit in a civil basilica, hearing cases from early in the morning until evening. According to the frankly propagandist preamble to *Novel* 82, Justinian's subjects deserved a court system that was 'speedy, easy to use and not subject to any delays'; the new system of *pedanei iudices*, however, seems to have been limited to Constantinople alone. In fact, less than a year before *Novel* 82 was promulgated, Justinian had forbidden plaintiffs from summoning provincials to Constantinople to defend minor suits; some of those who made the journey apparently never left, and died as beggars in the streets.[51]

In the language of the late Roman bureaucracy the provincial governor (*praeses* (*provinciae*), *praesidalis*, *rector* (*provinciae*)) was referred to as the *iudex ordinarius*, the 'ordinary judge' in civil and criminal cases.[52] Other courts of 'special jurisdiction' could, however, bypass

[51] *Nov. Iust.* 69 (Justinian to the People of Constantinople, 1 June 538). Compare *C.Th.* 11. 30. 47 (AD 386, given at Constantinople to Cynegius PP): litigants can travel to the imperial court if a judge has referred their case to the imperial consistory and they have not heard anything back for a year!

[52] See in general C. Rouchè, 'The Functions of the Governor in Late Antiquity: Some Observations', *Antiquité Tardive*, 6 (1998), 31–6.

the provincial governor's authority—in particular those connected with fiscal revenue.[53] The governor was expected to hear cases in public, either with the door of his private council chambers open and 'with everyone called inside' or before a tribunal 'crowded by throngs of people'.[54] As Luke Lavan has argued, we should perhaps think in general of late antique lawcourts as 'non-architectural spaces': they could be located in a city's forum, in a civil basilica, in bath buildings, or even in Christian churches.[55] An imperial courtroom was, however, carefully marked out from other quotidian spaces: according to the Christian writer Prudentius, a table was set up before the presiding *iudex* on which images of the emperors were placed.[56] The trial participants—and I include any 'audience' within this term—would thus have experienced the institutional authority of the courtroom through the presence of imperial insignia, as well as through the language, clothing, and bodily postures of the officials. We should not underestimate the theatricality of late Roman legal proceedings or the extent of the judge's role in creating a sense of social occasion. Clematius, then provincial governor of Palestine, was apparently so thrilled with his own judicial conduct that he wrote a letter to Libanius describing his personal arrest of a thief, his flow of eloquence in defeating the culprit's 'ingenious alibi', the arrival of a crowd at the trial, and, finally, 'the applause of the bystanders'.[57]

According to the third-century jurist Marcian, it was the duty of provincial governors to track down and punish thieves, kidnappers, and hijackers, as well as 'those who commit sacrilege against the gods'.[58] Governors could actively seek out offenders who threatened the peace

[53] In the 4th to 6th cents. the *rationalis*, a fiscal representative, usually heard cases concerning taxation and land that was claimed to be *bona vacantia* or *bona caduca*. See the discussion on Ammon Scholasticus in Ch. 4 below.

[54] Respectively, *C.Th.* 1. 16. 9 (Aquileia, AD 364) and *C.Th.* 1. 16. 6 (Constantinople, AD 331).

[55] L. Lavan, 'The Political Topography of the Late Antique City: Activity Spaces in Practice', in Luke Lavan and William Bowden (eds.), *Theory and Practice in Late Antique Archaeology* (Leiden and Boston: Brill, 2003), 314–37 at 325–7. Also Kaser and Hackl, *Das römische Zivilprozessrecht*, 554–5.

[56] Prudentius, *Peristephanon* 10. 5. 49–50, discussed by W. Loerke, 'The Miniatures of the Trial in the Rossano Gospels', *Art History Bulletin*, 43/3 (1961), 171–95.

[57] Libanius, *Ep.* 315. 1 (ed. Foerster), tr. S. Bradbury, *Selected Letters of Libanius from the Age of Constantius and Julian* (Liverpool: Liverpool University Press, 2004), no. 115, at 154.

[58] D. 48. 13. 4. 2 (Marcian, *Institutes*, 14); also D. 1. 18. 13 pr. (Ulpian, *On the Office of Proconsul* 7).

and security of their province by authorizing arrests and opening court proceedings ('inquisitorial' procedure), or they could alternatively wait for the cases to come to them via public *accusatio*. It was the latter 'adversarial' procedure, rather than the inquisitorial, that continued to be the most common means of initiating a criminal hearing in late antiquity.

Criminal trials, of course, had long fascinated Roman imaginations, and Christian martyr acts perhaps contributed to the trend.[59] In the course of a homily on Christ's passion narrative, a late fourth-century anonymous commentator on the Gospel of Matthew paints the following awe-inspiring scene, reminiscent as Brent Shaw has argued of Christian portrayals of martyrdom:

> The judge who will hear the cases of criminals in public places his tribunal in a high location . . . and you will see there the officials arranged in their proper order: in the middle of the judicial hearing chamber are placed the horrible devices of torture, which are painful not just to suffer, but even to see. There stand close at hand and at the ready the torturers themselves, crueller in their appearance than ghostly apparitions. The whole setting of the court is clothed in the dress of terror. When the criminals are led into the midst of this scene, even before any interrogation has actually begun by the judge, they are already broken by the terrible sight of the court itself.[60]

Not all criminal cases, however, lent themselves so readily to such dramatization. According to an imperial constitution issued at Milan in 395 to Pasiphilus, possibly *agens vicem PPO et PVR*, small-fry cases were being brought before governors 'under the pretence of being crimes': these included disputes over the boundaries of small tracts of land; slaves 'addicted to flight'; petty thefts; the seizure of an animal, or a slave, or a movable thing; and the contested possession of small cottages (*C.Th.* 2. 1. 8 pr.). The advantage to the litigant in classifying a trivial case as a 'crime' presumably lay in being able to avoid the lower courts and skip straight to the jurisdiction of the provincial governor or higher. The provincial governor's office staff, for their part, had at least one incentive in placing 'trivial' cases on the books: they got the fees. Section 2 of *C.Th.* 2. 1. 8 thus concludes with the decree 'that only those cases which are criminal are to be heard by your sincerity

[59] See B. Shaw, 'Judicial Nightmares and Christian Memory', *Journal of Early Christian Studies*, 11/4 (2003), 533–63.

[60] *Opus Imperfectum in Matthaeum, Hom.* 34. 31. 1, quoted from Shaw 'Judicial Nightmares', 540–1.

[Pasiphilus], those that the deserved and merited horror of an *inscriptio* has embraced'.[61]

A 409 or possibly 405 constitution, issued at Ravenna to Caecilianus PP, requires city magistrates to transfer those accused of robbery, violent assault, 'murder', debauchery, rape, and adultery to the governor's *iudicium* (*C.Th.* 9. 2. 5). Perhaps, however, there was genuine confusion on the ground: certain types of cases could be classified as falling under either 'criminal' or 'civil' jurisdiction, depending on the way in which the suit was pleaded. An individual dispossessed of property, for example, could pursue his opponent under civil law or criminal statutes (framing his adversary as either *dejiciens* or *invasor* respectively).[62] Thus the way was open for litigants with the inclination, and the necessary access to legal expertise, to strategically choose their legal venue by framing a plea accordingly.

Libanius weaves into a number of his *Orations* a satirical commentary on the types of cases heard before provincial governors. On the one hand, he accuses certain provincial governors of spending too much time on levying taxes and ensuring the corn supply, and not enough on court actions. And the time that is dedicated to judging cases is taken up with 'throttling and hacking the debtors'—thus leaving no opportunities for Libanius' prodigies to demonstrate their skills as advocates in 'long, fine discourses'.[63] On the other hand, still according to Libanius, there is a multitude of court hearings for trivial cases, but few for matters of any importance: 'I have often sat in attendance and listened to cases dealing with thirty staters, or twenty, or an acre of land, a few trees, a slave, a camel, an ass, a cloak or a jacket and things far less important still, with a galaxy of legal talent on each side and longwinded speeches from both.'[64] Whilst we should be cautious in taking Libanius' remarks at face value, the custom of

61 An *inscriptio personae* bound the accuser to serious penalties if the case was not proved; see *C.Th.* 9. 1 and *CI* 9. 2.

62 A. Chastagnol, *La Préfecture Urbaine à Rome sous le Bas-Empire* (Paris: Presses Universitaires de France, 1960), 91. Compare *C.Th.* 2. 18. 3 (AD 325 to Severus PU), which forbids litigants from dividing a single case up and pleading each 'issue' before different judges.

63 Libanius, *Oration* 62. 43 (ed. R. Foerster, *Libanii Opera*, iv. 368), tr. A. F. Norman, *Antioch as a Centre of Hellenic Culture as Observed by Libanius* (Liverpool: Liverpool University Press, 2000), 100–1. See also Libanius, *Oration* 45. 17 (= Norman, *Libanius, Selected Works*, ii. 174) and *Oration* 33. 7, 'Against Tisamenus' (= Norman, *Libanius, Selected Works*, ii. 200).

64 Libanius, *Oration* 45. 18 (= Norman, *Libanius, Selected Works*, ii. 174–6).

employing advocates in even minor cases is amply borne out by the papyri.

At the diocesan level there were the higher courts of the *vicarii* (with an authority delegated from the Praetorian Prefects), and above that the courts of the Praetorian Prefects and the prefects of the cities of Rome and Constantinople (all of whom judged *vice sacra*, in place of the emperor).[65] Finally, of course, there were the emperors themselves. Litigation undertaken at these higher level courts was expensive and perhaps mostly confined to late Romans of wealth and status: Justinian's *Novel* 71 implies that even the resources of sixth-century *clarissimi* might not stretch to employing procurators before the prefectural court.

From Constantine onwards, these higher level courts became increasingly linked to those at the provincial level through complicated procedures for the referral of judicial sentencing and the hearing of appeals. Magistrates could refer the judging of tricky cases to a court of higher jurisdiction via a report (termed a *relatio* or *consultatio*) to which any relevant documents were appended: the litigants could also forward their own statements on the case (*preces refutatoriae* or *libelli refutatorii*).[66] The higher *iudex* to whom the case was referred would examine this dossier and then issue a written decision, directed to the original presiding magistrate. There was no review on this decision, as Augustine noted in a letter written in 404: 'Is it not true that even in civil cases, when the right of judgement has been referred to a higher power, as long as circumstances remain unchanged, the verdict, from which no appeal is now allowed, is to be awaited without making any change in the course of the trial, so as not to prejudice the higher judge?'[67] Appeals, on the other hand, were supposed to be made by litigants after the presiding judge's final sentence had been delivered.[68] The request for

[65] Chastagnol, *La Préfecture Urbaine*, 100–20, gives a detailed examination of civil procedure in the court of the urban prefecture at Rome; for criminal cases, ibid. 85–100.

[66] Symmachus' *Relationes* 19 and 49 (*c*.384) provide detailed examples of the juristic and procedural tangles which could arise within the court of the urban prefecture.

[67] Augustine, *Ep*. 77. 2 (new edn. *CCSL* 31A, 82): 'cum in ipsis causis saecularibus, quando ad maiorem potestatem refertur arbitrium iudicandi, manentibus sicut erant omnibus rebus, exspectetur illa sententia, unde iam non liceat provocari, ne superiori cognitori fiat iniuria, si eius pendente iudicio aliquid fuerit commutatum?' See Augustine *Ep*. 78 for this procedure being adopted by the AD 397 Council of Carthage for ecclesiastical cases involving clerics.

[68] D. 49. 1–13, *C.Th.* 1. 5. 1–4, *C.Th.* 11. 30, *CI* 7. 62–70, *Nov. Iust.* 23, and *Nov. Iust.* 115. 1–2. See in general F. Pergami, *L'appello nella legislazione del tardo impero*, *AARC, Materiali per una palingenesi delle costituzioni tardo-imperiali*, serie terza 2 (Milan: Guiffré, 2000) and Matthews, *Laying Down the Law*, 201–21. In the 4th and 5th cents.

an appeal could be made orally and immediately, without recourse to a written petition: the papyrus *P.Col.* VII. 175, dated to 339, ends with the plaintiff making such an oral appeal against the final sentence (col. IV, ll. 176–7). The acts of the Council of Chalcedon (AD 451) refer to Eutyches making an oral appeal from an ecclesiastical sentence at the Council of Ephesus II (AD 449).[69] The onus of producing a written report (termed *litterae dimissoriae* or *apostoli*) fell upon the magistrates themselves some of whom, according to the drafter(s) of two Constantinian constitutions at least, took a request for an appeal as a personal insult to their judicial authority.[70] In 546, Justinian himself was alarmed when he learnt that litigants, advocates, and all those involved in cases heard on appeal *vice sacra* were using the 'garments', the 'feet-coverings', and the language that should be used in the emperor's actual presence alone (*Novel* 126, to Peter PPO).

THE MAKING OF A LATE ROMAN MAGISTRATE

Under the Late Empire, as in the preceding periods, there was no 'professional' training for judges as such. However, the career structures outlined in both legal and extra-legal source material suggests an increasing tendency for magistrates to have been trained as advocates prior to their promotion within the imperial bureaucracy. Moreover, 'forensic' modes of reasoning were taught via a rhetorical education, hence most judges would have had at least some familiarity with 'courtroom' argumentation—whether they had actually practised as advocates or not.

A constitution of Theodosius II issued at Constantinople in 442 implies that it was a frequent practice for the PPO to entrust the government of a province to advocates who had distinguished themselves in the *patrocinium causarum* either in the praefectural or provincial courts; Theodosius also allowed a retiring governor to resume his practice of advocacy 'by which he obtained his means of subsistence' (*CI*

there was no appeal from the praetorian prefects as immediate representatives of the Emperor; in this instance review proceedings were undertaken by a *supplicatio* addressed to the Emperor who could grant a renewed examination, but would assign it to the same court.

[69] *ACO* 2. 1. l, 185 and 819. I owe these references, with thanks, to Henry Chadwick.

[70] *C.Th.* 11. 30. 15 (posted Carthage, AD 329) and *C.Th.* 11. 30. 13 (issued at Heraclea, possibly also in AD 329).

2. 7. 9). Almost eighty years earlier the Emperor Julian had apparently attempted to restrict magistrates from becoming advocates again:

First of all, we should urge silence—without seeming to give orders—on those whose age and stature point to the desirability of rest . . . Will you, when you have settled controversies between disputing parties, promulgated edicts, dictated the law, will you go back to the sordid infights, the squalid clamour, will you turn back from honour to vice? Where then will be the ornaments of your dignities, if you return as a veteran to the same terrain where you began as a tiro? So, as I said, they will withdraw from the law court, those who have done their duty as judges.[71]

This text is from the opening lines of a constitution *de postulando* (concerning pleading), with a subscription of the Emperor Julian, dated 17 January 363 at Antioch. It was not included in either the Theodosian or Justinianic compilations, but was discovered in 1962 in a tenth–twelfth-century manuscript of the comedies of Terence housed in the Biblioteca Medicea Laurenziana, Florence. Although the *inscriptio* is lacking, the addressee was Apronianus, the prefect of the city of Rome. The drafter of the constitution, whom Nörr proposes was Julian himself, clearly holds the judicial functions of the magistrate in high regard; he includes the promulgation of edicts as one of his duties, alongside the settling of legal controversies.

Augustine also alludes to the progression from advocate to judge in a letter dated 414 and addressed to Macedonius, the vicar of Africa; 'Even you good men who are now judges, who have gained much experience by pleading men's cases in the law court, know how much more willingly you used to undertake a defence rather than a prosecution.'[72] Symmachus, *Letter* 9. 31 also comments on the high proportion of advocates who became magistrates. The relationship between forensic

[71] B. Bischoff and D. Nörr, 'Eine unbekannte Konstitution Kaiser Julians', *Bayerische Akad. der Wiss.* Phil.-Hist. Klasse, 58 (1963), 1–51, ll. 3–4 and 12–16: 'Adprimum illis suadere silentium nec | iussisse videamur, quibus quietem et aetas et dignitas porrigebat . . . An tu, cum controversias discep | tatorum absolveris, cum edicta proposueris, cum ius dixeris, ad | rabida litigia procacemque clamorem, ab honore ad vitia reverteris? Ubi igitur erunt infulae dignitatum, si ad idem emeritus redibis quo tiro | coepisti? Ergo, ut dixi, abstinebunt foro, qui iudicaverunt.' See also R. Andreotti, 'Problemi della constitutio de postulando attribuita all'imperatore Giuliano e l'esercizio della professione forense nel tardo impero', *RIDA* 19 (1972), 181–218 and A. Chastagnol, 'L'Empereur Julien et les avocats de Numidie', *Antiquités Africaines*, 14 (1979), 225–35. See also *N. Th.* 10. 2 (AD 439) and *N. Val.* 2. 2. 2 (AD 442).

[72] *Ep.* 153. 10, *PL* 3,657: 'andoquidem et vos viri boni qui nunc iudices estis, et in foro aliquando versati causas hominum suscepistis, scitis quam libentius defendere quam accusare soleretis'.

rhetoric and preparation for a public career was at least as important in the Late Empire as it had been in the first century BC, when Cicero stated that the practice of oratory was a necessary preparatory stage in the development of great Republican statesmen (*De Or.* 1. 34).[73]

During the fourth and fifth centuries a custom developed whereby a high-ranking magistrate could in fact delegate the examination of a case to an advocate attached to the bar of his court.[74] Promotion through the ranks of the imperial bureaucracy depended upon personal recommendation; thus how the aspiring advocate handled these delegated cases may well have affected his own chances of advancement. The opening stages of a case could accordingly take place before a magistrate, and the final stages, which were often held after a considerable time delay, before an advocate appointed *iudex datus*. The advantages of having your advocate reappear as your judge were not lost on Augustine: his *Sermon* 213 appeals to the convention as a means of reassuring his congregation about their treatment at the Last Judgment:

> If you had a case to be tried by some judge, and you instructed counsel, you would be defended by the advocate who would conduct your case as best he could; and if he did not complete it, and you heard that he was going to come as the judge, just imagine how overjoyed you would be, because the one who a short while before had been your advocate could now himself be your judge . . . We have him [Christ] as our advocate, need we fear Him as our judge? On the contrary, because we have sent Him ahead as our advocate, we can hope without a worry for his coming back as judge.[75]

It is in the light of this custom of delegating the judgment of cases to advocates that we should read the otherwise confusing constitution addressed to the urban prefect of Rome (AD 368): 'anyone who desires to be a pleader cannot act as advocate and judge in the same case, since a distinction must exist between those who decide cases and those who

[73] For the Early Empire, see Pliny, *Ep.* 1. 23 and [Ps-] Tacitus, *Dialogus de Oratoribus* 5.

[74] W. W. Buckland and A. B. McNair, *Roman Law and Common Law*, 2nd edn. (Cambridge: CUP, 1965), 6.

[75] Augustine, *Sermon* 213. 5 (*PL* 38. 1063): 'Si haberes causam apud aliquem iudicem agendam, et instrueres advocatum, esses susceptus ab advocato, ageret causam tuam sicut posset; et si non illam finisset, et audires illum iudicem venturum, quantum gauderes, quia ipse potuit esse iudex tuus, qui fuit paulo ante advocatus tuus? Et modo ipse pro nobis orat, ipse pro nobis interpellat; advocatum eum habemus, et iudicem timeamus? Imo, quia advocatum praemisimus, securi iudicem venturum speremus.'

argue them'.[76] In this instance, the emperors were thus more concerned about potential judicial abuses than Augustine the bishop was to be.

Justinian's *Novel* 158 (AD 544) outlines a fascinating case involving an advocate who reappeared as a judge in the same case. The *Novel*'s preamble states that petitions had been read before Justinian's consistory on behalf of a female petitioner named Thecla. In these petitions Thecla claimed that she had approached an advocate at the provincial court, named John, for advice about her possession of a certain inheritance. Having 'informed himself concerning the laws relating to this case', John had issued a written response in Thecla's favour. She (naturally) had then asked for the same advocate to be appointed as her judge. Despite his former opinion, however, John 'reached a verdict which was opposed to that which he had given in writing', apparently on the basis of a law of 'the sainted Theodosius' that had not been mentioned previously. John then, allegedly, put pressure on Thecla to accept his sentence. She, in turn, supplicated the Emperor—pleading that the law of Theodosius conflicted with one of Justinian's own constitutions (both laws having been included in Justinian's recently promulgated *Codex*). Justinian and his legal advisers were thus left to walk a legal tightrope, not least because one of the preambles to the Justinianic Code (*Const. Cordi* 3–4) explicitly stated that there were no conflicting laws contained within it. Justinian finally instructs Thecla's new judge to decide in her favour, once the truth of her allegations has been proved in his court. This case thus highlights both the procedural and legal complexities that could arise in the higher courts, as well as the potential pitfalls of having an advocate become a judge in the same case. The advocate is paid to win the case, the judge (in principle at least) is not. Justinian's *Novel* 158 also reminds us that 'codified' imperial constitutions could still be the subject of legal dispute and forensic argument.

In the absence of any formal training, the 'professional expertise' of an imperial magistrate may frequently have amounted to the sum of his previous experiences as an advocate.[77] Ammianus Marcellinus (29. 3. 6) tells the cautionary tale of Africanus, a 'busy' advocate at Rome

[76] *C.Th.* 2. 10. 5 = *CI* 2. 6. 6 pr. (AD 368/370, to Olybrius PP): 'Quisquis vult esse causidicus non idem in eodem negotio sit advocatus et iudex, quoniam aliquem inter arbitros et patronos oportet esse delectum.'

[77] Alternative routes apparently existed: Augustine, *Contra Academicos* 3. 16 (*c.*AD 386) bemoans the problem of judges who apply the philosophical system of scepticism to their reasoning in the lawcourts! Ammianus Marcellinus, *Res Gestae* 30. 4. 21, counts it as one of a number of disadvantages which advocates are liable to that 'they sometimes

and then a governor, who was apparently executed for requesting a change of provinces. Those who were more fortunate in their career advancement include Sextilius Agesilaus Aedesius, vicar of the Spains in 376 and former advocate in Africa and in the imperial consistory; Carterius, *consularis* of Syria in 380 and former advocate in Rome; and Maximinus, whose career path apparently progressed from advocate to *praeses Corsicae* (before 365), then *praeses Sardiniae* (365), *corrector Tusciae* (366), *praefectus annonae* (368/70), *vicarius urbis* (370–1), and *PPO Galliarum* (371–6).[78] Further biographical evidence is provided by the careers of late Roman bishops and ecclesiastics. Some trained as advocates prior to their episcopal appointments, and subsequently presided over their own episcopal hearings. The reason why the writings of these bishops are a valuable source for courtroom practice in the Late Empire is, in no small part, due to the simple fact that they themselves were trained in forensic rhetoric.[79]

THE *IUDEX* AS A 'CREATIVE' INTERPRETER OF LAW?

> A judge summons hearers, questions speakers, cross-questions those who deny, presses plaintiffs, dismays the guilty, reproaches accomplices, sentences confederates, delivers those convicted to their sentences.[80]

Under the late Roman *cognitio* procedure the judge was responsible for every stage of the trial from the summons to the sentence, and beyond. Bureaucratic magistrates, however, usually only held specific posts for up to two years—as the late fourth-century bishop Asterius of Amasea notes, the magistrate only possessed the canopy, the silver chariot, and the golden wand for a short time before they passed from him to the next appointment.[81] The judge's staff (*officium*), like the insignia of office

have to do with judges who have been trained in the wisecracks of Philistion or Aesop rather than in the school of Aristides the Just or Cato'.

[78] See Appendices I and II for more examples. [79] See Part II, Chs. 5–7 below.

[80] Peter Chrysologus (mid-5th cent.), *Sermon* 152. 5, *CCSL* 24B, 952, ll. 1144–46: 'Iudex audientes vocat, interrogat loquentes, regantes arguit, urget reos, percillet socios, conscios carpit, adducit complices, sententiae dat detectos.

[81] Asterius of Amasea, *Homily* 2. 5 (ed. C. Datema, *Asterius of Amasea. Homilies I–XIV: Text, Introduction, Notes* (Leiden: E. J. Brill, 1970), 19–20).

described by Asterius, were also attached to the court rather than to an individual. A late fifth-century register of staff attached to the court of the *praeses* of the Thebaid lists two advocates (*scholastici*), a legal expert (*assessor*), three chief clerks (*proximi*), an assistant and an 'under-assistant' (*subadiuva*), two stenographers (*exceptores*), five messengers (*singulares*), and a number of couriers (*cursores*).[82] We should perhaps also add the heralds and the judge's legal advisers (*assessores*, *iuris studiosi*, or *pragmatikoi*) to this list. Each of these officials was responsible for a particular sphere of forensic activity; they also functioned as the court's 'institutional memory' from one magisterial appointment to the next.

Late Roman literary and legal sources alike, however, tend to isolate the *iudex* from this forensic context. Ambrose, bishop of Milan and a former *consularis Aemiliae et Liguriae,* paints a vivid portrait of a 'good' judge during his exegesis of Psalm 118 'In praise of the divine law':

> The good judge does nothing arbitrarily nor in accordance with his own desires, but pronounces judgement in conformity with *leges* and *iura*. He respects the legal statutes and does not indulge his personal inclinations. He does not bring to the case any premeditated course of action, but judges in response to what he hears, and makes his decision in line with the nature of the case. He is deferent to the laws and does not contradict them, he looks at the merits of the case and does not alter them.[83]

Ambrose is here constructing an ideal 'Christian' template against which late Roman *iudices* could themselves be judged. He is also, however, speaking the same 'ideal' language as the late Roman chancery itself: a stress on impartial judgement, respect for *leges et iura,* and deference to the authority of the (imperial) laws are all common topoi in imperial constitutions.[84] Ambrose and a number of other 'educated' late Roman bishops were equally capable of inverting the 'good' template to criticize the 'bad' judicial practices of their day; if this amounts to a growing 'culture of criticism' in late antiquity, however, it should be viewed as a dissension from *within* the ranks and not from outside them.

[82] *CPR* 14. 39, discussed by Keenan, 'Egypt', 617.

[83] Ambrose, *Ex. Ps.* 118, *Littera 'Res'* 36 (*CSEL* 62, 462), dated to AD 386–90; 'Bonus enim iudex nihil ex arbitrio suo facit et domesticae proposito voluntatis, sed iuxta leges et iura pronuntiat, scitis iuris obtemperat, non indulget propriae voluntati, nihil paratum et meditatum domo defert, sed sicut audit ita iudicat et sicut se habet negotii natura decernit. Obsequitur legibus, non adversatur, examinat causae merita, non mutat.' Ambrose is using John 5: 30 as his 'proof text'.

[84] e.g. impartial judging, in accordance with *leges et iura*, *C.Th.* 2. 18. 1 (AD 321, given at Sirmium to 'Maximus') and *C.Th.* 1. 5. 3 (AD 331, to Maximus PU?); deference to imperial laws, *C.Th.* 1. 6. 9 (AD 384/385 to Symmachus PU).

The following scene, in which Ambrose imagines a *iudex* responding to the pleas of a convicted criminal, reads like a late fourth-century panegyric on 'rule of law' values:

Take a defendant convicted of a crime and guilty, who is not trying to construct lines of defense, but rather is resorting to prayer and twisting and turning at the knees of the judge. The judge will respond to him: I cannot act of myself. Justice, not power, is enshrined in the act of judgment. I am not standing in judgment over you, your deeds are, it is they that accuse you, they that condemn you. The laws pass judgment on you; and it is not for me to change them, but rather to safeguard them. Nothing comes out of me; rather, the nature of the case derives from you and is proceeding against you. I judge in accordance with what I hear, not what I want; and my judgment is true insofar as I give way to equity rather than to my will.[85]

In fact defending 'rule of law' values, in one form or another, was a conservative strategy of elite self-representation that stretched back to Plato, Aristotle, and the Roman jurists alike. This observation is not intended to imply that 'rule of law' values did not 'really' exist in Graeco-Roman society, nor that they were necessarily empty beliefs; it is, however, intended to widen our analysis of how cases were judged and decided within late Roman courtrooms. The idea that 'the Law' existed apart from a messy world of legal practice, and that it was objectively and rationally applied by an impartial judge (having been previously 'laid down' by an emperor), needs to be contextualized within a wider culture of late Roman forensic argumentation. Only then will it be possible seriously to reconsider late Roman judges, *iurisperiti*, and advocates as creative interpreters of law, rather than as individuals who simply applied imperial legislation (or not) on behalf of autocratic emperors.

First, we need to turn back to law in practice. Culturally specific rules concerning patronage relationships and socio-political status were built into the Roman legal system.[86] This could create informal expectations,

[85] Ambrose, *Ep.* 20 (ex 77), 11–12, (*CSEL* 82. 151–2): 'Constitue aliquem reum coargutum et convictum criminis, non astruentem defensionis genera, sed deprecantem ac volventem se ad genua iudicis. Respondet ei iudex: non possum a me facere quisquam. Iustitia in iudicando, non potentia est in iudicando. Ego non iudico, sed facta tua de te iudicant, ipsa te accusant, et ipsa condemnant. Leges te adiudicant, quas iudex non converto, sed custodio. Nihil ex me ego profero, sed ex te forma iudicii in te procedit. Secundum quod audio, iudico, non secundum quod volo; et ideo iudicium meum verum est, quia non voluntati indulgeo, sed aequitati.' Discussed by Shaw, 'Judicial Nightmares', 556–7.

[86] P. Garnsey, *Social Status and Legal Privilege in the Roman Empire* (Oxford: OUP, 1970).

as in the following third-century letter preserved on papyrus: 'If, as I hear, our prayers are answered and our lord and friend is to be holding a magistracy in the future, he and his brother can as a result of this give both of us protection with their friend . . . Whenever he [the magistrate] arrives among you, make yourself known to him.'[87] A litigant's expectations of receiving 'justice' could also be more formally grounded: high-ranking members of the senatorial aristocracy, for example, were 'naturally' accorded certain procedural privileges in their lawsuits. Moreover, formal orders of rank and dignity had to be observed when visitors were received by judges in their private council chambers and in 'extraordinary sessions'.[88] The right to enter the judge's private council chambers, together with the chance to influence the legal judgment by sitting with the magistrate during a trial (the *ius sedendi*), was extended to *illustres* and certain Palatine bureaucrats (*spectabiles* and eventually *clarissimi*), *defensores civitates*, and *sacerdotes provinciae* (the 'provincial priests' who under the Late Empire conveyed the decisions of provincial councils to the imperial court). In the early fifth century this valuable privilege was formally granted to (some) Christian bishops and defenders of the church (*defensores ecclesiae*).[89] Every late Roman court also had its own (unwritten) list of the 'usual' *honorati*, whom the official court herald would have known by sight.[90] Valerian of Cimiez, in the midst of a homily on humility and against pride, paints a psychologically nuanced picture of the behaviour of *honorati* in the courtroom:

Let us see what kind of man the proud man is when he is sitting with his peers in a law court, ready to offer an opinion. I can imagine the contests springing from the explosions of words, when one man is pressing for mercy and the other imagines that he is favouring justice—not so much because he is trying to preserve a reputation for good faith by giving the correct judgement but

[87] *P.Oxy.* LI. 3645.

[88] *C.Th.* 6. 7. 1 (given at Nasonoacum, AD 372, to Ampelius, Prefect of the City). See Matthews, *Laying Down the Law*, 221–2.

[89] *C.Th.* 6. 26. 5 (given at Trier, AD 389, to Constantianus PP) and *C.Th.* 6. 26. 16 (given at Ravenna, AD 413, to Faustinus PP). On the *defensores civitates* see *CI* 1. 55. 4 and Frakes, *Contra Potentiam Iniurias*, 133; on bishops and *defensores ecclesiae* see C. Humfress, 'A New Legal Cosmos: Late Roman Lawyers and the Early Medieval Church', in P. Linehan and J. Nelson (eds.), *The Medieval World* (London: Routledge, 2001), 557–73.

[90] Petit, *Les étudiants*, 248–9. *N.Th.* 15. 2. 1 (AD 444/441, given at Constantinople, addressed to Zoilus PP) recounts the case of Valerianus of Emesa, who (amongst other lawless acts) stormed the private chambers of the provincial governor, accompanied by 'a great horde of barbarians', and seated himself to the right of the magistrate.

because he is looking to impress a man of higher rank. He pretends to have some particular point of view in order to disagree with somebody else's opinion. He deems nothing right in the deliberations except what he alone has thought up. He thinks nothing just except what he has convinced himself of. He wants to be the only one listened to, and to be the only one to receive universal praise. And this is worse, there will be no shortage of people to take his side.[91]

In their courtrooms, at least, late Romans did not separate 'law' from 'society'.[92]

The parameters of the judge's reasoning also stretched beyond simply applying 'laws' to 'facts'. As Elizabeth Meyer has noted, 'In the courtroom every fact had to be embedded in the social understanding that helped determine character, motive, and the limits of possibility'.[93] Ancient rhetorical theory taught advocates how to manipulate persuasively this 'social understanding' in their client's favour. A relatively simple illustration is provided by a late fourth-century criminal trial recorded on papyrus. A defence advocate, Herminus, advises the judge to take the word of the defence witness Hermaion (a *curator* of Hermopolis) over that of the slave Acholius (who appears for the accusing side), as Hermaion 'is worthy of trust and the first of the hermopolitai'.[94] In other words, Hermaion should be believed because, given his social status and the integrity deriving from it, he is more likely to be 'telling the truth'. Similarly, having repeatedly accused an ex-duovir of lying, a fourth-century North African proconsul finally concludes: 'since you exercised the duovirate in your own territory your words ought to be trusted'.[95] From a theoretical perspective, we might conclude that 'truth', as understood in the courtroom, 'is a function not of discourse,

[91] Valerian, *Homily* 14. 5 on humility (James 4: 6), *PL* 52. 737: 'Videamus autem qualis sit hic superbus, cum inter aequales in iudicio sententiam daturus forte consederit. Videor mihi videre pugnas verborum eructatione compositas, cum unus misericordiae studeat, alter iustitiae favere se fingat; non ut recto iudicio fidem servet, sed ut studia personae superioris exspectet. Aliud enim sensisse se simulat, ut alterius disceptatione dissentiat. Non putat in consiliis rectum, nisi quod solus senserit; non putat iustum, nisi quod sibi ipse persuaserit. Vult solus audiri, ac solus omnium ore laudari; nec deest, quod pejus est, ex hac parte qui faveat.'

[92] Compare the recent debate within 'socio-legal studies' (itself taught as a separate discipline within modern law faculties) over whether we should correctly speak of 'law and society' or 'law in society'—see A. Sarat *et al.* (eds.), *Crossing Boundaries: Traditions and Transformations in Law and Society Research* (Evanston, Ill.: Northwestern University Press, 1998).

[93] Meyer, *Legitimacy and Law*, 217.

[94] *P.Lips.* 40, col. 2. 16, see also col. 3. 1. 5.

[95] Optatus, tr. M. Edwards, *Optatus: Against the Donatists* (Liverpool: Liverpool University Press, 1997), appendix II, 'The Acquittal Proceedings of Felix, Bishop of Abthugni', 179.

but of the enunciation of discourse'.[96] In practice, 'social profiling' was as much part of the judge's toolbox as the advocate's.

Augustine provides evidence for the impact that an advocate could have on a judge's decision-making in his commentary on Christ's Sermon on the Mount (*c*.392). Augustine states that Christ (the *advocatus*) has taught us the correct way to address our pleas/prayers (deliberately playing on the double meaning of *preces*) to God, the *iudex*. Some men, however, who have studied oratory choose to ignore the correct forms established by Christ himself and attempt to transfer their 'useless' study of oratory to an attempt to influence God by their own pleas, 'supposing that he just like a human judge will adduce the judgement from the words'.[97] As we shall see in Chapter 4, an advocate's arguments—if judged persuasive—could prompt a judge to interpret imperial 'laws' in ways never intended by their drafters. The preamble to Justinian's *Novel* 49 (issued in 537) claims that: 'The human condition, which is ever changing, never capable of remaining in a stable state, always becoming something else, brings havoc to the laws, so that that which has appeared to be well ordered, securely based, and shored up by meticulous observation, is often upset by multifarious supervening cases.'[98] In other words, according to the legislator, concrete cases prompted new laws.

Late Roman judges could not (legally) issue judgments that went against the 'sacred constitutions of emperors', as the early fourth-century juristic compilation known as the *Sentences of Paul* clearly states.[99] This does not, however, justify the conclusion that late Roman judges operated under an autocratic legal system in which they 'could not interpret, still less make', law for themselves.[100] Judges could, of

[96] B. Jackson, *Law, Fact and Narrative Coherence* (Liverpool: Deborah Charles Publications, 1988), 2 and 193.

[97] Augustine, *De Sermone Domini in Monte* (*CCSL* 35. 102–3, ll. 261–3); 'Et hoc nugatorii studii genus etiam ad deum prece flectendum transferre conantur, arbitrantes sicut hominem iudicem verbis adduci ad sententiam.' An interesting comment on the post-conversion activities of advocates!

[98] *Nov. Iust.* 49 (to John PP); compare the preamble to *Nov. Iust.* 98 (AD 539 to John PP).

[99] *Sent. Paul.* 5. 25. 4: A judge who pronounces against the sacred constitutions of emperors, or against a public law that has been read out in his presence, is deported to an island.

[100] Harries, *Law and Empire*, 29 and 117 (discussing Symmachus as a specific example); see also Meyer, *Legitimacy and Law*, 218: 'The emperor, and his officials, now make the rules; they are the authority, as what happens in court increasingly comes to show.'

course, bypass imperial laws by not allowing the recitation of specific constitutions in their courtrooms.[101] More to the point however, having heard the arguments advanced by advocates and having taken advice from their own legal experts, judges could, and did, arrive at conclusions that stretched the limits of those laid down by existing imperial legislation. Often those conclusions in turn provoked new imperial rulings on matters of substantive law.[102] We have seen a detailed example of the process above with the case of Thecla and John, first the advocate and then judge (*Nov. Iust.* 158). Judges, like emperors themselves (however much they protested to the contrary), were part of an ongoing process of legal interpretation and law-making, which was driven by concrete cases rather than abstract principles or values.

101 Libanius, *Oration* 33. 15–18 (= Norman, *Libanius, Selected Works*, ii. 208–10) accuses Tisamenus of deliberately suppressing the recitation of a law concerning decurions in his court; his *Oration* 45. 32–3 (= Norman, *Libanius, Selected Works*, ii. 190–2) also complains about the non-enforcement of imperial constitutions.

102 See Bianchini, *Caso Concreto*, 13–14, and Ch. 4 below.

3

Legal Experts and the Late Roman Courts

THE *IURISPERITUS* AND LEGAL SCIENCE

In his *Enchiridion*, excerpted at *Digest* 1. 2. 2, the mid-second-century jurist Pomponius gives an account of the origins and development of Roman law; after having outlined how the Twelve Tables came to be instituted he turns his attention to the beginnings of juristic science:

> After the enactment of these laws [the Twelve Tables], there arose a necessity for forensic debate, as it is the normal and natural outcome that problems of interpretation should make it desirable to have guidance from learned persons. This debate, and this *ius* which without formal writing emerges as expounded by learned men has no special name of its own like the other subdivisions of law designated by name (there being proper names given to these other subdivisions); it is called by the common name *ius civile*.[1]

For Pomponius the origins of juristic science thus lay in the disputes of the Forum, in the necessary interpretations of (statute) law given orally, on request, by those who were *iuris prudentes*. Hence the *iurisprudens* or *iurisperitus* was also known as the *iurisconsultus*.[2] Pomponius then announces his intention of listing the succession of *iurisconsulti* because 'the law cannot be coherent unless there is someone skilled in law by

[1] *D.* 1. 2. 2. 5: 'His legibus latis coepit (ut naturaliter evenire solet, ut interpretatio desideraret prudentium auctoritatem) necessarium esse disputationem fori. haec disputatio et hoc ius, quod sine scripto venit compositum a prudentibus, propria parte aliqua non appellatur, ut ceterae partes iuris suis nominibus designantur, datis propriis nominibus ceteris partibus, sed communi nomine appellatur ius civile.' The other subdivisions of law designated by name are given by Pomponius at *D.* 1. 2. 2. 12 as *lex* ('statute' law), *legis actiones* ('statutory actions at law'), plebiscite law, *ius honorarium*, *senatus consultum*, and *constitutio* (imperial enactment).

[2] A. Berger, *Encyclopaedic Dictionary of Roman Law* (Philadelphia: Transactions of the American Philological Society, 1953), 523.

whom it may be from day to day clarified'.[3] *Digest* 1. 2. 2. 35–53 then gives Pomponius' account of the men 'held in the highest honour by the Roman people': the jurists who developed and passed down legal principles through giving oral opinions, writing legal literature and teaching the *ius civile* (*instituere/instruere*, *D.* 1. 2. 2. 43). This activity in turn contributed to the creative expansion of the *ius civile*: the *iurisconsultus* was thus also *iuris auctor* and *iuris conditor*.

Classical Roman jurists (from the Late Republic until the mid-third century) built up the idea that 'Law' occupied an autonomous sphere within Roman social life; in other words, they developed the capacity 'to separate the discussion of legal rules from their possible application in actual circumstances'.[4] The classical jurists' reasoning, however, remained concrete; their method was to take cases, whether actual or hypothetical, and identify a common element that could be abstracted from the particulars. Even if we view this method as one of strict logical abstraction, it does not follow that the classical jurists wrote from a 'theoretical' rather than a 'practical' perspective.[5] The driving force for the creation of their 'autonomous' juristic science was that it should be applied back to concrete temporal situations, in search of a practical solution that fitted the particular circumstances. As Pomponius acknowledged, Rome's legal experts formed a distinct part of a broader culture of forensic argument.[6]

The extent to which the Roman jurists of the Early Empire actually engaged in daily forensic business has, however, been disputed. Schulz, for example, argued that during the Principate the leading jurists increasingly withdrew from what he terms 'cautelary jurisprudence' (assisting parties in private acts such as drawing up testaments and contracts). The 'real jurists', according to Schulz, concentrated on creatively elaborating the principles of juristic science—they abstained from advising

[3] *D.*1. 2. 2. 13: 'Post hoc deinde auctorum successione dicemus, quod constare non potest ius, nisi sit aliquis iuris peritus, per quem possit cottidie in melius produci.' For discussion see D. Nörr, 'Pomponius oder "Zum Geschichtsverständnis der römischen Juristen"', *ANRW* ii 15 (1976), 497–604.

[4] Lewis, 'Autonomy of Roman Law', 40. See also Harries, *Law and Empire*, 4, on the 'separateness of law as a discipline, with its own assumptions and intellectual tradition'.

[5] See Lewis, 'Autonomy of Roman Law', 45. *Contra* A. Watson, *The State, Law and Religion: Pagan Rome* (Athens, Ga: University of Georgia Press, 1992), 259: 'there is no sign that the jurists were even slightly interested in what happened in court'.

[6] See J. A. Crook, 'Once Again the *Controversiae* and Roman Law', in K. Lee, C. Mackie, and H. Tarrant, *Multarum Artium Scientia: Festschrift for R. Godfrey Tanner*, *Prudentia* suppl. (Auckland: University of Auckland, 1993), 68–76, at 69, discussing F. Lanfranchi, *Il diritto nei retori romani* (Milan: Guiffrè, 1938).

parties and instructing advocates, leaving this activity to 'lesser men, lawyers and mere scribes'. It was hence this latter 'subordinate class' that continued to exist in the Western Empire, long after the independent and creative output of the 'real jurists' had apparently been subsumed under an imperial monopoly of legal development. Little wonder, then, that Schulz and later modern Romanists have viewed post-classical legal development as 'inferior' to that of the classical period.[7]

The tendency to concentrate solely on the literary activities of the leading classical *iurisperiti* is reinforced by the way in which their *texts* have been transmitted via Justinian's early sixth-century *Digest*. The *Digest* presents us with a closed canon of 'authoritative' juristic texts, excerpts from which have been arranged systematically into a single and continuous whole, compiled with the needs of early sixth-century law students and practitioners in mind. The individual jurists excerpted in the *Digest* are identified by name; however the text as a whole was promulgated as if the jurists' words had been uttered from Justinian's own inspired mouth: 'for we ascribe everything to ourselves, since it is from us that all their authority is derived'.[8] According to Justinian, the jurists owed their authority to the imperial will. None of the 'canonical' jurists included in the *Digest*, however, dates from later than the early fourth century AD—hence the appearance that 'authoritative' jurisprudence itself came to an abrupt halt under the Late Empire. This Tetrarchic (or possibly Constantinian) cut-off point may have been an arbitrary decision on the part of the *Digest*'s compilers, but more likely perhaps reflects a genuine shift in the nature of jurisprudential literary output during the 'epi-classical period' (late third to early fourth century AD), when the first works to anthologize and epitomize classical juristic texts began to emerge.[9] Justinian's *Digest* thus casts a long shadow over how we assess the activities of classical *iurisperiti*: it focuses our attention on their 'authoritative' written output, rather than their (discursive) advice to clients, advocates, and magistrates.

[7] F. Schulz, *History of Roman Legal Science*, 2nd rev. edn. (Oxford: Oxford Clarendon Press, 1967), 111 and 277. Compare D. Ibbetson, 'High Classical Law', in A. Bowman, P. Garnsey, and D. Rathbone, *Cambridge Ancient History*, xi. *The High Empire A.D. 70–192*, 2nd edn. (Cambridge: CUP, 2000), 184–99, at 184 and 192.

[8] *Dig. Const. Deo Auctore* 6; also *CI* 1. 14. 12. 3 (529): 'leges condere soli imperatori concessum est, et leges interpretari solum dignum imperio esse oportet.' For a penetrating study of Justinian as legislator see M.-T. Fögen, 'Gesetz und Gesetzgebung in Byzanz: Versuch einer Funktionsanalyse', *Ius Commune*, 14 (1987), 137–58.

[9] D. Johnston, 'Epiclassical Law', in Bowman *et al.*, *Cambridge Ancient History*, xi. 200–7, at 201.

On the other hand, the *Digest* completely masks the existence of any post-classical *iurisperiti* at all—except of course those who were involved in the compilation of Justinian's legal *corpus* itself.

Whereas Justinian's *Digest* focuses exclusively on classical juristic works, the Theodosian Code (AD 438) contains only five imperial constitutions that mention works of classical jurisprudence.[10] Our Theodosian Code, of course, is not identical to the 438 original—even on the relatively simple level of textual transmission, as much as two-thirds of the first five books (which would have dealt with Roman private law) has not survived and books 6 to 16 may have entire rubrics missing.[11] Nonetheless, the Theodosian Code (as we have it) appears to suggest a fourth- and early fifth-century abandonment of jurisprudence in favour of 'the rigid establishment' of imperial legislation as the sole source of law.[12] If we turn to the original commission for the Theodosian Code, however, a different perspective emerges.

Theodosius II's first legal commission, set up in 429, was instructed to excerpt and systematically arrange imperial constitutions (with a general force) from Constantine onwards; having completed this first task, they were then to combine the result with the two Diocletianic Codes of Gregorianus and Hermogenianus to produce a final authoritative *Codex*, which would have the 'treatises and responses of jurists' attached to its titles.[13] What the Code's commissioners were asked to envisage in 429 was thus a single collection of juristic writings and *leges* (imperial constitutions) combined into an authoritative and referable structure. Moreover, the 429 constitution does not specify which 'treatises and responses of the jurists' were to be attached to the anticipated final

[10] Discussed by E. Volterra, 'Sul contenuto del Codice Teodosiano', *BIDR* 84 (1981), 85–124, at 98.

[11] G. Rotondi, *Scritti Giuridici*, i (Milan: Ulrico Hoepli, 1922), at 212. See also T. D. Barnes, 'Foregrounding the Theodosian Code', *Journal of Roman Archaeology*, 14 (2001), 671–85, at 676–7, and in general Matthews, *Laying Down the Law*.

[12] Ibbetson, 'High Classical Law', at p. 192, and compare S. Corcoran, 'The Tetrarchy: Policy and Image as Reflected in Imperial Pronouncements', in D. Boschung and W. Eck (eds.), *Die Tetrarchie: Ein neues Regierungssystem und seine mediale Präsentation* (Wiesbaden: Reichert Verlag, 2006), 31–61, at 49. On the rise of imperial legislation see J.-P. Coriat, *Le Prince législateur: La Technique législative des Sévères et les méthodes de création du droit impérial à la fin du Principat* (Rome and Paris: BEFAR 294, 1997).

[13] *C.Th.* 1. 1. 5 (AD 429, given at Constantinople to the Senate) = *Gesta* 4: 'Ex his autem tribus codicibus. [*sc.*, the Gregorian, Hermogenian and first Theodosian compilation], *et per singulos titulos cohaerentibus prudentium tractatibus et responsis*, eorundem opera, qui tertium ordinabunt, noster erit alius, qui nullum errorem, nullas patietur ambages, qui nostro nomine nuncupatus sequenda omnibus vitandaque monstrabit.'

Code: should we automatically infer that 'classical' juristic texts were meant, or might the 'treatises and responses' have included 'post-classical' works? The 429 plan was not realized, so we cannot know for sure—however, new post-classical juristic commentaries on imperial constitutions continued to be produced in both the Eastern and Western Empire.[14] Moreover, later Byzantine authors did not discount these post-classical juristic commentaries; despite Justinian's prohibition on consulting any text outside his compilation, they used post-classical works that predated Justinian and had been excluded by him.[15]

Most Romanists, however, would dismiss the idea that the lack of traditional 'first-rate' jurists after the beginning of the fourth century could be an accident of textual survival: 'From the reign of Constantine onwards there are many lawyers, but no more jurists in the traditional sense . . . as an individual source of law jurisprudence was dead'.[16] Under the Principate, jurists had given independent legal advice to imperial officials. From at least the second century, they were also being absorbed into the bureaucracy as career professionals.[17] In the late fourth and fifth centuries, emperors—particularly Eastern ones—may have deliberately promoted legal experts as the drafters of their constitutions, but the jurists' names are not recorded in this context.[18] Nor do we have records of the names of the countless assessors (legal advisers) who sat with magistrates when cases were being judged. By the early fourth century the large-scale commentaries on Roman civil law, in its

[14] Schulz, *History*, 274 n. 11: 'When Justinian, in his constitutions, speaks of controversies among the *veteres* or *antiqui*, or of *antiqua sapientia* or *antiquae dubitationes*, he is referring at times to the fifth century professors at Beirut, not to the classical jurists.' See also D. Simon, 'Aus dem Kodexunterricht des Thalelaios, B. Die Heroen', *ZSS, Rom. Abt.* 87 (1970), 315–94, and D. Daube, 'The Compilers' Use of a Revised Paul and Ulpian', *ZSS, Rom. Abt.* 90 (1973), 359–60. For the West see W. W. Buckland, 'The *Interpretationes* to *Pauli Sententiae* and the *Codex Theodosianus*', *Law Quarterly Review*, 60 (1944), 361–5, and N. Kreuter, *Römisches Privatrecht im 5. Jh. N. Chr.: Die Interpretatio zum westgotischen Gregorianus und Hermogenianus* (Berlin: Duncker & Humboldt, 1993).

[15] S. Riccobono, 'Il valore delle collezioni giuridiche bizantine per lo studio critico del *Corpus Iuris Civilis*', *Mélanges Fitting*, ii (Montpellier, L'Imprimerie Général du Midi, 1908), 460–75, at 465.

[16] O. Robinson, *The Sources of Roman Law: Problems and Methods for Ancient Historians* (London: Routledge, 1997), 48. The use of the term 'lawyer' is ambiguous but widespread—does it refer to advocates or 'lesser' *iurisconsulti* (as Schulz uses the term), or to the supposed new figure of the 'advocate skilled in law'?

[17] T. Honoré, *Emperors and Lawyers*, 2nd edn. (Oxford: OUP, 1994) and T. Honoré, *Ulpian: Pioneer of Human Rights*, 2nd edn. (Oxford: OUP, 2002). See also W. Kunkel, *Herkunft und soziale Stellung der römischen Juristen*, 2nd edn (Graz: Böhlau, 1967).

[18] See in general Honoré, *Law in Crisis*.

various branches, had already been written and post-classical law worked within this established framework.[19] Classical jurisprudence was thus still regarded as a formal source of 'Law' and late Roman *iurisperiti* themselves demonstrated considerable ingenuity in updating, glossing, reorganizing, and even faking 'classical' juristic texts—a process that Constantine, Valentinian III, and Theodosius II attempted to control in relation to the courtroom.[20]

Even if we view the emperors before Justinian as legal autocrats who put an end to creative and independent jurisprudence, their own imperial constitutions (like the twelve tables in Pomponius' account) still gave rise to forensic debate. Late Roman *iurisperiti* may no longer have contributed to the formal development of Law in their own names or had the same level of written juristic output as their classical counterparts; but, as we shall see, they still contributed to the forensic elaboration and development of the *ius civile* on a daily basis. The *iurisperiti* who engaged in forensic practice were not necessarily a 'subordinate class' who simply applied late Roman law; they could also test and stretch its boundaries through their practical casuistry.

From at least the early twentieth century the existence of skilled *iurisperiti* in the later Roman Empire has been the subject of intense scholarly debate. In 1907 Conrat published an article entitled 'Zur Kultur des römischen Rechts im Westen'; his detailed analysis of legal and literary references led him to conclude that the study and practice of the *scientia iuris civilis* was pursued throughout the Eastern and Western Empires in the post-classical period.[21] Collinet's exhaustive monograph *Histoire de l'école de droit de Beyrouth*, published in 1925 as the second volume of his *Études historiques sur le droit de Justinien*, established beyond doubt that juristic doctrines continued to develop in the law school at Beirut between the third and sixth centuries; and

[19] As argued by A. J. B. Sirks, 'Late Roman Law: The Case of *Dotis Nomen* and the *Praedia Pistoria*', *ZSS, Rom. Abt.* 108 (1991), 187–212; F. Pulitanò, *Ricerche sulla 'bonorum possessio ab intestato' nell'età tardo-romana* (Turin: Giappichelli, 1999); and Kreuter, *Römisches Privatrecht*, 121–54. See also Ch. 4 below.

[20] *C.Th.* 9. 43. 1 (to be joined with 1. 4. 1, 1. 4. 2, and 1. 4. 3). As Matthews, *Laying Down the Law*, 221, notes, Valentinian III's so-called 'Law of Citations' (AD 426) was originally issued together with 'some difficult rulings in testamentary law'; I would suggest that its concern with the textual authenticity of classical juristic texts arose out of a concrete case, or series of cases that reached the attention of the Palatine bureaux. Compare, however, Honoré, *Law in Crisis*, 117, which links the 'law of citations' with a programme of law reform in advance of the compilation of Theodosius II's Code.

[21] M. Conrat, 'Zur Kultur des römischen Rechts im Westen', *Mélanges Fitting*, i (Montpellier, L'Imprimerie Générale du Midi, 1907), 287–320, at 291 and 299–302.

in two articles from 1928 and 1929 he expanded his work on the law school at Beirut into a general theory on how law developed as a whole in the Late Empire, attributing advancements in doctrine almost exclusively to the professors of the Orient.[22] Collinet's conclusions prompted later twentieth-century scholars to speak of a continuing juristic tradition in the eastern half of the Empire alone. Amongst the most important detractors of the 'oriental' thesis was Riccobono. As outlined above in Chapter 1, Riccobono challenged the idea that late Roman law was developed by academic teachers in the East and argued that it evolved predominantly through the forensic practice of the West, perhaps overstating his case.[23] In 1949 Volterra, in turn, reformulated the debate by focusing upon the existence of flourishing post-classical law schools in the West.[24] Needless to say, his was not the last word in the East versus West debate. In a chapter entitled 'Juristenausbildung und Rechtsliteratur', Wieacker accepted Volterra's evidence for the existence of Western post-classical law schools—but he attacked the idea that this indicated any kind of specialized juridical formation ('fach-juristisch') in the West.[25] For Wieacker the Orient had precise evidence for schools and seats of legal specialization devoted to the study of the *ius civile*; the Occidental schools were not in the same league. The law schools of the West did not promote the study of *ius civile* but 'ius in foro' (*sic*); in other words, the West specialized in the forensic preparation of rhetoric and taught law only so far as it touched upon the needs of advocates. Recently the work of Detlef Liebs has challenged the idea that the Western Empire was jurisprudentially backward.[26] Combining Liebs's research with that of Honoré and Voss, we arrive at a much wider

[22] Collinet, *Histoire de l'école de droit de Beyrouth*, and 'Le Rôle de la doctrine et de la pratique dans le développement de droit privé romain au bas-empire', *RHDFE* 7 (1928), 551–83 and 8 (1929), 5–35.

[23] Riccobono, 'La prassi nel periodo post-classico', 349. Compare A. Guarino, *Storia del diritto romano* (Naples: Jovene, 1975), 54: the jurisprudence of the East tended to be abstract and abstruse, that of the West empirical and 'vulgarized'.

[24] E. Volterra, 'Appunti sulle scuole postclassiche occidentali', *Annali di Storia del Diritto*, 1 (1957), 51–65. This work was continued by Volterra's pupils Maria and Franca Piras in their *Les Écoles de droit dans l'Occident postclassique et dans la Gaule romaine* (Caen: Impr. Ozanne, 1971).

[25] F. Wieacker, *Recht und Gesellschaft in der Spätantike* (Stuttgart: Kohlhammer, 1964), 36—but see also his (final) revised view in Wieacker, 'Die krisen des späten Imperiums: Bemerkungen zu einem historiographischen Modell', *AARC* 10 (1995), 33–9.

[26] D. Liebs, *Die Jurisprudenz im spätantiken Italien (260–640 n. Chr.)* (Berlin: Duncker & Humblot, 1987); Liebs, 'Römische Jurisprudenz in Africa im 4. Jh. n. chr', *ZSS, Rom. Abt.* 106 (1989), 201–17; and Liebs, *Römische Jurisprudenz in Gallien (2 bis 8 Jahrhundert)* (Berlin: Duncker & Humblot, 2002). For discussion of Liebs's

picture of *iurisperiti* and their functions in the imperial bureaucracy; approaching a century after Conrat's article, Western post-classical *iurisperiti* are firmly back on the scholarly agenda.[27]

Having briefly outlined the existing scholarship and some of the problems inherent in it, I shall now turn to an analysis of the evidence for *iurisperiti* as forensic practitioners in the Late Empire. It will be argued, using underexploited sources such as 'theological' texts, that post-classical *iurisconsulti* were still active in the traditional sense of giving advice to private clients, advocates, and magistrates; and that they also functioned as teachers of Roman law in the Eastern and Western Empires.[28] Moreover, private teaching by practising *iurisperiti* continued to be available, alongside a formal legal education in the post-classical schools. The final section of this chapter will raise the question of whether the juristic opinions of postclassical *iurisconsulti* could still contribute to the development of law; although a detailed examination will have to wait until Chapter 4, when we analyse the interaction between late Roman *iurisperiti* and advocates.

POST-CLASSICAL *IURISPERITI* AND PRIVATE CLIENTS

In a letter written in 414 Augustine makes a clear distinction between an advocate and a *iurisperitus*:

In fact, taking something from someone against their will does not always constitute undue theft. Very often, people are unwilling to give due recognition to a doctor, or wages to a workman. If they receive their wages from employers

earlier work see M. Bianchini, 'Sulla giurisprudenza nell'Italia tardoantica', *Labeo*, 36/1 (1990), 85–115.

[27] e.g. Honoré, *Law in Crisis;* and W. E. Voss, *Recht und Rhetorik in den Kaisergesetzen der Spätantike* (Frankfurt/Main: Forschungen zur Byzantinischen Rechtsgeschichte 9, 1982). Also D. Nellen, *Viri litterati: Gebildetes Beamtentum und spätrömisches Reich im Westen zwischen 284 und 395 nach Christus,* 2nd edn. (Bochum: Brockmeyer, 1981), 128–36.

[28] A limited number of theological sources which refer to *iurisconsulti* and *iurisperiti* are noted by Conrat, 'Zur Kultur des römischen Rechts im Westen', esp. 299; G. Rotondi, *Scritti Giuridici*, i (Milan: Ulrico Hoepli, 1922), 558–61; Liebs, *Die Jurisprudenz im spätantiken Italien*, 62–3 (Ambrose as jurist), 65 (Alypius as jurist), 78–81 (five passages of Lactantius), 97–8 (one passage of Ambrose), 99–101 (two passages of Jerome), 101–4 (six passages of Augustine); Liebs, 'Römische Jurisprudenz in Africa', 204–5 and 210 (Augustine); see also now Liebs, *Römische Jurisprudenz in Gallien.*

who are unwilling, they do not receive them unjustly; rather, it would be unjust if they were not given to them. However, the fact that the advocate is paid for providing a just defence, and the iurisperitus for providing sound advice, does not mean that a judge ought to take money for a just judgement, or a witness for giving true evidence. The former appear for one side, the latter are engaged in investigating the issue between both sides.[29]

Augustine specifies that the advocate should receive money (from the client, the 'one side') for his 'just defence' and that the *iurisperitus* is likewise entitled to payment for 'sound advice'. The fact that this letter was addressed to Macedonius, the *vicarius Africae*, and refers to actual cases that were held before his court, suggests that Augustine was commenting upon contemporary practices rather than indulging in mere classical reminiscences. Over a century earlier, the Tetrarchic 'Prices Edict' had officially recognized the capacity of the *iurisperitus* to claim payment for his involvement in actual court proceedings. The edict distinguishes between the advocate and the *iurisperitus*; however, the fees due to each were fixed at the same tariff.[30] The phrase *advocatus sive iurisperitus* at s. 7. 72 of the Prices Edict should not be read as a hendiadys; as Tomulescu astutely notes, the text seems to identify the advocate with the legal expert, but this identification only operates on the level of their honorarium: both have the right to be paid for their services but the services themselves were distinct.[31] A constitution of Valentinian III (given at Rome in 452, addressed to the Praetorian Prefect Firminus) substitutes the contrast *advocatus/iurisperitus* for *causidicus/iurisconsultus*: 'The punishment for the defenders of the case, if they should assist and should conduct the case in the aforesaid extraordinary court, has been established as follows: the *causidicus* shall forfeit his office, the *iurisconsultus* shall lose his status and his citizenship, which shall be interdicted to him.'[32] This text clearly envisages the hiring of both a

[29] Augustine, *Ep.* 153. 23 (*PL* 3. 663–4), tr. E. M. Atkins and R. J. Dodaro, *Augustine, Political Writings* (Cambridge: CUP, 2001), 85–6.

[30] For general discussion of the Tetrarchic, 'Prices Edict' see Corcoran, *Empire of the Tetrarchs*, 2nd edn., 205–33, and M. Crawford, 'Discovery, Autopsy and Progress: Diocletian's Jigsaw Puzzles', in T. P. Wiseman (ed.), *Classics in Progress: Essays on Ancient Greece and Rome* (Oxford: OUP, 2002), 145–64.

[31] C. S. Tomulescu, 'Les Avocats dans l'édit du Maximum', *AARC* 2 (1976), 293–8, at 295. See also M. Travers, *Les Corporations d'avocats sous l'empire romain* (Paris: Thèse, 1894), 97.

[32] *N. Val.* 35. 1, s. 2: 'poena defensoribus negotii, qui in eodem extraordinario iudicio adfuerint atque egerint, huiusmodi constituta, ut causidicum officii amissio, iurisconsultum existimationis et interdictae civitatis damna percellant.' Discussed further in Part II below.

causidicus and a *iurisconsultus* to defend a case and, moreover, gives different penalties for each in the event that they help to plead a case before a particular court—in contravention of Valentinian's decree. Taken together, these texts from the late third century (the Prices Edict), the early fifth century (Augustine's *Ep.* 153), and the mid-fifth century (Valentinian's *Novel* 35. 1) provide a continuous picture of the advocate and *iurisperitus* active in distinct spheres of the same court cases.[33]

The role of the *iurisconsultus* in the Late Empire, as under the Late Republic and Principate, was to provide expert knowledge of the law. In the *De Oratore* Cicero gives the following definition: 'If however the question was, who is rightly named as a *iurisconsultus*, I should say it is the man who is an expert in the laws, and in the customary law observed by individuals as members of the community, and who is qualified to advise, direct the course of a lawsuit, and safeguard a client.'[34] Augustine, writing in 391, concisely states that a *iurisperitus* who is ignorant of many laws does not fulfil his profession.[35] Under the Early and Late Empire ignorance of 'carefully considered imperial constitutions' could not be relied upon as a defence in concrete cases.[36] To this end, litigants and/or their representatives might consult a *iurisperitus* (or several *iurisperiti*) for advice before a case reached the courts, and they might also engage a legal expert to be present 'on their side' in the courtroom during the trial proceedings. I shall examine the advice of *iurisperiti* outside the courtroom first, before turning to the activities of *iurisperiti* before late Roman judges.

[33] For an important discussion of the terminology *iuris peritus, iuris studiosus, iuris prudens/nomikos* in papyri from the 2nd and 3rd cents, see Crook, *Legal Advocacy*, 154–8. For the stability of this terminology in the later Empire see Conrat, 'Zur Kultur des römischen Rechts im Westen', 290–300, with references to Firmicus Maternus, *Matheseos libri* 3. 4. 4; Claudius Mamertinus, *Gratiarum actio Juliano* 20 and 25; scholiast on Juvenal 7. 123; Symmachus, *Ep.* 3. 23 and *Ep.* 5. 74; Cassiodorus, *Var.* 5. 4, *9.* 21, and 11 pr.; Boethius, *Comm. on Topics* 5. 8. 33–4; and Isidore of Seville, *Etymologies* 5. 7. 1 and 5. 24. 3.

[34] Cicero, *De Oratore* 1. 48. 212: 'Sin autem quaereretur, quisnam iurisconsultus vere nominaretur; eum dicerem, qui legum, et consuetudinis eius, qua privati in civitate uterentur, et ad respondendum, et ad agendum, et ad cavendum, peritus esset.'

[35] Augustine, *De Duabus animabus contra Manichaeos*, 5: 'improbo iurisconsultum multas leges ignorantem . . . quod suam professionem minus impleat, iure reprehendo', referred to by Liebs, *Die Jurisprudenz im spätantiken Italien*, 63 n. 9 and 103. Also Augustine, *En. Ps.* 145. 4.

[36] *C.Th.* 1. 1. 2 (addressed to Flavianus, Praetorian Prefect of Illyricum and Italy, AD 391): 'perpensas serenitatis nostrae longa deliberatione constitutiones nec ignorare quemquam nec dissimulare permittimus.' Honoré, *Law in Crisis*, 72, notes that this statement was originally issued in the context of a wider ruling on property law.

In the *De Quantitate Animae* (written at Rome in 388) Augustine provides (incidental) evidence of how the *iurisconsultus* might put his skills to use before a case reached the courts. Augustine's treatise on the soul is constructed in dialogue form, and draws throughout on metaphors constructed from forensic practice and other areas of everyday life—these mundane metaphors were intended to make opaque ideas concerning philosophy and theology easier for Augustine's (elite and select) audience to grasp. In the course of the text's dialogue, the character 'Augustine' suggests a definition for the philosophical concept of sensation. His interlocutor 'Evodius', however, objects to the definition, likening 'Augustine' to a *iurisperitus* who has drafted a formula that has been found deficient during a courtroom trial:

Evodius: What then shall we do? Will you allow this formula to make its way out of court in this condition? As for myself, I gave it as good a defence as I could, but you wrote the formula for the case that deceived us. Although I was unable to win the verdict, I was present in all good faith. That is enough for me. But if you are accused of calumny, what are you to do? You who are the author of the definition for this heated debate and the devisor of this shameful retreat under fire ?[37]

'Augustine' responds to this question by shifting the metaphor out of its specific courtroom context, and instead comparing his function to that of the *iurisperitus* in a private audience with his client:

Augustine: Is there anyone here to act as a judge to whom I or this definition must show respect? My role here, you see, is like that of a *iurisconsultus* brought in for private consultation, namely to attempt to prove you wrong for the sake of instructing you, so that you may stand prepared when you come into court.[38]

The importance of this passage is twofold. First, the *iurisconsultus* and his client (or his client's representative) might debate the case between themselves before the trial. The formulary system of the Late Republic and Early Empire was almost certainly no longer in use; however, cases were still constructed using *formulae* as definitions around which

[37] Augustine, *De Quantitate Animae* 57 (*CSEL* 93. 204): 'E. Quid ergo agemus? Patierisne illam de iudicio ita discedere? Quanquam enim ego ei defensionem qualem potui praebuerim, tu tamen ipsam litis formulam, quae nos decepit, composuisti. Et ego quidem tametsi obtinere non potui, bona fide adfui, quod mihi satis est: tu vero si praevaricationis arguaris, quid facias, a quo et producta est ut iurgaret audenter, et oppugnata ut turpiter cederet?'

[38] Ibid: 'A. Numquidnam est hic quisquam iudex, a quo huic vel mihi metuendum sit? Ego te privatim quasi adhibitus iurisconsultus, instruendi causa refellere volui, ut cum ad iudicium ventum fuerit, paratus assistas.'

to structure the pleading; the 'preparatory' role of the *iurisconsultus* was thus to ensure that the proposed formula for a given case was watertight and to propose objections that could conceivably arise during the courtroom proceedings.[39] Second, it is clear from Augustine's metaphor that the *iurisconsultus* was not expected to plead the case himself before the court. This fact is also borne out by the papyrological record: 'we do not find in the papyri *nomikoi* [legal experts] acting as pleaders'.[40]

A request from a client for private *responsa* could be made to several *iurisconsulti* for the same point of law. Cicero (*Ad Fam.* 7. 21) applies for *responsa* first to Trebatius, then to Servius, and finally to Ofilius, in the matter of succession to his friend P. Silius. Similarly, at *Digest* 33. 7. 16. 1, a man asks Cornelius Maximus for a *responsum* concerning a legacy and later appeals to Servius; the two jurists disagree. This practice continued in the later Empire. Ambrose envisages a heavenly realm in which legal experts constantly dispute the eternal laws amongst themselves.[41] Ammianus Marcellinus, on the other hand, constructs a more mundane vignette of two rival *iurisperiti* called upon to give legal opinions: 'a wife by hammering day and night on the same anvil—as the old proverb has it—drives her husband to make a will, and the husband insistently urges his wife to do the same. *Periti iuris* are brought in on both sides, one in a bedroom, the other, his rival, in the dining room to discuss disputed points.'[42] Humour aside, this passage also underlines the immediacy of the consultation between clients and legal experts. Oral answers are given to oral questions.

The immediate and oral characteristic of juristic opinions is (perhaps paradoxically) underscored by a letter written by Augustine, *c.*422, to a practising North African *iurisconsultus* named Eustochius. The text begins, 'Since you owe honest responses to all those who consult you, how much more do you owe such to us, the ministers of Christ . . .'.[43]

[39] Compare Cicero, *De Oratore* 2. 100–2. At Symmachus, *Ep.* 6. 74 (*c.*388) the *iurisconsultus* Prosdocius comments upon the 'inania fori' and the 'sutelae veterum formularum'.

[40] Crook, *Legal Advocacy*, 157.

[41] Ambrose, *Commentarius in Cantica Canticorum*, 3. 6 = *PL* 15. 1893.

[42] Ammianus Marcellinus, *Res gestae* 28. 4. 26: 'uxor, ut proverbium loquitur vetus, eamdem incudem diu noctuque tundendo maritum testari compellit, hocque idem ut faciat uxor, urget maritus instanter: et periti iuris altrinsecus adsciscuntur, unus in cubiculo alter eius aemulus in triclinio, repugnantia tractaturi.'

[43] Augustine, *Ep.* 24*, 1. 1 (*BA* 46B 382), 'Cum omnibus consultoribus tuis vera responsa fideliter debeas, quanto magis nobis ministris Christi . . .'

Augustine proceeds to request *responsa* on a number of detailed legal points concerning slavery and the status of the children of *coloni* (1. 3–5). At section 2. 1 Augustine specifies that he would also like to know what has been established either in jurisprudence or by imperial constitutions (*leges*) concerning those who function as managers; the question has been prompted by certain imperial laws which have been brought to Augustine's attention, with reference to a case pending adjudication in his episcopal court (section 2. 4). The *iurisconsultus* Eustochius is thus being asked to apply his knowledge of *ius et leges* in order to interpret a number of tricky imperial constitutions which Augustine has not been able to make sense of by himself; moreover, Augustine states that he has had these imperial constitutions copied and attached to the letter itself (2. 5). Augustine's closing line implies that Eustochius was more accustomed to receiving these requests for legal *responsa* in person than through a written letter.[44] Papyri from the Early Empire also refer to a *nomikos* being consulted about points of legal interpretation by letter, though we should still assume that oral consultation was more frequent.[45]

The *iurisconsultus* could also be requested to examine private legal documents that had become the subject of litigation. Gregory Nazianzen, writing in the Eastern Empire shortly before 372, asked the *nomikos* Caesarius to examine a contract concerning property, made by Gregory's cousins Eulalius and Helladius—and to resolve a legal dispute arising from it (*Ep.* 14). In order to avoid such litigation the expertise of the *iurisconsultus* could be sought before the contract was entered into. In the course of his exegesis of Psalm 118 Ambrose states: 'If you want to buy a tract of land, if you want to purchase a house, you get yourself someone more expert than yourself, you consider with care the legal regulations and, to avoid making some mistake, you do not trust in your own judgement.'[46] Ambrose's (homiletic) point is that, rather than employing these legal experts, men should seek their own salvation through the 'acquisition' of God the Father—employing as advisers Moses, Isaiah, Jeremiah, Peter, Paul, John, and the supreme

[44] Augustine, 6 (*BA* 46B. 387): 'obsecro ut me adiuues etiam corpore absentem, sicut soles adiuuare praesentem.'

[45] *P.Oxy.* 237; *PSI* 450. 2; *P.Yale* inv. 1530, discussed by Crook, *Legal Advocacy*, 157 n. 258.

[46] Ambrose, *Ex Ps.* 118, *Littera* 'Mem' 7: (*CSEL* 62, 286) 'Si agrum emere velis, si mercari domum, prudentiorem adhibes et quid iuris sit diligenter consideras et, ne in aliquo forte fallare, tibi ipse non credis.'

consiliarius Jesus himself. For the Eastern Empire, John Chrysostom gives a detailed account of the consultations taken with *iurisconsulti* before entering into a marriage agreement—again with a view to urging men to concern themselves with the state of their souls instead:

Now, say that you are about to get married. You enter into careful consultation with external *nomikoi*, you resort to them frequently, making anxious inquiry into what will happen if your wife dies childless, or if she leaves a son, or two or three survive her, then again, what use will she have of her father's property should he be alive, or should he be dead, what out of the inheritance will go to any brothers of hers, and what to the husband; likewise, you will want to know when she will be in control of all her property, so that no part of it will have to be yielded to another, and when on the other hand she will have to yield the whole of it. You pester them with questions of this kind, inquiring into all the ins and outs of the business, in order to make sure that none of the woman's property will go to any of her relations.[47]

Notably in this context, *C.Th.* 4. 21. 1 (given at Milan in AD 395, addressed to Petronius, vicar of Spain) states that the responses of all the *iurisconsulti* agree that a husband is excluded from succession to the property of an intestate wife when she has consanguineous male relatives surviving. Moreover, the AD 395 imperial constitution concludes by ordering that 'all frustrating contrivances shall be annulled'—thus suggesting that legal expertise had indeed been expended on trying to get round the prescriptions of the law.

Requests for advice from *iurisperiti* on the laws concerning succession and inheritance must have been commonplace, notwithstanding the example of a certain testator given at *D.* 31. 88. 17 (Scaevola): 'I, Licius Titius, have written this my will without the aid of a *iurisperitus*, following the promptings of my own heart rather than excessive and small-minded pedantry.'[48] The fourth-century Christian ecclesiastic Asterius of Amasea, however, offers the following dose of cynical realism, specifically for the benefit of the childless:

But if, being childless, you mean to transmit the inheritance to one of your friends, do not regard your will as an immutable law, a thing strong and

[47] John Chrysostom, *Laus Maximi et quales ducendae sint uxores* (*PG.* 51. 226–7).

[48] Compare Eusebius, *Vita Cons.* 4. 26, giving an account of the effects of Constantine's abrogation of the laws *Iulia* and *Papia Poppaea* with respect to the efficacy of last wills and testaments. Constantine's measure should perhaps be seen in the context of earlier juristic discussion.

incapable of being set aside. It will require but little exertion to make the writing invalid. Do you not see those who are constantly contesting wills in the courts, how by all kinds of attacks they wrest them by putting forward skilful legal interpretations, invoking the aid of eloquent orators, suborning witnesses, corrupting judges?[49]

Similarly, in the course of his homily against covetousness the Gallic bishop Valerian of Cimiez paints the following vignette concerning how wills could be contested on the grounds of legal interpretation, or through accusations concerning (procedural) fraud:

The corpse is not yet carried out, and already trust in the will has been destroyed by an interpretation of law. One man is disputing about his father's signature; another is in despair over the person of a brother. One man affirms that the will was not confirmed by witnesses; another gives as a reason that the will does not accord with the current circumstances.[50]

It is worth noting here that the famous AD 426 'Law of Citations'—which attempted to regulate the use of classical jurisprudential opinions in post-classical legal business—was originally promulgated as part of a much wider address to the Roman Senate that also covered succession and inheritance law.[51] It is thus quite plausible that the 'general' ruling concerning the use of classical juristic texts in 426 was prompted by a specific (possibly senatorial) inheritance dispute. Justinian also issued rulings on the specific deployment of classical jurisprudential writings in early sixth-century inheritance disputes. For example, a constitution issued in 531 and addressed to John of Cappadocia takes a case discussed by the jurist Ulpian, where Ulpian upholds the validity of a will when a possible mistake has been made in the stipulation of the testator's name.[52] Justinian's ruling declares that Ulpian's opinion

49 Asterius of Amasea, *Homily* 3. 8 (= Datema, *Asterius of Amasea*, 32).

50 Valerian of Cimiez, *Homily* 20. 5, *PL* 52. 753: 'Necdum funus effertur, et iam testamenti fides iuris interpretatione vacuatur, Alter de subscriptione patris disputat, alter de fratris persona desperate. Hic astruit scripturam non stare testibus, ille assignat testamentum non convenire temporibus.'

51 The so-called 'Law of Citations' is excerpted at *C.Th.* 1. 4. 3 (under the rubric *De responsis prudentum*); see also *CI* 1. 14. 2 (*C.Th.* 1. 1. 4a in Krüger's edn. of the Theodosian Code); *CI* 1. 14. 3 (= Krüger, *C.Th.* 1. 1. 4b); *CI* 1. 19. 7 (= Krüger, *C.Th.* 1. 2. 13); and *CI* 1. 22. 5 (= Krüger, *C. Th.* 1. 2. 14). The surviving passages concerning succession and inheritance are *C.Th.* 4. 1. 1; 5. 1. 8; 8. 13. 6; 8. 18. 9; 8. 18. 10; 8. 19. 1, and *CI* 6. 30. 18.

52 *CI* 6. 24. 14. This constitution should perhaps be seen in the context of Justinian's *quinquaginta decisiones*, a set of legal decisions concerning classical jurisprudence that paved the way for the *Digest*.

is too subtle: 'We hold that this opinion is incorrect, for no man can be found who is so ignorant, or rather such a fool, as not to know his own name.' For the drafter of this Justinianic constitution, common sense should trump late Roman juristic ingenuity.

Attempts to 'skirt' existing rules concerning the transmission of patrimony were certainly tried out on the ground: Ambrose specifically warns his Milanese congregation against seeking inheritances through the employment of 'cunning words', as this should be a practice alien to all Christian men.[53] Jerome's *Letter* 52. 6, on the other hand, states that certain Eastern churches had made use of a fiction of trusteeship in defiance of contemporary imperial legislation, so that monks and clerics could lawfully inherit properties that would otherwise be barred to them. In North Africa, Augustine's *Sermon* 47 refers to members of the schismatic Donatist church employing *iurisperiti* in order to find tricky *formulae* and loopholes in the law that would allow their testaments to stand. As we shall see in later chapters, imperial legislation against heretical beliefs and practices created manifold complexities in terms of concrete inheritance and succession cases.

The *iurisconsultus* could also assist in the actual drafting of legal documents (*cavere*). Ulpian implies that this activity might be undertaken by *iuris studiosi*, *advocati*, *tabellarii*, or *pragmatikoi*.[54] Whilst acknowledging the increasing visibility and prestige of *notarii* ('professional' short-hand writers) in the later Empire, we should note that *iurisconsulti* continued to help in the drafting of some types of legal documents (at least).[55] Dioscorus of Aphrodito (mid–late sixth century AD) was a *nomikos* employed in the Egyptian ducal bureaucracy; he also drafted records of formal arbitration settlements and crafted persuasive petitions on behalf of private clients—still leaving himself enough time to compose the poetry and prose that has earned him the (unjust) epithet of 'the worst poet of antiquity'.[56] With respect to

[53] Ambrose, *De Officiis* 3. 58 (ed. J. J. Davidson, *Ambrose De Officiis, I* 388); at *De Officiis* 3. 66, Ambrose (glossing Cicero's *De Officiis* 3. 61) refers to both *leges* and opinions of *iurisperiti* against fraud in legal business.

[54] *D.* 48. 19. 9. 4–7.

[55] On the rise of short-hand writing see H. C. Teitler, *Notarii and Exceptores: An Inquiry into the Role and Significance of Shorthand Writers in the Imperial and Ecclesiastical Bureaucracy of the Roman Empire. From the Early Principate to c. 450 A.D.* (Amsterdam: J. C. Gieben, 1985).

[56] B. Baldwin, 'Dioscorus of Aphrodito: The Worst Poet of Antiquity?', *Atti del XVII Congresso Internazionale di Papirologia*, 2 (1984), 327–31. See in general L. S. B. Mac Coull, *Dioscorus of Aphrodito: His Work and his World* (Berkeley, Los Angeles, and

Dioscorus' legal expertise, Mac Coull has perceptively noted its social context:

A legal document as it came from Dioscorus's pen was far from a dull, flat-footed, matter-of-fact record of a transaction. But it was also not simply a verbose exercise in the sound of one's own voice or the freakishly antiquarian hunt for obscure words. Even more so than a poem, a legal document was a mirror of his world, inasmuch as it was a working reality that actually effected something. One could not be too careful in the face of the law (especially as it had come to be understood by the 560's). The legal act and procedure were intimately bound up with their social context. As a practicing member of the Egyptian bureaucratic elite, Dioscorus consciously tried to do full justice (in every sense) to the problems that came his way.[57]

Dioscorus' 'Byzantine' style may have been peculiar to himself and his near contemporaries;[58] however, his work as a legal expert, drafting documents within a tight-knit social world, was not.

In the early fifth century Augustine's *Tractatus in evangelium Ioannis* 7. 10–11 refers explicitly to *iurisperiti* drafting pleas for imperial rescripts. Augustine's exegesis of the New Testament text is constructed around a clever contrast between drafting a plea/prayer to the Emperor and making a plea/prayer to God. Augustine attempts to frame his metaphor in such a way that it appeals directly to his intended audience and their own experience of contemporary legal realities. At the same time, of course, he is also reinforcing a particular 'theology of empire', in which the protocols for contacting the Christian God and the Roman Emperor are comparable—if not the same. Detlef Liebs quotes the opening sections of Augustine's text that refer to *iurisperiti*.[59] However, it is worth giving the passage in full, as Augustine's extended metaphor also clarifies why it was essential to seek the advice of an *iurisperitus* in particular, before submitting a petition to the imperial court:

If it is too much for you to fulfil the law, then make use of the covenant (*pactum*), make use of the bond (*chirographum*), make use of the petitions

London: University of California Press, 1988), esp. 16–56, and C. A. Kuehn, 'A New Papyrus of a Dioscorian Poem and Marriage Contract', *ZPE* 97 (1993), 103–15.

57 Mac Coull, *Dioscorus of Aphrodito*, 17.

58 On the evolution of a specifically 'Byzantine' style of legal rhetoric see A. B. Kovelman, 'From Logos to Myth: Egyptians Petitions of the 5th–7th Centuries', *Bulletin of the American Society of Papyrologists*, 28 (1991), 135–52.

59 Liebs, *Die Jurisprudenz im spätantiken Italien*, 103, and Liebs, 'Römische Jurisprudenz in Africa', 205. The following translation of Augustine's *Tractatus in Evangelium Ioannis* 7. 10–11 is my own, from the text at *CCSL* 36. 72–3.

(*preces*) that have been laid down and composed for you by the jurist who is in heaven (*iurisperitus caelestis*). For those who have a cause and wish to supplicate the Emperor seek a skilled jurist (*scholasticus iurisperitus*) to compose their petition (*preces*) for them, in case they should put their request in an unfitting manner, and not only fail to obtain what they seek, but receive punishment rather than a benefit (*beneficium*). When therefore the apostles wanted to petition their divine ruler (*imperatorem deum*) and did not know how to approach him, they said to Christ Lord, teach us how to pray; that is, you who are our *iurisperitus* and God's assessor and counsellor (*assessor . . . consessor Dei*), compose for us our prayers. And the Lord taught them out of the divine lawbook (*liber iuris caelestis*), taught them how to pray. And in his teaching he laid down a condition: forgive us our debts, as we forgive our debtors. If you do not frame your petitions in accordance with the law, you will become the guilty party (*reus*). Do you, in this state of guilt, tremble before the ruler (*imperatorem*)? Then offer the sacrifice of humility, offer the sacrifice of mercy, say in your prayers: Forgive me, as I forgive. What you say, do. What indeed will you do, where will you go, if in your prayers (*preces*) you have lied? You will lose the benefit of a rescript (*beneficium rescripti*), as they say before the tribunal, indeed you will not obtain a rescript at all. It is in accordance with forensic custom (*ius forense*) that he who has lied in his petition shall not profit from what he has obtained. Now that is the rule amongst men, for a man can be deceived; the emperor could be deceived, when you sent him your petition. You have made your request, and he to whom you addressed it does not know whether it is true or not. He left it to be refuted by your adversary. Thus, if you were found guilty of lying before the judge—because the one petitioned could not do otherwise than accord you the favour which you sought, as he was ignorant as to whether you had lied—you will lose the benefit of the rescript (*beneficium rescripti*) at the very place to which you have brought it. But God knows whether you are lying or speaking the truth, there is no question of his denying you a benefit in the context of a court (*in iudicio*). Rather, he does not permit you to obtain a benefit, because you had the audacity to lie to The Truth.

The procedure for private persons seeking and applying a rescript from the Emperor can thus be broken down from Augustine's text as follows; first the *iurisperitus* framed the plea using the correct conventions and forms, ensuring that the request was not made *contra ius*.[60] Persuasiveness is, of course, audience-relative—hence the need to employ a skilled

[60] See *D.* 1. 3. 14 (Paul); *C.Th.* 1. 2. 2 (given at Rome, AD 315); *CI* 1. 19. 7 (given at Ravenna, AD 426 to the Senate); and *CI* 1. 22. 6 (given at Constantinople, undated but according to Seeck AD 491).

jurist who could frame the request in a manner that fitted the relevant high-level imperial legal bureaux. We know from other late Roman sources that the advice of the *iurisconsultus* in drafting the petition could refer the client to the letter of the law as it stood, or could propose an equitable interpretation as a solution to their particular situation. *C.Th.* 1. 2. 3 (AD 316 or 317–18), for example, deals with rescripts where an interpretation has been interposed 'between equity and law': between the demands of a concrete case and the existing state of the law. *FIRA* 20 (308–12), a fragment from a fifth-century (jurisprudential?) *codex* found in Egypt, provides an example of this type of legal reasoning. The papyrus fragment is constructed around a passage from Ulpian's *Liber secundus disputationum* (the text of which also appears as the second part of *D.* 15. 1. 32 pr.). The form of the fifth-century text can be divided into four parts: first there is a categorical statement of what the law is, then Ulpian's juristic authority is produced to support it. Next a more extreme case is advanced with the same decision, and finally a contrary decision is pressed on the grounds of equity. A formal decision as to whether to grant such an 'equitable' judgment was reserved to the imperial authorities; however, independent *iurisperiti* would have most likely suggested the interpretation to their clients in the first instance.

It can be inferred from Augustine's account that it was standard practice for the client to relate the facts of the case to the *iurisperitus* for inclusion in the plea. Once completed, the *preces* would then be sent to the Palatine *magistri scriniorum*, whose staff were (in principle at least) constrained to act as if the related facts were accurate.[61] If the *preces* was deemed persuasive, an imperial rescript would be given—the petitioner (or their mandated representative or their advocate(s)) then had to lodge the rescript before a competent judge and prove the facts of the case, facing his or her adversary. If the facts were not proved then the judge would give a ruling that the *beneficium rescripti* should not be obtained. The *iurisperitus* was not responsible for checking the facts of the case at the time of drafting the petition; it was the petitioner who was held solely responsible for any false factual statements.[62] On the other hand, a *iudex* was not supposed

[61] On the different Palatine offices responsible for handling petitions see Honoré, *Law in Crisis*, 210.

[62] As clearly stated by *CI* 1. 22. 5 (AD 426, to the Senate): a petitioner who lies, but otherwise obtains an imperial rescript in conformity with the laws, shall not have the benefit of it; if 'excessive perversity' is found in his mendacity, 'he shall be abandoned to the severity of the judge'.

to hold a petitioner responsible for any genuine errors made by the petition's drafter.[63]

So far our discussion has focused on the activities of *iurisperiti* in extra-forensic judicial business or in the preparatory stages of litigation, but they could also be engaged to appear in the courtroom on behalf of their clients. As we shall see further in Chapter 4, the individual litigant or his/her advocate (or mandated representative) was responsible for the actual pleading of cases before the court. In fact, in order to plead a case at law a litigant or advocate did not necessarily have to consult a jurist at all. The legal issue in any case might be clear, and the judgement could then turn solely on a conjectural issue ('did the defendant do it?') or a qualitative issue ('why did the defendant do it?'). Where a legal issue was important, however, *iurisperiti* could appear before the court with the specific purpose of citing relevant points of law on behalf of their client. Hence Quintilian's advice to ambitious late first-century advocates, echoed by Marius Victorinus in the fifth century: the best orator will try to acquire a knowledge of the civil law himself so that he does not have to rely upon the promptings of *iurisperiti* in the courtroom.[64] Libanius is more explicit as to how this practice functioned. Whilst bemoaning the current promotion of *iurisperiti* to the positions of 'secretaries in the highest offices of state', Libanius states that previously they were content to merely bring their law books into court, and to 'stand, with eyes fixed on the orator waiting for the words "You read that, please"'.[65] Libanius' cleverly constructed argument—that 'previously' *iurisperiti* were entirely subservient to orators and waited on their word, but 'now' the situation is entirely reversed—should be treated with caution (as discussed in Chapter 1 above). Nonetheless, the picture of *iurisconsulti* bringing their own books of law into the courtroom and citing 'the law' accurately represents the collaboration that could take place between advocates and legal experts, when appearing before late Roman judges.

LEGAL EDUCATION IN THE LATE EMPIRE

There were three (possibly complementary) ways of studying law as a distinct science in the Late Empire: it was taught at specific law

63 *CI* 2. 9. 2 (AD 238).
64 Quintilian, *Inst. Or.* 12. 3. 1–10; compare Marius Victorinus, *RLM* 190. 24.
65 Libanius, *Oration* 2. 44, AD 380/1 (ed. and trs. A. F. Norman, Loeb, ii. 35).

schools, as a sideline subject at some rhetorical schools, and finally via private teachers through 'apprenticeship'. Legal training could also be augmented by practical experience in the bureaucracy, where *iurisperiti* undertook stints as assessors (legal advisers to judges and magistrates). In this section I shall give only a brief summary of the evidence, referring to more detailed treatments—where they exist—in footnotes.

A limited instruction in substantive law may have been provided at some rhetorical schools; Libanius, for example, apparently employed an individual to teach law as a subsidiary subject at his rhetorical school for a short time.[66] The extent to which this 'rhetorical' instruction qualified students to practise as *iurisconsulti* should not be overemphasized; from a study of the post-classical rhetorical handbooks it is clear that any legal principles taught by rhetoricians were concentrated on 'procedural' law, aimed at prospective advocates. I shall return to this point in Chapter 4.

In late antiquity the study of law at a specific *auditorium* was seen as a form of higher education, comparable with formal philosophical study or the training required in order to practise medicine.[67] *C.Th.* 14. 9. 3 (issued at Constantinople, 27 February 425 and addressed to the prefect of the city) provided imperial funding for a specific *auditorium* with three rhetoricians and ten grammarians specializing in Roman oratory and five 'sophists' and ten grammarians specializing in Greek (oratory), alongside three teachers who are 'authorities of more profound knowledge and learning': one to 'investigate the hidden secrets of philosophy' and two 'who shall expound the *formulae* of juristic science and leges'.[68] It is worth noting in this context that the same AD 425 constitution forbids those who teach publicly from taking private students, but explicitly permits 'those teachers who are accustomed to give such instruction privately within very many homes' to continue this activity. Private tuition is rarely mentioned in the late

[66] See in general A. Steinwenter, 'Rhetorik und römische Zivilprozess', *ZSS, Rom. Abt.* 64 (1947), 69–120, at 111–13; A Steinwenter, 'Die Briefe des Q. Aurelius Symmachus als Rechtsquellen', *ZSS, Rom. Abt.* 74 (1957), 1–25, at 8, and H. L. W. Nelson, *Überlieferung, Aufbau und Stil von Gai,* Institutiones (Leiden: Brill, 1981), at 39–40 and 103–4 n. 20.

[67] See Libanius, *Ep.* 1208.

[68] The AD 425 constitution was included in the Theodosian Code under the general rubric 'The pursuit of liberal studies in the cities of Rome and Constantinople', but was originally intended for Constantinople alone: for further discussion see F. De Marini Avonzo, 'I libri di diritto a Constantinopli nell'età di Teodosio II', *Annali della Facoltà di giurisprudenza di Genova*, 24/1–2 (1991–2), 103–13, at 104.

Roman legal sources, yet we should not overlook its importance and prevalence.

In the Eastern Empire there is firm evidence for public legal teaching in the cities of Beirut and Constantinople. Collinet suggests the zenith of the school at Beirut as beginning *c.*420 and reconstructs a list of named fifth-century professors—including a certain Auxonius, the brother of the Christian bishop of Beirut *c.*458.[69] Legal teaching may also have undergone some kind of reorganization at Constantinople during the 420s, on the basis of *C.Th.* 14. 9. 3, discussed above. *C.Th.* 6. 21. 1 (15 March 425, given at Constantinople) names the *iurisperitus* Leontius as a Professor of Law at the *auditorium* in Constantinople and accords him the codicils of the *comitiva primi ordinis* so that he might rank among the *ex vicariis* as a reward for his legal excellence. The pre-eminence of Beirut and Constantinople, together with that of Rome, was confirmed by Justinian as part of his early sixth-century overhaul of law and legal teaching; according to section 7 of his *Constitution Omnem* (one of the prefatory constitutions to the *Digest*) the formal teaching of law was only to be undertaken in these three cities and the instruction given at Alexandria, Caesarea, and 'other places' was to cease. Justinian's prohibition, of course, confirms that legal instruction had in fact been available outside his (newly sanctioned) golden triangle of Beirut, Constantinople, and Rome.

Papyrus fragments from the third to the sixth century testify to the availability of works of jurisprudence in Egypt. Extracts have been discovered from Gaius' *Institutes* (in papyri dated to the mid-third century); Paul's *Libri ad edictum* (fifth century), *Libri ad Plautium* (fourth century), and *Libri quaestionum* (fifth century); Papinian's *Responsa* (fourth/fifth century); Ulpian's *Disputationes* and *Libri ad edictum* (fourth century); a juristic fragment *Ad Legem Iuliam et Papiam* (fourth/fifth century); and a pre-Justinianic commentary *De pactis* (early sixth century).[70] The existence of these fragments and commentaries have led some modern scholars to suggest that formal schools of law, as

[69] Collinet, *Histoire de l'école de droit de Beyrouth*, 129 and 154–5. Also in general L. Jones Hall, *Roman Berytus: Beirut in Late Antiquity* (London: Routledge, 2004) and H. Wieling, 'Rechtsstudium in der Spätantike', *Juristische Schulung*, 40/1 (2000), 10–15.

[70] R. Taubenschlag, *The Law of Greco-Roman Egypt in the Light of the Papyri 322BC–640AD* (New York: Herald Square Press, 1944), at 26–7 and nn. 125–33. L. M. Zingale, 'Libri di dottrina romana e fonti papirologiche: Riflessioni in margine ad alcune recenti acquisizioni', *AARC* 15 (2005), 221–37, discusses recent developments in late Roman juristic papyrology

opposed to private instruction by individual *iurisperiti*, may have existed in late Roman Egypt. Whether formal schools existed in Egypt or not, Taubenschlag's astute observation stands: 'Since all these works were used for instruction in the law, they have undoubtedly influenced its practice.'[71] For example, students were taught a technique whereby a particular juristic text would be methodically compared to other relevant jurisprudential works, as well as related imperial constitutions.[72] Legal expertise entailed more than simply 'knowing' classical juristic texts or imperial 'legislation'; it demanded the capacity to reason out a (post-classical) solution from a relevant set of sources. This comparative technique was, of course, essential to practising *iurisperiti*, as we have already seen in the case of Augustine's requests to the North African *iurisconsultus* Eustochius. Egypt is thus perhaps, once again, only unique in terms of the extent to which the evidence for the late Roman interest in jurisprudence has been preserved.

Libanius, in his *Oration* 48. 22, suggests that there was a preference amongst Eastern students to study law at Rome, although this statement may simply be another weapon in his general attack against the teaching of law at Beirut. From at least the mid-third century, however, Rome does seem to have acted as a centre for legal study in the Western Empire: Symmachus' letters refer to both law professors and law students at Rome.[73] A number of fourth- to sixth-century texts also refer to individuals travelling from the Western provinces to Rome in search of a legal education.[74] Yet there is also evidence to suggest that a legal education was available elsewhere in the Western provinces. In 1914 Kübler argued for the existence of a school at Carthage, and as a result of the discovery of two inscriptions from the vicinity of Carthage this proposition has received support from Liebs and Lepelley.[75] In Gaul there is evidence for legal teaching (if not 'schools' of law) at Bordeaux,

[71] Taubenschlag, *Law of Greco-Roman Egypt*, 28 and 138, citing *PSI* 452 (4th cent), 'where decisions on fraudulent manumissions are evidently influenced by the legal literature'.

[72] For a possible early 4th-cent example of this comparative technique see F. M. D'Ippolito and F. Nasti, 'Frammenti Papiracei di un'Opera della Giurisprudenza Tardo Imperiale', *SDHI* 69 (2003), 383–98, and 'Diritto e papiri: Nuovi pareri giurisprudenziali da Phaun. III 45', *AARC* 15 (2005), 239–42.

[73] Liebs, *Die Jurisprudenz im spätantiken Italien*, 64 and 66–7.

[74] Augustine, *Conf.* 8. 6. 13 (on Alypius); Rutilius Namatianus, *De Reditu Suo* 1. 205–7; and Cassiodorus, *Variae* 1. 39, 4. 6, and 9. 21.

[75] See Liebs, 'Römische Jurisprudenz in Africa', 209, and C. Lepelley, *Les Cités de l'Afrique romaine au Bas-Empire II: Notices d'histoire municipale* (Paris: Études Augustiniennes, 1981), 200 n. 11.

Toulouse, Narbonne, Marseilles, Arles, and Lyon.[76] Nelson has raised the possibility of a law school at Verona, in which the famous palimpsest of Gaius might have been used for teaching purposes in the first half of the fifth century.[77]

For the most part, the career structures of assessors testify to a legal education prior to entering the imperial bureaucracy. A (possible) mid-third-century inscription records a certain Conon of Pamphylia who studied law at Beirut and acted as an assessor to governors in Judaea, Syria, and Bithynia.[78] The North African bishop Alypius studied law and, according to Augustine, sat as an assessor three times in the space of a single year at Rome; Alypius subsequently became unemployed and waited 'for someone else to whom he could sell his advice', before deciding to don his toga again and try his luck in Milan—where he was baptized a Christian.[79] The career of Floridus (365–427), on the other hand, followed a more circuitous route; he studied law, and then probably went on to practise as an advocate before becoming *praetor urbanus*, assessor to a provincial governor, and subsequently to a vicar, and then became himself *consularis Liguriae*. At this point Floridus apparently resigned his office to become assessor to the prefect of the city of Rome. Finally, Floridus took up the public teaching of law.[80] As a teacher, Floridus would have undoubtedly expounded his science using written texts; he was also equipped to pass on his practical experience of advising judges on disputed points of law in actual cases.

[76] Piras, *Les Écoles de droit*, 26–36, and Kreuter, *Römisches Privatrecht im 5. Jh. N. Chr.*, 116–17. Volterra, 'Appunti sulle scuole postclassiche occidentali', at p. 57, refers to 'numerous' epigraphical notices of *iuris periti, iuris studiosi, legis periti, iuris consulti*, and *iuris magistri* in Gaul and concludes that the centre of Western Roman law moved there in the post-classical period. For a more cautious assessment see now Liebs, *Römische Jurisprudenz in Gallien.*

[77] Nelson, *Überlieferung, Aufbau und Stil von Gai*, 40–6. We shall return to the post-classical handling of classical juristic texts in Ch. 4.

[78] J. F. Gilliam, 'A Student at Berytus in an Inscription from Pamphylia', *Zeitschrift für Papyrologie und Epigraphik*, 13 (1974), 147–50. Examples of 4th-cent. legally trained assessors include Euethius (Libanius, *Ep.* 1201) and Priscianus (Libanius, *Ep.* 936 and *Ep.* 939).

[79] Augustine, *Conf.* 8. 6. 13 (*BA* 14. 34): 'mecum erat Alypius otiosus ab opere iuris peritorum post assessionem tertiam, exspectans quibus iterum consilia venderet.' On assessors at Rome and their appointment see Chastagnol, *La Préfecture Urbaine à Rome*, 372–3.

[80] *CIL* vi. 31992. See *PLRE* ii. 481, Liebs, *Die Jurisprudenz im spätantiken Italien*, 66, and J. M. J. Chorus, 'L'Enseignement du droit romain en occident de 250–500: Essai de tableau', *Tijdscrift voor Rechtgeschiedenis*, 61 (1993), 195–204, at 201 n. 38.

The fact that assessors were expected to be trained legal experts is commented upon by Ammianus Marcellinus, who contrasts the Roman custom of employing assessors 'thoroughly versed in public law' with the judicial custom of the Persians.[81] This Roman self-image of the 'legally skilled' assessor assisting the 'unlearned' judge was not without its real-life complexities: for example, emperors attempted to ensure that assessors did not overstep their advisory role as experts in law and put their own signatures to official *libelli*—this act being reserved to the authority of the magistrate alone (*CI* 1. 51. 2). Assessors appear as a distinct bureaucratic office in early fifth-century imperial constitutions.[82] By the early sixth century, however, the links between advocates and assessors may have became stronger: in 529 Justinian ruled that an individual cannot act as both an advocate and an assessor (for a public magistrate) at the same time, but former assessors could resume the practice of advocacy if they so wished. Apparently some individuals had attempted to conceal the fact that they had acted as assessors for the same cases in which they had previously appeared as advocates—a situation replete with opportunities for fraud and judicial bias (*CI* 1. 51. 14). Justinian's ruling on advocates acting as assessors perhaps makes sense in the context of a constitution of the Eastern Emperor Leo, requiring that advocates who wished to become enrolled at high-ranking bureaucratic courts must first provide evidence of some formal legal instruction.[83]

COULD THE ADVICE OF POST-CLASSICAL *IURISPERITI* CONTRIBUTE TO THE CREATIVE ELABORATION OF ROMAN LAW?

Late Roman *iurisperiti* were expected to have had some sort of formal legal education and were active in the Late Empire advising private

[81] Ammianus Marcellinus, *Res Gestae* 23. 6. 82; see in general Harries, *Law and Empire*, 102–3.

[82] *C.Th.* 6. 15. 1 (given at Constantinople, AD 413, to Priscianus, prefect of the city): details changes to the honorific ranking of assessors and *C.Th.* 2. 10. 6 = *CI* 2. 7. 4 (given at Constantinople, AD 422, to Eustathius PP): regulating the ownership of the earnings of assessors who are under paternal power.

[83] *CI* 2. 7. 11 (addressed to the PPO, AD 460). On earlier expectations of some kind of legal instruction being advantageous to advocates at high-ranking bureaucratic courts see Ch. 1 above.

clients, aiding advocates in the forensic handling of lawsuits, and acting as assessors to Imperial magistrates. Could the advice and opinions of these late Roman *iurisperiti*, however, still affect the creative development of 'formal' law?

The imperial legislation of the Late Empire contains numerous references to determinate facts, persons, and concrete cases. As Bianchini has demonstrated, if we look behind any given constitution's normative content, a definite relation between a specific case that gave the *occasio legis* and the *lex* itself can sometimes be established.[84] I would go further and suggest that virtually all the 'general laws' in the Theodosian and Justinianic Codes were prompted by a concrete case (or with respect to the more 'administrative' rulings, a concrete situation). In 426 Valentinian III's (Western) chancellery specified that laws could be considered as having a 'general application' whether they had been prompted by a 'spontaneous impulse' of the Emperor, or by a petition or report (*relatio*), or a concrete lawsuit.[85] The first source, the spontaneous wish of the Emperor, might seem likely to us today to be the most prevalent—but this is a result of the specific editorial instructions given to the compilers of the Theodosian Code in particular.[86] The second prompt to general laws, according to Valentinian III, were petitions from private individuals or groups for clarification or modification of a particular legal point. In this instance the input of the *iurisperiti* was more direct. As we have seen, private individuals sought legal advice in constructing their petitions to the Emperor, and the imperial response could include rulings on substantive points of law (as well as straightforward grants of specific exemptions or privileges). Valentinian III's third source of general law lay in imperial responses generated by the *relatio* procedure: the practice whereby higher officials (magistrates) would request an imperial directive on a specific case or issue, sometimes concerning controversial legal points which had been raised during a legal

[84] Bianchini, *Caso concreto*, 1–2 and 100–1.

[85] *CI* 1. 14. 3 pr. (AD 426, to the Senate): 'sive eas nobis spontaneus motus ingressit sive precatio vel relatio vel lis mota legis occasionem postulaverit.' For the wider original context of this ruling see the discussion above on Valentinian III's 426 address to the Roman Senate.

[86] I have argued this point in detail in C. Humfress, 'Cracking the *Codex*: Late Roman Legal Practice in Context', *BICS* 49 (2006), 251–264. See also P. Ombretta Cuneo, *La legislazione di Costantino II, Costanzo II e Costante (337–361)* (Milan: Guiffré 1997), p. cxix: between AD 337 and 361 the constitutions in the *C.Th.* that (originally) had the character of *lex generalis* are few, and those issued as edicts even fewer.

proceeding. The input of *iurisperiti* in this instance could be twofold: first, the advice of legal experts to private litigants could be transmitted to the imperial court as part of the dossier on the case under referral. Second, *iurisperiti* acting as judicial assessors could suggest proposed legal revisions themselves—these suggestions would also be relayed to the imperial court.[87] Finally, we have concrete cases prompting the issuing of new constitutions: for example, in the post-Theodosian *Novels* we learn of the concrete cases of Valerianus of Emesa (*N.Th.* 15. 2), Leonius and Jucunda (*N.Val.* 21. 1), Micce and Pelagia (*N.Val.* 21. 2), and Domnina and Fortunatus (*N.Anth.* 3. 1. 2)—each of which gave the occasion for the posting of new 'general' edicts. If concrete cases did indeed prompt the issuing of imperial legislation (which they undoubtedly did[88]), then it seems a fair inference that *iurisperiti* (other than any legally expert drafters of the imperial text itself) could have had an input in prompting new imperial legislation. The advice of late Roman legal experts—whether given to private clients, imperial magistrates or indeed the Emperors themselves—could influence the promulgation of new imperial constitutions and thus contribute to the development of new 'statutory' legislation.

In fact the constitution *saepe nostra clementia* (*N.Th.* 1. 1), issued at Constantinople on 15 February 438, refers explicitly to the disputes of contemporary *iurisperiti* as a major motivating force behind the compilation of the Theodosian Code itself. In a flourish of bureaucratic rhetoric, the preamble to the *Novel* announces the legislator's deep puzzlement: despite all the pale complexions produced by all-night study sessions, scarcely 'one or two' persons have managed to attain complete mastery over the *ius civile*. Perhaps unsurprisingly, this particular passage has been used by some modern scholars to support the idea that *iurisperiti* in the Late Empire really were few in number and deficient in learning. Theodosius II's *Novel*, of course, needs to be read as a whole. Section 1 gives a list of perceived problems that are creating confusion and ambiguity in contemporary legal practice: the endless multitude of books, the diversity of actions, the difficulty of legal cases, and the mass of imperial constitutions. The drafter of this imperial text is not making a comment on the shortage of (learned) *iurisperiti*, but rather is charging

[87] e.g. *CI* 1. 50. 2 (given at Constantinople, AD 427): an imperial response accepting suggestions originally made from a Praetorian Prefect's office.

[88] Compare now also Millar, *Greek Roman Empire*, 207–14, on *suggestiones* and 'the routine of public persuasion'.

them as a profession with exploiting these perceived 'ambiguities' to their own advantage:

We have completed a true undertaking of our time . . . the decrees of previous emperors have been purged of interpretations (*purgata interpretatione*) and published by us, in order that no further may the *iurisperiti* dissimulate their ignorance by a pretended severity, while their formidable responses are awaited as though they proceed from the very innermost shrines, since it is now clearly evident with what validity a gift may be bestowed, by what action an inheritance may be claimed, and by what words a stipulation may be invested, in order that a definite or indefinite debt may be collected.[89]

In other words, the *iurisperiti* can engage in interminable controversies whilst issuing their 'formidable opinions' precisely because they are sufficiently skilled to exploit the endless multitude of books, the diversity of actions and the mass of imperial constitutions.[90] It can also be inferred from the passage quoted above that *iurisperiti* were often asked to advise on the topics of gifts, inheritances, and stipulations—thus supplementing the accounts of client and *iurisperiti* consultations discussed above.

From 1 January 438 the Theodosian Code was intended to comprise the sole source for daily legal practice, including the citation of imperial constitutions (from 313 to 438) in court, in both the Eastern and Western Empires.[91] There is, however, evidence to suggest that individuals continued to consult the two earlier Tetrarchic Codes.[92] Nor should we assume that the promulgation of the Code ended the practice of, or necessity for private consultations with *iurisperiti*. In 473, for example, the *magister militum Dalmatiae* sent a *relatio* to the Emperor Leo because he was unable to resolve a controversy between a woman

[89] *N.Th.* 1. 1, s. 1: 'verum egimus negotium temporis nostri . . . purgata interpretatione, retro principum scita vulgavimus, ne iurisperitorum ulterius severitate mentita, dissimulata scientia, velut ab ipsis adytis, exspectarentur formidanda responsa, quum liquido pateat, quo pondere donatio deferatur, qua actione petatur hereditas, quibus verbis stipulatio colligatur, ut certum vel incertum debitum sit exigendum.'

[90] Compare *C.Th.* 1. 4. 1 (AD 321): the notes of Ulpian and Paul on Papinian are to be destroyed, as the Emperor desires 'to eradicate the interminable controversies of *prudentes*'. This desire is usually read as referring to the controversies within the texts of classical jurists; however, it could just as well refer to contemporary disputes between legal experts.

[91] Accepting T. D. Barnes's argument in his 'Foregrounding the *Theodosian Code*', 685. On the authority of the 438 Code see *C.Th.* 1. 1. 6, s. 3 (given at Constantinople, AD 435).

[92] Liebs, *Römische Jurisprudenz in Gallien*, 100–2. Rescripts from the Tetrarchic Codes were, of course, included in Justinian's *Codex*.

and her brother, since both the parties were supporting their claim with many discordant jurisprudential and imperial opinions. Having argued for the healthiness of diverse jurisprudential opinions, the drafter of the imperial text decided to follow a *responsum* of the classical jurist Salvius Julianus (*CI* 6. 61. 5). In sum, it would be a mistake to assume that case-determined jurisprudence did not also play a part in a late Roman judicial structure apparently dominated by 'state' legislation.[93]

Provisions were made for authorized copies of the Theodosian Code to be held in the relevant Palatine offices, and under seal in the bureaux of provincial prefects. Even if we assume, for the sake of argument, that classical (and post-classical) jurisprudential writings—together with the Tetrarchic Hermogenian and Gregorian Codes—had no legal validity after 438, there would still have been a demand for literate individuals who could consult these authoritative copies of the Theodosian Code itself on behalf of disputants, litigants, and judges. Moreover, from a litigant's perspective, it might be worth applying considerable legal ingenuity to interpreting the Code. A constitution of Theodosius II, issued shortly after the promulgation of his Code, denounces any individual who 'embraces the words of the law' but strives against its intention—attempting to defend himself by a 'crafty prerogative of words'.[94] Just over a year and a half later the preamble to another Constantinopolitan constitution eloquently expounds the Emperor's munificence in providing laws for 'the common advantage of all'; but the drafter then goes on to state that the issuing of this particular constitution is necessary because 'certain persons attempt to distort by a wrong interpretation laws that have been most beneficially promulgated'.[95] The preamble to an imperial constitution promulgated by the Eastern Emperor Marcian in 454 states that:

If any regulation issued in the aforesaid laws should perhaps be rather obscure, it must be clarified by the interpretation of the emperor. Thus the ambiguity

[93] For the contrary argument see F. De Marini Avonzo, 'I rescritti nel processo del IV e V secolo', *AARC* 11 (1996), 29–39, at 30.

[94] *N.Th.* 9. 1 pr. (given at Constantinople, AD 438 or possibly 439, addressed to Florentius PP): 'Non dubium est, in legem committere eum, qui verba legis amplexus contra legis nititur voluntatem. Nec poenas insertas legibus evitabit, qui se contra iuris sententias scaeva praerogativa verborum fraudulenter excusat.'

[95] *N.Th.* 7. 3 pr (given at Constantinople, 29 Dec. 440, addressed to Cyrus PP): 'Sic nos in legibus maximis promulgandis non quid forte quibusdam separatim, sed quid universis in commune prodest, divinis sensibus ponderamus. Sed nonnumquam ea, quae saluberrime promulgantur, interpretatione (emend. Meyer) quidam non recta deformare contendunt.'

of every sanction shall be removed, and the alternate contention of litigants cannot divert doubtful points of law to their own advantage. Trial judges of cases also and those who preside over tribunals shall comply with the clear definition of the laws. They shall not waver while their sentences are suspended and fluctuate among uncertain decrees. For a clear and easy way to pronounce sentence is open to a judge whenever the law according to which he must judge is not ambiguous.[96]

It is worth noting that this attempt by Marcian to reserve all issues of legal interpretation to the Emperor's decision alone actually acknowledges the concrete attempts made by litigants, and presumably their legal advisers, to 'divert doubtful points of law to their own advantage'. It is in the nature of forensic disputes to exploit interpretative 'wriggle room', no matter how supposedly clear, unambiguous, and authoritative a legal statute is stated to be. On a practical rather than an ideological level, the drafters of imperial constitutions frequently had to play catch-up with legal arguments developed in forensic practice.[97]

Pomponius, looking back from the vantage point of the Antonine period into the mists of the Early and Middle Republic, knew that the natural habitat of jurists was and had always been the lawcourts. The extraordinary prominence of a few jurists of the Severan period and their works—favoured by late Roman emperors and canonized in Justinian's *Digest*—can distract our attention from the day-to-day operation of legal experts in and around the lawcourts, and can convey the false impression that jurisprudence *per se* entered a lean period from the end of the third century. *Iurisperiti* had long been, and continued to be an important structural element of the judicial system, active and influential at all levels. It happens that the late antique sources provide more than adequate evidence of the range and scope of the activities of *iurisperiti*, as they gave advice to private clients in matters of civil law, assisted individuals in drafting petitions

[96] *N. Marc.* 4 pr. (given at Constantinople, AD 454, addressed to Palladius PP): 'Si quid vero in iisdem legibus latum fortassis obscurius fuerit, oportet id imperatoria interpretatione patefieri, ut omnis sanctionis removeatur ambiguum, et in suam partem iuris dubia derivare litigatorum contentio alterna non possit, negotiorum quoque cognitores ac tribunalium praesides, apertam definitionem legum secuti, suspensis nutantibusque sententiis inter scita incerta non fluctuent. Plana enim et facilis ad pronuntiandum via patet iudici, quoties non est illud ambiguum, iuxta quod necesse est iudicari' (tr. Pharr *et al.*).

[97] For an example from 535 (i.e. after the promulgation of Justinian's *Corpus Iuris Civilis*) see *Nov. Iust.* 2: apparently prompted by a concrete legal case in which each side pleaded contradictory interpretations of different imperial constitutions.

to officials, guided advocates in persuading judges, and magistrates in reaching their verdicts; there is also some (limited) evidence for the post-classical production of independent juristic works, editions, and commentaries.[98] Finally, despite the impression that late Roman emperors liked to give that they themselves produced the law and monopolized its interpretation, the contribution of *iurisperiti* to the development of post-classical law is not to be discounted.

[98] On epiclassical and post-classical 'juristic' works see: E. Dovere, *De iure: Studi sul titolo 1 delle Epitomi di Ermogeniano* (Turin: Giappichelli, 2001); D. Liebs, 'Die pseudopaulinischen Sentenzen', *ZSS, Rom. Abt.* 112 (1995), 151–71 and 113 (1996), 132–242, and M. Bianchi Fossati Vanzetti (ed.), *Pauli Sententiae: Testo e interpretatio* (Padua: Cedam, 1995); F. Mercogliano, *Tituli ex corpore ulpiano: Storia di un testo* (Naples: Pubblicazioni della Facoltà di Giurisprudenza dell'Università di Camerino 44, 1997), *Scholia Sinaitica* (late 5th-/early 6th-cent. Greek commentary on Ulpian's *Ad Sabinum*), text in P. Krüger, T. Mommsen, and W. Studemund, *Collectio Librorum Iuris Anteiustiniani*, iii (Berlin: Weidmann, 1878/90; repr. Hildesheim, 1999), 267–82, and T. Honoré, *Ulpian: Pioneer of Human Rights*, 2nd edn. (Oxford: OUP, 2002), 206–26; M. De Filippi, *Fragmenta Vaticana: Storia di un testo normative*, 2nd edn. (Bari: Cacucci, 1998) and F. Betancourt Serna, *El libro anónimo* De Interdictis. *Codex Vaticanus Latinus No. 5766* (Seville: University of Seville, 1997); *Consultatio veteris cuiusdam iurisconsulti*, text in Krüger *et al.*, *Collectio*, iii, 203–20; W. Selb and H. Kaufhold, *Das syrisch-römische Rechtsbuch* (Vienna: Verlag der österreichischen Akademie der Wissenschaften, 2002); finally on the *Collatio Legum Mosaicarum et Romanarum* and the vexed question of its dating to the 390s, rather than to the age of Constantine, see now F. Lucrezi, 'Sulla data di redazione della Collatio alla luce di due costituzioni costantiniane', *AARC* 14 (2003), 599–613. For papyrological discoveries see the discussion above.

4

Late Roman Advocates

ASSESSING LATE ROMAN ADVOCATES

> It is the third hour. In come the advocates, the orators, the pleaders, summoned into the presiding judge's private office. Many plead cases, each as well as he can, according to the measure of his eloquence.[1]

Could post-classical advocates influence the development of late Roman law, on a case-by case basis, through their forensic pleading? In the previous chapter I have argued that post-classical *iurisperiti* were engaged in advising on legal points, and that this activity could not only contribute to the creative interpretation of law in the instant case, but was also capable of provoking 'new' imperial legislation. These *iurisperiti* were not responsible for pleading the cases they advised upon; this remained the domain of the advocate (*advocatus*, *causidicus*, *scholasticus*, *causarum orator*, *defensor*; *rhetor*, *scholastikos*, *dikologos*, *ekdikos*). Late Roman advocates operated at different levels; not all of their forensic activities, by any stretch of the imagination, contributed to the development of post-classical law. For example, advocates could take on humdrum 'notarial' business relating to the preparatory stages of a lawsuit—although the activities proper to a *notarius* (or *tabellarius*) and an *advocatus* remained distinct nonetheless. The jurist Ulpian provides a working definition in this respect: an advocate should be understood as anyone who had an actual role in pleading cases, but this definition does not extend to those who draft cases but do not appear before the

[1] *De Conversatione Cotidiana* 73 (a bilingual 4th-cent. school exercise) = A. C. Dionisotti, 'From Ausonius' Schooldays? A Schoolbook and its Relatives', *Journal of Roman Studies*, 72 (1982), 83–125, at 104: 'Fit hora tertia. Ingrediuntur advocati, causidici, scholastici, evocati in secretarium iudicis sui. Agunt plures causas, quisque ut potest secundum literarum facundiam.'

court.[2] According to the Ambrosiaster, a late fourth-century ecclesiastic writing in Rome: 'The advocate's *officium* is to plead the cause of his client in accordance with the due order of law.'[3] This 'duty' might amount to nothing more than simply appearing before a competent judge and stating the facts of a litigant's case; however, as we shall see, many late Roman advocates were trained in a higher level of technical rhetoric, which they could apply in the courtroom to the benefit of their clients—as and when the case demanded it.

It is a fundamental argument of this chapter that the late Roman schools of rhetoric continued to provide an essentially pragmatic training, primarily aimed at equipping forensic advocates for pleading in court. Late Roman rhetorical instruction provided an education not so much in 'legal' rhetoric as in 'forensic' rhetoric: it offered a training in formal systems of persuasive argumentation that advocates could call upon when preparing and pleading concrete cases. It was at the rhetorician's feet, for example, that a would-be advocate was taught to handle imperial legislation (when an instant case demanded it) as 'a resource for influencing the outcome of disputes', rather than ' a canon for deciding them'.[4] Existing scholarship on late Roman law is still dominated by research into imperial enactments and codification. Yet if we wish to understand legal development, the study of how late Roman advocates sought to utilize legislation in practice is at least as important as the study of that legislation itself. As with the *iurisperiti*, the creative handling of a concrete case by a late Roman advocate could provoke the framing of new imperial constitutions.

There are no modern studies devoted to advocacy between the fourth and sixth centuries AD *per se*; those that do discuss the later Roman Empire tend to address the period as a postscript on declining standards, framed by previous chapters on the quality and achievements of advocacy in the Late Republic and Early Empire.[5] Dictionary entries

[2] *D.* 50. 13. 1. 11 (Ulpian): 'Advocatos accipere debemus omnes omnino, qui causis agendis quoquo studio operantur: non tamen qui pro tractatu, non adfuturi causis, accipere quid solent, advocatorum numero erunt.' Ulpian's particular context in this passage is the clarification of an imperial rescript concerning the recovery of excessive *honoraria* paid to a *patronus causarum.*

[3] Ambrosiaster, *Quaestiones Veteris et Novi Testamenti*, 102 (*PL* 35. 2312, ll. 53–4): 'Hoc est officium advocati, ut secundum iuris ordinem suscepti sui causam peroret.' Compare Augustine, *En. Ps.* 147, *sermo ad plebem* 1.

[4] Heath, *Menander: A Rhetor in Context*, 294 at n. 33.

[5] e.g. the final chapter of A. Pierantoni, *Gli avvocati di Roma antica* (Bologna: N. Zanichelli, 1900) gives a graphic discussion of the 'decadence, anarchy and barbarity'

for *advocatus/causidicus*, with the important exception of Kubitschek's articles for Pauly-Wissowa, state as a matter of course that advocacy suffered a sharp decline in both moral and professional standards in the later Empire[6] and the standard textbooks on Roman law and procedure adopt a similar tone. Moreover, late Roman rhetoric itself has been accused of a 'retreat from reality', of existing in 'hermetic exclusion' and of 'being more and more exclusively diverted into mere epideictic' as opposed to the judicial/forensic or deliberative branches of rhetoric.[7] Malcolm Heath's learned monograph, *Menander: A Rhetor in Context* (2004), challenges these stereotypes, demonstrating a continuing connection between rhetorical instruction and practical advocacy right through to the sixth century.[8] Heath's final conclusion nonetheless ends with the suggestion that the bulk of advocates in the Late Empire were probably 'low-level', partially tracing this to a 'possible parallel in the codification of Roman law that began in the third century, which could also be seen as lowering the discipline's entry-threshold'.[9] The idea that legal codification somehow lessened the need for late Roman advocates to apply their rhetorical skills in court is something of a red herring; a 'codified' legal text can be as susceptible to rhetorical handling as a 'non-codified' one.

In his *Legal Advocacy in the Roman World* (1995) John Crook has confronted the many preconceived ideas that operate 'within this whole vast area of discourse', and in particular he challenges the 'major stereotype' that advocacy began its decline under the Principate, 'for the evidence is that it did no such thing'. Crook continues: 'The question

of late Roman advocacy; likewise K. Z. Méhész, *Advocatus Romanus* (Buenos Aires. Zavalia, 1971), ends with a chapter entitled 'Caracter, mentalidad y decadencia'.

6 The articles by Kubitschek are printed in *RE* i/1 (1st edn.), cols. 436–8 and *RE* iii/2 (1st edn.), cols.1812–13; see now art. 'Advocates', in G. W. Bowersock, P. Brown, and O. Grabar (eds.), *Late Antiquity: A Guide to the Postclassical World* (Cambridge, Mass.: Harvard University Press, 1999), 277–8.

7 P. A. Brunt, 'The Bubble of the Second Sophistic', *BICS* 39 (1994), 25–52, at 37; see also D. A. Russell, 'The Panegyrists and their Teachers', in M. Whitby (ed.), *The Propaganda of Power: The Role of Panegyric in Late Antiquity* (Leiden: Brill, 1998) and R. Browning, 'Education in the Roman Empire', in A. Cameron, B. Ward-Perkins, and M. Whitby, *Cambridge Ancient History*, xiv. *Late Antiquity: Empire and Successors A.D. 425–600*, 2nd edn. (Cambridge: CUP, 2001), 855–83, at 855 (quoting Kaster) and 862, with further bibliography.

8 In particular Heath, *Menander: A Rhetor in Context*, 277–331, on the 'relevance' and 'persistence' of judicial and deliberative rhetoric.

9 Ibid. 330–1. Similarly, M. Heath, 'Practical Advocacy in Roman Egypt', in M. J. Edwards and C. Reid (eds.), *Oratory in Action* (Manchester: Manchester University Press, 2004), 62–82, concludes (on the basis of Libanius) that, in the mid/late 4th cent., 'Oratory, it may have seemed, was no longer where the action was'.

whether or not advocacy (or jurisprudence, for that matter) declined in intellectual or moral stature as viewed with today's eyes is a quite different one from whether it retained or failed to retain its prestige or its role in the society of its own day, and the latter is the historical question which must occupy us.'[10] However, his concluding remarks—as least as far as they apply to the later Roman Empire—are not overly encouraging: 'There seems to be little evidence, actually, about the practice of the advocates in the late Roman Empire, when advocacy was corralled and channelled into a handmaid of the bureaucratic legal order.'[11] Yet Crook himself pinpointed an important source of evidence in the papyri from Egypt. Other underexploited sources, such as evidence from 'theological' material and late rhetorical handbooks, can in fact be combined with accounts from the more traditional primary sources to produce a comprehensive picture of late Roman forensic practice.

The aim of the present chapter is thus threefold: first, to argue that a 'formal' education in rhetoric provided a career-oriented training for advocates, second, to analyse some of the abundant historical evidence relating to the practice of advocacy in the Late Empire, and, third, to explore how late antique advocates contributed to legal development through their forensic rhetoric.

ADVOCATES IN THE LATER ROMAN EMPIRE

> No one so much as raises his eyes in a court of law, without an advocate.[12]

According to the author of the late fourth-century *Apocriticos* (possibly Macarios, bishop of Magnesia), employing an advocate was a *sine qua non* of late Roman litigation. It was not, however, a practice required by law.[13] Forensic speech could operate at the level of everyday discourse and there is evidence in the late Roman papyri for litigants going it alone. Forensic rhetoric, however, existed as a specialized technical

[10] Crook, *Legal Advocacy*, 180. [11] Ibid. 196.

[12] *Apocriticus*: 3.12. 16 = R. Goulet (ed.) *Macarios de Magnésie: Le Monogénès* (Paris: Librairie Philosophique J. Vrin, 2003), ii. 117, ll. 16–17.

[13] Although *C.Th.* 9. 2. 3 (AD 380, given at Constantinople, addressed to Eutropius PP) states a possible exception: having been summoned from afar in a case instituted by criminal accusation, the defendant should investigate the case against him 'by employing an advocate'.

discipline—where possible, it was presumably preferable to employ someone who was, or at least claimed to be, familiar with the type of persuasive pleading that worked in any (given) judicial context.

In the late Roman papyri we find advocates speaking on behalf of clients in formal arbitration disputes.[14] A letter included amongst the *spuria* of Sulpicius Severus demonstrates how forensic argument could also be employed by advocates seeking to settle a dispute *before* it became the subject of formal arbitration. The author of the letter, who describes himself as a retired advocate (*ex togato*), is in dispute with a practising advocate named Salvius—the letter's addressee—over the ownership of certain *coloni*. The letter's primary purpose is to invite Salvius to a private meeting to settle the dispute; naturally, given the context, the retired advocate is also concerned with showcasing his technical skill:

> I confess that while we were engaged in the field of battle I was often frightened by the arms of your eloquence, but according to my measure, I returned you blow for blow. I certainly learned along with you by what right and by which procedure the labourers ought to be revindicated, to whom a legal process is competent, and to whom the issue of a process is not competent.[15]

This letter thus gives us a rare glimpse of late Roman *togati* in action, but it also reminds us of how the mere threat of their forensic expertise could be deployed to 'encourage' an out of court settlement.

In court, an advocate did not appear *as* the litigant but rather spoke on his client's behalf—hiring an advocate thus did not excuse the parties to the case from being present at the judicial hearing.[16] In 320 an imperial constitution (which appears as a single sentence at *C.Th.* 2. 11. 1) specifies that the errors of advocates speaking before a competent court cannot harm the litigants; an earlier Tetrarchic rescript, however, records the same rule whilst making the client responsible for picking up on the advocate's mistake.[17] The Visigothic interpretation to

[14] On advocates pleading before arbitrators see *D.* 4. 8. 31 (Ulpian, *Edict*, book 13). *P.Oxy.* 3764 records two hearings from *c.*326 on the back of a roll of price-declarations—the first took place before a city official and the second before a delegated arbitrator; the same advocate (Ammonius) acts in both cases on behalf of different parties.

[15] Sulpicius Severus (*spuria*), *Ep. ad Salvium, PL* 20. 243, re-edited with commentary by C. Lepelley, 'Trois documents méconnus sur l'histoire sociale et religieuse de l'Afrique romaine tardive, retrouvés parmi les *spuria* de Sulpice Sévère', *Antiquités africaines*, 25 (1989), 235–62, at 240–51.

[16] *CI* 2. 9. 1 (AD 227): allegations made by advocates in the presence of litigants are to be understood *as if* they had been made by the litigants themselves.

[17] *CI* 2. 9. 3 (AD 294): a petitioner has tried to obtain an imperial rescript allowing an appeal from a judicial sentence, on the basis that his advocate made an error in not

C.Th. 2. 11. 1 goes further in demanding that the rule is only valid if the client has voiced an immediate objection to the error. Even having hired an advocate, a litigant still had to be present and moreover had to be prepared, if necessary, to take up an active role in the hearing.[18]

According to a Julianic constitution *de postulando* (on pleading), the practice of advocacy was flourishing in late antiquity: 'For men who are predisposed for that profession seem few, in a few ages just individuals, in many ages some. Our age has thrown up a whole number.'[19] Even if we are suspicious of this eloquent claim that advocates were *more* numerous in the Emperor Julian's age than at earlier times, there is no evidence to suggest a general late antique decline in numbers. Competition for forensic business could be fierce. Answering his critics (once again), Libanius claims that some of his former pupils have not been hugely successful as advocates because they do not go out indiscriminately hunting potential clients down (his classes teach moral decency as well as rhetoric); as to the rest whom he did not teach, Libanius continues, their tactics to secure business apparently include hiring publicists, flattering 'hawkers', and sending begging letters to neighbouring cities, as well as striking up agreements with court officials to guarantee themselves a share of cases and purchasing audiences from the magistrates' clerks.[20] Advocates could also pick up business by pleading before city councils, as well as on their behalf—the former venue may have been a lucrative source of income, given the number of decurions who apparently sought exemptions from their municipal obligations. This topic was, of course, dear to Libanius' heart and he paints an amusing vignette of such a 'plea for exemption' in his *Oration* 49 (nominally) addressed to the Emperor Theodosius: 'when a recruit was nominated up popped an advocate (*rhetor*), and after the exchange of a word or two, a notice of release followed—and they [the city

appealing within the given time limits and 'the error of an advocate cannot harm the litigant'. The rescript is denied on the basis that both the petitioner and the advocate had been present in the courtroom and *neither* of them had objected to the sentence, i.e. the petitioner should have corrected the advocate's 'mistake' at the time.

18 See Crook, *Legal Advocacy*, 65–6, making the same point with reference to the Late Republic and Early Empire.

19 Bischoff and Nörr, 'Eine unbekannte Konstitution', ll. 23–5 (discussed in Ch. 2 above).

20 Libanius, *Oration* 62. 41–2 (= Foerster, iv. 367). *C.Th.* 9. 1. 3 (AD 322, addressed to Agricolanus PP) warns advocates against 'rashly' accepting women as clients—in contravention of certain civil disabilities established against them.

officials] stayed dumb throughout'.[21] Late Roman advocates, then, can be found competing for business at a number of different municipal and provincial levels, as well as at the highest-ranking courts of the imperial bureaucracy. The practice of advocacy must have suffered, on the other hand, in those Western provinces affected by the fifth-century Vandal and Hunnic 'invasions'; the effects were, however, relatively localized and were met with attempts at imperial counter-measures.[22]

By the mid-fifth century it was a common practice for advocates to try to become officially enrolled as pleaders before particular bureaucratic courts. *C.Th.* 2. 10. 1–2 (given at Serdica on 1 November 319 and addressed to Antiochus, *praefectus vigilum*) formally attests to this practice of officially 'registering' advocates to plead cases before separate tribunals—whilst at the same time abolishing an earlier (non-extant) ruling that the number of advocates attached to a given court should be limited to a fixed number. Later imperial constitutions reinstated varying limitations on the numbers of advocates enrolled at a specific court at any given time, especially with respect to the higher (and more prestigious) venues of the courts of the Praetorian and Urban prefectures.[23]

The principle of Roman magistrates ensuring forensic assistance can in fact be traced back to at least the Early Empire. Ulpian states that, according to the praetor's edict, anyone who had not found an advocate for a number of reasons, including intrigues or duress on the part of his opponent, would be granted one by the praetor himself.[24] Late Roman magistrates were expected to uphold the same principle. An imperial constitution issued in 370 refers to the problem of litigants

[21] Libanius, *Oration* 49. 4, 'For the city councils', tr. Norman, *Libanius, Selected Works*, ii. 465 (slightly amended).

[22] *N.Val.* 2. 3. 1 (AD 443, given at Ravenna, addressed to Albinus PP Illyricum, Italy, and Africa): advocates who have fled from the Vandal invasion of North Africa can register at other courts, see also *N.Val.* 13. 1. 9 (445); *N.Val.* 32. 1. 6 (AD 451, given at Rome, addressed to Firminus PP): as a result of Alaric's invasions 'both advocates and judges' are lacking in certain regions of Italy—provincial advocates are thus henceforth granted perpetual tenure.

[23] For a summary account of the *numerus clausus*, the division between *statuti* and *supernumerarii* and the privileges and immunities associated with membership of a *collegium togatorum* see H. Weiling, 'Advokaten im spätantiken Rom', *AARC* 11 (1996), 419–63, at 429–34, and Kaser and Hackl, *Das römische Zivilprozessrecht*, 563–5.

[24] *D.* 3. 1. 1. 4 (Ulpian, *ad edictum*, book 6): 'Ait praetor: "Si non habebunt advocatum, ego dabo" nec solum his personis hanc humanitatem praetor solet exhibere, verum et si quis alius sit, qui certis ex causis vel ambitione adversarii vel metu patronum non invenit.'

hindering the course of justice by preventing their opponents from making an adequate defence—in this particular case, through retaining several advocates separately and thus tying up the most skilled pleaders; hence the constitution specifies that the judge should arrange for an equal distribution of *causidici* between the two parties. If a magistrate has instructed a given advocate to plead for a particular side and the advocate attempts to get out of that appointment with a 'unacceptable excuse', he is to be barred from ever pleading again.[25]

The advocates officially ranked as first (*primus*) amongst their cohorts were not necessarily those who had served longest, but those who displayed the highest technical merit.[26] Augustine uses this fact in a clever metaphor, designed to help his audience understand an otherwise potentially confusing statement at 1 Timothy 1. 15–16, that Christ was the first sinner among men:

> He [sc. Christ] called himself the first, not in the whole series of sinners, but in the magnitude of the sin. He considered the magnitude of his sin, for which he called himself the first of the sinners; just as among advocates for example, some are called first. This one is first, not because he has been handling cases for more years than the others, but because from the time he began he has surpassed them.[27]

The *primus advocatus* was thus expected to have achieved his coveted position through demonstrations of his technical skill in pleading lawsuits. Moreover, in the later Roman Empire the top-ranking advocate(s) attached to each court were promoted as *advocati fisci* (advocates who pleaded on behalf of the imperial treasury)—a highly prestigious and remunerative career move.[28]

The official ranking of advocates within their cohorts was part of a general formalization of regulations governing *advocati statuti* ('statutory advocates', as opposed to the 'supernumeraries'). Being actively enrolled to plead before a particular tribunal offered access

[25] *CI* 2. 6. 7 (AD 370, addressed to the Urban Prefect, Olybrius).

[26] *Contra* Jones, *Later Roman Empire*, 510, who assumes that promotion was by length of service.

[27] Augustine, *Sermon* 176. 3 (*PL* 38. 951): 'Primum se dixit, non peccatorum ordine, sed peccati magnitudine. Magnitudinem peccati sui adtendit, unde se primum dixit peccatorum; quomodo dicuntur inter advocatos, verbi gratia, primi: primus est iste, non quia plures annos habet, ex quo causas agit; sed quia ex quo coepit, ceteros superavit.'

[28] On the *advocati fisci* see the constitutions collected under *C. Th.* 10. 15 and *CI* 2. 8; also *CI* 2. 7. 10 (452), 2. 7. 12 (463), 2. 7. 21 (500), 2. 7. 22 (505), and 2. 7. 23 (506).

to potential clients and a steady income, and could also establish powerful patronage relationships. Those of modest backgrounds and/or resources, from the time of Cicero onwards, had always regarded advocacy as a means of social advancement.[29] It was also an attractive profession for those who already had property to lose, as in the case of a certain Chrysogonus who—according to Libanius—wanted to become enrolled as an advocate at the tribunal of the governor of Phoenicia in order to protect his ancestral estates. Libanius implies that merely being enrolled as an advocate at the provincial governor's court will be enough to put a stop to the current lawsuit pending against Chrysogonus' property, as well as deterring any future claimants.[30] The families of established sixth-century Oxyrhynchite landowners count a number of 'statutory' advocates amongst their members—perhaps motivated by concerns similar to those of Chrysogonus. Acceptance onto the register of statutory advocates did not, however, guarantee that an advocate would actually be employed in pleading cases; the presiding magistrate was responsible for summoning the advocates by name, and could thus make or break their reputations. In a letter addressed to Alexander, governor of Syria, in 363, Libanius reminds him that:

> It's a big deal for such fellows [sc. newly enrolled advocates] that the judge says, 'where is so-and-so?'—these little words produce a crowd of people fleeing for protection to the man judged worthy of them . . . We hear that many governors made the reputation of many men who had been unknown and who acquired a name for themselves. Even now they point to the good advocates and say among themselves, 'Rufinus wanted this fellow, Himerius that fellow, someone else that other fellow'.[31]

It was, of course, a common topos that advocates of a higher social standing pleaded cases to *enhance* their reputations, whilst those of a low social status sought out cases for the profit.[32] Conversely, once an advocate had finally become established at court it could prove difficult to leave: a friend of Basil of Cappadocia claimed that he wanted

[29] For the later Empire, see Honoré, *Law in Crisis*, 7.

[30] Libanius, *Ep.* 1208 (Foerster) to Marius, governor of Phoenicia.

[31] Libanius, *Ep.* 838. 7–8 (Foerster), tr. S. Bradbury, *Selected Letters of Libanius from the Age of Constantius and Julian* (Liverpool: Liverpool University Press, 2004), 132–3.

[32] On payment and honoraria for advocates see *D.* 50. 13. 1. 10 (Ulpian); *CI* 2. 6. 3 (AD 240); *CI* 4. 6. 11 (294); *C.Th.* 2. 10. 3–4 (325/?326); *C.Th.* 8. 10. 2 (344); and *CI* 2. 6. 6. 3–5 (368). For the 5th and 6th cents. see A. A. Dimopoulou, *La Rémunération de l'assistance en justice* (Athens: Éditions ant. N. Sakkoulas, 1999).

to abandon advocacy for a life of Christian contemplation, but the magistrates were pursuing him 'like a deserter'.[33]

Theodosius II consolidated the privileges available to advocates at the higher ranking bureaucratic courts; by 428 all *togati* (advocates) attached to the Eastern courts of the Praetorian and Urban prefectures had been awarded senatorial rank. A later Theodosian constitution extended a package of lesser privileges and exemptions to all those who pleaded before judges with a rank of *spectabilis*—it also specified that no duties, other than the office of arbitrator, should be imposed on such advocates.[34] Finally, in 440, Theodosius laid down that all advocates already enrolled at the courts of the PPO or the PU, and their children, should be freed from a cohortal or lower status, although other long-standing restrictions on decurions acting as advocates persisted.[35]

Personal recommendation continued to be the main avenue through which imperial magistrates recruited statutory advocates. Both Libanius and Ausonius, for example, wrote letters of recommendation to legal officials on behalf of their students, and Symmachus also acted as a patron to young *causidici*.[36] This was the point at which patronage networks

[33] Basil, *Letter* 150, (from the edn. by R. Deferrari, *Basil. Letters 59–185* (Cambridge, Mass.: Loeb, 1928), 362. Ps-Palladius, *On the Races of India and the Brahmans* allegedly records the travels of a (4th-century?) Theban *scholasticus*, who left for India 'because he was fed up with legal practice'—see J. D. M Derrett, 'The Theban Scholasticus and Malabar in c.355–60', *Journal of the American Oriental Society*, 82/1 (1962), 21–31.

[34] *C.Th.* 6. 2. 26 (428, given at Constantinople, addressed to Proculus PU), and *N.Th.* 10. 1. 4 (439/444) addressed to Florentius PP). Compare *N.Val.* 2. 2. 3 (442, posted at Rome), *CI* 2. 7. 14 (469, given at Constantinople), *CI* 2. 7. 16 (474, given at Constantinople), *CI* 2. 7. 17. 1 (474, addressed to the *PP Illyricum*), *CI* 2. 7. 20pr. (497, given at Constantinople), and *CI* 2. 7. 26 pr. (514, given at Constantinople). For Justinian's measures, see below.

[35] *CI* 2. 7. 8 (440, addressed to Cyrus PP). Attempts to prevent decurions from acting as advocates beyond the city to which they owe their compulsory obligations include *C.Th.* 12. 1. 46 (AD 358, addressed to Martinianus, vicar of Africa): no laws have ever granted advocates exemption from compulsory municipal services; *C.Th.* 12. 1. 77 (AD 372, given at Trier to Probus PU): judges are conniving with decurions who are enrolled as advocates, helping them to jump the queue by nominating them as provincial governors before they have risen through the ranks of the municipal council; *CI* 2. 7. 2 (AD 378, given at Ravenna): curials cannot 'go from one place to another in order to act as advocates'; *C.Th.* 12. 1. 98 (AD 383, given at Constantinople): if any decurion attempts to evade their compulsory services 'under the plea of holding the office of an advocate', the PP must compel both them and their sons to perform their obligations; see also *C.Th.* 16. 1. 116 (387), *C.Th.* 12. 1. 152. 3 = *CI* 2. 7. 3 (396), *N.Th.* 10. 1 pr. (439) and *N.Val.* 32. 1. 7 (451).

[36] See e.g. Appendix I below, entries for Anticles and Diognetus; and Appendix II, entries for Epictetus, Felix, Helpidius, Iulianus, Martyrius, and Anonymous 3.

could be called upon with respect to a good family name or influential backer, or to a famed teacher. A candidate's level of study could also be used to persuasive effect: in a letter of recommendation addressed to a *comes sacrarum largitionum,* Symmachus highly commends two individuals for having undertaken formal legal study, in addition to their familiarity with forensic customs and practice (*Ep.* 5. 74). Magistrates seem to have been free to enrol whom they wished as advocates, within certain parameters (such as preferential rules regarding the enrolment of sons of existing statutory advocates); however, a set of selection criteria peculiar to individual courts undoubtedly evolved.

A 442 constitution of the Emperor Valentinian III, addressed to the PP Faustus, specifies that a *causidicus* who wished to be enrolled at a bureaucratic court must be 'examined' by the magistrate with respect to his studies, character (*mores*), birth status, and whether he had performed any compulsory municipal services to which he was obligated.[37] The preamble to the constitution records that Faustus himself had suggested these criteria to the Emperor—hence the constitution should be understood as 'formalizing' and 'generalizing' a practice that already existed at the highest level courts.[38] A later ruling of the Eastern Emperor Leo, on the other hand, confined its measures specifically to the court of the PP *Orientis*: an advocate could not be registered at this court unless he had first 'undergone examination' before the governor of the province where he was born (to establish that he had no prior obligations); in addition to this requirement, *iurisperiti* also had to certify under oath that the candidate was 'learned in the science of jurisprudence'.[39] This particular rule perhaps helps to explain why, out of the seventeen members who served on Justinian's second commission for his *Codex*, eleven were advocates from the court of the PP *Orientis*.

In the later fifth and early sixth centuries, examination of an advocate's 'mind' and 'character' also began to include the criterion of their religion. A constitution issued at Ravenna in 418, addressed to Palladius PP, had forbidden 'those of the Jewish *superstitio*' from seeking entry into the imperial service, but had also ruled: 'We do *not* prohibit Jews *instructed*

[37] *N. Val.* 2. 2. 1 (442, given at Rome).

[38] Julian's *Const. de Postulando*, discussed above, lists the ideal 'qualifications' for an advocate at ll. 25–6, 'optimos eligi velimus, animo prius, deinde facundia. Nam studiorum secunda gloria est, prima mentium.'

[39] *CI* 2. 7. 11. (460, given at Constantinople), partially modified by *CI.* 2. 7. 17 pr. (474). Compare *CI* 2. 7. 26. pr. (514, given at Constantinople).

in liberal studies from acting as advocates.'[40] Exactly fifty years later in the Eastern Empire, however, a constitution of the Emperor Leo states that no one would be admitted to practise as an advocate before the prefect's court, nor any provincial one, unless he had first been 'admitted into the holy mysteries of the Catholic *religio*' (i.e. baptized a Catholic).[41] The drafter of Leo's text possibly anticipated difficulties in enforcing the law: if any evasive scams or fast tricks were attempted, then the magistrate's office staff were to be fined a hundred pounds of gold, whilst the advocate who had attempted to circumvent the regulation was to be barred from pleading, his property confiscated, and his person sentenced to perpetual exile. Penalties were also laid down against any provincial governor complicit in the deceit. Even if we read Leo's constitution as a 'symbolic' enactment, rather than as a law that was actually meant to be enforced, it nonetheless suggests that forensic culture was changing in the later fifth century (at least in the East). In 527 the Emperors Justin and Justinian ruled that not even 'the most learned *causidici*' could be put on the register of advocates if they were heretics. The constitution continues with the statement that advocates, 'more than others, should have an accurate understanding of the divine precepts, as they live their lives among books'.[42] This 527 ruling prepared the way for Justinian's later changes to forensic procedure, concerning, for example, the swearing of all legal oaths on Christian gospel texts, placed within the courtroom for the duration of the trial.[43]

This increase in fifth- and sixth-century imperial regulations concerning the practice of advocacy should not, however, be seen as proof that late Roman advocacy was a mere 'handmaid of the bureaucratic order'. A significant number of the imperial constitutions governing

[40] *C.Th.* 16. 8. 24: 'Sane Iudaeis *liberalibus studiis institutis* exercendae advocationis non intercludimus libertatem'; *N.Th.* 3. 1. 3 and 8 (AD 438, given at Constantinople, addressed to Florentius PP) prohibits Jews and Samaritans from acting either as a *defensor civitatis* or as an apparitor for any cases other than those concerning the civil law. Compare *C.Th.* 16. 5. 42 (AD 408, given at Ravenna, addressed to Olympius, master of the offices, and Valens, count of the household troops): those who are *hostile* to the Catholic sect cannot hold Palatine offices.

[41] *CI* 2. 6. 8 (468, given at Constantinople): 'Nemo vel in foro magnitudinis tuae vel in provinciali iudicio vel apud quemquam iudicem accedat ad togatorum consortium, nisi sacrosanctis catholicae religionis fuerit imbutus mysteriis.' See also *CI* 1. 4. 15.

[42] *CI* 1. 5. 12. 7–9 (527).

[43] For further discussion see C. Humfress, 'Judging by the Book: Christian Codices and Late Antique Legal Culture', in W. Klingshirn and L. Safran (eds.), *The Early Christian Book* (Washington, DC: Catholic University of America Press, 2007), 141–58.

the practice of advocacy were issued in response to petitions from individual groups of advocates who either wanted to clarify their status, or sought the extension of privileges and immunities based on precedents already granted to other corporate bodies. The piecemeal extension of the advocates' right to hold a *peculium* provides a good example. In 422 the Emperor Theodosius II gave advocates at the court of the PP *Orientis*, who were still under paternal power, the right to vindicate their professional profits to their own ownership, after the death of their fathers. This *beneficium* was presumably granted after the advocates themselves had petitioned it—perhaps pleading an analogy with the practice granted to military soldiers (*CI* 2. 7. 4 and *C.Th.* 2. 10. 6). In 426 the same privilege was extended to the advocates of the Urban Prefect at Constantinople (*CI* 2. 7. 5, to Cyrus PU) and in 439 to the advocates at the court of the prefect of Illyricum (*CI* 2. 7. 7). In 442 all advocates enrolled at the Western provincial courts were granted the same *beneficium*, apparently in response to a *suggestio* made by the Praetorian Prefect of Italy (*N.Val.* 2. 3. 4). In 469 the *scholastici* (advocates) of Alexandria had all their privileges confirmed by the Emperor Leo, in direct response to a wide-ranging petition that they had drafted and sent to the Emperor themselves (*CI* 2. 7. 13). The fact that the advocates' privileges were extended and confirmed in a piecemeal fashion should alert us to the fact that other *collegia*, such as churches and other ecclesiastical organizations, were granted their *beneficia* via similar processes of individual petition and response.

In the Justinianic legislation, in particular, we find a group of constitutions issued in direct response to requests from forensic corporations for clarification of substantive legal principles and procedural issues.[44] For example, *CI* 6. 38. 5 responds to the advocates of Illyricum who had apparently queried the legal scope of the term 'family'; *CI* 6. 58. 12 responds to the advocates of Caesarea, concerning the status of a child born to a woman over 50 years of age; and *CI* 8. 4. 11 alleviates the doubts of Illyrian advocates concerning the possession of vacant property without express legal authority. Taken as a whole, the preambles to these constitutions imply that the issues to be resolved have arisen in the context of recent concrete cases pleaded in the courts. Bonini assumes that the process of consultation was initiated by Justinian himself, but

[44] *CI* 2. 3. 30, 5. 37. 25, 6. 58. 12, and 8. 37. 14 (*Caesariana advocatio*); *CI* 6. 38. 5, 2. 7. 29, and 8. 4. 11 (*Illyriciana advocatio*); and *CI* 8. 40. 27 (*Palaestina advocatio*).

admits that there is no evidence for an explicit request for collaboration from the Emperor to the advocates.[45] I would suggest, to the contrary, that this group of constitutions do not testify to a Justinianic innovation in the legal system, but rather to a continuation of the traditional collaboration between the imperial chancellery and forensic practitioners. The preambles to these Justinianic texts provide us with explicit evidence of what is implicit in the surviving sections of earlier imperial constitutions: that late Roman advocates, as members of increasingly influential corporate bodies, could directly provoke the promulgation of new imperial constitutions through their forensic practice.

FORENSIC RHETORIC AND THE POST-CLASSICAL SCHOOLS

> Whoever hastens to take part in disputes of the law,
> Learned in the ways of rhetoric,
> Let him read and reread this work on the art,
> and he shall forge his renown.[46]

The fourth-century *Ars Rhetorica* of Chirius Fortunatianus opens with this hexameter poem, promising success in the courtroom to those who master the handbook's contents. The intended audience for Fortunatianus' rhetorical treatise was thus aspiring forensic orators. Modern scholarship, however, tends to obscure this continuing connection between rhetorical training and forensic practice in the later Roman Empire, through a focus upon the 'literary' or 'cultural' effects of late antique education.[47] Marrou's classic work, *Histoire de l'éducation dans l'antiquité* (1948), denies that the study of late Roman rhetoric equipped its graduates with any technical competence: the products of the late rhetorical schools were 'rhetors with a mere gift for words—or, if you

[45] R. Bonini, '"Interrogationes" forensi e attività legislativa giustinianica', *SDHI* 33 (1967), 279–319.

[46] Chirius Fortunatianus, *Ars Rhetorica* i. 1–3, *RLM* 81: 'Quisquis rhetorico festinat tramite doctus/Ad causas legesque trahi, bene perlegat artis/Hoc opus et notum faciat per competa callem.' My thanks to Catherine Edwards for her help with this passage.

[47] For the Early Empire see E. P. Parks, *The Roman Rhetorical Schools as a Preparation for the Courts under the Early Empire* (Baltimore: Johns Hopkins University Press, 1945); A. Steinwenter, 'Rhetorik und römische Zivilprozess', *ZSS, Rom. Abt.* 64 (1947), 69–120; and Crook, *Legal Advocacy*, 163–7 and 180–1. Heath, *Menander: A Rhetor in Context*, esp 217–331 is the exception—he argues for the continued prevalence and relevance of forensic rhetoric into the Late Empire.

prefer, for literature'.[48] Peter Brown likewise makes no mention of any practical link between rhetoric and forensic advocacy in his *Power and Persuasion in Late Antiquity: Towards a Christian Empire* (1992); the rhetor is ranked along with the sophist and the professional poet as 'vocational followers of the muses'.[49]

The fact that Fortunatianus chose to open his technical rhetorical treatise with a hexameter poem is—of course—telling; like Apuleius, Ausonius, Martianus Capella, and Dioscorus of Aphrodito, he wished self-consciously to display both his forensic and 'literary' talents.[50] In fact, a proficiency in forensic rhetoric demanded the mastering of tools and techniques which we today might more readily associate with literary theory wholesale: how to construct character and motive persuasively, for example, or how to order the temporal sequencing of a narrative to achieve the maximum effect relative to audience and argument. The forensic bias of Greek and Roman rhetorical instruction even appears within the plots of ancient Graeco-Roman 'romance' novels: 'No extant ancient novel is without some form of court-room case where school rhetoric can be practised with a vengeance.'[51] Or as Anderson memorably puts it: 'The sophistic Eros is not just quiver and arrows and a bare bottom; there is a satchel crammed with *progymnasmata* [preliminary rhetorical exercises] as well.'[52] According to Graeco-Roman rhetorical theory, a skilled 'sophist' aimed at entertaining an audience, arranging different words as a painter arranges different colours, whilst a good advocate aimed at winning his audience's trust and conviction. It should be no surprise, however, that some of the individuals whom we might more readily identify with the 'second sophistic', and the (newly

[48] H. I. Marrou *Histoire de l'éducation dans l'antiquité* (Paris: Éditions du Seuil, 1948), tr. G. Lamb, *A History of Education in Antiquity* (London: Sheed & Ward, 1956). 311. See also Jones, *Later Roman Empire,* 1003–4.

[49] P. R. L. Brown, *Power and Persuasion in Late Antiquity: Towards a Christian Empire* (Madison: University of Wisconsin Press, 1992), 33–7.

[50] For Apuleius see S. J. Harrison, J. L. Hilton, and V. J. C. Hunink, *Apuleius: Rhetorical Works* (Oxford: OUP, 2001); for Ausonius see H. Sivan, *Ausonius of Bordeaux: Genesis of a Gallic Aristocracy* (London and New York: Routledge, 1993); for Martianus Capella's practice as an advocate see his *De Nuptiis Philologiae et Mercurii* 6. 577: 'desudatio curaque districtior tibi forensis rabulationis partibus illigata aciem industriae melioris obtudit'; and for Dioscorus of Aphrodito see Ch. 3 above.

[51] R. F. Hock, 'The Rhetoric of Romance', in S. Porter, *Handbook of Classical Rhetoric* (Leiden: Brill, 1997), 450. For a provocative argument concerning the relationship between judicial, deliberative, and epideictic rhetoric see J. Walker, *Rhetoric and Poetics in Antiquity* (Oxford: OUP, 2000).

[52] Hock, 'Rhetoric of Romance', 462, quoting G. Anderson, *The Second Sophistic: A Cultural Phenomenon in the Roman Empire* (New York: Routledge, 1993).

canonized) 'third sophistic', were either educated as advocates or appeared themselves before the courts in concrete cases.[53]

A formal training in rhetoric had a wider cultural function in both classical and post-classical antiquity; put simply, it shaped and reproduced an *ethos* for the literate elite. We should not solely think in terms of a shared high-level *paideia* of an Ambrose, an Ausonius, or a Symmachus here; some teachers of rhetoric in the cities of Graeco-Roman Egypt, for example, may have systematically taught their pupils to a level where they were 'equipped to take orders and pass them on' but 'rather less well equipped to answer their superiors back'.[54] Rhetoric could function as a means of social control partly, at least, because it taught techniques for training and controlling the self. The 'discipline' of formal rhetorical study might thus also function as part of a propaedeutic preparation for a higher level study of philosophy.[55] Finally, we have Libanius (in the late 380s/early 390s) referring to the 'sacred rites of oratory', to the 'Muse's holy ground', and to 'initiation into the rites of Hermes'—perhaps in an attempt to teach his students the cultural and 'religious' significance of their studies, as much as a personal plea that they show proper reverence to their teacher.[56] We can acknowledge all of these social, cultural, political, even 'religious' dimensions to late Roman rhetoric, without losing sight of the fact that it also functioned as a practical preparation for forensic advocacy.

'By far the largest part of the huge mass of rhetorical technography extant from late antiquity is concerned with techniques of judicial and

[53] E. Bowie, 'Literature and Sophistic', in A. K. Bowman, P. Garnsey, and D. Rathbone (eds.), *Cambridge Ancient History*, xi. *The High Empire A.D. 70–192*, 2nd edn. (2000), 898–921, at 902: 'We must remember that sophists undertook real forensic cases'; also noted by Heath, *Menander: A Rhetor in Context*, 78–83 and 290–1. On the so-called 'third sophistic' see E. Amato, A. Roduit, and M. Steinrück, *Approches de la troisième sophistique: Hommages à Jacques Schamp* (Brussels: Latomus 296, 2006), including discussions of Libanius, Gregory of Nazianzus, Gregory of Nyssa, Synesius of Cyrene, and Ausonius.

[54] T. Morgan, *Literate Education in the Hellenistic and Roman Worlds* (Cambridge: CUP, 1998), 225.

[55] For instruction in the disciplines of the liberal arts as a preparation for philosophy see the influential thesis of P. Hadot, *Arts libéraux et philosophie dans la pensée antique* (Paris: Études Augustiniennes, 1984), taken up by B. Studer, *La riflessione teologica nella chiesa imperiale (sec. iv e v)*, Sussidi Patristici dello Istituto Patristico Augustinianum, 4 (Rome: Sussidi Patristici dello Istituto Patristico Augustinianum 4, 1989), 99–104; and R. Lim, *Public Disputation, Power and Social Order in Late Antiquity* (Berkeley: University of California Press, 1995), 61–2.

[56] Libanius, *Oration* 3. 35 and *Oration* 58. 5.

deliberative speech.'[57] Heath has argued this case primarily with regard to the Greek rhetorical technography. The same conclusion, however, holds good for the Latin rhetorical handbooks. Julius Victor's *Ars Rhetorica*, probably written in the late fourth century, is almost entirely dedicated to the explication of forensic rhetoric, as is that of Chirius Fortunatianus.[58] The *De Rhetorica* of (Pseudo-)Augustine and the *Institutiones Oratoriae* of Sulpitius Victor are both focused on 'rhetorical techniques and exercises relevant to forensic cases'.[59] Even in Martianus Capella's highly 'literary' allegory on the seven liberal arts, rhetoric makes her triumphal entry preceded by the (legendary) founders of judicial rhetoric, Corax and Tisias—who call her daughter—trailing a retinue headed by the great forensic orators Demosthenes and Cicero.[60] Having announced her arrival, Martianus has 'Rhetoric' expound her forensic art to the assembled Olympian gods—and, of course, to the more mundane mid-fifth-century audience of Martianus' text. As Leff has argued, Latin rhetorical technography had always focused primarily upon forensic speaking; however, the late antique authors 'exaggerate this emphasis to the point of excluding all other oratorical genres'.[61] Boethius, writing in sixth-century Ostrogothic Italy, even complains that the fourth-century rhetorician, Marius Victorinus, was not seriously committed to logic as an enquiry for its own sake; his concern was essentially for its 'utility to the orator and advocate in court'.[62]

[57] Heath, *Menander: A Rhetor in Context*, 278, also p. xi, Menander 'was above all an expert in judicial and deliberative oratory, and precisely as such exemplary for an age in which rhetoric retained, for good practical reasons, a primary interest in techniques of judicial and deliberative persuasion.'

[58] C. Iulius Victor, *Ars Rhetorica Hermagorae Ciceronis Quintiliani Aquili (? = Aquila Romanus) Marcomanni Tatiani*, *RLM* 373–448; Chirius Fortunatianus, *Ars Rhetorica, libri III*, *RLM* 81–134.

[59] M. C. Leff, 'The Material of the Art in the Latin Handbooks of the Fourth Century AD', in B. Vickers (ed.), *Rhetoric Revalued: Papers from the International Society for the History of Rhetoric* (New York: Center for Medieval and Early Renaissance Studies, 1982), 71–8, at 74. On the (pseudo-)Augustine, *De Rhetorica* see *RLM* 137–51. M. Heath, 'The Substructure of *Stasis*-Theory from Hermagoras to Hermogenes', *Classical Quarterly*, 44 (1994), 114–29, at 117–21 dismisses Augustine's authorship—however, the case is not closed; Sulpitius Victor, *Institutiones Oratoriae ad M. Silonem Generum*, *RLM* 313–52.

[60] Martianus Capella, 'Liber de Arte Rhetorica', 3 (from his *De Nuptiis Philologiae et Mercurii*), *RLM* 452–3; on techniques of allegorical personification in handbooks of the liberal arts see G. Moretti, 'Il manuale e l'allegoria. La personificazione allegorica delle arti liberali come tradizione del genere manualistico', in M. S. Celentano (ed.), *Ars—Techne: Il manuale tecnico nelle civiltà greca e romana* (Chieti: Edizioni dell'Orso, 2003), 159–86.

[61] Leff, 'Material of Art', 75.

[62] As noted by H. Chadwick, *Heresy and Orthodoxy in the Early Church* (Aldershot: Variorum, 1991), 116.

The tools of post-classical rhetoric included classical texts. A late Roman rhetorician named Eusebius apparently produced a commentary on Cicero's *De Inventione* (no longer extant), as did the rhetorician Grillius (partially extant).[63] Marius Victorinus' *Explanationes in Ciceronis Rhetoricam* contains painstaking analyses of Cicero's *De Inventione* and *Topica*—both focused on the forensic branch of rhetoric. Cicero's oratorical works also appear in Christian polemic: in the opening pages of his *Contra Rufinum*, Jerome (perhaps sardonically) advises his adversary to unroll Cicero's *Ad Herennium*, his *De Oratore*, in which—as Jerome states—'Cicero introduces the most eloquent men of that time, Crassus and Antonius, engaged in argument', and his *Orator*.[64] Commentaries on Demosthenes' orations and Menander's corpus of treatises on judicial and deliberative rhetoric also circulated in late antiquity.[65] Post-classical rhetoricians, however, did not concern themselves with the minutiae of complex rhetorical techniques simply out of an uncritical reverence for the authority of classical literature.[66] In chapter 19 of the (Pseudo-)Augustine *De Rhetorica*, the author disputes Hermagoras' earlier teaching on a finer point of Greek *stasis* theory, stating: 'I completely disagree, and I say so despite the stature of the man. For authority is not always to be deferred to, at any rate, when it is bettered by reason.'[67] In his *Ep.* 118 Augustine himself refused a request from a certain individual for instruction in Cicero's *Orator* and *De Oratore*, with the putdown that he would answer questions on forensic rhetoric

[63] Eusebius, noted by Grillius, *RLM* 598. 20 and Rufinus, *RLM* 581. 18; Grillius = *Excerpta ex Grilli commento in primum Ciceronis librum de inventione*, *RLM* 596–606. See also 'Incerti auctoris tractatus de attributes personae et negotio sive commentarius in Ciceronis *de inventione* I.24–28', *RLM* 305–10.

[64] *PL* 23. 409. F. Marx, *Incerti auctoris de ratione dicendi ad C. Herennium lib iv iterum* (Leipzig: Teubner, 1894), 7, cites this passage as the first attribution of the *Ad Herennium* to Cicero in Latin literature.

[65] On commentaries to Demosthenes see C. A. Gibson, *Interpreting a Classic: Demosthenes and his Ancient Commentators* (Berkeley: University of California, 2002), 13–69; for a 5th-cent. advocate reading both commentaries on Demosthenes and the works of Menander see *P. Berol. 21849* discussed by R. Kaster, *Guardians of Language: The Grammarian and Society in Late Antiquity* (Berkeley: University of California Press, 1988), 111; T. Hauken, *Petition and Response: An Epigraphic Study of Petitions to Roman Emperors A.D. 181–249*, ii (Bergen: Norwegian Institute at Athens, 1998), 288; and Heath, *Menander: A Rhetor in Context*, 94–5 and 296–7.

[66] M. L. Clarke, *Rhetoric at Rome* (London: Cohen & West, 1953), 139–40, still reflects most current scholarship with his judgement that the late rhetoricians 'are of minor interest and do not deserve to be read on their own account' as 'original thought is as lacking as literary charm'.

[67] (Pseudo-)Augustine, *De Rhetorica* 19 (*RLM* 149, ll. 3–4).

'if anyone proposed those difficulties to be analysed and solved, not out of the books of Cicero, but in their own right'. The bishop of Hippo, like other late Roman rhetoricians, was not interested in the classical texts alone, but in their practical application.

It is one thing to argue that the technical output of late Roman Latin and Greek rhetoricians was predominantly focused on forensic rhetoric, and another thing to prove that a 'formal' education in rhetoric provided a career-oriented training for advocates.[68] In other words, were the late Roman rhetorical treatises related to instruction at the rhetorical schools? Late Roman teachers of rhetoric such as Eumenius, Lactantius, Ausonius, Alethius, and Augustine each understood their task as encompassing the training of accomplished forensic speakers.[69] The same is true of Libanius at his school in Antioch, where the tongues of orators were taught to mesmerize audiences 'like snowflakes on a winter's day'.[70] Libanius' *Oration* 34. 25 states (rather more prosaically) that he expects his pupils to become advocates, governors, or *curiales*; and his *Oration* 62 diligently recounts their 'shining' successes in these three positions.[71] Petit attempted a statistical analysis of the known eventual careers of Libanius' ex-students: he identified over forty 'functionaries', twenty-five advocates, twenty-two *curiales*, ten professors of the liberal arts, three bishops, and one doctor.[72] Out of the forty or so named as 'functionaries', approximately half had started out as advocates. Libanius even once claimed that, if a student was really pushed for resources, a mere two years spent frequenting his classes could lead to brilliant success at the bar.[73]

Aspiring advocates could also, of course, learn the skills of the trade by watching advocates in action. Practising advocates in both the Early

[68] For an important discussion of 'formal' instruction in rhetoric using papyrological evidence, and the sociology of Roman education in general, see Morgan, *Literate Education*, 190–239.

[69] For Eumenius see C. Lécrivain, 'Note sur le recrutement des avocats dans la période du bas empire', *MEFR* 5 (1885), 276–83, at 282; for Lactantius, his *Inst Div.* 3. 13; for Ausonius, his *Praef.* 1. 17; for Alethius, see Ausonius, *Prof. Burd.* 2. 7; for Augustine, see his *Confessions* 3. 3–4, 4. 2 and *Eps.* 93, 117, and 118. Kaster, *Guardians of Language*, 105, notes a number of 4th-cent. rhetoricians who also practised at the bar.

[70] Libanius, *Ep.* 503. 3 (Foerster), tr. Bradbury, *Selected Letters*, 84.

[71] Libanius, *Oration* 62. 37, 41, and 50 (Foerster, iv. 364–5, 367, and 371).

[72] P. Petit, *Les Étudiants*, 154–70. See also P. Petit, *Les Fonctionnaires dans l'œuvre de Libanius: Analyse Prosopographique* (Paris: Centre de recherches d'histoire ancienne, 1994).

[73] Heath, *Menander: A Rhetor in Context*, 217–54, discusses Libanius' curriculum and teaching programme.

and Late Empire seem to have taken on 'apprentices', who may have simply been taught what they needed to know on the job. Anyone, moreover, could frequent the lawcourts in the *fora*/*agorai* of the major cities. Recalling his student days at Rome, Jerome states that, rather than attending his rhetorical classes and exercising his mind in 'fictitious disputes', he preferred to run to the forum and learn his technique from watching 'the most skilled orators vehemently attacking each other'.[74] Hilary of Poitiers, on the other hand, assumed that a mid-fourth-century audience would take it for granted that classroom *controversiae* naturally led to courtroom pleadings:

That which is always observed, according to our recollection, in every branch of learning, is that when someone has been instructed from the beginning and for a very long time in some insignificant exercise and has become familiar over an extended period of time with the more humble task, then he is permitted to experiment in the things to which he has been accustomed . . . so those who have completed the forensic battles in the classroom are then admitted to the disputes in tribunals.[75]

A fifth-century text, probably written in Mesopotamia within a monastic context, also treats a formal education as a technical preparation for advocacy. The author gives the following passage as one proof amongst several that the natural order of things always proceeds from lesser to greater:

For anyone who wants to learn to read, the first step is to learn the symbols. When he has become first in this, he goes on to the school of the Romans, and is the last of all. Again, when he has risen to the top of that school, he goes on to the school of literature (*grammata*), and is again, last of everyone there, a tiro. Then when he has become the learned one (*scholastikos*) he is the novice,

[74] Jerome, *Comm. in Epist. ad Gal.* 1. 2. 11–12 (*PL* 26. 340): 'Aliquoties cum adulescentulus Romae controversias declamarem et ad vera certamina fictis me litibus exercerem, currebam ad tribunalia iudicum, et disertissimos oratorum tanta inter se videbam acerbitate contendere.'

[75] Hilary of Poitiers, *De Trinitate* 1. 34, *CCSL* 62. 32, the passage reads in context: 'Quod autem in omni genere doctrinarum observari semper meminimus, ut si qui diu tenui primum exercitatione longoque usu humilioris studii fuerint eruditi, tum iam ad rerum ipsarum quibus inbuti sunt experimenta mittantur,—ut cum iam bene luserint bella militaturi, in militiam protrahantur; aut cum forenses lites scholaris materiae temptauerint, tunc mittantur ad tribunalium pugnas . . . idipsum nos in hac maxima et gravissima totius fidei intellegentia facere curauimus.' On the school *controversiae* see M. Winterbottom, 'Schoolroom and Courtroom', in B. Vickers (ed.), *Rhetoric Revalued* (New York: Center for Medieval and Early Renaissance Studies, 1982), 59–70, and Crook, 'Once Again the *Controversiae* and Roman Law'.

in the last place, out of all the advocates (*dikologoi*). Having again reached the pinnacle he becomes the dux (*hegemon*) there. And when he has become the master (*archon*), first of all, he takes on an assessor (*sugkathedros*) as an aide.[76]

This depiction of the *scholastikos* as *already* a neophyte advocate highlights the close association between the type of higher level literate education taught via formal 'school' instruction and forensic practice under the Late Empire.[77]

Advanced-level rhetoric taught both the formal 'discovery' of facts and arguments (*inventio*, *heuresis*), as well as how to plead them effectively in court. Part of the advocate's art lay in constructing the most plausible narrative for a case, according to the brief that he had been given; in other words, the raw facts of a dispute (as relayed by the client to the advocate) had to be transformed into a persuasive account that would win over the judge.[78] The skills necessary for identifying the most plausible 'facts' and arguments were taught via *stasis* theory and other techniques of 'invention'. How to use demonstrative logic to structure a given argument effectively was also taught by the rhetorician (*dispositio*, *taxis*)—as were specific techniques for swaying emotion. An understanding of character was also essential: when reasons and motives had to be assigned to the 'facts' on which a given case turned, the characters of the 'actors' (primarily the litigants) had to be constructed accordingly. As Quintilian teaches:

The narrative will be credible (1) if we consult our own hearts first and so do not say anything contrary to what is natural; (2) if we give notices and reasons before events (not all events, but those on which the inquiry turns); (3) if we set up characters approximate to the actions which we wish to be believed; for

[76] Makarios of Egypt/Symeon of Mesopotamia, *Homily* 15. 41, *PG* 34. 603. See Rouché, 'Functions of the Governor', 34.

[77] Matthews, *Laying Down the Law*, 57–8, specifies that the term *scholasticus* denotes 'not just an academic but an advocate or pleader at law'; Heath, *Menander: A Rhetor in Context*, 297, argues that the term could cover teachers of rhetoric, advocates, holders of a range of official posts, and honorific addresses to educated men. Sources that equate *scholastici* with advocates in particular include: *FIRA* ii. 332; *P.Cairo Maspero* III. 67329; *P.Oxy.* 902; *P.Lond.* 922 and 1686; *P.Cairo Maspero* 67117.14; *C.Th.* 8. 10. 2 (344); *C.Th.* 1. 29. 3 (368). Theodoret of Cyrhus, *Ep. Sirm* 46 (*SC* 98. 120–2) is addressed to a *scholasticus* Peter, known to be an advocate from his letters addressed to Isidore of Pelusium; and the *Scholasticus* Ammon (= *P. Ammon*) was a practising advocate from Panopolis.

[78] A. Carcaterra, 'Le operazione dell' avvocato: Euristica e logica a fronte della "narratio" dell' interessato', *SDHI* 52 (1986), 73–105, at 77–8, discusses the relationship between the private *narratio* which a client gave to an advocate and the technical *narratio* made by that advocate before a court of law (*narratio ante iudicem*).

example, an alleged thief should be covetous, an adulterer lustful, a murderer rash; if we are for the defence we take the opposite line; and (4) if we also specify places, times, and the like.[79]

A constitution (most probably) issued in 370 to the Urban Prefect at Rome provides a late Roman legislative perspective on this rhetorical handling of 'character':

Advocates shall, above all things, defend the cases of those who retain them in such a way as to do nothing more than the success of the actions demands, *and they shall not employ abuse and slander*. They must do whatever the case requires, but refrain from vituperation; for if anyone should be so bold as to think his case should be conducted not by argument but by personal invective, he shall suffer loss of reputation.[80]

An advocate who went beyond the 'plausible' into the realms of 'abuse and slander' risked the censure of the court. Rhetorical school thus also taught would-be advocates how to construct their own *ethos*, learning how to create and sustain an impression of moral authority and credibility, as well as how to hold their togas in court for maximum impact.[81]

The late Roman documents known as the *narratio* papyri show these rhetorical techniques in action. Despite some disagreement amongst papyrologists, it is now generally accepted that these papyri contain a rhetorical presentation of a case at law, constructed by a *rhetor* (advocate) responsible for the case.[82] As Lewis and Schiller have noted, the techniques of classification and arrangement employed in the *narratio* papyri demonstrate that late Roman advocates 'were well acquainted with the schemes of rhetoric set forth by earlier as well as more contemporary rhetoricians, and were still trained in the art'.[83] The

[79] Quintilian, *Inst. Orat.* 4. 2. 52. Tr. Russell, Loeb edn. ii. 245–7.

[80] *CI* 2. 6. 6. 1 (AD 368/370 to Olybrius PU): 'Ante omnia autem universi advocati ita praebeant patrocinia iurgantibus, ut non ultra, quam litium poscit utilitas, in licentiam conviciandi et maledicendi temeritatem prorumpant: agant, quod causa desiderat: temperent ab iniuria. nam si quis adeo procax fuerit, ut non ratione, sed probris putet esse certandum, opinionis suae imminutione quatietur.'

[81] See e.g. Fortunatianus, 15–23 = *RLM* 130–4.

[82] The group includes *P.Princ.* 119 (*c.*325); *P.Col.* 174 (4th cent.); *P.Vindob. Gr. Inv.* 39757 (early 4th cent.); *P.Lips* 41 (late 4th cent.); *P.Thead.* 16 (after 307); and *P.Köln Panop.* 31 (early 4th cent.). For discussion, with reference to earlier bibliography see Crook, *Legal Advocacy*, 114–18, and Harries, *Law and Empire*, 107–10.

[83] N. Lewis, and A. A. Schiller, 'Another "Narratio" Document', in A. Watson (ed.), *Daube Noster* (Edinburgh: Edinburgh University Press, 1974), 187–200, at 194. Compare J. L. Fournet, 'Entre document et litterature: La Pétition dans l'antiquité

later Latin rhetorical handbooks, moreover, also include explanations of technical terms of Roman legal procedure.[84] For example, in his commentary on Cicero, Marius Victorinus discusses the advocate's technical use of *praescriptiones* and *exceptiones*—both of which identified the existence of certain conditions that would block the plaintiff's claim.[85] *P.Oxy.* 3579 (AD 325) provides an example of a defence advocate pleading such a 'demurrer', with the additional brio: 'The demurrer I have announced is brilliant and legally absolutely spot-on.'[86] At least part of this defence advocate's self-assurance was probably drawn from his rhetorical studies—whether it was justified or not is unknown, as the papyrus breaks off with the presiding judge adjourning the hearing so that the 'Lord's day' could be observed. The discipline of post-classical rhetoric could thus serve a dual function: it was both a technical preparation for pleading concrete cases in court, as well as an introduction to the principles of legal procedure with which practising advocates were expected to be familiar.

THE CONTRIBUTION OF ADVOCATES TO THE DEVELOPMENT OF LATE ROMAN 'LAW'

> An advocate only succeeds to the extent that he impresses his judge.[87]

Under the various late Roman civil *cognitio* procedures advocates could be involved in every phase of the lawsuit, from the *principium litis* (including the registering of the case, the summons, the response of

tardive', in D. Feissel and J. Gascou (eds.), *La Pétition à Byzance* (Paris: Centre de Recherche d'Histoire et Civilisation de Byzance, 2004), 61–74, on the rhetorical dimension of late antique petitions.

[84] On forensic procedure in the later Greek rhetorical handbooks, see Heath, *Menander: A Rhetor in Context*, 317–21.

[85] *Praescriptio* and *exceptio* = Victorinus, *RLM* 277. Compare Fortunatianus, *RLM* 97–8. Heath, 'Practical Advocacy in Roman Egypt', 78, and Heath, *Menander: A Rhetor in Context*, 319, argues that the development of the issue of objection in (Greek) *stasis* theory was prompted by the forensic practice of lodging a *paragraphe* (= *praescriptio*). See in general Kaser and Hackl, *Das römische Zivilprozessrecht*, 488–551.

[86] Quoted from Crook, *Legal Advocacy*, 112.

[87] Jerome, *Ep.* 57. 1 (*CSEL* 54. 504).

the defendant and the prescribing of the necessary *cautiones*), through the *medium litis* (formally encompassing the *narratio* of the plaintiff and the *contradictio* of the defendant before the judge) to the *definitum negotium* (the administration of proofs up to the definitive sentence).[88] If appointed, defence advocates would also be at hand throughout a public/'criminal' trial.

The papyri suggest that the majority of cases that did make it to at least some preparatory stage of pleading dealt with routine property disputes, or with questions of liability for taxation or claims of various types of 'oppression'. There may be some dispute as to each side's pleading of the 'facts', but the legal basis of the case was often relatively straightforward. A petition from the archive of Aurelius Sakaon, for example, opens with the lines: 'Your majesty has commanded, my lord *praeses*, in conformity with an imperial command, that no one be subjected to undue levies, but that each meet his proper burdens.'[89] The legal principle referred to here is general, to the point of being obvious—what are really at stake are factual questions concerning who owes what to whom (in rhetorical theory, this case could be said to turn on a 'conjectural issue'). Nonetheless, the drafter included the 'command' of the provincial governor at the beginning of this document because it adds a rhetorical punch to the plea: the same *praeses* who issued the command, in accordance with the Emperor's wishes, now has the (lucky) chance to put his own words into action by accepting this case and deciding in favour of the 'wronged' petitioner. An appeal to the command (or we might say the 'law') of the *praeses* is part of this potential litigant's rhetorical strategy.

From the perspective of forensic rhetoric, at least, it would be a mistake to focus solely on whether laws and legal principles were 'applied', 'vulgarized', or even 'developed' in late antiquity. We should ask first how they were handled in practice. Todd has explained one crucial conceptual distinction at stake here, with reference to the understanding of law in classical Athens: 'ancient rhetorical theorists classify laws as a form of evidence, whereas we would tend to speak of evidence being used to demonstrate matters of fact and laws being

[88] On the involvement of advocates in the *principium litis*, see Chastagnol, *La Préfecture Urbaine*, 375.

[89] *P. Sakaon* 41, ll. 3–4 (dated 14 July 322), tr. G. M. Parássoglou, *The Archive of Aurelius Sakaon: Papers of an Egyptian Farmer in the Last Century of Theadelphia* (Bonn: Habelt, 1978), 100–1.

the rules on the basis of which those facts are to be judged'.[90] Like the ancient Greek theorists, late Roman rhetoricians taught techniques for pleading written laws as evidence, rather than approaching them simply as authoritative 'rules'. In the late Roman papyri, as in the earlier material, the direct appeal to a specific legislative pronouncement is relatively infrequent—more common are persuasive appeals to equity or justice couched in general terms. The late Roman rhetorical handbooks, however, do give detailed accounts of how to come to grips with pleading particular written laws as 'evidence' in concrete cases.

Under the heading 'documents brought as proof', Martianus Capella covers how to treat various types of ambiguity in a written law, as well as arguments from 'the letter and the spirit'; the persuasive handling of 'contradictory' and 'conflicting' laws; and the forensic uses of various types of 'syllogism' (reasoning by analogy, reasoning from consequence, reasoning from greater to lesser, and reasoning from contraries).[91] The rhetorical handbooks also taught arguments from the 'intention of the lawgiver' under the heading of pleading 'non-artistic' or 'documentary' proofs as evidence. Hence from the Greek technography, a set of second- or third-century notes known as 'The Art of Political Speech' by Anonymous Seguerianus includes the following advice in a chapter 'on *pisteis*': 'In the case of non-artistic proofs (we refute) laws either by an ambiguity and saying that not this but something else is signified, or turning from the wording and examining the intent of the lawgiver we conclude from what has been said that the subject is something else, or we ourselves bring up another law.'[92] Contracts and 'oracular pronouncements' could be subjected to the same techniques.

A rescript of Justinian, surviving only in an inscription from Didyma, hints at a broader context for handling imperial constitutions in late antiquity.[93] The inscription first gives the Justinianic constitution itself: a pragmatic sanction issued at the imperial court in Constantinople

[90] S. C. Todd, 'The Language of Law in Classical Athens', in P. Coss (ed.), *The Moral World of the Law* (Cambridge; CUP, 2000), 17–36, at 30.

[91] Martianus Capella, 'Liber de Arte Rhetorica', 15–16 = *RLM* 461–2. Compare Fortunatianus, *Ars Rhetorica* 2. 8–9 = *RLM* 87–8.

[92] The text has recently been edited by M. Patillon, *Anonyme de Séguier: Art du discours politique* (Paris: Les Belles Lettres, 2005); the translation given here is from M. R. Dilts and G. A. Kennedy (eds.), *Two Greek Rhetorical Treatises from the Roman Empire: Introduction, Text, and Translation of the Arts of Rhetoric, attributed to Anonymous Seguerianus and to Apsines of Gadara* (Leiden: Brill, 1997), 188.

[93] D. Feissel, 'Un rescrit de Justinien découvert à Didymes (1er avril 533)', *Chiron*, 34 (2004), 285–365.

in response to a petition directed in the first instance to the PP *Orientis*. It then records the relevant extract from the (bilingual) *gesta praefectoria* of the Eastern Prefecture (lines 36–56) and a further related declaration of the governor of Caria (lines 57–64). No doubt, when this inscription was commissioned, the aim was to emphasize the legitimate authority of the pragmatic sanction, by carefully monumentalizing every stage of its issuing. However, this inscription also reminds us that 'the text' of an imperial constitution could be copied (for a price of course), together with surrounding material from the *acta* of the various sessions in which it was discussed and transmitted.[94] Hence advocates and other interested parties could (potentially at least) access written *gesta* that recorded the various verbal processes associated with a given constitution's transmission. All of this material could be pleaded as 'evidence'—if a concrete case demanded it. Ultimately, it was up to the presiding magistrate and his legal advisers (*assessores*) to decide whether an advocate's handling of any given legal text stretched the boundaries of acceptable forensic practice or operated outside of them.[95]

Even relatively straightforward cases could, however, be made to turn on an issue of legal definition. In rhetorical theory a 'definitional issue', strictly speaking, involved denying the name or classification given to an act, rather than simply denying the act itself. As Martianus Capella phrases it, 'another name is put on a deed' so that the consequences following from the first 'name' can be negated.[96] To take a modern example, a defendant pleading 'involuntary manslaughter' in response to a charge of 'first degree murder' admits the killing, but reclassifies the act—with consequences for the judicial sentencing if the plea is admitted. A Ciceronian example frequently discussed in the later Latin material advises negating a charge of sacrilegious theft by admitting that the item was stolen, at the same time as reclassifying the place where the theft occurred (e.g. pleading that the item was taken from a *domus*, rather than a temple). As Alida Wilson puts it, 'events which occur in

[94] Kelly, *Ruling the Later Roman Empire*, 82, notes that John Lydus composed a daily summary of business (*cottidiana* or *regesta*) transacted in the Praetorian Prefect's court at Constantinople.

[95] An advocate could of course be held responsible for the pleading of forged documents, as at *D.* 48. 10. 13. 1 (Papinian, *Replies*, book 15): an advocate removed from the order of decurions for ten years for reading out a forged document before a court with the governor presiding. Other underhand forensic tactics are evident in *C. Th.* 11. 30. 11 (321).

[96] Martianus Capella, 'Liber de Arte Rhetorica', 10 = *RLM* 458.

the world are not self-labelling'.[97] In Part III we shall return to the uses made of the rhetorical 'issue of definition' in the prosecution and defence of heresy cases in late Roman courts.

Where a case was held to turn on a 'definitional issue' any resulting reclassification would be constructed with the interests of a particular litigant in mind. The archive of Ammon *Scholasticus*, a practising advocate from Panopolis (Egypt), contains a series of documents that record one such legal dispute.[98] A certain Eugeneios (identified as a member of the imperial *comitatus*, possibly a legal secretary) claimed that Ammon's deceased brother Harpocration had died without heirs—the latter's estate, comprising of three slaves who had been left in the care of a certain Conon at Alexandria, was according to Eugeneios *bona vacantia*. Eugeneios duly obtained an imperial rescript granting the slaves to him, 'if no one should lay opposing claim to them and no one should appear proving legal claim to their ownership'.[99] Ammon's papers suggest that Eugeneios travelled to Alexandria and lodged his imperial rescript before the *rationalis*; he also took possession of the slaves and delivered them to the same fiscal representative. Eugeneios also delivered a summons to Ammon to appear before the *rationalis* in court. It was at this point that Eugeneios seems to have doubted whether his imperial rescript could withstand Ammon's claim to his deceased brother's inheritance: Eugeneios thus redefined his case as a claim for 'runaway slaves'. The 'facts' of the case were (according to Ammon) changed accordingly—Eugeneios now pleaded that he had found the slaves as runaways and was thus entitled to possess them as 'ownerless' property, neatly bypassing Ammon's own claim based on intestate inheritance. Although we are reliant on Ammon's account of the case, the fact that Eugeneios' new 'redefinition' held a certain potential seems to be supported by Ammon's decision to agree to formal arbitration. The arbitrator's decision that the three slaves should be split between the two parties (!) was set aside, however, by the unexpected discovery of sealed wills belonging to Harpocration. The narrative cannot be reconstructed beyond the point at which Ammon is summoned once

[97] Quoted from N. MacCormick, *Rhetoric and the Rule of Law: A Theory of Legal Reasoning* (Oxford: OUP, 2005), 70.

[98] *P.Ammon* 1, nos. 5–25. I have followed the editor's suggestions as to the course of the dispute.

[99] *P.Ammon* 1. 13, ll. 45–7, and 15, ll. 5–6. For general discussions of late Roman fiscal *delatores* and cases concerning *bona vacantia* and *bona caducia*, see Jones, *Later Roman Empire*, 486, and Harries, *Law and Empire*, 94.

again to appear before the *rationalis*, presumably so that the wills could be officially opened. Notwithstanding its surprise ending, the case between Ammon and Eugeneios thus demonstrates the potential for individuals to redefine the legal basis to a given dispute—framing a case one way rather than another, in their own interest.

Reasoning from rules, as Neil MacCormick once argued, can only take us so far: 'Problems of interpretation, of classification and of relevancy are endemic to legal thought and to the law's processes'.[100] MacCormick subsequently revised his position that 'law' might be 'perennially arguable', with the qualification that 'the immediate and concrete persuasiveness of an argument is not necessarily the same as its soundness'.[101] This proposition was intended to contribute to a wider current debate over how a commitment to the 'Rule of Law' (with capital letters) might be viewed as functioning within contemporary understandings of legal argumentation: 'Now, however, it seems to me that the whole enterprise of explicating and expounding criteria and forms of good legal reasoning has to be in the context of fundamental values that we impute to legal order.'[102] Hence in his most recent work to date, MacCormick (like a number of modern legal scholars) approaches the study of rhetoric in an attempt to 'cast light on the character of argument in law'.[103] My perspective here, on the other hand, has focused on a technical branch of ancient rhetoric, where 'laws' were already held to exist within a domain of rhetorical argumentation. Moreover, advocates—practitioners of this ancient 'forensic' rhetoric—were taught to plead a case so as to win it for their clients. We might conclude that this perspective still applies to lawyers today, although MacCormick attempts to qualify its impact by claiming ultimately that modern lawyers must restrain themselves out of respect for the Rule of Law: 'Obfuscating tactics beyond these constraints can be and are from time to time utilized by lawyers. That is not within the legitimate rhetoric of their profession, but it is a betrayal of it.'[104] Advocates, ancient and modern, may well applaud this statement as a grand 'rhetorical turn' in itself. Late Roman *iudices* were, of course, expected to judge according to certain socio-legal criteria—and ideas concerning the 'soundness' and 'justness'

[100] N. MacCormick, *Legal Reasoning and Legal Theory* (Oxford: Clarendon Press, 1994), p. xiii.

[101] MacCormick, *Rhetoric and the Rule of Law*, 19.

[102] Ibid. 1. [103] Ibid. 22–3. [104] Ibid. 280.

of legal decisions certainly troubled Roman *iurisperiti* and the drafters of imperial constitutions. From the perspective of the practical life of late Roman law, however, questions of interpretation, classification, and relevancy were endemic. One explanation for this fact, as already suggested, relates to an appreciation of late Roman rhetoric as a technical discipline used in the construction of *forensic* arguments, on behalf of a client. A second explanation, however, relates to the very nature of late Roman 'sources of law'. In other words, the potential for late Roman advocates to handle law 'creatively' was due in no small part to the nature of the legal sources themselves.

The promulgation of the late Roman imperial 'law-codes' by no means made either advocates or *iurisperiti* redundant. After 438, however, litigants and forensic practitioners could potentially access a defined body of imperial constitutions that had been officially designated as 'general' (even if only by the mere fact that they had been promulgated as part of the Theodosian Code itself). In 426 an imperial constitution addressed to the Roman Senate had already attempted to classify authoritatively those laws 'that should be observed by all persons as general'.[105] According to this *oratio*, 'general law' could be found in a number of sources, including final judgments given in response to concrete cases: 'For [the] emperors have resolved that decisions that have been made in particular cases settle the outcomes of similar cases too.'[106] Hence a *lex generalis* was not necessarily phrased in either 'general' or 'abstract' terms. As John Matthews has explained, it is easy to misunderstand how the concept of *generalitas* operated in late Roman law:

> Indeed, part of the problem may be that it is so easy to fall victim to a simple logical fallacy: 'General laws' are not like categorical moral imperatives ('Do your duty,' 'Conduct yourself in a civilised manner,' 'Be kind to your neighbour,'), precepts to be observed by all at every time and in every place, but enactments on specific subjects, large or small, *to be obeyed in all relevant circumstances*; it is in this last phrase that *generalitas* is to be sought.[107]

[105] *CI* 1. 14. 2 and 1. 14. 3 (6/7 Nov. 426, given at Ravenna, *ad senatum*)—discussed in Ch. 3 above. Matthews, *Laying Down the Law*, 96–7, convincingly demonstrates that these texts, extant only in *CI*, were originally part of *C.Th.*

[106] *CI* 1. 14. 3: interlocutory judgements and concessions made 'in particular cases to certain cities, or provinces or associations' were explicitly excluded from this category.

[107] Matthews, *Laying Down the Law*, 70. Compare Honoré, *Law in Crisis*, 129: 'To summarise, a law is general if, judging by form or content, the emperor intends to apply it widely; but there is an assumption that when he replies to a petition from a private

Laws could therefore be understood as 'general' without being necessarily 'universal'—as in the case of 'general' laws that were only applicable to particular provinces or places.[108] They could also be understood as 'general' despite the fact that they were framed with reference to a specific case. Two examples out of many in the Theodosian Code will serve to illustrate this point. *C.Th.* 8. 17. 4 (AD 412, given at Ravenna to Johannes PP) gives the solution to a concrete case and explicitly declares it applicable to all similar cases (*in simili causa*); *C.Th.* 11. 36. 20 (AD 369, addressed to Claudius—possibly proconsul of Africa), issued in response to the concrete case of Bishop Chronopius, establishes a rule 'to hold in this case and in all other ecclesiastical cases' (*quod in hac causa et in ceteris ecclesiasticis fiat*). These judgments are thus specific to a single case, but a litigant (or their advocate, perhaps acting on advice from *iurisperiti*) was permitted to extend their application through reasoning by analogy. The drafters of such imperial constitutions might have intended these 'analogous' extensions to develop in a limited sense; however, explicit criteria of relevance are rarely specified within the imperial texts themselves. It would be left to the *iurisconsulti* and the advocate in court to convince the judge that any analogy drawn was a legitimate extension. Attempts to broaden the scope of case-specific decisions issued in the form of imperial rescripts were particularly susceptible to 'creative' forensic arguments.

Rescripts continued to be issued throughout the later Empire to private individuals, corporate groups, imperial officials, cities, and provinces.[109] Penalties were established against petitioners who sought

individual or a consultation by a judge he means to confine the reply to the person or case that has prompted it. This approach does not guarantee that general laws will be impartial and will be conceived in the interests of all, but it helps.'

[108] As stated in the 'new' clause included in the AD 435 instructions for the compilation of *C.Th.*—discussed by Matthews, *Laying Down the Law*, at 65 and 70. For Justinianic modifications to this principle see *CI* 8. 10. 13 (AD 531, to John PP): it is unworthy of Justinian's time for law to be observed in one way at Constantinople and in another in the provinces.

[109] On the use (and abuse) of rescripts under the Late Empire see Matthews, *Laying Down the Law*, 13–16; Honoré, *Law in Crisis*, 161–2 and 210–11; F. De Marini Avonzo, 'I rescritti nel processo del IV e V secolo', *AARC* 11 (1996), 29–39; L. Maggio, 'Note critiche sui rescritti postclassici, I, Il c.d. processo "*per rescriptum*" ', *SDHI* 61 (1995), 285–312; L. Maggio, 'Note critiche sui rescritti postclassici II. L'Efficacia normativa dei rescritti *ad consultationes* e dei rescritti *ad preces emissa*', *AARC* 14 (2003), 359–80; and D. Feissel, 'Pétitions aux empereurs et formes du rescrit', in D. Feissel, and J. Gascou, *La Pétition à Byzance* (Paris: Centre de Recherche d'Histoire et Civilisation de Byzance, 2004), 33–52.

rescripts so that they might 'be able to evade what has already been enacted'.[110] Petitions were made, however, asking for the issuing of rescripts granting specific 'privileges' or 'exemptions' relative to the law in force. *C.Th.* 11. 1. 33 (AD 424), addressed to the Praetorian Prefect of Illyricum, illustrates the 'rescript system' in operation with respect to the remission of tax liabilities. The constitution opens with the general principle that each province must pay its due with respect to taxes. It then proceeds to list those to whom exemptions have been granted in response to their petitions: certain (unspecified) provinces can 'follow the examples of the Macedonians' and assume the payment of half the amount of taxes that are due; the Achaeans, however, have protested that they can only pay a third and their debt is also reduced; the 'sacrosanct Church of the City of Thessalonica' gets a full exemption as a result of its efforts, with the explicit qualification that only its own taxes would be alleviated as 'the *res publica* must not be injured by the burden of tax exemptions of extraneous persons, by a misuse of the name of the Church'.[111] The last caveat provides an interesting hint at attempts to extend the specific exemption, through interpretations of what or who might classify as the 'church of the City of Thessalonica'.

Imperial constitutions frequently state the rule (in one form or another) that the application of a 'concessionary' rescript should not be extended beyond the instant case for which it had been issued.[112] A 'concessionary' rescript was, strictly speaking, contrary to law (*contra ius*); it could not be used procedurally to open a legal hearing unconnected with its immediate application, nor could it be pleaded in court in any cases unrelated to its original scope.[113] Rescripts granting *beneficia* and exemptions could, nonetheless, be cited as *persuasive* precedents by petitioners seeking analogous 'one-off' grants. For example, the privileges granted to palace functionaries in the West (*C.Th.* 6. 23. 3, AD 432) may have prompted palace functionaries in the East to ask for the same treatment (*C.Th.* 6. 23. 4, AD 437). Members of the ecclesiastical

[110] *CI* 1. 16. 1 (AD 384, *ad senatum*).

[111] *C.Th.* 11. 1. 33: 'Sacrosancta Thessalonicensis ecclesia civitatis excepta, ita tamen, ut aperte sciat, propriae tantummodo capitationis modum beneficio mei numinis sublevandum nec externorum gravamine tributorum rem publicam ecclesiastici nominis abusione laedendam.'

[112] See the constitutions collected under *CI* 1. 19, 22, and 23.

[113] For further discussion of rescripts *contra ius* see D. V. Simon, *Konstantinisches Kaiserrecht: Studien anhand der Reskriptenpraxis und der Schenkungsrecht* (Frankfurt/Main: Forschung zur Byzantinische Rechtsgeschichte 2, 1977), 10–16.

hierarchy were particularly skilled in this type of reasoning, pleading that what had been granted to one particular church should be extended 'by analogy' to another. Ecclesiastics were also not averse to arguing that privileges previously granted to 'pagan' imperial cults should be extended by analogy to Catholic churches. The granting of *beneficia* and exemptions was, of course, part of the traditional Roman ideology of the 'responsive' emperor—in this respect rescripts granted *contra ius* (and *adnotationes*, pragmatic sanctions, etc.) continued to fulfil an important socio-political function.

In forbidding the extension of rescripts granted *contra ius*, the Emperors nonetheless left the way (relatively) open for the 'creative' extension of case-specific rescripts that conformed to *ius*. The extension of rescripts issued in accordance with law could be interpretative and thus integral to the law in force, or innovative: 'Though rescripts had the force of law, they purported to declare existing law, which they typically describe as certain, clear, or settled. They did not purport to make new law, though in practice they could not wholly avoid doing so, any more than can modern judges, at least interstitially.'[114] However, there is some evidence to suggest that by the end of the fourth century the imperial authorities were attempting to prevent such rescripts from being pleaded in analogous cases. Tony Honoré cites *C.Th.* 10. 1. 15 (AD 396, issued at Ravenna, addressed to Paulus, count of the imperial household) and *C.Th.* 1. 2. 11 (AD 398, issued at Constantinople, addressed to Eutychianus PP) and concludes that: 'After 398 rescripts were never to recover the general force they had earlier possessed.'[115] The constitution of 396, however, refers only to rescripts granting titles to those who occupy imperial property; the law of 398 singularly restricts the extension of a particular type of rescript, given in reply to *consultationes* from imperial magistrates. Within certain limitations, then, rescripts conforming to *ius* remained a valid source for the construction of legal arguments in court and late Roman advocates accordingly cited these rescripts in cases that they were not originally

[114] Honoré, *Emperors and Lawyers* (2nd edn.), 41. See also *CI* 1. 23. 2 (AD 270): what is stated in a rescript is eternal, as long as it conforms to *ius*—discussed by W. Turpin, 'The Law-Codes and Late Roman Law', *Revue internationale des droits de l'antiquité*, 3rd ser. 32 (1985), 339–53, at 350.

[115] T. Honoré, 'Eutropius' Lawyer (396–9) and Other Quaestors of Arcadius (394–408)', *ZSS, Rom. Abt.* 112 (1995), 172–94, at 190. See also Honoré, *Law in Crisis*, 161–2 and 209–10.

issued for.[116] For example, we find rescripts being read into court *acta* as 'evidence' during legal processes associated with the 'Donatist' and 'Arian' controversies.[117]

The practice of pleading case-specific imperial decisions in later cases may have prompted forensic practitioners to copy and/or compile private collections of rescripts.[118] The text of the so-called *consultatio veteris cuiusdam iurisconsulti,* a juristic work that should probably be attributed to Gaul post-506, is divided into nine sections, the last of which contains a collection of nineteen constitutions on the subjects of inheritance and *pacta.* Seven rescripts are taken 'ex corpore Hermogeniani' (from the collection of rescripts known as the *codex Hermogenianus*), ten 'ex corpore Gregoriani' (from the *codex Gregorianus*) and two constitutions 'ex corpore Theodosiani' (from the *codex Theodosianus*).[119] The seven cited as from the Hermogenian Code are all dated within the space of a single year (364–5) and include a number issued to private petitioners.[120] The Hermogenian Code was, of course, originally compiled under the Tetrarchy; hence the copying of rescripts dating from the reign of Valentinian 'ex corpore Hermogeniani' suggests some kind of updating to this Code—which underscores its continuing practical relevance. We should probably, however, think in terms of an individual copyist doing the updating, rather than any kind of 'official' new edition(s).[121] Sections 4–6 of the *Consultatio,* on the other hand, contain three theoretical legal discussions, supported by excerpts from the *Pauli Sententiae* and the Hermogenian Code (thus incidentally providing evidence about late Roman methods of legal reasoning).[122] The remaining sections of the text give solutions to concrete questions put to the 'author'—the putative *iurisconsultus* of the text's (possibly early-modern) title—by a

[116] For a concrete example see Andreotti, 'Problemi della constitutio de postulando attribuita all'imperatore Giuliano', 192: a rescript issued 17 Jan. 363 and read out before the *praefectus urbis,* Ampelius, in 371. On imperial constitutions in general being *lecta apud acta/actis* see Matthews, *Laying Down the Law,* 185.

[117] See Ch. 9 below.

[118] F. Von Schwind, *Zur Frage der Publikation im römischen Recht: Mit Ausblicken in das altgriechische und ptolemäische Rechtsgebiet* (Munich: Beitr. zur Papyrusforsch. 31, 1940), 165 and 182, examines the question of the publication of rescripts; he suggests that they may have been catalogued and held in public archives for consultation and copying.

[119] *FIRA* ii. 610–13.

[120] For further discussion see E. Volterra, 'Le sette constituzioni di Valentiniano e Valente contenute nella *Consultatio Cuiusdam Veteris Iurisconsulti*', *BIDR* 85 (1982), 171–204.

[121] I owe this point to discussions with Simon Corcoran.

[122] *FIRA* ii. 599–606.

questioner, in the manner of a *consultatio* with a client or advocate. Tellingly, the material employed to resolve these concrete questions includes arguments from rescripts.[123]

The *Codex Gregorianus*, another collection of Tetrarchic rescripts, seems to have been circulating in some form in early fifth-century North Africa. In the course of writing his treatise *De Adulterinis Coniugiis* (AD 420) Augustine had occasion to consult a rescript of the Emperor Antoninus apparently from a copy of the *Codex Gregorianus*; he reproduces the rescript word-for-word, having introduced it with the explicit statement that: 'The following are the words of the Emperor mentioned above, as they appear in the *Gregorian Code*.'[124] Augustine effectively pleads Antoninus' rescript as evidence in the theological case that he is arguing. If handled carefully, a trained rhetorician (such as Augustine) could thus use a rescript as if it were 'general'—it was up to a judge to accept or reject the argument. We should perhaps also note the instructions to the compilers of Justinian's *Codex* in this context: rescripts addressed to certain individuals, or originally issued by pragmatic sanction, may obtain the effect of general laws where they have been included in the new Code (AD 528, *Const. Haec.* 2). The potential for case-specific rescripts to be interpreted in 'general' terms was thus acknowledged *before* Justinian reissued them all under his own authority.

The fact that late Roman forensic practitioners continued to treat case-specific rescripts as having a potential for wider application has, however, been understood as one symptom of a general late Roman 'crisis in the certainty of law'. Under that perspective, forensic practitioners faced grave problems in seeking to 'apply' the law in court: they had to cope with a large number of frequently mutually-contradictory legal sources of differing validity, application, and force, as well as facing problems in terms of distinguishing 'general' from 'special' laws.[125] This 'crisis of certainty', however, can be viewed from another angle: what we may term a problem in evaluating the sources of law could in fact

123 *FIRA* ii. 594–8 and 606–10.

124 Augustine, *De Adulterinis Coniugiis* 2. 7 (*CSEL* 41. 389–90), discussed by J. de Churruca, 'Un rescrit de Caracalla utilisé par Ulpien et interprété par Saint Augustin', in R. Feenstra and A. S. Hartkamp (eds.), *Collatio iuris romani études dédiées à Hans Ankum* (Amsterdam: Gieben, 1995), 71–81.

125 G. Purpura, 'Dalle raccolte di precedenti alle prime codificazioni postclassiche: Alcune testimonianze papiracee', *Ann. Sem. Giur. Univ. Palermo*, 42 (1992), 675–93, at 678.

be a late Roman advocate's (or litigant's) greatest strength; it provided them with room for manœuvre in their argumentation. The forensic practice of the Late Empire may well have been 'much more a matter of assembling and applying the relevant legislation, the appropriate imperial constitutions, the edicts of the prefects, the current of decisions and other such norms'.[126] But the crucial terms here are 'relevant' and 'appropriate'. If the text of a relevant imperial constitution or rescript admitted an interpretation in favour of the client that was not explicitly *contra ius*, then the duty of the advocate was to seek to persuade the court that this interpretation should stand.[127] Similarly, if a 'law' appeared to be outside the scope of a case, but could be classified in such a way that its application became relevant to furthering the client's plea, then an advocate would appeal to it accordingly.

P.Col. VII. 175 provides a concrete example of such forensic activity.[128] The papyrus records a dispute over liability for taxation before the *syndikos* of Arsinoe in 339. The petitioners are represented by a *rhetor* (advocate) named Theodorus, the respondents by a *rhetor,* Alexandros. The *syndikos* is aided by two *assessores*. We can reconstruct a plausible version of the 'facts' of the case as follows.[129] The petitioners (Herois and Taesis, sisters present in court through a *cognitor* Neilos) inherited farmland from their father, but then seemingly abandoned the estate. The community, however, was still responsible for paying the taxes—thus the *praepositus pagi* assigned cultivation of the abandoned land, under compulsion, to certain villagers. The sisters subsequently returned and, according to the defence, demanded payment for the 'rent' of the land; the villagers claim that they paid up and promptly returned the responsibility for the land's cultivation. The sisters were now complaining that the land turned over included a parcel which was not theirs, but from the estate of a certain Atisios. The subject of the present litigation thus

[126] Crook, *Legal Advocacy*, 195.

[127] *CI* 3. 1. 14. 4 (AD 530) states that advocates had to swear oaths on copies of the Gospels, promising to 'do everything for their clients that they consider to be just and honourable', and employ all of their learning on their client's behalf. Justinian also specifies, however, that advocates must refuse to take a 'disgraceful' or 'absolutely hopeless' case—or withdraw when information to this effect becomes known to them.

[128] New material has been added to the text edited as *P.Col.* VII. 175 by B. Kramer and D. Hagedorn, 'Zum Verhandlungsprotokoll P. Columbia VII 175', *ZPE* 45 (1982), 229–41 (as noted by Crook, *Legal Advocacy*, 104 n. 192).

[129] Heath, *Menander: A Rhetor in Context*, 317, and Heath, 'Practical Advocacy in Roman Egypt', 76, gives a slightly different reconstruction with less emphasis on the 'background' to the instant case.

included the ownership of the land; however, it is the tax burden that is uppermost in the minds of all concerned—neither petitioner nor respondent actually *wants* to claim ownership. I shall analyse the specific case as recorded in the papyrus first, before turning to the significance of the two advocates' arguments.

The papyrus opens with the *recitatio* of documents relevant to the institution of the case before the *syndikos* (apparently a *iudex datus*, appointed by the prefect). The *rhetor* Theodorus then asserts the petitioners' claim that they have been wrongly burdened with taxes and reads out the original petition to the court (l. 22). Alexandros, the defence advocate, interrupts Theodorus' *narratio* with the statement '*paragraphomai*', 'I object' (l. 23), and the *syndikos* grants him permission to plead his (procedural) exception. The papyrus gives Alexandros' words in direct speech (*oratio recta*):

> It would have suited my clients to plead the case before the higher court in order to have our opponents undergo punishment when their malice became evident. For there is nothing but malice in the petition which they submitted to the Prefect. And now I shall formally depose before this esteemed court the objection which I just now offered in order to prove to your excellency that our opponents have set the court in motion against us totally without reason. I have come before the court, relying on a divine and venerated law of our masters, the eternal Augusti, which provides that if anyone is in possession of property for a period of forty years, his possession is in no way to be removed from him nor is the date of the inception of possession to be investigated.[130]

The defence advocate's claim here is that there is 'no case to answer'—the imperial rescript should be understood as a bar to the petitioner's plea.[131] The fact that it is an imperial *rescript* that Alexandros cites here (in a case for which it was not originally issued) has been convincingly demonstrated by Simon Corcoran.[132] Alexandros proceeds to plead the defence's version of the facts, stressing that the petitioners' father had been in undisputed possession for the entire forty years and that the petitioners themselves had admitted their inherited ownership when they received rent from the villagers (a claim later disputed by the petitioners, who state that no rent was paid). Alexandros then appeals

[130] *P.Col.* VII. 175, ll. 24–38 (tr. Bagnall and Lewis).

[131] Crook, *Legal Advocacy*, 104 n.194.

[132] Most recently Corcoran, 'The Tetrarchy: Policy and Image', 49. Maggio, 'Note critiche sui rescritti postclassici II', 377–80, suggests that the 'rescript' pleaded by Alexandros was in fact a *lex generalis*.

once again to the provisions laid down in the imperial constitution, but this time with a slight change of emphasis: 'If a period of forty years has elapsed with a person in possession of property, no one is in any way to proceed against his property or dissolve his long-standing possession' (ll. 39–40). In other words, no one—including the petitioners themselves—can simply repudiate responsibility for the land that they own. At this point the *syndikos* grants permission for a formal *recitatio* of the entire imperial rescript, now revealed as Constantinian. The process subsequently moves on to an interrogation of both the parties to the dispute and a number of witnesses, undertaken by the *syndikos*. His final sentence (also given in direct speech) accepts the relevancy of the Constantinian rescript to the case:

> therefore, it follows from the divine and venerated law itself, and from the long-standing possession, and is in accordance also with the testimony of Germanos the headman of the village of Karanis, that Herois and Taesis are to retain ownership of the said plots, and are to pay the imperial taxes on them as in the past, since they possess also the house and the entire estate registered in the same name. For it is not the place of my mediocrity, since a divine law is applicable, to disturb a longstanding possession. (ll. 70–74)

The defendant's victory was thus assured, in no small part, by their advocate's skilful pleading of an earlier imperial rescript.

This papyrus provides the only extant text of the rescript on *longissimi temporis praescriptio*. The first editors argued that its date lay between 325 and 333, and that it was originally issued in the form of a Latin constitution addressed to a Roman senator, Agrippinus. The fact that it is quoted by an Egyptian advocate in Greek translation, in a trial of 339, is thus worthy of note in itself. The Constantinian rescript was itself innovative: it decided that forty years' possession established ownership without the need to prove that said possession had begun lawfully (as in previous constitutions).[133] The original intention behind the Constantinian rescript was thus to provide a safeguard for possession. In the 339 dispute, however, the advocate Alexandros turns the intention of the legislator on its head. As Crook states, Constantine's rescript is here used 'as a weapon, to pin the possessors down against their will so that they will not escape tax liability'.[134] The *syndikos*, moreover, accepted the advocate's 'stretching' of the rescript and delivered sentence accordingly.

[133] As noted by Bagnall and Lewis in their commentary to *P.Col.* VII. 175.
[134] Crook, *Legal Advocacy*, 106.

If an advocate's 'creative' interpretations were endorsed in the magistrate's final sentence (as in the papyrus just discussed), then his reasoning could also in turn influence the outcome of future cases. I have already argued that there was an intrinsic link between concrete cases and the issuing of new imperial constitutions. There was, however, a further means though which a late Roman advocate could contribute to the development of law in practice: the creation of a type of 'persuasive' case-law from *res iudicatae.* By offering the *exempla* of previous sentences, advocates could provide magistrates or arbitrators with models of practical judging, even if these *exempla* were not binding in themselves.[135] The incorporation of *praeiudicia* into 'dossiers' for instant cases appears in fourth- and fifth-century North African forensic practice, with particular reference to the Donatist dispute.[136] A short extract included at *CI* 1. 14. 11 (attributed to the Emperors Leo and Zeno and dated AD 474) implies that pleading such *exempla* might have been particularly effective when magistrates were confronted by *novum ius* (imperial constitutions not yet established by long-standing use). In fact, Justinian's 529 ruling that 'judgement should be given not on the basis of precedents but rather laws' is perhaps itself evidence for a tendency among judges to follow previous judgments.[137]

The practical importance of *praeiudicia* can be demonstrated by the fact that they too were copied and gathered into collections, arranged according to particular subject-matters. For example, the early second-century papyrus *BGU* I. 114 (= Mitteis, *Chrest*, 372) collects together previous judgments on proprietary difficulties arising from the fact that soldiers' unions could not count as legal marriages; from the late second/early third century *P.Strass.* I. 22 (= Mitteis, *Chrest*, 374) collects

[135] For a detailed discussion see U. Vincenti, *Il valore dei precedenti giudiziali nella compilazione giustinianea,* 2nd edn. (Padua: Cedam, 1995), reviewed by M. Valentino, 'Il precedente giudiziale: esigenza di certezza e problema sistematico', *Labeo,* 44/2 (1998), 292–7. It should be noted that 'interlocutory' judgments could not be legally pleaded as precedents.

[136] See Ch. 9 below.

[137] *CI* 7. 45. 13 (AD 529, addressed to the PP Demosthenes); the constitution as a whole specifically concerns imperial *consultationes*: 'Let no judge or arbiter imagine that *consultationes* are to be followed which he thinks have not been rightly judged—and even more so sentences of the most eminent prefects and other dignitaries (for if an inadequate judgement has been made, then this should not be carried over so as to produce error in other judges, *since judgement should be given not on the basis of precedents but rather laws*), not even if the sentences in question represent the judgements of the most exalted prefecture or of some very high magistrate. For we order all our judges to follow truth and the directions of the laws and of justice.'

judgments concerning rules of prescription; and a curious papyrus from the late fourth/early fifth century appears to be a collection of previous sentences concerning 'criminal' offences against women (*BGU* IV. 1024).[138] The editors of *P.Oxy.* 3758 (AD 325) suggest that this papyrus was also put together to form a collection of seven *praeiudicia* on inheritance law, extracted from the daybook of the curator of the city. These collections had a number of possible practical uses, ranging from 'persuasive precedents' to be laid before a judge in analogous future cases, to 'casebooks' from which advocates (and perhaps *iurisperiti* too) could get a sense of what sentences to expect in relation to a particular question or issue.[139]

In the later Roman Empire, then, a specific rhetorical training was available which taught the techniques of what we can properly term 'forensic' (courtroom) rhetoric. Most late Roman advocates, like their earlier counterparts, did not have to handle the law 'jurisprudentially' and the advice of *iurisconsulti* remained a source for the advocate's construction of their case-material. However, the very fact that advocates were ultimately responsible for pleading that law, for example, sometimes appealing to imperial constitutions as demurrers or reciting legal texts as 'evidence' in a given case, meant that they too could contribute significantly to the development of Roman law on the ground. Even if we view late Roman law as a formal 'top–down' system, it is clear that existing law had to be constantly extended to cover new factual situations as and when they arose—this 'formal' extension was achieved through interpretation and classification, whether academic (for example, in the case of the professors in the late Roman law schools) or practical (in the case of the imperial chancellery). But in both cases these new legal interpretations or pronouncements had to be tested in the courts. Law was forged in practice, not just made in imperial constitutions or law books. As it was the business of the forensic practitioner to interpret 'the law', not for the greater coherence of imperial legislation, but for the good of their client(s), the application of general laws or

138 See J. G. Keenan, 'Roman Criminal Law in a Berlin Papyrus Codex', *Archiv*, 35 (1989), 15–23.

139 For examples of advocates handling various types of *praeiudicia*, see *P.Fam.Tebt.* 24 (AD 124); *P.Cairo Preis.* 1 (2nd cent.); *P.Oxy.* 2340 (AD 192); *P.Lond. inv.* 2565 = SB 7696 (AD 250); and *P.Berl.Zill.* 4 (AD 350). For the Early Empire see R. Katzoff, 'Precedents in the Courts of Roman Egypt', *ZSS* 89 (1972), 256–82, and 'Sources of Law in Roman Egypt: The Role of the Prefect', *ANRW* ii/13 (1980), 808–44.

principles to concrete cases could stretch, and even on occasion subvert, the original content of those legal premises. Moreover, as a result of the structural organization of the late Roman system, persuasive courtroom argumentation could—and did—give rise to new normative legal decisions.

The advent of a Christian Empire at the beginning of the fourth century created a need for existing law to be extended to cover whole new situations of fact; existing categories were stretched in order to create new ones. In the particular case of anti-heresy law, new classifications and forensic arguments were elaborated on an almost day-to-day basis. Previous scholarship has focused on imperial legislation as the motivating force. I shall argue, to the contrary, that a body of laws against heresy and heretical practices was developed by forensic practitioners, acting in concrete cases and employing all the rhetorical techniques specific to their training (Part III). I will now turn to the argument that at least some of these forensic practitioners operated from within the church (Part II).

II

FORENSIC PRACTITIONERS IN THE SERVICE OF THE LATE ANTIQUE CHURCH

5

Introduction and Background

FROM APOSTOLIC TO IMPERIAL CHURCH

When the days of Pentecost were come, they were all together in one place. And suddenly a sound came from heaven as if a strong wind was approaching, and it filled the whole house where they were sitting. And it appeared to them like split tongues of fire, alighting on each one of them. And they were all filled with the Holy Spirit, and began to speak in different languages, as the Holy Spirit gave them the power to do.[1]

To early Christians looking back, the missionary advance of Christianity was (at least partly) founded upon this unique event: the sending of the gift of effective speech from God to the apostolic founders of his church, through the power of the Holy Spirit. During the struggles and schisms suffered by early Christian communities in their attempts to establish an internal structure, part of the bishop's particular claim to be listened to 'lay in his being the successor of God's fisherman'.[2] What certain bishops, such as Irenaeus at Lyons and Hippolytus (possibly at Rome), claimed to inherit through 'apostolic succession' to the fishers of men thus included the power of effective speech—understood as a spiritual gift received from the Christian God, via the Holy Spirit.[3]

[1] *Acts of the Apostles*, 2. 1–4 (tr. from Jerome's *Vulgate*). For a possible reconstruction of the original context for 'Luke–Acts' see J. G. Gager, 'Where does Luke's Anti-Judaism Come from?', in H. Zellentin and E. Iricinschi (eds.), *Heresy and Identity in Late Antiquity* (Tubingen: Mohr Siebeck, 2007), 300–15; on Luke's *pneuma* as a giver of 'insight and boldness of speech' see R. P. Menzies, *The Development of Early Christian Pneumatology with Special Reference to Luke–Acts* (Sheffield: JSOT Press, 1991).

[2] H. Chadwick, 'The Role of the Christian Bishop in Ancient Society', in *Protocol of the 35th Colloquy* (Berkeley: Centre for Hermeneutical Studies, 1980), 1–14, at 14.

[3] On the concept of 'spiritual authority' in relation to both individual bishops and the episcopal office see C. Rapp, *Holy Bishops in Late Antiquity: The Nature of Christian Leadership in an Age of Transition* (Berkeley, Los Angeles: University of California Press, 2005), 16, 29, and 56–8. For discussion of the 'Hippolytus question' see J. A. Cerrato, *Hippolytus between East and West: The Commentaries and the Provenance of the Corpus* (Oxford: OUP, 2002).

In his continuation of Eusebius' *Historia ecclesiastica*, Rufinus, writing in 402 or 403, depicts an incident at the Council of Nicaea (325) in which the power of 'inspired' speech was put to the test. Rufinus' narrative is carefully constructed in order to highlight a difference between the skilled technical speech that can be mastered in this world and the eternal simplicity of the Word of God. According to Rufinus, rumours of the gathering council drew philosophers, dialecticians, and rhetoricians 'of great renown and fame', as well as bishops, priests, and laymen, to Nicaea. A certain renowned philosopher, we are told, 'used to hold ardent debates each day with our bishops, men likewise by no means unskilled in the art of disputation, and there resulted a magnificent display for the learned and educated men who gathered to listen'.[4] The rhetorically skilled bishops, however, were unable to get the better of this philosopher's arguments, 'for he met the questions proposed with such rhetorical skill that whenever he seemed most firmly trapped, he escaped like a slippery snake'.[5] The assembled bishops were thus embarrassed when an elderly unlettered confessor who had endured persecution and 'knew only Christ Jesus and him crucfied', came forward and challenged the philosopher. The elderly confessor challenged the philosopher with a simple profession of Christian faith. The short speech that Rufinus then puts in the philosopher's mouth underscores the lesson that our author intends to teach through this narrative episode. Turning to his disciples and the assembled crowd, the philosopher proclaims:

> Listen, O learned men: so long as it was words with which I had to deal, I set words against words and what was said I refuted with my rhetoric. But when power rather than words came out of the mouth of the speaker, words could not withstand power nor could man oppose God. And therefore if any one of you was able to feel in what was said what I felt, let him believe in Christ and follow this old man in whom God has spoken.[6]

In Rufinus' early fifth-century story, then, a divinely given power of speech trumps all the educated expertise of the assembled *litterati* (a

[4] Rufinus of Aquileia, *Church History* 10. 3, all translations are quoted from P. R. Amidon (tr.), *The* Church History *of Rufinus of Aquileia Books 10 and 11* (New York and Oxford: OUP, 1997), 10–11.

[5] On 'logical disputation' as a form of extra-conciliar entertainment compare Socrates, *HE* 1. 8. Sozomen, *HE* 1. 17, on the other hand, has the philosophers in the same story intervene with malicious intent in the council itself, apparently because they were angry at the recent suppression of paganism!

[6] Rufinus, *HE* 10. 3.

category which includes both the philosopher and the Christian bishops skilled in dialectic and rhetoric) and the philosopher departs from the city of Nicaea a believing Christian.[7]

The idea of power gifted from god(s) via 'inspired' speech was by no means a peculiarly Christian one.[8] The traditional expectation that a 'wise and divine man' would possess the power of effective speech is neatly demonstrated by a series of questions posed in the *Apocriticos* of Macarios (of Magnesia): why when Christ appeared before Pontius Pilate did he not 'address a few words before the governor, worthy of a divine and wise man'? Shouldn't Christ have behaved more like the divinely inspired philosopher Apollonius, when he was summoned to appear before the Emperor Domitian?[9] The tradition of divinely 'gifted' speech found a renewed emphasis in fourth- and fifth-century redactions of Christian martyr-acts—where the would-be martyr is portrayed as steadfastly refusing the services of human advocates present at the trial-hearing, preferring to bear witness through plain, direct speech aided by the *parakletos* alone (the Holy Spirit, understood in the sense of 'helper'/'comforter').[10] The hero of Rufinus' story at *HE* 10. 3 is portrayed, of course, as just such a 'confessor' who had withstood persecution under Diocletian.[11] At the same time as acknowledging Rufinus' early fifth-century stress on the continuing power of spiritually gifted speech, we should also note that he has constructed his narrative at *HE* 10. 3 in such a way that Christian

[7] The power of the Word vs 'words' is also found as a *topos* in anti-heretical polemic, e.g. in Ambrose *De Fide ad Gratianum* 2. 77–8: 'Let therefore vain questions about words fall silent, because the kingdom of God, as it is written, consists not in verbal persuasion but in the demonstration of power', a passage quoted at the Council of Chalcedon in 451, having been read out from the acts of the first session of the council of Ephesus, 22 June 431 (R. Price and M. Gaddis (ed. and tr.), *The Acts of the Council of Chalcedon* (Liverpool: Liverpool University Press, 2005), 306).

[8] e.g. Socrates (*HE* 1. 17) compares the Christian Bishop Alexander with Julian 'the Chaldean', arguing that the power of the former in silencing a philosopher with a command not to speak was in no way inferior to the power of the latter in cleaving a wall in two by the 'power of a word'. See, in general, D. Potter, *Prophets and Emperors: Human and Divine Authority from Augustus to Theodosius* (Cambridge, Mass.: Harvard University Press, 1994).

[9] *Apocriticos* 3. 52. 1, tr. from Goulet, *Macarios de Magnésie, Le Monogénès*, V. ii. 72. An account of Apollonius' appearance before Domitian is given in Philostratus, *Life of Apollonius of Tyana* 8. 10.

[10] The Holy Spirit as *parakletos* is found at John 14. 16, 14. 26, 15. 26 and 16. 7. For a 5th-cent. example of the (polemical) use of the term to mean a forensic advocate see Augustine, *Contra Litteras Petiliani* 3. 16. 19 (*BA* 30. 622 ll. 3–9).

[11] As also stressed by R. Lim, *Public Disputation, Power, and Social Order* (Berkeley, Los Angeles: University of California Press, 1995), 191–9.

bishops educated in dialectical reasoning and rhetoric nonetheless appear as a fixed part of the Constantinian landscape.

Historians now tend rightly to problematize the traditional historiographical picture of early Christian communities founded on (Weberian) 'charismatic' authority, gradually giving way to the 'institutional' authority that supposedly dominated the post-Constantinian era.[12] Late Roman bishops, on the other hand, could represent the transition from apostolic fishermen to post-Constantinian bishops in stark terms. Preaching at roughly the same time as Rufinus was writing, Augustine explains to his congregation:

> You see, if Christ had begun by choosing an orator, the orator would say 'I was chosen for the sake of my eloquence'. If he had chosen a senator, the senator would say 'I was chosen because of my rank'. If he had first chosen the emperor, the emperor would have said 'I was chosen because of my authority'. All these types have to keep quiet for a little while and be put on one side; let them keep quiet—they are not being left out, they are not being ignored, they are just being put to one side for a time, in that they are likely to boast about themselves in themselves. Give me, he says, that fisherman, give me a common man, give me an uneducated man, give me one whom the senator doesn't deign to talk to, not even when he's buying fish. That's the one to give me, he says, if I fill that one, it will be obvious that it's I who am doing it. Though I am also going to do it with the senator, the orator, and the emperor, though it's more certainly me with the Fisherman . . . The Emperor is best brought along through the Fisherman.[13]

The apostolic fishermen still held authority in the age of senators, orators, and emperors—as Augustine's *Sermon* 43.6 also states, 'nowadays a professional orator wins great acclaim if he is able to understand the fisherman'.[14] A distinct shift from the fisherman to the Christian orator was, nonetheless, part of God's providential plan for man's salvation. The same theme reappears in 'Mainz' *Sermon* 62 (*Contra Paganos*),

[12] Three different, but potentially complementary, perspectives are offered by L. Nasrallah, *An Ecstasy of Folly: Prophecy and Authority in Early Christianity* (Cambridge, Mass.: Harvard University Press, 2004); Rapp, *Holy Bishops in Late Antiquity*, and M. Gaddis, *There is No Crime for those who have Christ: Religious Violence in the Christian Roman Empire* (Berkeley, Los Angeles: University of California, 2005), 251–82.

[13] Augustine, *Sermon* 43. 6 (tr. E. Hill, *Augustine, Sermons*, ii. *(20–50) on the Old Testament* (Brooklyn, NY: New City Press, 1990), 241).

[14] It is tempting here to see a reaction to the Emperor Julian's characterization of Christian doctrine as 'the degenerate error of ignorant fisherman-theologians' (Julian, *Ep.* 55 = Bidez 90, quoted from R. Smith, *Julian's Gods: Religion and Philosophy in the Thought and Action of Julian the Apostate* (London and New York: Routledge, 1995), 190).

where Augustine explains that Christ came to earth, 'so that god-made man might teach humility':

> To this humility it might seem nothing can be added, yet from those very human elements he did not choose that which men boast about. He did not choose parents who were noble and endowed with some dignity. He chose to be born of a woman who was married to a carpenter, lest anyone, opposed to justice for the poor and undistinguished, glory in the celebrity of his own parents, and puff himself up unhealthily with pride . . . But perhaps someone might say 'though he was of humble birth, he wanted to boast in the nobility of his disciples.' Yet he did not choose kings, or senators, or philosophers, or orators. Rather he chose ordinary people, poor men, unlettered men, fishermen. Peter was a fisherman, Cyprian an orator. If the fisherman had not faithfully come before, then the orator would not have humbly followed.[15]

According to Augustine's eschatology the age of the (humble) Christian orator, heralded from at least the time of Cyprian, had arrived.

Charlotte Rouché has drawn attention to a broader context for a late antique public rhetoric of praise focused on learning and education, with reference to civil and ecclesiastical officials alike. From the middle of the third century onwards, inscriptions erected in honour of provincial governors tend to be in epigram form and increasingly praise the governor 'for his personal merits rather than as a member of Roman society'; Rouché also notes that 'the verse medium is the same as that used for prominent local citizens or bishops, and that this is 'a medium which emphasises the learning of all those involved'.[16] The emergence of this late Roman 'shared language of praise' also 'alerts us to the possibility that the distinction between public roles in civic and ecclesiastical contexts was not always clearly drawn'.[17] It is perhaps within this wider epigraphic context that we should place Jerome's late fourth-century *De Viris Inlustribus* (alongside the more usual Suetonian parallels): as noted by Maxwell, Jerome comments on the rhetorical skill of virtually all his Christian entries.[18] By *c*.570 even the educational achievements of Christ himself did not go unrecognized: pilgrimage tours to Nazareth

[15] Augustine, 'Mainz' *Sermon* 62. 60 (tr. from the text edited by F. Dolbeau, *Augustin d'Hippone: Vingt-six sermons au peuple d'Afrique* (Paris: Institut d'études Augustiniennes, 1996), 137–8, ll. 1446–52 and 1459–63).

[16] C. Rouché, 'The Functions of the Governor in Late Antiquity: Some Observations', *Antiquité Tardive*, 6 (1998), 31–6, at 33.

[17] Rapp, *Holy Bishops in Late Antiquity*, 171.

[18] J. L. Maxwell, *Christianization and Communication in Late Antiquity: John Chrysostom and his Congregation in Antioch* (Cambridge: CUP, 2006), 33.

apparently included a visit to a synagogue, where devout Christians could venerate 'the book in which the Lord wrote his ABC'.[19]

CHRISTIAN RHETORIC AND THE 'THIRD SOPHISTIC'

The specific idea of a 'Christian rhetoric', gradually transforming its content and techniques from the apostolic to the imperial church, frames the discussions of many modern scholars who seek to explore questions concerning the 'rise of Christianity'.[20] As Cameron stated in the opening paragraph of her 1991 monograph, *Christianity and the Rhetoric of Empire*:

> It is no longer a novelty to hold that societies have characteristic discourses or 'plots,' or that the development and control of a given discourse may provide a key to social power, or even that an inquiry into the dissemination of knowledge by oral or written means ought to be high on the agenda for historians. A religion that succeeded (if slowly) in establishing itself as the prevailing religious system of the wider society to which it was at first only marginal, and laid a quite exceptional emphasis throughout this process on the verbal articulation of the faith, must cry out for analysis in these terms.[21]

Cameron also noted that this 'new' (in 1991) scholarly orientation demands the application of techniques of (post)modern literary analysis; it necessitates a move away from analysing the social and institutional dimensions of Christianity to a focus upon Christian 'modes of expression'. Treated under this methodology, however, the 'rhetoric

[19] *Piacenza Pilgrim*, 5 (quoted from J. Wilkinson, *Jerusalem Pilgrims before the Crusades*, 2nd ed. (Warminster: Aris & Philips, 2002), 131). The same synagogue apparently also exhibited the bench on which Christ sat for his lessons, which Christians could pick up and drag around, but Jews could not (a claim that undoubtedly attempts to redress the Jewish/Christian power balance, from the Christian pilgrim's perspective)!

[20] e.g. B. Studer, *La riflessione teologica nella chiesa imperiale (sec. iv e v)*, Sussidi Patristici dello Istituto Patristico Augustinianum, 4 (Rome: Istituto Patristico Augustinianum, 1989); F. Young, *Biblical Exegesis and the Formation of Christian Culture* (Cambridge: Cambridge University Press, 1989), 49–116; A. Cameron, *Christianity and the Rhetoric of Empire: The Development of Christian Discourse* (Berkeley, Los Angeles: University of California Press, 1991); Brown, *Power and Persuasion*; M. Vessey, 'The Forging of Orthodoxy in Latin Christian Literature: A Case Study', *Journal of Early Christian Studies*, 4 (1996), 495–513, and now F. Young, L. Ayres, and A. Louth (eds.), *The Cambridge History of Early Christian Literature* (Cambridge: CUP, 2004).

[21] Cameron, *Christianity and the Rhetoric of Empire*, 1.

of Christianity' appears to have little in common with the technical forensic rhetoric of the Late Empire, analysed in Part I above; it can be characterized rather as a 'series of overlapping discourses always in a state of adaptation and adjustment, and always ready to absorb in a highly opportunistic manner whatever might be useful from secular rhetoric and vocabulary'.[22] More importantly, what the Christian orators are seen to have absorbed from 'secular rhetoric and vocabulary' tends to be limited to the epideictic sphere of oratory—the only branch of rhetoric that, according to most modern scholars, managed to struggle on past the Principate in the context of Greek and Latin civic life. Through epideictic rhetoric, and more specifically through following the 'plots' laid by orators of the Second Sophistic, the Christian writers and speakers of the fourth century could convert their rhetoric into a 'power rhetoric in political terms'.[23] Hence, 'in the revived urban culture of the fourth century, Christian bishops succeeded to the place of the epideictic orators of the Second Sophistic; and their speeches were more political than the earlier ones ever could be'.[24] The idea of Christian bishops succeeding to 'the epideictic orators of the Second Sophistic' has recently contributed to the coining of a new term: the 'Third Sophistic', which includes on its honorary roll-call the fourth-century bishops Gregory of Nazianzus, Gregory of Nyssa, and Synesius of Cyrene.[25]

The theme of Christian bishops as heirs to the 'ornamental' or 'show-piece' rhetoric of the Second Sophistic was a common preoccupation of earlier studies on the formation of 'Christian' rhetoric. Baldwin, in an article written in 1925 and entitled 'St Augustine and the Rhetoric

[22] Ibid. 5. [23] Ibid. 122.

[24] Ibid. 135, see also 81–4. Maxwell, *Christianization and Communication*, 36, likewise argues for a continuity between 'pagan second sophistic writers' and Christian preachers; as does M. M. Mitchell, 'Reading Rhetoric with Patristic Exegetes: John Chrysostom on Galatians', in A. Y. Collins and M. M. Mitchell, *Antiquity and Humanity: Essays on Ancient Religion and Philosophy Presented to Hans Dieter Betz on his 70th birthday* (Tubingen: Mohr Siebeck, 2001), 333–55, at 344: 'The great orator-bishops like the Cappadocians and Chrysostom in many ways occupied the social positions that had been held by sophists in an earlier day, and exercised their elegant rhetorical skill precisely on behalf of the "unlettered truth" of the gospel'. Compare Bruce W. Winter, *Philo and Paul among the Sophists: Alexandrian and Corinthian Responses to a Julio-Claudian Movement*, 2nd edn. (Grand Rapids and Cambridge: Eerdmans, 2002).

[25] E. Amato, A. Roduit, and M. Steinrück (eds.), *Approches de la troisième sophistique: Hommages à Jacques Schamp* (Brussels, Latomus 296, 2006), esp. the essay by J. Schamp, 'Sophistes à l'ambon: Esquisses pour la Troisième Sophistique comme paysage littéraire', 286–338. See also Ch. 4 above.

of Cicero', acknowledges Augustine's literary debts to Cicero but concludes that 'Augustine had been himself, in Plutarch's sense and in Strabo's, a sophist'.[26] Similarly, Barry—in a 1924 dissertation entitled *St. Augustine the Orator: A Study of the Rhetorical Qualities of St Augustine's Sermones Ad Populum*—almost exclusively traces the influence of the Second Sophistic on Augustine's rhetorical formation. Having analysed Augustine's technical deployment of 'figures of argumentation' in minute detail Barry claims that: 'All the devices of the court room taken together occur 2201 times in the sermons, imparting life to style. They have an interest, historical rather than rhetorical, showing how the old devices were clung to, on account of their attic associations.' Barry thus painstakingly enumerates the influence of forensic rhetoric on Augustine's *Sermons*, but she interprets this as support for her conclusion that 'Augustine's oratory rings true to a sophistic fullness of expression'.[27]

In the 1991 monograph *Rhetoric and Homiletics in Fourth Century Christian Literature*, Oberhelman also argued that the rhetoric of fourth-century Christian authors was reflective of a 'contemporary sophistic style' and linked this firmly to 'the pagan schools of rhetoric'.[28] Once again, we encounter the idea of late antique rhetorical schools providing a 'literary' socio-cultural formation alone.[29] Moreover, when viewed in the context of an evolving 'Christian rhetoric', the rhetorical schools themselves can (naturally) be unmasked as the standard-bearers of a specifically 'pagan' *paideia*. Thus, we find, the 'Christian' orators' utilization of the 'pagan' educational models of the past presented them with an 'often agonized' dilemma: was it possible to participate—in good conscience—in a 'pagan' educational system that 'could be represented as contrary to their professed beliefs'?[30] Julian's attempt to limit Christian access to the educational system (referred to by Julian himself and reported by Ammianus Marcellinus) revealed the stress lines—looking

[26] C. S. Baldwin, 'St Augustine and the Rhetoric of Cicero', *Proceedings of the Classical Association*, 22 (1925), 24–6, at 24.

[27] M. I. Barry, *St Augustine the Orator: A Study of the Rhetorical Qualities of St Augustine's Sermones Ad Populum* (Washington, DC: Catholic University of America, 1924), 225. Compare M. Comeau, *La Rhétorique de saint Augustin d'après les* Tractatus in Ioannem (Paris: Gabriel Beauchesne, 1930), which sets out to examine Augustine's rhetorical models in his *Tractates on John*, but exclusively treats the influence of Neoplatonism, the Second Sophistic, and 'Gorgianic figures'.

[28] S. M. Oberhelman, *Rhetoric and Homiletics in Fourth-Century Christian Literature* (Atlanta, Ga: American Philological Association, 1991), 2 and 120.

[29] Young, *Biblical Exegesis*, 249, refers to the rhetorical schools' 'literary-philological tradition' in a discussion of John Chrysostom's homilies on 1 Corinthians.

[30] Cameron, *Christianity and the Rhetoric of Empire*, 139.

back some eighty years or so later the ecclesiastical historian Socrates attributed a single motive to Julian's measure: 'to exclude the children of Christian parents' from 'the acquisition of argumentative and persuasive power'.[31] Julian, Basil of Caesarea, Gregory of Nazianzus, Jerome, and the church historians Socrates and Sozomen, amongst others, were all well aware of the relationship between knowledge and power.[32] As Foucault argues, 'any system of education is a political way of maintaining or modifying the appropriation of discourses, along with the knowledges and powers which they carry'.[33] The reign of the apostate Emperor Julian thus no doubt served to heighten the consciousness of some educated Christians in terms of their reliance on a 'pagan' classical inheritance, but this should not by any means be equated with a general antithesis between a 'pagan' rhetorical education and Christianity—the latter could and did make extensive use of the former.

In the chapters that follow I shall argue that there is an alternative 'discourse' that also tells a story about the development of 'Christian' rhetoric and the establishment of Christianity in the later Roman Empire: namely, the practice of forensic rhetoric by individuals within the Christian church.[34] I shall also suggest that the practice of forensic rhetoric helped to determine Christian power relations within the late Roman world because it was governed by practical, case-specific applications. I have already argued in Part I that the teaching and practice of forensic rhetoric was flourishing in late antiquity and it was career-specific in the sense that it offered a particular rhetorical formation, which frequently in turn governed access to political power in a concrete social and institutional context. Forensic rhetoric was still a stepping-stone to career advancement in the late Roman world; it could

[31] Julian, *Ep.* 61b (ed. Bidez) = *Ep.* 36 (ed. Wright); Ammianus Marcellinus, *Res Gestae* 22. 10. 7 and 25. 4. 20; and Socrates, *HE* 5. 18, quoted from Young, *Biblical Exegesis*, 72. For discussion see Matthews, *Laying Down the Law*, 274–7.

[32] Basil of Caesarea, *Address to Young Men on Reading Profane Literature*; Gregory of Nazianzus, *Oration* 4. 61–63; Jerome, *Ep.* 22. 30 to Eustochium; Socrates, *HE* 3. 16; and Sozomen, *HE* 5. 17–18.

[33] M. Foucault, *L'Ordre du discours* (Paris: Gallimard, 1971), tr. Ian McLeod in R. Young (ed.), *Untying the Text: A Post-Structuralist Reader* (Boston: Routledge & Kegan Paul, 1981), 48–78, at 64.

[34] Honoré, *Law in Crisis*, 4–5, notes that 'a number of lawyers and advocates became prominent Christians, even bishops' (with a reference to Detlef Liebs); Heath, *Menander: A Rhetor in Context*, 87–9, 262, and 264–5, notes that some Christian Fathers were educated in forensic rhetoric; see also B. Sirks, 'Instruction in Late Antiquity, the Law and Theology', *AARC* 15 (2005), 493–513, at 499: 'Christian students were thus also prepared for pleading on [*sic*] the forum'.

also function as a stepping-stone to advancement in an imperial church. Christian communities needed skilled forensic practitioners in order to exploit the structures of Empire to their advantage. Moreover, the access of elite Christian 'orators' to the centres of late imperial political power relied less on their absorption of political theories or philosophical concepts from the Second (or indeed the Third) Sophistic, than on their practical education as forensic practitioners. When Augustine suggested that the age of the fisherman had been superseded by that of the 'orator', he meant 'orator' in the traditional Roman sense of the word.

FORENSIC ELOQUENCE 'IN THE SERVICE OF GOD'

In his *Epistle* 2* Augustine gives us his definition of an orator, and it is a traditional Ciceronian one of a good man skilled in forensic dispute:

> What that most prolific and well-endowed teacher of this same art said is so very true: 'Eloquence with wisdom has been of the greatest benefit to states but eloquence without wisdom has been very harmful and never beneficial'. Whence the ancients thought that not the eloquent man, for eloquence can exist without wisdom, but the orator should be defined in this way: they would say that he is a 'good man skilled in forensic speaking'. If what is expressed in the first words of this definition is lacking, what is left will be harmful indeed. Therefore, they knew and said that when the rules of rhetoric are taught to fools, orators are not being produced but weapons are being put into the hands of madmen.[35]

For Augustine rhetoric could be put either to a good or a bad use, depending on the moral quality of the person exercising it.[36] The only way to ensure the use God intended in his gifts of rhetorical ability is for individuals to apply it in the service of the church. Hence the context of sections 12–13 of *Ep.* 2*: Augustine's advice to a father on the future direction of his son's career as an orator. This can be further compared to Augustine's exhortation in *Ep.* 69 to the advocate Castorius, to devote his eloquence to the service of God. Augustine was well aware that the position of the church in the Empire demanded men of Castorius' ability. Moreover, techniques of forensic argument

[35] Augustine, *Epistle* 2*, 12 (= *BA* 46B. 88), tr. R. B. Eno, *St Augustine Letters 1–29**, 29. The quotations are from Cicero, *De Inventione* 1. 1 and *De Oratore* 3. 55.

[36] Augustine, *De Doctrina Christiana* 4. 2. 3.

were not just needed in practical contexts, such as pleading for imperial privileges and exemptions, but could also be applied in doctrinal controversies.

The importance of verbal argumentation and public disputations in shaping Christian theological controversies was highlighted by Richard Lim in his monograph, *Public Disputation, Power and Social Order in Late Antiquity*. Lim sets out to explore the 'salient cultural parameters' which determined 'competitive disputation in Christian theological enterprises'.[37] Having acknowledged the importance of public verbal dispute and argument, Lim identifies the 'salient cultural parameters' of disputation in Christian contexts as Graeco-Roman beliefs concerning persuasion and proof in philosophical circles; hence chapter 2 analyses 'disputation, dialectic and competition among Platonist philosophers'. The fourth-century Christian controversies that are analysed in Lim's remaining chapters are each treated under the perspective of verbal argument as 'dialectic' and 'philosophy'. Lim's thesis concerning the influence and impact of philosophical debate is important and undoubtedly correct, but at the same time there is virtually no recognition of the legal arena, or more specifically of forensic rhetoric, as a possible 'cultural parameter'—the only reference comes in the final paragraph of the monograph where Lim briefly suggests that:

> Roman legal scholars who study the Theodosian Code, for instance, should find much of interest in the construction of authority in nearly contemporaneous church councils, since the legal and conciliar authorities of the time were fashioned by an elite that was, if not identical in composition, then at least of like temperament. Their habits of mind and discourses on power, seldom articulated in theoretical terms, must yet remain one of the central concerns of any student of late antiquity.[38]

My aim, then, in what follows is to argue for forensic rhetoric as a further crucial 'salient cultural parameter'. In particular, Part III (chapters 8 and 9 below) will explore how techniques of forensic rhetoric, alongside traditions of philosophical debate, contributed to the formation and development of Christian theological controversies. I shall briefly turn to church councils and the elaboration of early canon law in Chapter 7.

The application of forensic techniques of argument has been identified in the earliest period of the Judaeo-Christian era, in the writings of St

[37] Lim, *Public Disputation*, pp. x–xi.
[38] Ibid. 235; compare Meyer, *Legitimacy and Law*, 243.

Paul and Philo.[39] I should note in this context that the impact of Roman legal institutions on Jewish society and in particular early rabbinical material has long been recognized.[40] It has also been argued that the earliest Judaeo-Christian writers were skilled at 'borrowing' substantive principles of Roman law and applying them metaphorically to expand principles of Christian dogma.[41] Finally, it is now generally accepted that the rhetorical schools under the Early and Later Empire influenced a wide range of patristic exegesis (at least in a 'literary' sense).[42] In the post-Constantinian church, however, these various existing relationships between 'law' and 'theology' underwent a dramatic transformation as the Christian church itself entered into the imperial legal arena. The fact that leading ecclesiastics had been trained as forensic practitioners in the rhetorical schools now had wide-scale concrete and immediate applications, and no more so than in the field of distinguishing 'right' from 'wrong' Christian belief. Verbal disputation in a court of law was a new avenue through which orthodoxy and heresy could be defined. The dialectic of the courtroom could also offer a singular advantage over philosophical disputation, in that it produced a legally enforceable judgement as to the winner and the loser. From the fourth century onwards it thus became essential that some ecclesiastics at least

[39] T. Mommsen, 'Die Rechtsverhältnisse des apostel Paulus', *ZNW* 2 (1901), 81–96; B. Sampley, ' "Before God I do Not Lie" (*Gal.* 1. 20): Paul's Self-Defence in the Light of Roman Legal Praxis', *NTS* NS 23 (1976), 477–82; H. D. Betz, 'The Problem of Rhetoric and Theology According to the Apostle Paul', in A. Vanhoye (ed.), *L'Apôtre Paul: Personnalité, style et conception du ministère* (Leuven: Leuven University Press, 1986), 16–48; and compare J. Gager, *Re-inventing Paul* (Oxford: OUP, 2002), 70–9 and 80–2. On Philo as a 'practical lawyer learned in Greek and Roman jurisprudence as well as the Jewish law', see E. R. Goodenough, *The Jurisprudence of the Jewish Courts in Egypt: Legal Administration by the Jews under the Early Roman Empire as Described by Philo Judaeus* (New Haven: Yale University Press, 1929).

[40] S. Lieberman, 'Roman Legal Institutions in Early Rabbinics and in the *Acta Martyrum*', *Jewish Quarterly Review*, 35 (1944), 1–57. See now in general S. Schwartz, *Imperialism and Jewish Society* (Princeton: Princeton University Press, 2001).

[41] On the metaphorical use of Roman legal concepts in the New Testament see O. Eger, 'Rechtswörter und Rechtsbilder in den Paulinischen Briefen', *ZNW* 18 (1918), 84–108; G. Cavigioli, 'Impronte di diritto romano nel carteggio di s. Paolo e nella volgata del nuovo Testamento', *ACII* ii (Rome: Pontifical Institute, 1935), 91–100, and A. N. Sherwin-White, *Roman Society and Roman Law in the New Testament* (Oxford: Clarendon Press, 1963).

[42] F. Young, 'The Rhetorical Schools and their Influence on Patristic Exegesis', in R. Williams, *The Making of Orthodoxy: Essays in Honour of Henry Chadwick* (Cambridge: CUP, 1989), 182–99. See also G. Clark, ' "Spoiling the Egyptians": Roman Law and Christian Exegesis in Late Antiquity', in R. Mathisen, *Law, Authority and Society in Late Antiquity* (Oxford: OUP, 2001), 133–47.

were skilled in a specialized power of speech: that of forensic oratory as practised by the *advocatus*.

THE RELATIONSHIP BETWEEN ROMAN JURISPRUDENCE AND THEOLOGY

If the link between late Roman ecclesiastics and the practice of forensic advocacy has been in general neglected by previous scholarship, the wider relationship between Roman *jurisprudence* and Christian theology has not. Sir Henry Maine, writing in the second half of the nineteenth century, specifically drew attention to the latter:

> The great point of inquiry which is here suggested has never been satisfactorily elucidated. What has to be determined, is whether jurisprudence has ever served as the medium through which theological principles have been viewed; whether, by supplying a peculiar language, a peculiar mode of reasoning and a peculiar solution of many of the problems of life, it has ever opened new channels in which theological speculation could flow out and expand itself.[43]

Maine arrived at his 'great point of inquiry' by posing three fundamental questions concerning legal development. How did ancient law develop, what was its connection with the early history of society, and what is its relation to modern ideas? Maine viewed law in early societies, and in particular Roman law, as having contributed modes of thought, avenues of reasoning, and a technical language to the sciences of politics, moral philosophy, and theology. Furthermore, Maine saw the relationship between Roman jurisprudence and Western theology as particularly intimate:

> For some centuries . . . all the intellectual activity of the Western Romans had been expended on jurisprudence exclusively . . . It was impossible that they should not select from the questions indicated by the Christian records those which had some affinity with the order of speculations to which they were accustomed, and that their manner of dealing with them should not borrow something from their forensic habits. Almost everybody who has knowledge enough of Roman law to appreciate the Roman penal system, the Roman theory of the obligations established by Contract or Delict, the Roman view of Debts and of the modes of incurring, extinguishing, and transmitting them,

[43] H. J. S. Maine, *Ancient Law: Its Connection with the Early History of Society and its Relation to Modern Ideas*, 16th edn. (London: Murray, 1897), 355.

the Roman notion of the continuance of individual existence by Universal Succession, may be trusted to say whence arose the frame of mind to which the problems of Western theology proved so congenial, whence came the phraseology in which these problems were stated, and whence the description of reasoning employed in their solution.[44]

Characteristically, Maine made these thought-provoking remarks almost in passing. The argument from Roman jurisprudence to theology that he outlines, however, has attracted a more systematic treatment from later scholars.

A similar perspective to that of Maine's frames a series of detailed, mostly early twentieth-century, studies on individual late Roman 'theologians' who thought like classical Roman *iurisperiti*.[45] The North African theologian Tertullian has provoked a minor scholarly industry in this respect, due primarily to the fact that some extracts from a minor second–third-century jurist named Tertullian were included in Justinian's *Digest*.[46] The hypothesis that Roman jurisprudence and theology

[44] Maine, *Ancient Law*, 358–9.

[45] On Cyprian of Carthage see T. G. Fogliani, *Contributo alla ricerca di riferimenti legali in testi extragiuridici del III sec. d.c.* (Modena: Bassi & Nipoti, 1928) and A. Beck, *Römisches Recht bei Tertullian und Cyprian: Eine Studie zur frühen Kirchenrechtgeschichte* (Halle: Max Niemeyer Verlag, 1930); on Lactantius, Arnobius, and Minucius Felix, C. Ferrini, 'Le cognizioni giuridiche di Lattanzio, Arnobio e Minucio Felice', *Memorie dell'Accademia delle Scienze di Modena*, 2nd ser. 10 (1894), 195–210; on Asterius of Amasea, E. Volterra, 'Considerazioni teologico-giuridiche di Asterio di Amasea', *Rivista italiana per le scienze giuridiche*, NS 4 (1929), 3–10; on the Ambrosiaster, O. Heggelbacher, *Vom römischen zum christlichen Recht: Iuristische Elemente in den Schriften des sogenanntes Ambrosiaster* (Freiburg, Switzerland: University Press, 1959); on Jerome, G. Violardo, *Il pensiero giuridico di San Girolamo* (Milan: Società Editrice 'Vita e pensiero', 1937); on Augustine, F. Martroye, 'Saint Augustin et la jurisprudence romaine,' *BSNAF* (1916), 210–14; E. Albertario, 'Di alcuni riferimenti al matrimonio e al possesso in Sant' Agostino', *Rivista di filosofia neo-scolastica,* supplemento speciale al vol. 23 (1931), 367–76; M. Roberti, 'Contributo allo studio delle relazioni fra diritto romano e patristica tratto dall'esame delle fonti Agostiniane', *Rivista di filosofia neo-scolastica,* supplemento speciale al vol. 23 (1931), 305–66; D. Nonnoi, 'Sant' Agostino e il diritto romano', *Rivista italiana per le scienze giuridiche*, 12 (1934), 531–622, and F. G. Lardone, 'Roman Law in the Works of St Augustine', *Georgetown Law Journal*, 21 (1933), 435–56. Also now J. Gaudemet, *Le Droit romain dans le littérature chrétienne occidentale du IIIe au Ve siècle* (Milan: Guiffrè, 1978)—with reference to Tertullian, Minucius Felix, Cyprian, Arnobius, Lactantius, Ambrose, the Ambrosiaster, Jerome, and Augustine.

[46] For modern discussions see R. Klein, *Tertullian und das römische Reich* (Heidelberg: C. Winter, 1968); T. D. Barnes, *Tertullian: A Historical and Literary Study* (Oxford: OUP, 1971); R. Martini, 'Tertulliano giurista e Tertulliano padre della chiesa', *SDHI* 41 (1975), 79–124; D. I. Rankin, 'Was Tertullian a Jurist?', *Studia Patristica*, 31 (1997), 335–42; and R. Martini, 'Ancora a proposito di Tertulliano', *Bullettino dell'Istituto di diritto romano Vittorio Scialoja*, 39 (2003), 117–26. For further discussion see Ch. 6 below.

demanded a similar 'frame of mind' has also been used to support the idea of a late Roman braindrain from one discipline to another: starting from the traditional premise of a dramatic decline in the level of legal science in the fourth and fifth centuries, Peter Stein suggested that 'the best brains' had been 'attracted away from law to theology'—thus apparently accounting for both the 'triumph' of Christianity and the sterility of late Roman legal science.[47]

If we now turn to Lactantius' *Institutiones Divinae* (*Divine Institutes*)—a work written just before Constantine came to power and touched up under his reign, described by Gaudemet as 'le premier exposé complet de la doctrine chrétienne rédigé en Latin'—we can see that modern scholarship on the relationship between late Roman theology and late Roman law has approached this text from a number of different angles.[48] For the sake of example, I shall focus on the following (much quoted) passage from book 1 of the *Institutes*:

> And if certain people who are professional experts in fairness have published *Institutes of Civil Law*, for the settlement of lawsuits and quarrels between citizens in dispute, then we shall be all the more right to publish the *Institutes of God*, in which we shall not be discussing gutters or water-theft or common afray, but hope and life, salvation and immortality and God, for the eternal settlement of superstition and error, which are foul and lethal.[49]

Ferrini and Felice, both writing in 1894, followed by Carusi in 1906, treat this passage as one example amongst many of Lactantius' familiarity with juristic vocabulary, pointing towards his individual 'legality of mind'.[50] Using Ferrini's list of textual correspondences between juristic

[47] P. Stein, 'Roman Law', in J. H. Burns (ed.), *The Cambridge History of Medieval Political Thought c.350–c.1450* (Cambridge: CUP, 1988), 37–47, at 40. Compare E. M. Pickman, *The Mind of Latin Christendom, 375–496* (Oxford: Clarendon Press, 1937), 58 n. 37.

[48] Gaudemet, *Le Droit romain dans le littérature chrétienne,* 54.

[49] Lactantius, *Divine Institutes* I. 1. 12 (*SC* 326. 34–6, ll. 71–9): 'Et si quidam prudentes et arbitri aequitatis Institutiones civilis iuris conpositas ediderunt, quibus ciuium dissidentium lites contentionesque sopirent, quanto melius nos et rectius Divinas Institutiones litteris persequemur, in quibus non de stillicidiis aut aquis arcendis aut de manu conserenda, sed de spe, de vita, de salute, de immortalitate, de Deo loquemur, ut superstitiones mortiferas erroresque turpissimos sopiamus?' Tr. A. Bowen and P. Garnsey, Lactantius, *Divine Institutes* (Liverpool: Liverpool University Press, 2003), 58–9.

[50] Ferrini, 'Le cognizioni giuridiche', F. Felice, 'Su le idee giuridiche contenute nei libri V e VI delle Istituzioni di Lattanzio', *Rivista internazionale di scienze sociali e discipline ausiliarie*, 5 (1894), 581–6, and Z. B. Carusi, 'Diritto romano e patristica', *Studi giuridici in onore di Carlo Fadda*, ii (Naples: Pierro, 1906), 71–97.

vocabulary and Lactantius' terminology, Amarelli sought to specify exactly which work of classical Roman jurisprudence Lactantius sought to imitate, opting for Ulpian's *Institutes*.[51] The impetus to establish a specific juristic model for Lactantius' work was driven by Amarelli's wider project to prove that Lactantius envisaged a practical application for his *Institutes*, by providing the Emperor Constantine with a blueprint from which to construct a new system of private law for a Christian empire; his thesis, however, has not attracted the support of later scholars.[52] In his *Le Droit romain dans le littérature chrétienne occidentale du IIIe au Ve siècle*, Gaudemet expanded upon a similar method; his aim, however, was to explore the borrowing of 'concepts' from one intellectual field to another, the use of legal genres by theologians and the application of legal metaphors to religious contexts.[53] Accordingly, Gaudemet begins from a premiss contrary to that of Amarelli: the *Divine Institutes* may have adopted the form of the 'petits manuels' in which Roman jurists discussed the essentials of law, but Lactantius intended to write a religious not a legal treatise, in which the topics were *de spe, de vita, de salute, de immortalitate Dei*.[54] Here we approach the understanding of a relationship between law and theology founded on a two-societies view of late antiquity: 'La loi de Dieu' is incompatible with 'la solution juridique romaine'—one is grounded in Christian theology, the other in a 'pagan' Empire. Hence Gaudemet saw serious difficulties in attempting to reconcile the new religion and traditional Roman society.

In an important article, 'Contributo allo studio delle relazioni fra diritto romano e patristica tratto dall'esame delle fonti Agostiniane'—published in 1931—the Italian scholar Roberti had already noted the same 'serious difficulties' in reconciling Christianity and Roman law. Roberti questioned the perspective adopted by humanist scholars such as Hugo and Montesquieu, who had sought to either prove or disprove the proposition that Christianity had exercised an influence over the development of substantive principles of Roman law; instead Roberti argued that the Church Fathers had consciously intended to create a new system of Christian jurisprudence that was entirely autonomous

[51] F. Amarelli, *Vetustas Innovatio: Un'antitesi apparente nella legislazione di Costantino* (Naples: E Jovene, 1978), 133–45—a section entitled 'Lattanzio, lettore di Ulpiano'.

[52] Ibid. 103–33. Amarelli's premise has been challenged by R. Martini, 'Sui pretesi modelli giuridici delle Div. Inst. di Lattanzio', *Atti del Seminario Romanistico Gardesano III* (Milan: Guiffrè, 1988), 423–32.

[53] Gaudemet, *Le Droit romain*, 12–13.

[54] Ibid. 54.

from classical pagan law: 'In our opinion the distinctive character of the relationship between Patristics and Roman law, especially the classical and pagan law, lies in the autonomy of the theoretical constructions attempted by the Fathers of the Church, who never took into consideration—knowingly—the pagan works, not only that, they frequently distanced themselves decisively from them.'[55] Moreover, the juristic principles of this 'nuovo sistema di diritto Cristiano' were based solely on Christian ethics, reasoned out from evangelical teaching and the Pauline epistles, with each Father of the Church slowly constructing the new edifice from the materials provided by their predecessors—until 'la theoria completa' had been developed (an evolution that Roberti saw as complete by the time of Augustine).[56] The Church Fathers are thus revealed as autonomous Christian 'jurists' in their own right. Moreover, Roberti concluded with a veritable sting in the tail: 'Every theory which until now has been attributed to either the "Byzantine spell" or to a modification introduced by the last emperors, from Theodosius to Justinian, can be found already in the works of the Fathers—a new source for legal science.' Thanks to the juristic elaborations of the Church Fathers, according to Roberti, the development of ecclesiastical law outstripped the development of its main competitor, the secular late Roman law.

The Italian Roman lawyer Biondo Biondi elaborated on Roberti's perspective in three volumes of painstaking research published between 1952 and 1954, which he significantly titled *Il diritto romano cristiano*.[57] Biondi's earlier research, however, had focused upon the legislative principles of the Emperor Justinian; principles in which Biondi identified the official merging of an 'autonomous ecclesiastical law' with 'late Roman state legislation'.[58] For Biondi, then, the age of Justinian heralded the advent of a true *diritto romano-cristiano*. The Church Fathers of the previous centuries had prepared the way for Justinian through their autonomous 'Christianization' (equated by Biondi with 'vulgarization') of classical legal concepts. They had thus laid the foundation for the

[55] M. Roberti, 'Contributo allo studio delle relazioni fra diritto romano e patristica tratto dall'esame delle fonti Agostiniane', *Rivista di filosofia neo-scolastica*, supplemento speciale al vol. 23 (1931), 305–66, at 314.

[56] Ibid. 322.

[57] B. Biondi, *Il diritto romano cristiano*, i–iii (Milan: Guiffrè, 1952–4).

[58] See in particular B. Biondi, 'Religione e diritto canonico nella legislazione di Giustiniano', *ACII*, (Rome, 1935), 3–19, and Biondi, *Giustiniano primo principe e legislatore cattolico* (Milan: Pubblicazioni della Università cattolica del Sacro Cuore, 1936).

jurisprudence of a Byzantine Empire—a jurisprudence in which the priests (*sacerdotes*) of the church truly became the jurists of the 'state' and the classical jurists of old were revealed as the high priests of law in a Christian empire. Biondi's framework is still influential, in one form or another, today.[59]

This book seeks to reformulate the debates outlined above by arguing that law and theology had a natural point of contact in late Roman ecclesiastics because many drew on a late Roman programme of career-orientated education—more specifically, leading ecclesiastics and 'theologians' were skilled in a variety of forensic contexts and applied their techniques, case-by-case, in the service of the church (Chapter 6). This approach does not rely upon identifying *juristic* terminology or concepts in theological writings, nor does it focus upon individual theologians who 'thought like *jurists*' in a generic sense of the term. The forensic training of ecclesiastics helped them to participate in the legal hierarchy of the imperial bureaucracy: pleading at the imperial court for privileges and exemptions, arguing for the extension of case-specific rescripts before prefects and proconsuls, seeking the promulgation of new imperial legislation and then transforming its content by applying it to analogous cases. This concrete interaction between 'church' and 'state' even resulted in the creation of a new category of late antique legal practitioner: the *defensor ecclesiae*.[60] In other words, in the later Roman Empire, theology interacted with Roman law on a concrete day-to-day basis.

[59] See J. Gaudemet, *La Formation du droit séculier et du droit de l'église aux IV et V siècles*, 2nd edn. (Paris: Sirey, 1979); Crifò, G., 'Romanizzazione e cristianizzazione: Certezze e dubbi in tema di rapporto tra cristiani e istituzioni', in G. Bonamente and A. Nestori (eds.), *I cristiani e l'Impero nel IV secolo: Colloquio sul Cristianesimo nel mondo antico. Atti del convegno Macerata 17–18 dicembre 1987* (Macerata: Università degli studi di Macerata, 1988), 75–106; and F. Amarelli, 'Cristianesimo e istituzioni giuridiche romane: Contaminazioni e influenze recuperi', *Bullettino dell'Istituto di diritto romano Vittorio Scialoja*, 39 (2003).

[60] For discussion see C. Humfress, 'A New Legal Cosmos: Late Roman Lawyers and the Early Medieval Church', in P. Linehan and J. Nelson (eds.), *The Medieval World* (London: Routledge, 2001), 1–45.

6

Ecclesiastics as Forensic Practitioners

JUDGES

> And so judge as you are surely to be judged, even as you have Christ for both partner and assessor and counsellor and spectator with you in the same case.[1]

Pre-Constantinian Christian communities developed various practices that encouraged their members to settle legal disputes within their own communities of the faithful, without recourse to 'external' lawcourts or members outside the group. In this context the *Didascalia Apostolorum*—translated into Syriac, possibly in the early fourth century, from a non-extant third-century Greek text—contains one of the earliest systematic treatments of the involvement of Christian bishops in dispute resolution.[2] At 2 46. 1–2 the *Didascalia* paraphrases a number of precepts from the Gospel of Matthew: it is better not to have lawsuits with anyone; however, if a process is unavoidable the parties should not bring the case before a 'heathen' court, even if that entails forfeiting a patrimonial inheritance.[3] Sections 2. 49. 1 to 2. 50. 3 establish the bishop's hearing as an alternative recourse to justice for litigious members

[1] *Didascalia Apostolorum* 2. 47. (tr. R. H. Connolly, *Didascalia Apostolorum: The Syriac Version Translated and Accompanied by the Verona Latin Fragments* (Oxford: Clarendon Press, 1929), 111–12.

[2] On the Syriac and Latin translations ibid. p. xviii. M. Metzger, *Les Constitutions Apostoliques*, i (*SC* 320) gives the later 4th-cent. Latin reworking of the text and also discusses the Arabic and Ethiopian translations. On the 'Semitic Christian traditions' of the *Didascalia Apostolorum* see Vööbus, *CSCO* 401. 5—noted by C. Fonrobert, 'The Didascalia Apostolorum: A Mishnah for the Disciples of Jesus', *Journal of Early Christian Studies*, 9/4 (2001), 438–509, at 484. For discussion of the text in the context of early Christian dispute resolution see Harries, *Law and Empire*, 191–5 and Rapp, *Holy Bishops*, 244–5.

[3] Matt. 17: 24–7, 18: 21–2, and 21–2. For discussion, with bibliography, see G. Schöllgen, *Die Anfänge der Professionalisierung des Klerus und das Kirchliche Amt*

of the community and specify a number of procedural guidelines that ought to be followed, with an explicit analogy to the practice of civil magistrates.[4] The text is also careful to point out how the bishop's sentence differs from that of a secular judge: 'For the word of sentence which you decree ascends straightaway to God; and if you have justly judged, you shall receive of God the reward of justice, both now and hereafter; but if you have judged unjustly, again you shall receive of God a recompense accordingly.' Before drawing any conclusions, however, about the nature of episcopal tribunals in the pre-Constantinian church on the basis of the *Didascalia Apostolorum*, it is worth pausing to ask what kind of context our earliest extant version of the text was drafted within.

As argued by Charlotte Fonrobert, the author of the *Didascalia Apostolorum* knows:

> of places and towns in Syria with Jewish and Christian presence, in which community boundaries remain fluid, in which people do not conform to models of Judaism and Christianity promoted by our (rabbinic or patristic) heresiologists, and in which people experiment, even convert from one community to another and import with them their former experience into the newly chosen community.[5]

This reading of the *Didascalia*'s intended audience acts as a salient reminder that, although the administrative units of the early church were undoubtedly modelled on the pattern of the civil administration (cities and provinces), religious communities on the ground did not come in neat packages. Fonrobert also argues that the author of the *Didascalia Apostolorum* chose a very particular literary framework (for a polemical purpose), namely 'the so-called Apostolic Council', which according to Acts 15 also took place in Syria.[6] The work is thus effectively pseudepigraphical: 'In its retelling of the Council, based on Acts 15, the *Didascalia* puts into the mouths of the apostles that "it seemed to us in one mind (Acts 15. 25) *to write this catholic* Didascalia *for the confirmation of you all*".'[7] In sum, our earliest extant text of the *Didascalia Apostolorum* offers an early fourth-century Syriac translation

in der Syrischen Didaskalie (Münster Westfalen: Aschendorffsche Verlagsbuchhandling, 1998), 133.

[4] When the bishop sits 'to judge' he should follow certain procedures for the admission of the parties (Connolly, *Didascalia Apostolorum*, 112, ll. 25–9); he must establish the character of the parties (112, ll. 29–114) and he should follow the example of civil magistrates in making a full inquiry into the facts of the case (115, ll. 5–19).

[5] Fonrobert, 'Didascalia Apostolorum', 489.

[6] Ibid. 489–90.

[7] Ibid. 490.

of a third-century Greek text which in turn tried to imagine, for polemical purposes, what Christ's Apostles *would have* laid down in the first century AD. What the Didascalia says about dispute settlement, then, cannot be read as a straight description of pre-Constantinian Christian practice 'on the ground'.[8]

Jill Harries has argued that the language used in the *Didascalia Apostolorum* and the fourth-century Latin *Constitutiones Apostolorum* is 'that of healing, not judgment' and that the bishop acted primarily as the 'physician of his flock'.[9] Christian bishops, however, had a number of different cultural models of self-representation to draw upon, including that of the Roman secular magistrate (the *iudex*). The task of reconciling litigious sinners, using threats of penance and excommunication if necessary, was certainly not comparable to a bureaucratic trial procedure. Pre-Constantinian bishops, however, were also instructed to preach that the gaze of all the 'faithful in Christ' should be fixed on the Day of Judgment to come. Hence the exhortation at *Didascalia Apostolorum* 2. 18:

> For it behoves the bishop to be by his doctrine a restrainer of sins and an example and an encourager of righteousness, and by the admonition of his teaching a director of good works, and one who praises and magnifies the good things which are to come and are promised by God in the place of life everlasting; a proclaimer also of the wrath to come in the judgement of God, with threatening of the grievous fire which is unquenchable and intolerable.[10]

Or as Augustine put it *c.*413/414 to Macedonius, the vicar of Africa: 'We act as our Episcopal powers allow us to; we sometimes use the threat of human judgement; but emphatically and always we use the threat of divine judgement.'[11] Christ's tribunal could be represented as more terrifying and powerful than that of any secular magistrate, using language and imagery borrowed from the latter. As Brent Shaw has argued, 'There is no doubt that bishops appropriated the judicial experience and preached it.'[12] Valerian, bishop of Cimiez in the mid-fifth century, advised his congegration that neither the murderer who was acquitted by a corrupt civil court, nor the adulterer who was accused

[8] Schöllgen, *Die Anfänge*, 133, notes that there is 'very little evidence' for pre-Constantinian Christian judicial proceedings.

[9] Harries, *Law and Empire*, 192, and Rapp, *Holy Bishops*, 244.

[10] *Didascalia Apostolorum*, 2. 18 (Connolly, *Didascalia*, 54).

[11] Augustine, *Ep.* 153. 21 (tr. from E. M. Atkins and R.J. Dodaro (eds.), *Augustine, Political Writings* (Cambridge: CUP, 2001), 84).

[12] Shaw, 'Judicial Nightmares' at 549, see also 555–62.

as such but then let off with a pardon, nor the perjurer who kept his right hand(!) should be thought to have escaped punishment: 'Dead men have their sins still clinging to them, unless before their demise they purged them away through the intercession of their tears before God. Hell, armed with due punishments, awaits its prisoner.'[13] Bishops may well have been approached as 'reconcilers' and 'mediators' (in a non-technical sense of the term), but they were also understood, by their Christian contemporaries at least, as judges who would themselves be judged.

In a letter addressed to the Catholic bishops, written sometime after the Council of Arles in 314, the Emperor Constantine expressed his own reluctance to judge concerning synodical decisions: 'They demand my judgment when I myself await the judgment of Christ. For I tell you, as is the truth, that the judgments of the bishops should be regarded as if God himself were in the judge's seat. For these have no power either to think or to judge except as they are instructed by Christ's teaching.'[14] Here Constantine is referring specifically to bishops acting in council, but it is easy to see how this statement could be extended to cover the judgment of bishops in a different context. The problematic text of *C.Th.* 1. 27. 1 (dated by Seeck to 318) gives the first extant reference to the bishop's 'court' (*iudicium*) in an imperial constitution.[15] It too expresses a reverence for episcopal judgment similar to that just quoted from Constantine's 'Letter to the Catholic Bishops'. The text as we have it excerpted at *C.Th.* 1. 27. 1 does not, however, set out to define the nature of episcopal jurisdiction over legal cases, but rather addresses a specific 'procedural' issue under Roman law. In fact, as

[13] Valerian of Cimiez, *Homily* 1 (*PL* 52. 694): 'Defunctis corporibus salva sunt crimina, nisi fuerint prius apud deum lacrymarum intercessione purgata: exspectat enim reum suum gehenna debitis armata suppliciis.'

[14] Appendix 5 to Optatus Milevitanus, ed. K. Ziwsa (*CSEL* 26. 209): 'Meum iudicium postulant, qui ipse iudicium Christi expecto, dico enim, ut se veritas habet, sacerdotum iudicium ita debet haberi, ac si ipse dominus residens iudicet. Nihil enim licet his aliud sentire vel aliud iudicare, nisi quod Christi magisterio sunt edocti.' Tr. M. Edwards, *Optatus: Against the Donatists* (Liverpool: Liverpool University Press, 1997), 190.

[15] Matthews, *Laying Down the Law*, 94–5 and 124: *C.Th.* 1. 23–7 are missing in our extant manuscripts, but Mommsen restored two titles to *C.Th.* 1. 27 from the *Sirmondian Constitutions* (nos. 17 and 18). These two texts were both included in the *CI* at 1. 4. 6 and 1. 4. 8, together with a third (= *CI* 1. 4. 7), which *Krueger* correctly restored to his *C.Th.* edn.—thus giving us three extant constitutions under the rubric of *C.Th.* 1. 27 (as opposed to Mommsen's two). On the problems associated with the heading, text, and subscript of *C.Th.* 1. 27. 1 in particular see Corcoran, *The Empire of the Tetrarchs*, 2nd edn., 284–6 (rejecting Licinius as the issuer).

we shall see, the (few) late Roman imperial constitutions that refer to episcopal jurisdiction have too often been taken as 'founding laws', or as laws that regulate or define the scope and functions of the *episcopalis audientia* (the 'bishop's hearing'), whereas in fact they were responses to concrete situations. They carry implications about the nature of the bishop's 'court', but their purpose was not to define it.[16]

The particular circumstances that provoked the issuing of *C.Th.* 1. 27. 1 in 318 can be reconstructed as follows: having begun legal proceedings before a *iudex* (probably the provincial governor), some litigants have subsequently decided to transfer the same case to an episcopal 'court'. The constitution reinforces the fact that there is a due process that must be followed in these circumstances: in other words, having already begun their case before a magistrate, litigants cannot just abandon that process without any formalities and seek judgment in the bishop's 'court'.[17] The text implies that the magistrate must halt the proceedings and grant a transfer of the case to the *Christiana lex*; once the judgment has been given by the bishop, it should be treated as sacrosanct. However, the litigant was still required to return to the (original) magistrate's court and disclose the verdict that he had received from the bishop. The bishop's verdict was thus to be formally pronounced by the magistrate before whom the case had originally been lodged.[18]

[16] For modern literature on the late Roman *episcopalis audientia* see in general: W. Selb, 'Episcopalis audientia von der Zeit Konstantins bis zur Novelle XXXV Valentinians III', *ZSS, Rom. Abt.* 84 (1967), 162–217; E. Herrmann, *Ecclesia in Re Publica* (Berne: Lang, 1980), 207–31; F. J. Cuena Boy, *La episcopalis audientia: La justicia episcopal en las causas civiles entre laicos* (Valladolid: University of Valladolid, 1985); M. R. Cimma, *L'episcopalis audientia nelle costituzioni imperiali da Costantino a Giustiniano* (Turin: Giappichelli, 1989); G. Crifò, 'A proposito di episcopalis audientia', in *Institutions, société et vie politique: Collection de l'École Française de Rome*, 159 (1992), 397–410; J. C. Lamoreaux, 'Episcopal Courts in Late Antiquity', *Journal of Early Christian Studies*, 3/2 (1995), 143–67; P. G. Caron, 'I tribunali della Chiesa nel diritto del Tardo Impero', *AARC* 11 (1996), 245–63; Harries, *Law and Empire*, 191–211; Frakes, *Contra Potentium Iniurias*, 198–9; O. Huck, 'A propos de CTh 1,27,1 et C. Sirm 1: Sur deux textes controversés relatifs à l'episcopalis audientia constantinienne', *ZSS, Rom. Abt.* 120 (2003), 78–105; and Kaser and Hackl, *Das römische Zivilprozessrecht*, 641–4.

[17] John Crook noted this point on an earlier draft, but it has taken me years to fully understand his astute and incisive comment here!

[18] *C.Th.* 1. 27. 1 (= *CI* 1. 4. 6); the following text is from the database of the *Projet Volterra I, Law and Empire AD 193–455*: 'Iudex pro sua sollicitudine obseruare debebit, ut, si ad episcopale iudicium (eds.; lacuna in Ber.; 'ereasa ad aepost.' Par.; 'de re aliqua ad episcopos' sugg. Momm.) prouocetur, silentium accommodetur (..]modetur, Berol.; accommodet, Par.) et, si quis ad legem Christianam negotium transferre uoluerit et illud iudicium obseruare, audiatur (Ber.;..]etur, Par.), etiamsi negotium apud iudicem sit inchoatum, et pro sanctis habeatur, quidquid ab his fuerit iudicatum: ita tamen, ne

The general principle that cases could be transferred from one forum to another was standard: for example, there is late Roman evidence for a number of attempts at 'forum-shopping' from the jurisdiction of 'ordinary' *iudices* to the various 'courts of special jurisdiction', including those of *collegia* who claimed jurisdiction over their own members in relevant cases.[19] The text excerpted at *C.Th.* 1. 27. 1 does not specify *why* a litigant might wish to transfer a case from a magistrate to a bishop: it may have been that one party or both, for whatever reasons or changed circumstances, now believed that the dispute would be resolved with less time and/or expense, or more 'justly' via the bishop's *iudicium*, or it may have been that the request for transferral perhaps involved some kind of claim to privileged clerical jurisdiction. Nor should we assume that 'legal' parameters always governed such situations; whom you knew, how much you were willing to pay, and what lengths you were able or willing to go to must have played their part in (most?) such cases. From the drafter's perspective, then, the 318 constitution seeks to 'remind' magistrates that, even if a case has already opened before them, they should allow litigants to transfer a case to the bishop's 'court'. At the same time the drafter 'reminds' litigants that, if their case has already begun before a magistrate, they must follow certain formal procedures and not just receive judgment from a bishop, without the presiding magistrate's knowledge. Thus the 318 constitution does not invest bishops with 'civil *cognitio*', nor does it in any sense establish arbitration as the only 'permissable' form of episcopal judgment.[20] Finally, we should note that *C.Th.* 1. 27. 1 says nothing about any dispute that might be brought for the bishop's judgment in the first instance—that is not part of the 318 consitution's particular focus.

If we suppose that the 333 Constantinian rescript which survives as *Sirmondian Constitution* 1 is genuine, then it too can be understood along broadly similar lines.[21] As this rescript survives outside

usurpetur in eo, ut unus ex litigantibus pergat ad supra dictum auditorium et arbitrium suum enuntiet. Iudex enim praesentis causae ('praesentes partes audire et causae' sugg. Momm.) integre habere debet arbitrium ut omnibus accepto latis pronuntiet.' My thanks to Peter Garnsey and Anthony Bowen for their advice on this text.

19 See Jones, *Later Roman Empire*, 484–94.

20 J. Gaudemet, *Les Institutions de l'antiquité*, 3rd edn. (Paris: Montchrestien, 1991), 232, argues that *C.Th.* 1. 27. 1 established the right of litigants to appeal to bishops as arbitrators, whilst G. Vismara, *La giurisdizione civile dei vescovi* (Milan: A. Guiffré, 1995), 40, sees the constitution as officially investing the bishop with civil *cognitio*.

21 As noted by Matthews, *Laying Down the Law*, 122–5, the Lyons manuscript of the 'Sirmondian' collection dates to the second half of the 7th cent., but the private

the Theodosian and Justinianic Codes its preamble is extant.[22] In this preamble we learn that the issuing of the rescript itself was prompted by the Praetorian Prefect Ablabius, who had raised certain queries relating to episcopal *sententiae* (sentences or judgments).[23] The drafter of the rescript directs Ablabius' attention to previous Constantinian constitutions on this matter and reaffirms the ability of litigants to transfer their cases to the bishop's 'court', as in the 318 text discussed above. In addition, the 333 rescript underscores the right of one party to request this transfer without the agreement of the other and at any stage in the proceedings.[24] This 333 ruling does not, of course, prima facie, preclude both parties *under a different scenario* from requesting a transfer to episcopal 'arbitration'—that is not the issue at stake here; if both parties to a dispute agreed that they wished to opt out and seek a bishop as a formal arbitrator, then the presiding magistrate could presumably be expected to grant such a demand.[25] There is late Roman evidence for litigation beginning before provincial governors and ending before arbitrators and vice versa.[26]

collection may have been put together earlier. See also Liebs, *Römische Jurisprudenz in Gallien*, 135–7.

[22] Matthews, *Laying Down the Law*, 127–8, ventures that 'it is just possible' that *Sirm.* 1 'was included in the now mainly lost title in Book 1 of the [*Theodosian*] *Code* but escaped the interest of the compilers of the *CI* and the *Breviarium*'.

[23] *Sirm.* 1 pr. (text as edited by the *Projet Volterra I* database): 'Satis mirati sumus grauitatem tuam, quae plena iustitiae ac probae religionis est, clementiam nostram sciscitari uoluisse, quid de sententiis episcoporum uel ante moderatio nostra censuerit uel nunc seruari cupiamus, Ablabi, parens karissime atque amantissime. Itaque quia a nobis instrui uoluisti, olim promulgatae (W; prorogatae, alii) legis ordinem salubri rursus imperio propagamus.'

[24] Ibid: 'Quicumque itaque litem habens, siue possessor siue petitor uel inter initia litis uel decursis temporum curriculis, siue cum (dum, W) negotium peroratur (peroperatur, W Berol.), siue cum iam coeperit promi sententia, iudicium elegerit sacrosanctae legis antistitis, ilico sine aliqua dubitatione, etiamsi alia pars refragatur, ad episcopum (episcopale iudicium, W) personae litigantium dirigantur.'

[25] Although an opinion of the 3rd-cent. jurist Paul from his commentary on the *Edict*, book 13 (= *D.* 4. 8. 32) may have caused some confusion in early 4th-cent. courts: it states that individuals appointed to priesthoods can be exempted from acting as arbitrators, in recognition of both the honour due to them and 'the majesty of the god for whose rites the priests ought be free'.

[26] e.g. *CI* 2. 4. 40 (381) specifies procedures for abandoning arbitration and taking the case to court; *C.Th.* 11. 30. 63 (405), on the other hand, refers to regulations of the 'ancient law' on litigants obtaining arbitrators in the presence of a magistrate; compare also Justinian, *Novel* 93 (539): a certain Hesychius lodged an appeal on a civil case with the Praetorian Prefect, but whilst the case was pending both parties agreed to appoint arbitrators; having subsequently abandoned the arbitration, Hesychius was

What was at issue in *Sirmondian Constitution* 1, it seems, was the reluctance of civil judges to enforce the bishop's *sententia* 'whatever its nature' (as the text states). Ablabius' original query may in fact have related to a specific case, where a certain bishop had given an improper *sententia*, from Ablabius' perspective at least, most likely in a case concerning a minor. We could thus imagine the following plausible scenario: a bishop has heard a particular case referred to him from Ablabius' court, without the minor's guardian being present and has thus contravened an established rule of Roman legal procedure; one of the litigants has reported this decision back to the Praetorian Prefect (in accordance with the principle noted from *C.Th.* 1. 27. 1), but an interested party has complained about the irregularity of the bishop's judgment; should Ablabius, under such circumstances, reopen the case and review it himself?[27] The imperial response is no: the 333 constitution clearly specifies that lawsuits judged 'by either Praetorian or Civil law' and ended by episcopal *sententiae* cannot be subject to further review.[28] The implication is thus that if a bishop has not followed standard Roman legal principles in his judging, a litigant has no recourse to an appeal. The Praetorian Prefect, who 'holds the top rank of the courts', and all the rest of the *iudices* are simply responsible for executing the bishop's judgment—their duties do not include reviewing the details of *sententiae* that bishops have already pronounced. Once again, reference is made to the bishop's 'sacrosanct' authority in this context.[29] The bishop's judgment is thus understood by the drafter of the rescript to be of a different quality to that of 'ordinary' judges. For the same reason, the rescript also states that the testimony of a single bishop must be accepted by every judge, even if there is no other witness. It is plausible, given the context, that this ruling refers to a specific situation

now attempting to reopen the same appeal before the prefect—his opponent lodges an objection but Justinian permits the case to be returned to the PP.

[27] *Sirm.* 1: 'Sanximus namque, sicut edicti nostri forma declarat, sententias episcoporum quolibet genere latas (inlatas, Florus) sine aliqua aetatis discretione inuiolatas semper incorruptasque seruari; scilicet ut pro sanctis semper ac uenerabilibus habeantur, quidquid episcoporum fuerit sententia terminatum. Siue itaque inter minores siue inter maiores ab episcopis fuerit indicatum, apud uos, qui iudiciorum summam tenetis, et apud ceteros omnes iudices ad exsecutionem uolumus pertinere.'

[28] Ibid: 'Omnes itaque causae, quae uel praetorio iure uel ciuili tractantur, episcoporum sententiis terminatae perpetuo stabilitatis iure firmentur (incorrupte f., Berol.), nec liceat ulterius retractari negotium, quod episcoporum sententia deciderit.'

[29] Ibid: 'Multa enim, quae in iudicio captiosa praescriptionis uincula promi non patiuntur, inuestigat et publicat sacro sanctae religionis auctoritas.'

in which a bishop may have been called into a magistrate's court to render an account of his judging, at the request of one of the parties involved.[30] The bishop's word was (in theory at least) to be understood by the magistrate as the end of the matter. The 333 rescript, then, does appear to grant a privileged position to Christian bishops, on the basis of their divinely given capacity to both tell the truth and search it out.[31] The rescript is not concerned, however, with defining whether bishops should be understood as 'judges' or 'arbitrators'—both avenues of approach were open to litigants, amongst others.

We still find various avenues of approach available in the later fourth century.[32] Ambrose's *Ep.* 24 describes a dispute over a family legacy involving a bishop and his brother (a *vir consularis*), that was lodged before the court of the Praetorian Prefect.[33] The advocates (*togati*) of both parties subsequently requested a transfer of the hearing from the prefect's jurisdiction and requested that (Bishop) Ambrose act as their *iudex* (judge). Ambrose, however, replied that he would only accept the case as an arbitrator.[34] We might be justified in thinking of Ambrose as a peculiarly high-level operator, due to his family connections and his previous career path dispensing justice in the imperial bureaucracy; nonetheless his *Ep.* 24 suggests that bishops themselves could have some say over the form in which they agreed to hear cases.

The piecemeal nature of fourth- and early fifth-century imperial constitutions on episcopal legal jurisdiction suggests that Emperors only

[30] Compare *C.Th.* 11. 39. 8 (= *CI* 1. 3. 7), an excerpt from proceedings held in the imperial consistory on 29 June 381: Gothofredus argues that Theodosius intended to exempt 'clerics' from being bound to give an account of their sentences on referred cases before a civil magistrate; Gothofredus linked *C.Th.* 11. 39. 8 to canon 1 of the fifth council of Carthage, where it was agreed to petition the Emperors so that if a civil case was referred to the 'judgment of the church', and one of the parties was unhappy with the outcome, the cleric who gave the sentence should not be dragged into court to testify as to his judgment. Justinian, *Novel* 123. 7 should be seen as significantly broadening the scope of the original Theodosian constitution.

[31] Compare Eusebius, *Vita Const.* 4. 27. 2: Eusebius refers to a Constantinian constitution that forbade governors from subverting or ignoring the decisions of bishops made in council, on the grounds that Christian 'priests' were superior to civil magistrates (might this also be related to Constantine's 'Letter to the Catholic bishops' (= Optatus *App.* 5), quoted above?).

[32] Notwithstanding the Emperor Julian's apparent repeal of 'all the laws giving judicial powers to bishops': Harries, *Law and Empire*, 199.

[33] Discussed by Vismara, *La giurisdizione civile*, 65–76, and J. Harries, 'Resolving Disputes: The Frontiers of Law in Late Antiquity', in R. W. Mathisen, *Law, Society and Authority in Late Antiquity* (Oxford: OUP, 2001), 68–82.

[34] Ambrose, *Ep.* 24. 3, *CSEL* 82. 1, 170–5 at 171, ll. 28–9. Also, compare Ambrose's advice on episcopal judgment in cases of patrimonial litigation at *De Officiis* 2. 125.

legislated in this area when prompted by concrete case-specific instances; it is tempting, but not necessarily accurate, to make broad generalizations from fragments of text excerpted and placed under general rubrics by the compilers of the Theodosian and Justinianic Codes. For instance, the excerpted text at *C.Th.* 16. 2. 23, given at Trier on 17 May 376 and addressed to 'Artemius, Eurydicus, Appius, Gerasimus and all other Bishops', implies a situation in which named bishops have written to the Emperor Gratian because (other?) 'clerics' were being dragged before magistrates on charges relating to 'ecclesiastical dissensions' and 'slight offences relating to religious observance'. The imperial constitution responds by clearly upholding *privilegium fori* in ecclesiastical matters: 'clerics' shall be heard 'in their own places and by the synods of their own diocese', but (as was standard practice) any claim to *privilegium fori* was not valid in criminal actions. This 376 constitution does not, then, limit episcopal 'courts' to *only* hearing cases pertaining to ecclesiastical or religious matters—Gratian simply reaffirms that this is part of their scope, in response to a concrete request to do so. *Sirmondian Constitution* 3 (issued at Constantinople, possibly in 384 and addressed to Optatus PP) deals with a similar set of circumstances but, due to the fact the text has been transmitted in its almost complete state in the *Sirmondian Constitutions*, it also gives us the name of the bishop whose authority had apparently been threatened: Timothy of Alexandria. The text also implies that the specific problem here is with (schismatic) bishops hauling other clerics before the 'secular' courts. The Emperors are once again responding to specific petitions, as *Sirmondian Constitution* 3 states: 'Supplications have been read out in the imperial consistory whereby the episcopal piety makes some plea and contests in that tribunal.'[35]

CI 1. 4. 7 (= *C.Th. Krueger* 1. 27. 2), issued in 398 and addressed to the PPO Eutychianus, should perhaps be understood from the same perspective: as a particular response to an actual case or at least a set of circumstances,[36] rather than as part of a general late fourth-century

35 *Sirm.* 3 (tr. Pharr *et al.*), discussed by Matthews, *Laying Down the Law*, 161 and Honoré, *Law in Crisis*, 34–5. Compare the highly excerpted text at *C.Th.* 16. 11. 1, given at Padua in 399 and addressed to the then proconsul of Africa—which should be read in the context of the Donatist controversy.

36 Matthews, *Laying Down the Law*, 210, convincingly reads *CI* 1. 4. 7 as part of a much more extensive constitution addressed to Eutychianus, of which other fragments occur at *C.Th.* 11. 30. 57, 9. 40. 16, 9. 45. 3, 16. 2. 33, and possibly also 16. 2. 32. The context appears to have been problems with monks (perhaps in Constantinople?).

'policy' to assimilate episcopal jurisdiction to procedures of (formal) arbitration.[37] The text, as excerpted in the Justinianic Code, reads: '*If people are agreed* [my italics] that they want to litigate before the "priest" of the sacred law, they will not be prevented from doing so, but they will make use of his court, at least as regards a civil dispute, as that of one who sits voluntarily as judge.'[38] In other words, if both parties wish to have a bishop settle their dispute, their decision is to be respected—as long as they abide by the relevant formalities. However, continues *CI* 1. 4. 7, a bishop 'cannot and should not involve himself with people who, it has been established, have been summoned to an examination before a designated judge, and have stayed away rather than willingly attended'.[39] The drafter is thus concerned with preventing bishops from simply interfering or interposing themselves in cases that have already been begun before a designated judge. On this reading, *CI* 1. 4. 7 (which should, remember, be restored to *C.Th.* 1. 27. 2) fits neatly with the imperial concerns (as argued above) of the Constantinian constitution excerpted at *C.Th.* 1. 27. 1.[40] Moreover, the excerpted text included at *C.Th.* 1. 27. 2 (= Krüger *C.Th.* 1. 27. 3), issued in the West in 408 and addressed to the Praetorian Prefect Theodorus, again confirms the judgments of bishops who have acted as formal arbitrators—this time specifically in situations where the bishop has been approached directly 'without the knowledge' of the magistrate. This 408 constitution was almost certainly provoked by a particular query, perhaps from the Praetorian Prefect Theodorus himself.[41] In sum, none of the imperial constitutions that I have discussed so far have

[37] Harries, *Law and Empire*, 201: 'By 398, it was argued that Episcopal jurisdiction could be assimilated to the procedure of arbitration'; also Honoré, *Law in Crisis*, 4: 'This conciliation procedure, later termed *episcopalis audientia*, was rationalized by the lawyers as a form of civil arbitration (compromissum), open to both clerics and laymen, to which both parties must agree.'

[38] *CI* 1. 4. 7: 'Si qui ex consensu apud sacrae legis antistitem litigare uoluerint, non uetabuntur, sed experientur illius, in ciuili dumtaxat negotio, arbitri more residentis sponte iudicium.'

[39] Ibid.: 'Quod his obesse non poterit nec debebit, quos ad praedicti cognitoris examen conuentos potius afuisse quam sponte uenisse constiterit'.

[40] Compare *C.Th.* 2.1.10 (also issued in 398 and addressed to the same PPO Eutychianus) on 'Jewish' arbitrators and their *sententiae*. As noted by Millar, *Greek Roman Empire*, 124–5, the text excerpted at *C.Th.* 16. 8. 2 (= *CI* 1. 9. 15) subsequently stripped the then Patriarch Gamaliel of his authority in this respect (amongst other things), in response 'to a complaint from the region [of Palestine]'.

[41] Perhaps a litigant had dug up the juristic opinion of Paul (as noted above = *D.* 4. 8. 32) and cited it in a petition to the Praetorian Prefect's court as 'evidence' that a judgment delivered by a bishop as arbitrator should not stand?

sought to limit bishops to *only* acting in legal cases as arbitrators. Nor should these constitutions be read as evidence for an 'interventionist zeal' for issuing 'laws' about episcopal hearings or as evidence for a 'hazy awareness on the part of the imperial lawyers' concerning Christian dispute resolution.[42] The imperial constitutions discussed above are not statements of 'imperial policy', but are in fact reactions to a series of precise *ad hoc* questions that had arisen out of daily legal practice.

Even if we were to suppose for the sake of argument that everyone in the later Roman Empire knew exactly how 'correctly' to define the nature of episcopal 'legal' jurisdiction and could explain precise sets of procedural rules which governed its operation in a number of different contexts, we should still expect to find some individuals attempting to subvert those clearly defined rules by working them to their own advantage. Given the state of our evidence it is difficult to make any definitive statements about how episcopal 'legal' jurisdiction was in fact understood at any given time, by any particular individual or group. Nonetheless, we *do* know that some late Roman litigants (perhaps guided by the advice of advocates and/or *iurisconsulti*) attempted to 'forum-shop', for example, by pleading *praescriptio fori* as a jurisdictional 'dodge'; that some challenged a bishop's authority to act as a *iudex datus* or as an arbitrator in their case; and that others attempted to frame persuasive appeals from episcopal *sententiae*, prompting the repetition of imperial constitutions forbidding this course of action. The drafter of Valentinian III's *Novel* 35 (given at Rome in 452 and addressed to the PP Firminus) seems to have had exactly these types of situations in mind, when he set out to define the nature of the *episcopalis audientia* by adopting a legislative 'once and for all' tone.

The opening lines of Valentinian III's *Novel* 35 read: 'There have often been differences of opinion about the Episcopal court. That this complaint may not proceed further, it is necessary that a sanction be issued by the present law.'[43] In fact this 452 constitution has a much broader scope than simply the episcopal 'court'; there is a real sense that the text is taking stock of previous legislation covering a variety

[42] In contrast to the current scholarly consensus, as outlined by Harries, *Law and Empire*, 202–3.

[43] *N.Val.* 35 (Firminus PP and Patrician, given 15/16/25/26 Apr. 452 at Rome): 'De episcopali iudicio diversorum saepe causatio est: ne ulterius querella procedat, necesse est praesenti lege sanciri.'

of different topics.[44] The preamble to *N.Val.* 35. 1 refers explicitly to constitutions contained in the *Codex Theodosianus* (438) and the drafter is obviously working with the Code open before him; section 8, moreover, refers to the fact that various rules on succession stand in need of clarification, 'since they were not clearly expressed in the previous constitutions'.[45] Given this context, we might surmise that after January 438 litigants, judges, and clerics in the Western provinces had been consulting the Theodosian Code and applying the various constitutions within it as 'general laws'—various queries had arisen in legal practice as a result.

With respect to ecclesiastical 'legal' jurisdiction, Valentinian III's *Novel* 35 states that disputes between clerics, or disputes between the laity, can be settled by a bishop's judgment—as long as the litigants concerned have completed the correct formalities (i.e. have made a *compromissum*). Otherwise, bishops cannot judge because they have no 'court', except in cases concerning religion (in accordance, the drafter specifies, with certain constitutions included in the Theodosian Code).[46] If a lawsuit arises between clerics, and either one party or both refuses to have their case heard by a bishop, then it should be judged 'according to public statutes and common law'. *Novel* 35 thus allows the clergy to opt out of ecclesiastical jurisdiction, and even enables one cleric to compel another to do so.[47] Section 2 of the *Novel* further clarifies that a plaintiff who is a cleric must follow the forum of the defendant (presumably a layperson),

44 Subjects covered by the constitution include episcopal arbitration (pr.); ecclesiastics and the courts (ss. 1–2); that no clerics or monks can be *inquilini*, slaves, or *coloni* (s. 3); that no clerics can engage in trade (s. 4); that the *defensor ecclesiae* and other clerics cannot be decurions (s. 5); that clerics will be returned to their original status, with some exceptions (s. 6); that clerics are not to interfere with legal cases (s. 7); rules on succession (s. 8); various rules on dowry (s. 9); procedural exemptions for Africans who suffered under the Vandals (s. 12); the duty of a plaintiff to pursue a case once officially begun (s. 14); various clarifications on the giving of securities and appeals (ss. 15–18); and finally the status of a child born to a fugitive *colona*.

45 In comparison, s. 11 of *N.Val.* 35 annuls a Novel of Theodosius II.

46 *N.Val.* 35 pr.: 'Itaque cum inter clericos iurgium vertitur et ipsis litigatoribus convenit, habeat episcopus licentiam iudicandi, praeeunte tamen vinculo compromissi. Quod et de laicis, si consentiant, auctoritas nostra permittit: aliter eos iudices esse non patimur, nisi voluntas iurgantium interposita, sicut dictum est, condicione praecedat, quoniam constat episcopos [et presbyteros] forum legibus non habere nec de aliis causis secundum Arcadii et Honorii divalia constituta, quae Theodosianum corpus ostendit, praeter religionem posse cognoscere.'

47 *P.Princeton* 55 (481) records the formal arbitration sentence for a group of ecclesiastics who chose to have their case heard by a group of advocates—having originally lodged it before an imperial magistrate.

unless the defendant has agreed to a hearing before a bishop. If any advocates or *iurisconsulti* acting on behalf of said cleric (i.e. the plaintiff) persist in pleading the case before a bishop, they are to be punished.[48] An analogous ruling can be found at Theodosian Code 2. 1. 9 (Arcadius and Honorius to Archelaus, Augustal Prefect, given at Constantinople, 397), where it is stated that civil cases are not to be lodged before a military court without an imperial rescript; if an advocate nonetheless conducts such a case then he shall be fined ten pounds of gold. In both the 452 and the 397 constitutions, then, the drafter expects that litigants will attempt to continue to lodge 'illicit' cases at the courts of bishops and military officers, with the collusion of forensic practitioners.[49]

Valentinian III's *Novel* 35 also states that a plaintiff who is a layperson can compel an adversary who is a cleric *of any rank* to answer charges in a 'public court'. Section 1 of the text clarifies that this rule also applies to bishops, but offers a special privilege: a bishop can appoint a procurator when summoned to appear before a magistrate having been accused of certain 'criminal' actions (forcible entry, seizure, and 'atrocious outrages').[50] Any penalty enforced in such cases, however, would still fall on the mandator(!). As the text itself notes, procurators could not usually be appointed to act in any 'criminal' cases.[51] The drafter thus expresses the Emperor's reverence for religion, at the same time as ensuring that a magistrate could judge a bishop in both criminal and civil suits. In this respect Valentinian III's 452 *Novel* contrasts markedly with Justinian's *Novel* 86 (539): according to the drafter of Justinian's constitution, bishops were to supervise the judicial activity of provincial governors and in certain cases report back directly to the Emperor himself.[52]

[48] As also noted by Honoré, *Law in Crisis*, 264. F. Martroye, 'Les Plaidoiries devant la jurisdiction episcopale au IVe siècle', *BSNAF* (1918), 136–9, does not seem to have been aware of this text when he concluded that advocates did not plead in cases heard by bishops.

[49] See also *CI* 1. 3. 25 (Marcian to Constantine PP, 456), esp. ss. 1 and 2.; *CI* 1. 4. 13 (Marcian, 456); *CI* 1. 3. 32 (given at Constantinople, 472); *CI* 1. 3. 36, s. 2 (given at Constantinople, 484).

[50] On bishops and violence see L. Dossey, 'Judicial Violence and the Ecclesiastical Courts in Late Antique North Africa', in R. W. Mathisen, *Law, Society and Authority in Late Antiquity* (Oxford: OUP, 2001), 98–114, and Gaddis, *There is No Crime*.

[51] Compare the discussion at the fourth session of the Synod of Constantinople (16 Nov. 448), Schwartz, *ACO* II. 1. 1, 563–4: Eutyches wishes to speak through an *entoleus* (an agent or representative) and Bishop Meliphthongus wants to refer the decision of whether he can or not to the Emperor.

[52] For further discussion see H. Jaeger, 'Justinien et l'episcopalis audientia', *RHDFE* 38 (1960), 214–62.

So far I have discussed the bishop's 'court' from the almost exclusive perspective of relevant late Roman imperial constitutions; this has been necessary because, as Claudia Rapp has commented, 'The laws on the judicial powers of bishops have become something of a touchstone in the evaluation of the relation between emperor and church during the period when Christianity was gaining public recognition.'[53] Under my proposed reading, however, these 'laws', at least up until Valentinian III, are in fact imperial reactions to a series of highly specific procedural questions that arose *out of the practice of the bureaucratic courts.* If we now turn to evidence from outside the Codes, we can see that case-specific circumstances could also provoke a more 'informal' interaction, or even collaboration, between fourth- to sixth-century imperial magistrates and bishops. Gregory of Nazianzen relates one such instance concerning a divorce case: Verianus, a citizen of Nazianzus, wanted his daughter to divorce her husband, and the Prefect Olympius asked Gregory to interrogate the woman and report back to him. According to Gregory, the divorce was contrary to Christian law, 'but the Roman law may judge otherwise'.[54] This type of more informal consultation between 'secular' and episcopal legal judgment also occured in the prosecution of heresy cases. Imperial constitutions could specify that membership of a certain named Christian sect should be deemed by law heretical; however, the successful application of that general law to a particular case depended on the extent to which the individual defendant could be subsumed under the heretical 'category' specified by the legislation. A magistrate might thus call upon the theological expertise of a bishop as either 'expert' witness or 'expert' prosecutor.[55]

If we leave the questions of juridical classification to one side and adopt a more 'bottom–up' perspective on the bishop's involvement with legal disputes, there is evidence from the early fourth century onwards to suggest that the structural organization of the *episcopalis audientia* came increasingly to mirror that of the bureaucratic courts. This was partly, as we shall see in Chapter 7, a development that occurred across the Eastern and Western Empires; but it also no doubt depended on individual bishops, their own backgrounds and social networks, and the specific nature

[53] Rapp, *Holy Bishops*, 242.

[54] Gregory Nazianzen, *Eps.* 144–6. (ed. P. Gallay, *Saint Gregoire de Nazianze, Lettres*, ii (Paris: Les Belles Lettres, 1967), 35–8)

[55] See Part III below.

of the episcopal see over which they held authority. Ambrose in Milan was apparently besieged by litigants.[56] Augustine in North Africa claimed that he too judged cases 'concerning gold, silver, farms and herds' on a daily basis.[57] We should not assume, however, that the increasingly 'civil' apparatus of the *episcopalis audientia* convinced everyone: writing in 386, Libanius contrasts a charge being lodged before Flavianus, the bishop of Antioch, with a charge brought before 'a real court of law'.[58]

Documentary evidence from the fourth and fifth centuries suggests that procedural norms for lodging a case before a bishop could be adapted directly from late Roman law. *P.Oxy.* VI. 903 is an example of a *libellus conventionis*, submitted to a bishop, requesting the initiation of civil proceedings and providing an account of the legal foundation of the plaintiff's claim.[59] *P.Lond. Inv.* 2217, dated to the late fifth century and addressed to the 'most holy and most pious bishop Apa Theodorus', ends with the plaintiff's request that the bishop issue a summons for the defendant to appear in court.[60] With regard to the procedures followed by a bishop himself, canons from the church councils of Arles (314) and Hippo (415) refer to Roman procedural regulations governing the capacity of witnesses and the evaluation of evidence in the context of bishops' judicial hearings.[61] Passages from Basil of Caesarea's mid-fourth-century *Moralia* also lay out the conduct of the episcopal 'judge' with specific reference to the norms and principles of Roman procedure.[62] Gregory Nazianzen, moreover, states that Basil's

[56] See Augustine, *Confessions* 6. 3. 12.

[57] Augustine, *Ep.* 33. 5, discussed by Harries, *Law and Empire*, 204. See in general F. Martroye, 'Saint Augustin et la compétence de la jurisdiction ecclésiastique au Ve siècle', *MSNAF* 70 (1910), 1–78; C. Gebbia, 'S. Agostino e l'episcopalis audientia', *L'Africa Romana*, 8 (1989), 683–99; S. Toscano, 'Casi di ordinaria giustizia nelle epistole Divjak di Agostino', *AARC* 11 (1996), 541–63; and N. Lenski, 'Evidence for the Audientia Episcopalis in the New Letters of Augustine', in R. Mathisen (ed.), *Law, Society and Authority in Late Antiquity* (Oxford: OUP, 2001), 83–97.

[58] Libanius, *Oration* 30. 19 (tr. A. F. Norman, Loeb ii. 118).

[59] The factual circumstances of this case are discussed by J. Lamoreaux, 'Episcopal Courts in Late Antiquity', *Journal of Early Christian Studies*, 3 (1995), 143–7, at 157. See also J. Lammeyer, 'Die "audientia episcopalis" in Zivilsachen der Laien im römischen Kaiserrecht und in den Papyri', *Aegyptus*, 13 (1933), 200–1.

[60] The papyrus is re-edited and translated, with commentary, by H. I. Bell, 'The Episcopalis Audientia in Byzantine Egypt', *Byzantion*, 1 (1924), 139–44.

[61] As noted by F. Bossowski, 'Quo modo usu forensi audientiae episcopalis suadente non nulla praecepta ad instar iuris graeci aut hebraici etc. in iure romano recepta sint, exponitur', *ACII* 1 (1935), 361–410.

[62] Basil, *Moralia* 51. 4–5 (*PG* 31. 761). On the handling of disputes within monastic communities see Basil, *Regulae Fusius Tractatae* 49, 'de iis quae in controversiam veniunt inter fratres' (*PG* 31. 1037–40).

case-specific judgments were collected and used as precedents by other bishops when delivering sentences in analogous cases, again suggesting a comparison with forensic practices as discussed in Part I above.[63]

A further correspondence between 'secular' and ecclesiastical judicial practices lies in the fact that, in both spheres, cases were usually open to public attendance. The prologue to *P.Lips.* 43 records that the case was heard in the gateway of the Catholic church and was attended by both ecclesiastical and civic officials.[64] Moreover, a number of Christian basilicas were in fact converted judicial basilicas. Examples from North Africa include a church at Tipasa, situated in the forum and converted from a civil to a Christian basilica in the early fifth century; two churches at Lepcis Magna, both converted from civil basilicas during the fifth or early sixth centuries; and a basilica at Sabratha, converted during the fourth century.[65] The internal architecture of the civil tribunal may equally have been appropriated in Christian contexts.[66] In some instances, then, the *episcopalis audientia* assimilated the very fabric of late Roman judicial architecture.

As in bureaucratic trial-proceedings and cases settled by arbitration, *notarii* seem to have been employed to record *sententiae* delivered in episcopal hearings.[67] The papyrus *SB* 6097 (fourth century) records an ecclesiastical sentence that was conserved in a private archive. Records of ecclesiastical sentences may have been deposited in city archives, in addition to their conservation in episcopal registers or private collections:

63 Gregory Nazianzen, *Oration* 43, 'in laudem Basilii Magni', 34 (*PG* 36. 541).

64 On the places where legal audiences before bishops were held see L. Lavan, 'The Political Topography of the Late Antique City: Activity Spaces in Practice', in L. Lavan, and W. Bowden (eds.), *Theory and Practice in Late Antique Archaeology* (Leiden and Boston: Brill, 2003), 314–37 at 325.

65 For Tipasa and Lepcis Magna see I. Gui, N. Duval, and J.P. Caillet, *Basiliques chrétiennes d'Afrique du Nord*, i (Paris: Collection des Études Augustiniennes 129, 1992), 27–9; for Sabratha see N. Duval, 'Une basilique chrétienne à deux absides à Sabratha?', *RE Aug.* 33 (1987), 269–301. H. Rheinfelder, *Kultsprache und Profansprache in den romanischen Ländern* (Florence: Genf, 1933), 78, suggests that the adoption of the term 'basilica' by Christians in the early 4th cent. was motivated by its judicial connotations. For further discussion see J. M. David, 'Le Tribunal dans la basilique: évolution fonctionnelle et symbolique de la république à l'empire', in *Architecture et société de l'archaïsme grec à la fin de la république romaine* (Paris and Rome: Collection de l'École française de Rome 66, 1983), 219–41.

66 H. Leclercq, 'Chaire episcopale', in F. Cabrol (ed.), *Dictionnaire d'archéologie chrétienne et de liturgie*, i (Paris: Letouzey et Ané, 1913), 19–75.

67 See in general, Teitler, *Notarii and Exceptores*. M. A. Handley, 'One Hundred and Fifty-Two Addenda to PLRE from Gaul, Spain and Britain', *Historia* (2005), 93–105, at 94, includes a previously unnoted(!) *notarius* (*c*. 471–94) to a certain Bishop Basilius, who was buried at Aix and a 6th-cent. *notarius* to Caesarius of Arles, buried at Arles.

Augustine, *Ep.* 88 (406) mentions that the records of a case heard before the episcopal 'court' at Hippo could be consulted in the municipal archives. During the fifth century the papal *scrinium* apparently archived copies of judicial acts relevant to ecclesiastical 'legal' processes at Rome, including records of sureties, oaths, donations, testaments, accusations, and manumissions.[68]

From the fourth century onwards there is also evidence for some bishops being assisted by lay *assessores* in their adjudication of cases: *P.Lips.* 43 records the earliest extant example of an episcopal (arbitration) sentence from Egypt, and a certain Bishop Plousianos is attended by lay advisers in a matter concerning laws of inheritance. For the Eastern Empire, the sixth-century *Life of Euthymius* by Cyril of Scythopolis (himself apparently the son of a *scholastikos*) mentions a certain Eudoxius who acted as a legal adviser to a bishop.[69] Finally, from at least the mid-fifth century, the bishop of Rome seems to have acquired a permanent staff of lay *assessores* and *iurisperiti*—Pope Leo refers to their involvement in the 443 prosecutions against crypto-Manichees (*Ep.* 15). In addition to Valentinian III's *Novel*, discussed above, there is some further (limited) evidence to suggest that advocates could be hired to plead before episcopal hearings. For example, Basil of Caesarea describes the procedure for freeing slaves via an ecclesiastical process (*manumissio in ecclesia*) as involving turning up on the appointed day and hiring advocates on the spot—thus suggesting not only that advocates were used in ecclesiastical manumissions, but also that they were hanging around churches and episcopal residences hoping to pick up clients.[70]

Individual bishops could also opt to delegate the adjudication of cases; again, in keeping with the practices discussed in Chapter 2 above, certain bishops seem to have preferred their delegated 'judges' to have had some previous training as advocates. The ecclesiastical historian

[68] On the papacy's development of a 'central' archive see C. Pietri, *Roma Christiana: Recherches sur l'Eglise de Rome, son organization, sa politique, son idéologie de Miltiade à Sixte III (311–440)* (Rome: Bibliothèque des Écoles Françaises d'Athènes et de Rome, 1976), 675–6, and O. Bucci, 'La genesi della struttura del diritto della Chiesa latina e del diritto delle Chiese Cristiane Orientali in rapporto allo svolgimento storico del diritto romano e del diritto bizantino', *Apollinaris*, 65 (1992), 93–135, at 131.

[69] For discussion of Cyril of Scythopolis see B. Flusin, *Miracle et histoire dans l'œuvre de Cyrille de Scythopolis* (Paris: Études Augustiniennes, 1983). On bishops' legal advisers see also Cyril's *Life of Sabas* 75.

[70] Basil, *Homily* 13. 3; II, 116, A, B. On this passage see S. Giet, *Les Idées et l'action sociales de saint Basile* (Paris: Librairie Lecoffre, 1941), 86.

Socrates claims that Silvanus, bishop of Troas, had formerly been a rhetorician who learnt his art at the school of a certain 'Troilus the sophist'; as bishop of Troas, Silvanus stopped the practice of delegating cases to clerics to judge, once it came to his attention that they were making money out of the disputants; Silvanus instead had all the case documents delivered to himself and then summoned a pious lay advocate to whom he committed the adjudication of the case. Through this action, according to Socrates at least, Silvanus acquired a high reputation amongst 'all classes of persons'.[71] Similarly, in a letter addressed to a certain Elias, a practising lay *scholastikos*, Theodoret, bishop of Cyrhus, requests that the former assume adjudication of a case involving church property. The letter begins with a general exhortation to Elias's practice of his forensic art:

> Legislators have made laws in aid of the oppressed and advocates have practised the orator's arts to help those that stand in need of fair defence. You, my friend, have studied eloquence and the law. Now put your art into practice and use it to put down the oppressors, help those that are oppressed by them and defend them with the law as with a shield.[72]

The case that Theodoret asks Elias to hear involves a certain Abraham, who has been settled 'for a long time' on an estate belonging to the church and has committed a number of crimes; Theodoret does not wish Abraham to be delivered to the 'authorities', but asks Elias to hear the victims of the crimes and then compel Abraham to restore what he has stolen. Rather than delegating cases to a lay advocate, Epiphanius (the fourth-century bishop of Constantia in Cyprus) apparently preferred to delegate cases to his deacon Sabinus who held the office of *defensor ecclesiae*. According to his biographer, Epiphanius preferred to exploit the 'in-house' forensic expertise of an advocate for the church.[73]

'Secular' forensic practice, then, clearly had an important impact on the structural development and functioning of ecclesiastical jurisdiction in legal matters; we can even speak of the dim beginnings of a mirroring between forensic offices in the 'secular' and 'ecclesiastical' spheres from at

[71] Socrates, *HE* 7. 37, discussed by Jones, *Later Roman Empire*, 480, and T. Urbaincznk, *Socrates of Constantinople: Historian of Church and State* (Ann Arbor: University of Michigan Press, 1997), 111–12. *CI.* 1. 4. 29 (530) sought to regulate the legal fees and tips charged in episcopal hearings.

[72] Theodoret, *Ep. Sirm.* 10 (*SC* 98. 36–8).

[73] Polybius, *Life of Epiphanius* 55 (*PG* 41. 93A). Polybius claims that Sabinus 'dedicated his entire day to judging lawsuits' (although one wonders here whether there is a connection with the claims made by Possidius in his *Life of Augustine*, 12).

least as early as the fourth century.[74] In the following sections, however, I shall widen the parameters of our discussion beyond late Roman courtrooms and episcopal hearings by discussing the evidence for the forensic training and practice of key ecclesiastical figures. Up to this point I have deliberately left the question of 'Christian' versus 'pagan' or 'secular' education to one side, in favour of stressing how skills learnt in the rhetorical schools and in forensic practice were applied in a wealth of different ecclesiastical/theological contexts.[75] Of course, late Roman ecclesiastics came from a wide variety of social contexts, including uneducated and humble backgrounds: coal-burners, farmers, soldiers, labourers, fullers, shepherds, and linen weavers to name but a few.[76] We should thus not assume, by any means, that all ecclesiastics were literate, let alone literary. The marked late antique rise in the use of rhetorical topoi stressing the power of the simple and the unlettered *vis-à-vis* the worldly, however, is undoubtedly related to the fact that ecclesiastical appointments were increasingly made on the basis of education (and wealth).

Around the same time as the Emperor Justinian laid down that members of the clergy could not be ordained unless they were acquainted with letters, a Syrian scribe was copying out the story of a heated altercation between a 'simple', 'unlettered' elderly monk (who nonetheless evidences a dazzling array of rhetorical devices and a finely honed skill for scriptural exegesis) and a certain advocate (*dikanikos*), a 'man of the world' (*kosmikos*) skilled in 'wisdom' (*sophos*).[77] In the course of their dispute over the nature of justice and the ascetic life, the monk advises the advocate to 'follow up [his] secular training in rhetoric and law by embracing the spiritual law also, and undertake labor in the cause of piety and religion' (section 2). The advocate, 'wearied by the arguments', eventually exclaims:

[74] See also Ch. 7 below.

[75] For a discussion relating to 'how Greek *paideia* came to be replaced by Christian education' see S. Rubenson, 'Philosophy and Simplicity: The Problem of Classical Education in Early Christian Biography', in T. Hägg and P. Rousseau, *Greek Biography and Panegyric in Late Antiquity* (Berkeley, Los Angeles, and London: University of California Press, 2000), 110–39.

[76] See Rapp, *Holy Bishops*, 156, 172–83, and 199–203, with further bibliography.

[77] Justinian, *Novel* 123. 12 (546) and Mark the Hermit, 'Disputation with an advocate', in G.-M. de Durand, Traités. *Marc le Moine: Introduction, texte critique, traduction, notes et index*, *SC* 455 (Paris: Éditions du Cerf, 2000), ii. 26–92. The only extended discussion of this text that I am aware of is by T. Ware, 'The Ascetic Writings of Mark the Hermit' (Oxford, D.Phil. thesis, 1965).

Monk, I wonder at the machinations of your mind, not to mention your astuteness, in which though you accuse others, you yourself indulge. Lacking a liberal education, you take refuge in divine folly, claiming that that is the highest wisdom and pleasing to God, to which you join prayer and labour undertaken out of piety, so that you use piety to paper over your obvious lack of education (*apaideusia*).[78]

With that, the advocate gets up and leaves, but nonetheless makes a promise to return the next day; the text continues, 'the old man, permitting him to leave, turned around and groaned'. Even if we conclude that this story is purely 'fictional', the rhetorical situation that it portrays was not: individuals who had trained and/or practised as forensic advocates and *iurisperiti* were a fixed part of late Roman ecclesiastical and monastic life.

LEGAL EXPERTS

The question of whether the minor classical *iurisperitus* 'Tertullianus'—fragments of whose works *De Castrensi Peculio Liber Singularis* and *Quaestionum Libri Octo* appear in the *Digest*[79]—should be identified with the second-century Church Father of the same name has exercised scholarly imaginations since late antiquity itself. Tertullian himself is silent on whether he either studied or practised Roman law, leaving no evidence save his deployment of a certain 'juridical phraseology', and his case offers a caution against drawing firm conclusions concerning educational backgrounds on the basis of late Roman hagiography.[80] The 1906 exchange between Schlossmann and De Labriolle neatly illustrates the problems involved in using 'stylistic' criteria to judge concerning legal expertise: the same textual evidence can be used to justify opposing conclusions. After carefully weighing up Tertullian's *phraseology*, Schlossmann argued that, although it is drawn from the ideas and institutions of law, it is often superficial and sometimes does not correspond to true juridical concepts: the theologian was not the jurist.[81] De Labriolle countered with the assertion that, regardless of

78 Mark the Hermit, *Disputation with an Advocate*, 14.

79 The juristic fragments are collected by Lenel, *Palingenesia iuris civilis*, ii, col. 341–3.

80 Eusebius, *HE* 2. 2. 4; Lactantius, *Divine Institutes* 5. 1. 23 and 5. 43; and Jerome, *De Vir. Inl.* 53. Beck argues that Jerome used details gleaned from the 'jurist' Tertullian's work *De castrensi peculio liber singularis* in his biographical listing for the 'theologian' Tertullian.

81 H. Schlossmann, 'Tertullian im Lichte der Jurisprudenz', *ZSS, Kan. Abt.* 27 (1906), 251–75 and 407–30

the accuracy of Tertullian's copying of judicial phrases, his *method of argumentation* 'perfectly conformed to the mentality of a jurist'.[82] It was left to Steinwenter, in his important 1932 review of Beck's monograph *Römisches Recht bei Tertullian und Cyprian*, to advance the debate by moving it away from a question surrounding a coincidence of identities. According to Steinwenter, Beck's assembly of extracts from Tertullian's texts—intended to show him as a jurist—in fact revealed him as an *advocatus*.[83] However, as Sider has more recently argued:

> It is not enough simply to note traditional rhetorical sequences in the development of [Tertullian's] thought. The formative power of these canons can be truly gauged only when we have perceived how skilfully he can adapt, rearrange, and transpose the orders prescribed by the textbooks, for such freedom implies a total absorption of the rules into one's thinking.[84]

As with the advocates discussed in Chapter 4 above, Tertullian was not concerned with rigidly following the rules of forensic rhetoric when they did not suit his polemical, apologetic, and on occasion exegetical purposes.[85]

In common with many early Christian authors, Tertullian's treatises are full of references and allusions to Roman law and legal practice.[86] 'Theologians' (from St Paul onwards) shared in his technique of stretching 'Christian' doctrine by applying legal metaphors to it—a practice which Gaudemet aptly terms *la construction juridique au service de la théologie*.[87] For example, in the *De Testimonio Animae* forensic practice provides Tertullian with a dramatic rhetorical framework; in the

[82] P. De Labriolle, 'Tertullien jurisconsulte', *NRHDFE* 30 (1906), 5–27.

[83] A. Steinwenter, *ZRG, Rom. Abt.* 52 (1932), 412–16, reviewing Beck, *Römisches Recht bei Tertullian und Cyprian.*

[84] R. D. Sider, *Ancient Rhetoric and the Art of Tertullian* (Oxford: OUP, 1972), 126.

[85] T. D. Barnes, *Tertullian: A Historical and Literary Study* (Oxford: OUP, 1971); G. Eckert, *Orator Christianus: Untersuchungen zur Argumentationskunst in Tertullians Apologeticum* (Stuttgart: Franz Steiner Verlag, 1993); D. I. Rankin, 'Was Tertullian a Jurist?', *Studia Patristica*, 31 (1997), 335–42; and R. Martini, 'Ancora a proposito di Tertulliano', *Bulletino dell'Istituto di diritto romano Vittorio Scialoja*, 39 (2003), 117–26, all argue for Tertullian 'the Church Father' as skilled in forensic rhetoric.

[86] I. Vitton, *Concetti giuridici nelle opere di Tertulliano* (Rome: L'Erma di Bretschneider, 1924, reissued 1972), 17–55, gives the most exhaustive catalogue of Tertullian's legal terminology—arranged according to subject divisions within Roman law.

[87] Gaudemet, *Le Droit romain dans le littérature chrétienne*, 30. Gaudemet cites as examples: Tertullian's famous extended metaphor of the Christian community as a corpus (*Apology* 39. 1); his metaphor of baptism as a pact with the Holy Spirit (*De Pudicitia* 12); and his treatment of the metaphor of sinner as debtor and Christ as creditor (*De fuga* 12 and *De anima* 35).

De Praescriptione Haereticorum it dictates his subject-matter. Tertullian styled the latter as a text whereby the controversy between 'Catholics' and 'heretics' would be ended once and for all on a technical point of Roman law: *praescriptio*, a juridical objection through which a defendant sought to bar the suit in the form in which the plaintiff entered it.[88] His first defence denies heretics the right to use scripture as their judicial proof and is thus a *praescriptio* of evidence.[89] The second defence is the prescription of time: only the universal Catholic Church has communion with the Apostolic Church.[90] Tertullian thus drew his anti-heretical arsenal from the advocate's rules of procedure, rather than the jurist's concepts of substantive law. Whereas the *De Praescriptione Haereticorum* uses Roman procedural law to construct a general defence against all heresies, the treatises *Adversus Hermogenem*, *Adversus Marcionem*, and *Adversus Praxean* employ forensic argumentation in an attempt to silence specific individuals. In each of the three texts, Tertullian visualizes court scenes in which the 'heretical' defendant (or often a 'heretical' opinion of the defendant—personified for dramatic effect) is subjected to cross-examination, according to the techniques outlined under the 'qualitative' *stasis* of forensic rhetoric.[91] Tertullian, then, literally subjected his adversaries to trial by treatise. He thereby created a rhetorical template which set an important precedent for later Christian authors, who were writing at a time when heretics were subject to actual civil and criminal prosecutions.[92] Walter Ullmann was right to trace the 'legalism' of the medieval papacy back to Tertullian; however, this 'legalism' was that of the advocate, rather than the (*Digest*) jurist.[93]

Tertullian aside, evidence for other ecclesiastics and prominent lay Christians as *iurisconsulti* has been relatively neglected—with the

[88] For further discussion see J. K. Stirnimann, *Die praescriptio Tertullians im Lichte des römisches Rechtes und der Theologie* (Freiburg, Switzerland: Paulusverlag, 1949) and A. Sergène, 'Tertullien "de praescriptione hereticorum" XXXVII, 4 et la "longi temporis praescriptio"', in *Études offertes à Jean Macqueron* (Aix-en-Provence: University of Aix-en-Provence, 1970), 605–12.

[89] *De Praescriptione* 1–15 (*CCSL* 1. 187–99).

[90] Ibid. 21 (*CCSL* 1. 202–3).

[91] e.g. *Adversus Marcionem* 2. 20 (with discussion in Sider, *Ancient Rhetoric*, 82–3).

[92] Including the 'apostate' Emperor Julian: at *Against the Galileans* 41e Julian imagines himself in a court of law accusing Christian 'dogmas' and his opponents must respond to his points before they bring counter-suits. 'Trial by treatise', of course, had a much wider Graeco-Roman context (including e.g. Plato's *apologia* for Socrates and Apuleius' for himself).

[93] W. Ullmann, *A History of Political Thought: The Middle Ages* (London: Penguin, 1965), 20.

exception of the third-century Gregory 'Thaumaturgus', bishop of Neocaesarea, whose account of his early life provides one of the first references to the famous law school at Beirut.[94] The fifth-century church historian Sozomenus mentions a certain Triphyllius, bishop of the Ledri, who had practised law at Beirut and was later rebuked by Spyridon, a wonder-working peasant bishop, for substituting the word 'couch' for 'bed' whilst preaching the Gospel of Matthew; thus, states Sozomenus, Spyridon taught the people how 'to keep the man who is proud of his learning under control'.[95] Also within the Eastern Empire, the polemicist Asterius of Cappadocia, branded a 'many-headed sophist' by Athanasius, may in fact have trained as a *iurisconsultus*.[96] This biographical detail is particularly interesting in the light of Asterius' involvement in the protracted and complex legal wranglings of the post-Nicaean (so-called) 'Arian' party.[97]

In the Western Empire, the legal education of Sulpicius Severus at Bordeaux is clearly documented by his contemporary Paulinus of Nola, who states that Sulpicius had practised a forensic career before his baptism in 389.[98] According to his 'hagiographer', the fifth-century Bishop Germanus of Auxerre had studied rhetoric in Milan and then law at Rome, before becoming an advocate at the court of the Praetorian Prefect. Germanus' life before his ordination had been 'part of God's secret design': his eloquence prepared him for preaching, his knowledge of law prepared him to act with justice, and his wife acted as a 'witness to his chastity'(!).[99] The civil career of Ambrose from legal *assessor* to *Consularis*

94 Gregory Thaumaturgus, In *Originem* 5 (62). Gregory does not seem to have continued his law studies at Beirut, despite the fact that Jerome, *De Vir. Inl.* 65, Socrates, *HE* 4. 27, and Cassiodorus, *Hist. Tripart.* 8. 8 state the contrary. For discussion see J. M. Mélèze-Modrzejewski, 'Grégoire Le Thaumaturge et le droit romain: A propos d'une édition récente', *RHDFE* 49 (1971), 312–24.

95 Sozomenus, *HE*. 1. 11.

96 Athanasius, *De Synodis* 18. Jerome, *De Vir. Inl.* 94, lists Asterius' literary output—all of these works were thought lost until Richard and Skard discovered a number of his expositions on the Psalms, now edited by W. Kinzig, *Asterius, Psalmenhomilien* (Stuttgart: Anton Hiersemann, 2002). See also M. Vinzent, *Die theologischen Fragmente, Asterius von Kappadokien; Einleitung, kritischer Text* (Leiden: Brill, 1993).

97 For Asterius the *iurisconsultus*, see E. Skard, 'Eine Bemerkung über spätrömisches Strafrecht in einer Homilie des "Sophisten" Asterios', *Symbolae Osloenses*, 25 (1947), 80–2. On Asterius' doxology see R. P. Vaggione, *Eunomius of Cyzicus and the Nicene Revolution* (Oxford: OUP, 2000), 66–7.

98 Paulinus of Nola, *Ep*. 5. 5.

99 'Constantius of Lyons', *Vita Sancti Germani*, *SC* 112 (ed. R. Borius) 1. 122–4. Compare the educational background in the *Vita Sancti Desiderii*, discussed by P. Riché,

Aemiliae et Liguriae in 374 is outlined by his contemporary biographer, Paulinus (a former ecclesiastical notary and deacon at Milan).[100] In the Middle Ages Ambrose's reputation as a legal scholar was further enhanced by the claim of the Nestorian bishop of Nisibis and Armenia, Ebed-Ieshu (d. 1318), that Ambrose had made a collection of laws on the order of the Emperor Valentinian.[101] Although no support can be adduced for Ebed-Ieshu's specific claim, the existence of the *Sirmondian Constitutions* testifies to the fact that late antique ecclesiastics were indeed independently compiling 'collections' of imperial legislation.[102]

Alypius, the future bishop of Thagaste, studied law at Rome before serving three times as *assessor* to the court of the imperial fisc, one of the most prestigious appointments available to late Roman *iurisperiti*.[103] During his episcopacy Alypius' skills as a *iurisperitus* were much in demand. At the 411 'council of Carthage' he was named second, after the Primate Aurelius, amongst the mandated Catholic *actores*. This election may well have been influenced by his forensic reputation: the 411 conference was not merely a council of 'Catholic' and 'Donatist' bishops, but a legal procedure according to the *ius publicum*. Accordingly, the imperial mandate instituting the proceedings made allowances for each side to institute seven *actores*, seven *consiliarii*, and four *notarii* to draft the records.[104] The *acta* testify to Alypius' interventions at key moments

Education and Culture in the Barbarian West, Sixth through Eighth Centuries, tr. J. J. Contreni (Columbia, SC: University of South Carolina Press, 1976), 14.

[100] Paulinus of Milan, *Vita Amb.* 2. 5 (412/13). On Ambrose's legal knowledge see Liebs, *Die Jurisprudenz im spätantiken Italien*, 62–3; J. Gaudemet, 'Droit séculier et droit de l'église chez Ambroise', in G. Lazzati (ed.), *Ambrosius Episcopus: Atti del Congresso internazionale di studi Ambrosiani nel XVI. centenario della elevazione di sant'Ambrogio alla cattedra episcopale*, i (Milan: Vita e pensiero, 1976), 286–315; and B. Hebein, 'St Ambrose and Roman Law' (St Louis University, Ph.D, thesis, 1970).

[101] Ebed-Ieshu, *Collectio Canonum Syndicorum tractatus*, iii, noted by E. Volterra, 'Collatio Legum Mosaicarum et Romanarum', *Memorie della classe di scienze morali, storiche e filologiche, Accademia Nazionale dei Lincei*, 6th ser. 3 (1930), 3–123, and Nelson, *Überlieferung, Aufbau und Stil von Gai. Institutiones*, 109 n. 9.

[102] The compilation was almost certainly made in an ecclesiastical context. For further discussion see M. Vessey, 'The Origins of the Collectio Sirmondiana: A New Look at the Evidence', in J. Harries and M. Wood, *The Theodosian Code* (London: Duckworth, 1993), 178–99.

[103] See Alypius 8, *PLRE* i. 47. Compare Maximus, bishop of Pavia, 495–514 (Maximus 14, *PLRE* ii. 746) who held the important post of adviser to the *comes sacrarum largitionum* before his episcopal appointment.

[104] The 'Catholic' *actores* and *consiliarii* are listed at *SC* 195. 670, ll. 374–85. The 'Donatist' *actores* are named at *SC* 195. 798–800, and an (incomplete) list of their *consiliarii* is given at *SC* 224. 924. For discussion of the personalities of the 411 'Catholic' and 'Donatist' *consiliarii* see *SC* 194. 105–6.

in the preliminary dispute concerning the juridical basis of the case between Catholics and Donatists.

Alypius' pivotal intervention in the *cause célèbre* of the North African church, the 'Apiarian incident', also stands as testimony to his training as a *iurisperitus*. The background to this case is complex. In early 418 Apiarius, a presbyter of the diocese of Sicca Veneria in Africa Proconsularis, was condemned by his Bishop Urbanus for an unknown offence; Apiarius deserted the African courts and sought redress from the bishop of Rome. In the late summer of 418, Pope Zosimus sent legates to Africa with a *commonitorium* supporting Apiarius. The papal legates held a preliminary audience with the Primate Aurelius in September 418, but it was not until Easter 419 that Zosimus' papal successor renewed his predecessor's commission to the legation. A council was summoned for Carthage on 25 May 419.[105] The proceedings of the 419 council were brilliantly structured by the North African bishops in a sustained defence against the contents of the papal *commonitorium*. The papal brief had cited two canons, thought to be from the Council of Nicaea, in support of Rome's intervention in the Apiarian case; Aurelius requested that the papal legates commence by reading those canons aloud.[106] Having then presented Zosimus' written documentation, the papal delegation opened debate on the first canon of the *commonitorium*. Barely into his *peroratio* the legate was silenced by a formal intervention from Alypius:

> Concerning this canon, we wrote to the Pope last year, and we declare for the record, that we will observe that which was established at Nicaea. I am compelled to say this as when we inspected our Greek copies of the canons of the Nicene Synod, I do not know why, but we were in no way able to find the canons cited by you [*sc.* the papal side].[107]

Alypius had spent the winter months of 418–19, as he must have spent many months as a *iurisconsultus*, comparing two versions of a written juridical text and constructing a watertight legal defence around the results.[108] Aurelius' request that the legates open with a reading

[105] Following Cross, 'History and Fiction', 240–3. See also J. E. Merdinger, *Rome and the African Church in the Time of Augustine* (New Haven and London: Yale University Press, 1997), 111–35.

[106] *CCSL* 149. 89–90 ll. 15–27.

[107] Ibid. 91, ll. 72–7.

[108] A parallel can be found in Augustine's requests to the *iurisconsultus* Eustochius (*Ep.* 24*), see Ch. 3 above.

of the (henceforth disputed) canons had been an orchestrated move. Alypius thus proposed that authentic copies of the Nicene Council should be sought from Constantinople, Alexandria, and Antioch and any decision delayed until those copies arrived in Africa. Meanwhile the bishops would observe the disputed canon, but would incorporate their own African texts into the record of the present council.[109] The debate surrounding the second canon followed exactly the same premiss and structure, with Bishop Novatus and Augustine now applying Alypius' forensic techniques.[110] The arrival of the Nicene canons from Constantinople confirmed Alypius' defence, and a legal dossier (the 'Apiarian Codex') was accordingly drafted as a triumphant vindication of the African church's case.[111]

ADVOCATES

Ossius bishop said: I consider it necessary that this be gone into with all care and attention: If some rich man or forensic advocate is thought worthy of becoming a bishop, he should not be established (in this station) until he has served as lector and deacon and presbyter, that he may ascend to the highest grade of bishop (if he is worthy) one step at a time.[112]

At the Council of Serdica in 343 Bishop Ossius highlighted the fact that forensic advocates were of crucial importance to the (Western) post-Constantinian Church, through his tacit admission that they were being promoted straight to episcopal seats.[113] This practice, however, also posed certain dilemmas for a late Roman papacy intent on a rhetoric of other-worldly separation. Two decretals of Pope Siricius (384–98) raise the question of whether those who have distinguished themselves in forensic careers should be admitted to the priesthood at all—Siricius, *Ep*. 6. 3 forbids their consecration, basing his interdiction on the apostolic precepts of the early church, but his *Ep*. 10 (*Ad Gallos*)

[109] *CCSL* 149. 91, ll 86–93. [110] Ibid. 92–3.
[111] This dossier was meticulously structured; see *CC* 149. 101–49.
[112] Council of Serdica, Greek Canon X = H. Hess, *The Early Development of Canon Law and the Council of Serdica*, 2nd edn. (Oxford: OUP, 2002), 232. Compare Latin Canon 13 = Hess, 220 and Theodosian Canon 13 = Hess, 248.
[113] For further discussion of the so-called 'canons' of the Western bishops who met at Serdica see Barnes, *Athanasius and Constantius*, 78–80, and Hess, *Early Development of Canon Law*, 95–140.

offers an elegant solution: imperial functionaries can be consecrated after they have undertaken penance.[114] In the early fifth century Pope Innocent I directed the attention of the bishops of Spain to a rather more concrete problem: Christians were still busying themselves in forensic practice after they had received baptism, and some of these were being ordained—of whom Innocent mentions a certain Rufinus and Gregorius.[115] It is to individuals such as these that I shall now turn, analysing the evidence for their training as *advocati* and briefly outlining a number of different ecclesiastical contexts in which they made use of their forensic skills.[116]

A number of key late Roman bishops in the Eastern Church had received an education in forensic rhetoric. According to Jerome, Gregory bishop of Nazianzus, the 'Christian Demosthenes', had been educated by the 'sophist' Polemon, amongst others.[117] Basil of Caesarea attended rhetorical schools at Caesarea, Constantinople, and Athens, and his younger brother Gregory was a teacher of rhetoric before he was raised to the see at Nyssa; their father had been a famous rhetorician at Neocaesarea.[118] At *Vita Macrinae* 27, Gregory states that his brother returned to Caesarea in 356 in order to begin his own career as an advocate:

When the mother had arranged excellent marriages for the other sisters, such as was best in each case, Macrina's brother the great Basil returned after his long period of education, already a practised rhetor. He was puffed up beyond measure with the pride of oratory and looked down on the local dignitaries, excelling in his own estimation all the men of leading position. Nevertheless Macrina took him in hand, and with such speed did she draw him also to the

[114] Siricius, *Ep.* 6. 3 (*PL* 13. 1166A) and *Ep.* 10. 13 (*PL* 13. 1190A). A. Lenox-Conyngham, 'The Judgement of Ambrose the Bishop on Ambrose the Roman Governor', *Studia Patristica*, 17/1 (1982), 63–5, at 64, makes an interesting suggestion that Siricius' decretals may provide the context for Ambrose's condemnation of his former career at *De Paenitentia* 2. 8. 67.

[115] Innocent I, *Ep.* 3. 7 (*PL* 20. 490–1), see also his *Ep.* 37. 5 (*PL* 20. 604B). Innocent I endowed a corporation of seven lay *advocati* to represent the church of Rome in the civil courts.

[116] See also the brief discussions in Honoré, *Law in Crisis*, 4–5; Heath, *Menander: A Rhetor in Context*, 292–6; and Rapp, *Holy Bishops*, 182.

[117] Jerome, *De Vir. Inl.* 117; also Socrates, *HE* 4. 26. See in general, C. Castelli, 'L'esemplarità retorica di Gregorio di Nazianzo: Spunti per una riflessione', in Amato *et al.* (eds.), *Approches de la troisième sophistique*, 63–79.

[118] Further discussion in G. Kustas, 'Saint Basil and the Rhetorical Tradition', in P. J. Fedwick, *Basil of Caesarea: Christian, Humanist, Ascetic*, i (Toronto: Pontifical Institute of Medieval Studies, 1981), 221–79.

mark of philosophy that he forsook the glories of this world, and despised fame gained by forensic speaking, and deserted it for the busy life where one toils with one's hands.[119]

Part of Basil's later 'toil with his hands' included penning the *Moralia* (first published with a preface entitled *De Iudicio Dei*), the *Regulae Fusius Tractatae* and the *Regulae Brevius Tractatae*, which still today collectively form the legislative basis for the principal monastic rule of the Greek Church. Gregory of Nyssa, on the other hand, deployed his considerable rhetorical skill against the (so-called) 'Ariomaniac' Eunomius of Cyzicus, pointedly criticizing the latter's attempt to employ forensic rhetoric against him.[120] Little wonder, perhaps, that Gregory wrote to two students of rhetoric asking them to show his treatise 'Against the Heretic' to their teacher (probably Libanius).[121] Gregory was also used to consulting archives at the lawcourts: in section 3 of his treatise *On Virginity* he advises his audience to 'go to the law-courts and read through the laws there', so that they might learn all 'the shameful secrets of marriage' from 'the strange variety' of relevant crimes mentioned in the legal texts.

Amphilocius of Iconium became the metropolitan bishop of the new province of Lycaonia in 373 at Basil's request—having previously attended the lectures of Libanius in Antioch and practised as an advocate at Constantinople between 362 and 365.[122] His forensic skills are clearly in evidence at the Synod of Side (390), where he presided over the drafting of legal condemnations against the sects of Messalians, Euchites, and Adelphians.[123] From the beginning of his episcopacy, Amphilocius had been active in promoting legal formulae for the exclusion of named

[119] Gregory of Nyssa, *Vita Macrinae* 27 (tr. W. K. Lowther Clarke, *St Gregory of Nyssa, The Life of St Macrina* (London: SPCK, 1916), 27–8). Photius, *Bibl. Cod.* 141 (*PG* 103. 420–1) comments that Basil's discourses could be used as models of forensic style, thus rendering Plato and Demosthenes redundant.

[120] Gregory of Nyssa, *Against Eunomius*, esp. 2. 4, 2. 7, and 5. 2–4. On Eunomius' own background, which included short-hand and rhetoric, see Vaggione, *Eunomius of Cyzicus*. 1–14.

[121] Gregory of Nyssa, *Ep.* 15 to John and Maximianus, discussed by R. Kaster, *Guardians of Language: The Grammarian and Society in Late Antiquity* (Berkeley and Los Angeles, University of California Press, 1988), 79, and Maxwell, *Christianization and Communication*, 31–32.

[122] Amphilocius 4, *PLRE* i. 58; Heath, *Menander: A Rhetor in Context*, 294 (describing Amphilocius as an advocate and teacher) and Maxwell, *Christianization and Communication*, 36–41 (discussing Amphilocius as a 'rhetor and lawyer' who 'preserved the attributes of the traditional sophist').

[123] The proceedings are noted in Photius, *Bibl. Cod.* 52.

heretical sects, and Theodoret (*HE* 5. 16) mentions Amphilocius' petitions before the Emperor Theodosius I against the 'Arian heretics'. The historian also specifies that Amphilocius' second audience before Theodosius resulted in 'an edict forbidding the congregation of heretics'. Hence perhaps the drafter's use of Amphilocius as a touchstone for orthodoxy at *C.Th.* 16. 1. 3 (given at Heraclea, 381, to Auxonius, proconsul of Asia).[124] Amphilocius' contemporary, Optimus, bishop of Agdamia (Phyrgia) and Antioch, had been educated by Libanius and had practised as an advocate; he is also mentioned in *C.Th.* 16. 1. 3 as 'permitted to obtain the Catholic churches'.[125] Asterius, the metropolitan bishop of Amasea in Pontus, had also received a rhetorical education and may have practised as an advocate in Constantinople before his ordination.[126] A member of the laity rather than a cleric, the historian Sozomenus practised advocacy in Constantinople and may even have been active in the courts whilst he was engaged in writing his *Ecclesiastical History*: at 2. 3. 10–11 he refers to a certain Aquilinus, with a note in the present tense that he 'pleads cases in the same courts as I do'.[127]

The fifth-century ecclesiastical historian Socrates may not himself have practised as an advocate;[128] but he was certainly familiar with the legal scene at Constantinople. His *Ecclesiastical History* discusses a number of *rhetors* who evidently became 'Novatian' ecclesiastics at Constantinople, including Sisinnius (d. 427), an orator with senatorial connections and the 'Novatian' bishop of Constantinople, and Ablabius, an 'eminent orator from the school of Troilus', who was ordained as a presbyter at Constantinople by Chrysanthus (the then bishop of the 'Novatians' at Constantinople and himself a former *consularis* of Italy and *vicarius* of the British Isles). Ablabius was later ordained 'Novatian' bishop at Nicaea, where Socrates claims that 'he

[124] See Part III below.

[125] Kaster, *Guardians of Language*, 73, also noting Apollinarius of Laodicea as a 'rhetorician and bishop'.

[126] For discussion of Asterius' legal knowledge (rather than his rhetorical techniques) see E. Volterra, 'Considerazioni teologico-giuridiche, di Asterio di Amasea', *Rivista italiana per le scienze giuridiche*, NS 4 (1929), 3–10.

[127] 'Salamanes Hermeias Sozomenus 2', *PLRE* ii. 1023–4. For further discussion see G. Greatrex, 'Lawyers and Historians in Late Antiquity', in R. Mathisen (ed.), *Law, Society and Authority in Late Antiquity* (Oxford: OUP, 2001), 148–61.

[128] For discussion of whether Socrates deserves his epithet 'scholasticus', see M. Wallraff, *Der Kirchenhistoriker Sokrates: Untersuchungen zu Geschichtsdarstellung, Methode und Person* (Göttingen: Vandenhoeck & Ruprecht, 1997) and Urbainczn k, *Socrates of Constantinople*, 4–6.

also taught rhetoric at the same time'.[129] Returning to Constantinople, Socrates (amongst other writers) also stresses the rhetorical education of John 'Chrysostom', claiming that he 'prepared himself for the practise of civil law' but eventually decided to follow 'the example of Evagrius, who had been educated under the same masters and had some time before retired from the tumult of public business'. Socrates states that Chrysostom thus 'laid aside his legal habit and applied his mind to a reading of the sacred scriptures'.[130] Finally, Socrates also styles Chrysostom's successor as patriarch at Constantinople, Proclus the former bishop of Cyzicus, as being devoted to both rhetoric and the rhetorical schools—before he turned to preaching Christian sermons.[131]

A background in forensic advocacy was not confined to leading bishops in the East. Naucratius, the elder brother of Basil and Gregory of Nyssa, had practised as an advocate before he retired into monastic solitude at the age of 22, certain other late Romans also seem to have deserted the lawcourts in favour of the monastic life.[132] Theodore (the future bishop of Mopsuestia in Cilicia), on the other hand, apparently wavered between forensic and monastic practice: having studied rhetoric under Libanius he subsequently entered a monastery near Antioch, only to leave in order to become an advocate. In two letters, *Ad Theodorum Lapsum*, John Chrysostom took it upon himself to persuade him to return to monastic life.[133] Around 383 Theodore was consecrated as a priest and in 392 he was elevated to the episcopacy; his *Disputatio cum Macedoniano* probably dates to the same year and merits examination within the context of Theodore's former practice as an advocate. The treatise is in fact the record (or a later summary) of a disputation held at Anazabos in which Theodore defended the divinity of Christ against adherents of

[129] Socrates, *HE*. 6. 22. 20 (Sisinnius) and *HE* 7. 12 (Ablabius).

[130] This account of Chrysostom's education and background is not without its difficulties; for discussion see A. H. M. Jones, 'St John Chrysostom's Parentage and Education', *Harvard Theological Review*, 46/3 (1953), 171–3, and D. G. Hunter, 'Libanius and John Chrysostom: New Thoughts on an Old Problem', *Studi Patristica*, 22 (1989), 129–35.

[131] Socrates, *HE* 7. 41 and 43.

[132] 'Naucratius', *PLRE* i. 618; also 'Anastasius 3', *PLRE* ii. 78; 'Athanasius 5', *PLRE* ii. 176; and 'Eulogius 1', *PLRE* i. 294. On the 'reception' of imperial constitutions within monastic contexts see C. Neri, 'Ci sono testimonianze giuridiche nelle fonti monastiche?' *AARC* 15, (2005), 107–17.

[133] John Chrysostom, *Ad Theodorum Lapsum* (*PG* 47. 277–316).

the beliefs of 'Macedonius'.[134] *CTh* 16. 5. 11 (given at Constantinople, 383, to Postumianus PP) had classified 'Macedonians', amongst others, as heretics; it also granted the right to expel 'Macedonians' specifically to those who observed religion 'correctly'.[135] Theodore's *disputatio* may be styled a theological debate, but in the context of the preceding legislation it assumes the significance of a judicial enquiry.[136]

Still within the Eastern Empire, Eusebius, bishop of Dorylaeum, provides an example of a former advocate who transferred his forensic skills to theological controversy. Eusebius was an advocate at Constantinople *c.*426–30: Leontius of Byzantium describes him as a *dikanikos*, Evagrius refers to him as a *rhetor*, and Theophanes and Georgius Cedrenus as a *scholastikos*.[137] Whilst still practising as an advocate, Eusebius achieved notoriety as a result of his outspoken opposition to the 'Marian doctrines' of Nestorius, bishop of Constantinople. Following his episcopal consecration, Eusebius wasted no time in bringing accusations of heresy against Eutyches, who expounded a doctrinal position at the opposite extreme to Nestorianism. If Eusebius' proficiency in handling these 'fluid' doctrinal debates was *perhaps* informed by his training as an advocate, his behaviour at church councils definitely was. For example, at the opening of the fifth session of the Synod of Constantinople (17 November 448) a question arose as to whether Eutyches had now assented 'to all the pronouncements of the holy fathers at Nicaea and at Ephesus and all those of the blessed Cyril'. Eusebius' following exchange with Flavian, then patriarch of Constantinople, betrays his forensic training. Eusebius asks, 'Has he [Eutyches] now come to give his assent? My accusation relates not to the future but to the past. Have I already lost my case because some people have given him a formula

[134] The text is only extant in a Syriac version, ed. R. Graffin and F. Nau, *Théodore de Mopsueste, Controverse avec les Macédoniens* (Paris: Patrologie Orientalis 9, 1913).

[135] See also *C.Th.* 16. 5. 12 (given at Constantinople, Dec. 383, addressed to Postumianus PP) and *C.Th.* 16. 5. 13 (given at Constantinople, Jan. 384, addressed to Cynegius PP).

[136] Compare the *Altercatio Heracliani*, *PL suppl.* I, 345–50 (a public 'debate' between the pro-Nicene Heraclianus before Germinius, bishop of Sirmium) and Augustine, *Collatio cum Maximino Arianorum episcopum*, *PL* 42. 683–708 (Maximus 'the Arian', debates with Augustine having apparently been sent to Hippo on the orders of the governor Sigisvultus).

[137] 'Eusebius 15', *PLRE* ii. 430–1; Leontius Byz., *Contra Nestorianos et Eutychianos* III (*PG* 86. 1389) and Evagrius, *HE* 1. 9. On Evagrius' own forensic practice, see P. Allen, *Evagrius scholasticus: The Church Historian* (Louvain: Spicilegium Sacrum Lovaniense, 1981).

and said to him, "Give in to necessity: assent or sign"?' To this Flavian responds that no one is letting Eusebius drop his charges or excusing Eutyches from the necessity of defending his past. Eusebius counters with the following interjection:

> I demand that his statement [sc. Eutyches' credal subscription] not prejudice my case. I have reliable witnesses in whose presence he taught, and inculcates, perverse doctrines and embarked on disputation. When I urged him not just once or twice but many times to hold orthodox views, he still refused. Say to people in prison, 'From today stop stealing', and they will all promise to.[138]

Eusebius' point is that, having lodged a formal accusation against Eutyches as a heretic, that accusation should stand regardless of whether Eutyches now repented and conformed to the 'correct' doxology. Less than three years later we find that Eusebius has lodged two petitions against Dioscorus, bishop of Alexandria, the first adressed to the Emperor and the second to the bishops assembled at the Council of Chalcedon itself. Eusebius' petition to the Emperor, a copy of which was read out as 'evidence' at the session of Chalcedon held on 13 October 451, accused Dioscorus of sharing the beliefs of the now deposed and anathematized 'heretic' Eutyches, thus building on the earlier case and extending it by analogy. The petition to the 451 council, on the other hand, sought to annul the decisions of a previous church council (Ephesus II) to anathematize Dioscorus' teaching, and 'to make him pay the [ecclesiastical?] penalty of his crimes'. Dioscorus, however, countered Eusebius' pursuit with forensic tricks of his own.[139]

From the late fifth and early sixth centuries ecclesiastical advocates in the Eastern Empire were also admitted to the lower ranks of the clergy. Ioannes, an *ecclesiae scholasticus* at Amida, is described by the ecclesiastical historian Zacharius as a devout man and an eloquent speaker.[140] From the early sixth century Rufinus, an *ecclesiae scholasticus* of Ephraem, patriarch of Antioch, was employed in ecclesiastical prosecutions of suspected heretics. The relentless tactics used by Rufinus

[138] Schwartz, II.1.1, 423–4; tr. Price and Gaddis, *The Acts of the Council of Chalcedon*, i. 209.

[139] Price and Gaddis, *The Acts of the Council of Chalcedon*, ii. 41–3. Dioscorus obstructs the hearing of the second petition at the 451 Council partly by refusing to acknowledge that there were two processes, with the same prosecutor, but different charges, lodged separately before emperor and bishops.

[140] 'Iohannes 39', *PLRE* ii. 603. The ecclesiastical historian Zacharias practised as an advocate at Constantinople before his election as bishop of Mytilene ('Zacharias 4', *PLRE* ii. 1194–5).

when questioning John of Tella about his beliefs apparently resulted in a protest from the defendant.[141]

Bishops in Egypt knew how to exploit the forensic training of their ecclesiastical colleagues. Jerome (*De Vir. Inl.* 99) and Sozomen (*HE* 4. 9) both refer to the mid-fourth-century bishop of Thmuis, Serapion, as a *scholasticus* and praise the power of his eloquence. His skills were also noted by his metropolitan bishop Athanasius: on 19 May 356 Athanasius sent Serapion, together with four other Egyptian bishops and three Alexandrian priests, to the court of the Emperor Constantius with instructions to placate Constantius and refute the 'calumnies' of the 'Arians'.[142] Serapion's forensic skills were probably well exercised at the imperial court; according to the oft-quoted opinion of the ecclesiastical historian Theodoret, the Emperor Constantius treated the Christian church as a house of judicial business rather than the house of God.[143]

The links between forensic and ecclesiastical practice are equally apparent in the Western Empire. Juvenal famously described North Africa as a *nutricula causidicorum.*[144] This epigram can just as well be applied to the North Africa of the later Empire, with the qualification that many of her *causidici* now turned their talents to the defence of the Christian church. The early fourth-century writer Lactantius was neither cleric nor advocate; but he himself states that 'the practice of pleading imaginary cases' has helped him personally, as his 'plentiful command of rhetoric' can now be used 'to plead the cause of truth to its end'.[145] Pleading imaginary cases was part of Lactantius' work as a professor of rhetoric, the aim of which—he states—was to prepare young men for practice in the forum.

In the *Divine Institutes* (composed in the first decades of the fourth century) Lactantius presents us with a neatly packaged trio of former Christian rhetors with North African connections: Minucius Felix, Tertullian, and Cyprian.[146] The third-century Christian apologist Minucius Felix was a noted *causidicus*, who was born in North Africa but

141 'Rufinus 14', *PLRE* ii. 957.

142 Barnes, *Athanasius and Constantius*, 112.

143 Compare the 5th-cent. Alexandrian-born Isidore of Pelusium: according to his *Ep.* 1. 311, Isidore petitioned the Emperor Theodosius II to prevent Ephesian court officials from assuming judicial authority in matters of faith. See in general, E. Lyon, 'Le Droit chez Isidore de Péluse', *Études d'histoire juridique offertes à Paul Girard*, ii (Paris: Librairie Paul Geuthner, 1913), 209–22.

144 Juvenal, *Sat.* 7, 148–9.

145 Lactantius, *Div. Inst.* 1. 1. 10 (tr. Bowie and Garnsey, Lactantius, *Div. Inst.* 58).

146 Ibid. 5. 1. 22–4.

practised at Rome.[147] In contrast with Tertullian's *Apologia*, Minucius Felix structured his apologetic work (the *Octavius*) as a philosophical dialogue on the *veritas* of Christianity rather than its legality. However, the dramatic setting for the *Octavius* is forensic: the debate is conducted on the beach at Ostia whilst the three disputants are on their annual vacation from the courts at Rome.[148] The *feriae Augustae* were used as a dramatic setting by Cyprian in his *Ad Donatum* (written after 246), a highly stylized *apologia* for his own conversion. Later hagiography suggests that Cyprian was skilled in rhetoric, perhaps even holding a position in the imperial bureaucracy or practising as an advocate before his appointment as bishop of Carthage in 248–9.[149] Whether this is true or not, Cyprian may well have been the first writer, secular or ecclesiastical, to find a legal formula for the practice of leaving pious bequests to the Christian church.[150] He was certainly capable of adopting a legalistic attitude towards schismatics and heretics: neither, according to Cyprian, can be said to have any *potestas* or legal capacity.[151]

In the case of North Africa's own particular late Roman ecclesiastical schism, many of the leading 'Donatist' bishops were skilled rhetoricians and forensic advocates.[152] In fact the historical situation of the dissident church demanded that its bishops act before civil judges, in front of audiences held by municipal magistrates and provincial governors, and before the Emperor himself.[153] The forensic expertise of leading early fifth-century 'Donatist' bishops was very much on display at the 'Conference' of Carthage, as can be illustrated from the *Gesta* of 411.

[147] Minucius Felix, *Octavius* 2. 3 and 28. 3; also Jerome, *De Vir. Inl.* 58: 'Minucius Felix, Romae insignis causidicus, scripsit dialogum christiani et ethnici disputantis, qui Octauius inscribitur', and *Ep.* 70. 5: 'Minucius Felix, causidicus Romani fori, in libro, cui titulus "Octauius" est, et in altero contra mathematicos.'

[148] Minucius Felix, *Octavius* 2. 3: 'sane et ad vindemiam feriae iudiciariam curam relaxaverant'. Compare Cicero, *De Natura Deorum* 1. 15.

[149] *Vita Caec. Cypr.* 1. 1 (*CSEL* 3. 1. xc). Also Lactantius, *Div. Inst.* 5. 1. 21. G. W. Clarke, 'The Secular Profession of St Cyprian of Carthage', *Latomus*, 24 (1965), 633–63 at 638 concludes that Cyprian cannot be viewed as a 'lawyer' (*iurisconsultus*).

[150] T. G. Fogliani, *Contributo alla ricerca di riferimenti legali in testi extragiuridici del III sec. d.c.* (Modena: Bassi & Nipoti, 1928), 40–3; see now also A. Hoffmann, *Kirchliche Strukturen und römisches Recht bei Cyprian Karthago* (Paderborn: Schöningh, 2000).

[151] Cyprian, *Ep.* 69. 1 (CCSL 3. 2. 470, ll. 9–10): 'dicimus omnes omnino haereticos et schismaticos nihil habere potestatis ac iuris'.

[152] On Marculus, a rhetorician who became a mid-4th-century 'Donatist' martyr, see Kaster, *Guardians of Language*, 73.

[153] See Ch. 9 below.

The seven bishops mandated as *defensores* (‘*actores*’) of the ‘Donatist’ church at the ‘Conference’ were Protasius of Tubanae, Gaudentius of Thamugadi, Primianus of Carthage, Montanus of Zama, Adeodatus of Mileu, Emeritus of Caesarea, and Petilianus of Constantine. We know almost nothing by way of biographical information concerning the first two named bishops, and their single interventions during the 411 debate reveal little about their background or education.[154] Primianus (the ‘Donatist’ primate) confesses that he had no forensic training; however, as a result of this admission he mandates Victor, bishop of Thabbora, to act in his place.[155] Victor had practised as an advocate in the secular courts. The very fact that Primianus excluded himself from the proceedings on account of his lack of forensic expertise, and moreover appointed a former advocate in his stead, testifies that forensic practice was regarded as a desirable prerequisite for a ‘Donatist’ *defensor.* Montanus and Adeodatus both reveal a forensic background in their argumentative techniques and in their familiarity with technical points of procedural law.[156] Emeritus ably introduces and handles a host of pre-judicial *praescriptiones* (*de tempore, de mandato, de persona, de causa*) in a manner typical of a skilled *advocatus.* In fact we know from Augustine that Emeritus had practised at the Numidian bar.[157] Augustine also informs us that Petilianus, the most celebrated of the ‘Donatist’ bishops, had practised for a time as an advocate with some success.[158] Concerning Petilianus, Lancel concludes that: ‘A la Conférence de 411, il le fit surtout en avocat’.[159] He also notes that Petilianus and Emeritus work together at key stages in the development of the ‘Donatist’ case. In a practice analogous to that of the ‘secular’ advocates already discussed in Chapter 4 above, Petilianus acts as the lead *advocatus*, instructing his junior colleague to take over his argument at agreed points in the (preliminary) hearing.

[154] S. Lancel, *Actes de la Conférence de Carthage en 411*, i, *SC* 194 (Paris: Éditions de Cerf, 1972), 198–200.

[155] Ibid. 201–2. See also *Gesta* 1. 157 (*SC* 195. 804, ll 8–10) and 1. 201 (*SC* 195. 868, ll. 115–21).

[156] Lancel, *SC* 194. 203. On Adeodatus as an *advocatus* see also Mandouze, *Prosopographie Chrétienne*, 36.

[157] Lancel, *SC* 194. 279–80 and 208–9, judging Emeritus ‘plus méthodique, plus précis, plus acharné à attaquer comme à se défendre, l’avocat numidie le surclassa finalement par le nombre, la vigueur et la qualité tactique de ses interventions’.

[158] Augustine, *Contra litt. Petil.* 3. 16. 19 (*BA* 30. 622).

[159] Lancel, *SC* 194. 234. See further the entry, ‘Petilianus’ at *PLRE* ii. 861 and also Ch. 9 below.

Out of the seven Catholic *actores* mandated at the 411 conference we know of five who had some experience of forensic practice, of whom Augustine of Hippo is one.[160] In his early life Augustine followed the *cursus* of the late Roman educational system. To the newly minted bishop looking back, his educational formation had been providentially foreordained, despite the fact that he believed himself to have been driven by 'secular' ambition at the time.[161] During his study of grammar and rhetoric undertaken first in his home town of Thagaste and then in the provincial capital of Carthage, Augustine claims that he had examined all the textbooks on eloquence so that he could distinguish himself as a rhetor, in the hope of one day winning fame as a *causidicus* in the lawcourts:

My studies which were deemed respectable had the objective of leading me to distinction as an advocate in the law courts, where one's reputation is high in proportion to one's success in deceiving people. The blindness of humanity is so great that people are actually proud of their blindness. I was already top of the class in the rhetor's school, and was pleased with myself for my success and was inflated with conceit. Yet I was far quieter than the other students (as you know, Lord), and had nothing whatever to do with the vandalism which used to be carried out by the wreckers . . . This was the society in which at a vulnerable age I was to study the textbooks on eloquence. I wanted to distinguish myself as an orator for a damnable and conceited purpose, namely delight in human vanity . . .[162]

In book 4 of the *Confessions*, Augustine gives an account of his own experience of teaching the liberal arts in a publicly appointed position at Carthage. Augustine defines the purpose of his teaching quite precisely:

In those years I used to teach the art of rhetoric. Overcome by greed myself I used to sell the eloquence that would overcome an opponent. Nevertheless, Lord, as you know, I preferred to have virtuous students (virtuous as they are commonly called). Without any resort to a trick, I taught them the tricks of rhetoric, not that they should use them against the life of an innocent man, but that they might save the life of a guilty person.[163]

160 Catholic *actores* with otherwise attested forensic skill: Possidius of Calama (see Augustine, *Ep*. 105. 4 and *Contra Cresconius*. 3. 46. 50); Fortunatianus of Sicca; Vincentius of Culusi; Alypius (discussed above); and Augustine (discussed below).

161 Discussed by C. Lepelley, 'Un aspect de la conversion d'Augustin: La rupture avec ses ambitions sociales et politiques', *BLE* 88 (1987), 229–46.

162 Augustine, *Confessions* 3. 3. 6–4. 7, tr. H. Chadwick, *Saint Augustine Confessions* (Oxford: OUP, 1991), 38.

163 Augustine, *Confessions* 4.2.2, tr. Chadwick, *Saint Augustine Confessions*, 53.

This last sentence, incidentally, should not be seen as a case of a higher Christian morality imposing itself upon forensic practice. As Augustine himself was undoubtedly well aware, the theme of advocacy as an honourable profession, in which the advocate strove to ensure that the prosecution prove their case even when his client appeared guilty, was already an established rhetorical *topos* when Cicero applied it in his *De Officiis* (2. 51). The fact that at least some of Augustine's students were destined for careers as advocates should come as no surprise in the light of Chapter 4 above. Augustine's task of teaching the art of rhetoric in Rome (to which he was lured by the expectation of higher fees and more disciplined students) should be read in the same context.[164]

In Augustine's 'conversion' to Christianity it is the sale of *eloquentia* and not the practice of it that assumes importance. In the culmination to the Pauline conversion scene in book 8 of the *Confessions*, Augustine (and in a parallel narrative Alypius), having 'confessed' the Catholic faith, announces his intention to withdraw from the *sale* of his profession.[165] Both Augustine and Alypius, however, were fully aware that the Catholic church needed trained forensic practitioners—hence rather than casting off their old selves completely, they dedicated their skills to the Christian God. Both also apparently delayed their retirement from their 'secular' careers until the official end of the judicial year and the beginning of the *feriae Augustae*; a fact that was not missed by Augustine's contemporaries. In 408 Augustine's ('pagan') correspondent Vincentius wrote that it was well known by all that, after his conversion, Augustine had devoted himself to legal disputes.[166]

The recently published 'Divjak' letters highlight the fact that Augustine took on the responsibility of preparing case-dossiers for certain members of his congregation when they faced trial in the secular courts, for example, in property or inheritance disputes and also in cases involving the laws on slavery. That Augustine was accustomed to looking up

[164] Augustine's relationship with the 'liberal arts' can, of course, be set within a broader context, see M. Vessey and K. Pollmann (eds.), *Augustine and the Disciplines: From Cassiciacum to Confessions* (Oxford: OUP, 2005). There is no chapter devoted to rhetoric in the volume.

[165] Compare Possidius of Calama, *Vita Aug.*, 2: 'Renuntiavit etiam scholasticis, quos rhetoricam docebat, ut sibi magistrum alium providerunt, eo quod servire Deo ipse decrevisset.'

[166] Augustine, *Ep.* 93.

previous cases in the municipal and proconsular records himself, and then applying them to pressing legal matters, is evident from *Eps.* 24*, 28*, and 29*.

From the innumerable contexts in which Augustine applied his expertise in forensic rhetoric I shall take a single illustrative example: *Sermon* 52 (*De Trinitate*), delivered before his congregation at Hippo *c.*410–12.[167] *Sermon* 52 is deliberately and self-consciously constructed around an elaborate rhetorical conceit: Augustine presents himself as an advocate defending the case that the Trinity is inseparably three-in-one, for his client, God (named in section 1), before his judges, the congregation, gathered to hear the sermon (appealed to in section 8). Augustine opens his defence with a statement of his mandate to plead/preach, 'at the Lord's command', received through the passage of the Gospel just read out to the congregation.[168] Augustine then proceeds to a statement of his argument, introducing the evidence on which his defence will be founded: the Gospels of Matthew 3: 14–17 and Mark 1: 11. In section 2 Augustine establishes the credibility of that evidence as being 'not a bundle of opinions and prejudices but a summary of Biblical testimonies, not riddled with heretical rashness, but founded on apostolic truth'. Sections 3, 4, and 5 present further testimonies from scripture, and in section 6 Augustine names his adversaries: they are the 'Patripassians' (also known as 'Sabellians' or 'Modalists'): 'heretics' who persist in incorrect interpretations of the evidence (i.e. scripture). Section 7 then presents an imagined objection from one of these heretics, as if it had been recorded *ad verbatim*: the 'heretic' accuses Augustine of having contradicted himself in his opening statement of the case. Augustine gives a concise response to this objection and concludes with the following statement:

Now we seem to have rid ourselves of this objection, but perhaps only through my formula; let us see if it is also through the divine formula of the case. It

167 On Augustine's knowledge of Roman jurisprudence and legal concepts (rather than his techniques of forensic argument) see F. Martroye, 'Saint Augustin et la jurisprudence romaine', *BSNAF* (1916), 210–14; E. Albertario, 'Di alcuni riferimenti al matrimonio e al possesso in Sant' Agostino', *Rivista di filosofia neoscolastica*, supplemento speciale al vol. 23 (1931), 367–76; M. Roberti, 'Contributo allo studio delle relazioni fra diritto romano e patristica tratto dall'esame delle fonti Agostiniane', ibid. 305–66; D. Nonnoi, 'Sant' Agostino e il diritto romano', *Rivista italiana per le scienze giuridiche* 12 (1934), 531–622; F. G. Lardone, 'Roman Law in the Works of St Augustine', *Georgetown Law Journal* (1956), 435–56, and Gaudemet, *Le Droit romain dans le littérature chrétienne occidentale*, 127–64. None of these texts mention Augustine's *Sermon* 52.

168 Augustine, *Sermon* 52. 1 (*PL* 38. 354–5).

is up to me then to demonstrate by the evidence of the holy books that the birth of the Son was the work of both Father and Son, likewise his passion and resurrection . . . Let us prove each point. You are appointed as judges; the case has been stated, let the witnesses step forward. Let's suppose you, the judges, say to me what is usually said to advocates: 'Bring the proofs of your proposition'. I certainly will, and I will also read out to you the text of the heavenly law. You have listened carefully to my statement of the case; listen even more carefully now to my proof of it.[169]

With this sentence Augustine closes his *narratio* and opens his presentation of the *probationes* (the proofs). Incidentally, the records of a trial preserved in *P.Oxy.* 3758 (325) verify Augustine's statement concerning the usual request to advocates to 'bring the proofs of their proposition'.[170] Augustine then continues his rhetorical appeal to correct forensic procedure:

The first thing I have to bring proof of concerns the birth of Christ, how the Father effected it and the Son effected it, although what Father and Son effected together belongs only to the Son. I refer you first to Paul as a suitable *iurisperitus* in divine law. *Causidici* today, you see, also have a Paul who declares the laws for litigants, not for Christians. I refer you, I repeat, to the Paul who declares the laws of peace, not of litigation.[171]

With this statement Augustine quite brilliantly establishes himself as a truly Christian *causidicus*, substituting the *Sententiae* of the Roman jurist Paul for the New Testament of Paul the Apostle as his pleader's handbook. Sections 10 to 20 complete his presentation of the proofs upon which the case is founded. In the closing paragraph of section 20 Augustine self-consciously acknowledges his elaborate rhetorical conceit

[169] Augustine, *Sermon* 52. 4. 8 (*PL.* 38. 357–8): 'De quaestione ista videmur iam expediti; sed forte verbis meis, videamus etiam utrum verbis divinis. Pertinet ergo ad me sanctorum Librorum testimoniis demonstrare, nativitatem Filii et Patrem operatum et Filium; ita passionem; ita resurrectionem . . . Probemus singula, judices auditis, causa proposita est, testes procedant. Dicat mihi iudicium vestrum, quod solet causas agentibus dici: Doce quod promittis. Doceo plane adiuvante Domino, et coelestis iuris recito lectionem. Intente audistis proponentem, audite intentius iam probantem' (tr. Edmund Hill).

[170] *P.Oxy.* 3758, ll. 98–131. The magistrate first instructs the defending advocate to 'produce the evidence to justify your case' and then addresses the court: 'Let him (the advocate) produce the proofs to justify his case or let him withdraw'.

[171] Augustine, *Sermon* 52. 4. 9 (*PL* 38. 358): 'De Christi nativitate mihi primo docendum est, quomodo eam et Pater fecerit, et Filius fecerit, quamvis nonnisi ad Filium pertineat quod fecit Pater et Filius. Paulum recito, idoneum iuris divini consultum. Nam et causidici habent hodie Paulum dictantem iura litigatorum, non Christianorum. Recito, inquam, Paulum dicantem pacis iura, non litis' (tr. Edmund Hill, slightly adapted).

to the listening congregation: he states that he preached the sermon today 'with the greatest trepidation', lest he 'delight the wit of the clever, and bore the less clever to tears'.

Sermon 52 is a single example of the way in which Augustine adapted his expertise in forensic rhetoric to the service of the church. In this instance, the forensic context was introduced as an elaborate rhetorical model, through which he could persuade his audience that his interpretation of a particular doctrinal issue was the correct one. In Part III, however, we shall examine some rather more concrete applications of Augustine's expertise in the actual prosecution of 'heretics'.

The later years of Augustine's life were occupied with the 'heresy' of Pelagius and more specifically the challenges posed by the 'Pelagian' Julian of Eclanum. In a series of important studies Noel Cipriani has drawn attention to the importance which forensic techniques of rhetoric play in Julian's *Ad Florum* and *Ad Turbantium*.[172] According to Augustine, Julian made his living by teaching rhetoric in Sicily following his exile in 418. The *commonitorium* of Marius Mercator implies that Julian was not the only Pelagian with a forensic background: Pelagius himself had reputedly studied law at Rome. Moreover, Caelestius—one of the original exponents of 'Pelagian' doctrines—may have been a former advocate. Both Pelagius and Caelestius conducted their own defences against charges of heretical opinion laid before the ecclesiastical courts.[173] Unlike the Donatists, however, the Pelagians did not pursue their cause through the secular courts, but through doctrinal polemic which directly appealed to the *mores* of forensic debate.

Still within the Western Empire, the late fourth-century 'Ambrosiaster', probably writing at Rome, seems to have had some type of forensic background.[174] We are on surer ground with the early

[172] N. Cipriani, 'Aspetti letterari dell'Ad Florum di Giuliano d'Eclano', *Augustinianum*, 15 (1975), 125–67; N. Cipriani, 'La morale pelagiana e la retorica', *Augustinianum*, 31 (1991), 309–27; and N. Cipriani, 'L'Ad Florum di Giuliano', in *Opere di Sant' Agostino, Polemica con Giuliano*, Nuova Biblioteca Agostiniana, 19/1 (Rome: Citta nuova, 1993), pp. vii-xix. C. Baxter, 'Notes on the Latin of Julian of Eclanum', *Bulletin du Cange*, 21 (1929), 5–54, notes Julian's 'striking use of legal terminology'.

[173] Caelestius was questioned and condemned at Carthage in 411; versions of the *acta* survive in Augustine's *De Gestis Pelagii* and Marius Mercator's *Commonitorium super nomine Coelestii*; Pelagius was questioned and acquitted at the synod of Diospolis in 415. Following his acquittal, Pelagius appealed to Pope Innocent against the 'calumny' of his accusers (see Augustine, *De Gratia Christi* 30. 32).

[174] 'Ambrosiaster' and Roman law: F. Cumont, 'Ambrosiaster et le droit romain', *Revue d'histoire et de littérature religieuse*, 8 (1903) and O. Heggelbacher, *Vom römischen*

fifth-century Christian poet Prudentius who tells of his own rhetorical training and his practice as an advocate.[175] Paulinus, bishop of Nola, a former pupil of Ausonius at Bordeaux, had practised advocacy before being appointed *consularis* of Campania and then bishop within the same province (395).[176]

In his *Commentary on the Epistle to the Galatians*, Jerome describes himself as a young student, frequenting the judicial tribunals in the Roman forum so that he could watch the most skilled advocates vehemently attacking each other.[177] Jerome seems to have been formally educated by the famous Roman professor of rhetoric, Marius Victorinus, who himself applied his forensic expertise to theological disputes against 'the Arians'.[178] Monceaux argues that as a young man, Jerome orientated himself 'towards the lucrative glories of the advocate's profession'.[179] In any event, after Jerome's first (short) period of asceticism, Pope Damasus appointed him as the individual responsible for replying to synodal *consultationes* addressed to the papal court.[180] Jerome's polemical treatises *Contra Helvidium* and *Adversus Iovinianum* are replete with allusions to forensic practice and would repay careful study in this context.

In this chapter I have sought to demonstrate the forensic expertise of certain key late Roman ecclesiastics and lay Christians. This expertise was not simply gleaned from a general late Roman 'legal culture'; as in Part I, the biographical evidence (within the limits noted at various points above) suggests a career-orientated education. The training of leading ecclesiastics in forensic rhetoric may provide one explanation

zum christlichen Recht: Iuristische Elemente in den Schriften des sogenanntes Ambrosiaster (Freiburg, Switzerland: Universitätsverlag, 1959).

[175] Prudentius, *Praefatio* 8–9 and 13–18 (Loeb, i. 271).

[176] 'Meropius Pontius Paulinus 21', *PLRE* i. 681–3; see in general C. Conybeare, *Paulinus Noster: Self and Symbols in the Letters of Paulinus of Nola* (Oxford: OUP, 2000).

[177] Discussed in Ch. 4 above. It seems that Jerome may have continued this hobby of watching advocates: in his *Ep.* 40 he confesses to laughing 'at a *causidicus* who has no clients'.

[178] On Jerome and Marius Victorinus see Jerome, *Chron.* s.a. 354 (= Eusebius, *Werke*, *GCS* 7): 'Victorinus rhetor et Donatus grammaticus, praeceptor meus, Romae insignes habentur. e quibus Victorinus etiam statuam in foro Traiani meruit,' and *in Gal.* pr: 'Caium Marium Victorinum, qui Romae me puero, rhetoricam docuit.' On Marius Victorinus, see also Jerome, *De Vir. Inl.* 101, and P. Hadot, '"De lectis non lecta conponere" (Marius Victorinus, Adversus Arium II 7). Raisonnement théologique et raisonnement juridique', *Studia Patristica*, 1 (1957), 209–20.

[179] P. Monceaux, *St Jerome: The Early Years*, tr. F. J. Sheed (London: Sheed & Ward, 1933), 49.

[180] Jerome, *Ep.* 123. 10 (*PL* 22. 1052).

as to why canon law was largely developed through similar techniques as late Roman law. The creative elaboration of these two legal systems was thus reciprocal, rather than parallel, as we shall see in the following chapter. In other words, the development of early canon law in late antiquity was framed by a constant case-specific interaction between forensic practitioners within the church and forensic practice outside the church.

7

Forensic Expertise and the Development of Early 'Canon Law'

ROMAN LAW AND 'ECCLESIASTICAL' LAW

> Question: How does governance by God on behalf of angels and humanity take place?
> Answer: Through lawgiving.[1]

In the early 540s the Emperor Justinian's top legal official, the *quaestor* Junillus Africanus, composed a Latin treatise in Constantinople entitled *Instituta Regularia Divinae Legis* (*Institutes of the Principles of Divine Law*) and addressed it to a certain Primasius, bishop of Hadrumetum, North Africa. According to Junillus, he had written the text for all individuals 'who burned with a passion for understanding the divine books': it was intended as a guide to unlocking the 'very principles' that operate in divine law, through the study of sacred scripture. Junillus further explained that his *Institutes* had been inspired by a certain exegete named Paul, 'who was educated at the Syrian school in the city of Nisibis, where the Divine Law is taught in a disciplined and orderly fashion by public teachers in the same way that in secular education grammar and rhetoric are taught in our cities'.[2] If we are to trust Junillus' characterization, then the Syrian school at Nisibis was almost unique in its institutionalized approach to scriptural exegesis and it was perhaps this particular aspect of 'disciplined and orderly' instruction by 'public teachers' that attracted the attention of Justinian's *quaestor*.[3] Junillus,

[1] Junillus, *Handbook of the Basic Principles of Divine Law* 2. 5, tr. M. Maas, *Exegesis and Empire in the Early Byzantine Mediterranean* (Tubingen: Siebeck, 2003), 182.

[2] Ibid. 118–20.

[3] On biblical exegesis and the 'schools' of Alexandria and Antioch see Young, *Biblical Exegesis*; on Constantinopolitan 'schools' see H. Schlange-Schöningen, *Kaisertum und*

however, was not the only sixth-century individual leading a double life of legal and theological exegesis. According to his hagiographer the *scholastikos* Zacharius, Severus, the future bishop of Antioch (512–18), was an exemplary student at the law school of Beirut—mastering the civil law from Monday through to Saturday morning, then studying sacred scripture and the Church Fathers on a Saturday afternoon, before spending Sunday at church services.[4] In the hagiography of the early sixth-century East, then, 'lawyers' read scripture and saints read law. The medieval recovery of Justinian's *Digest* opened up new possibilities for the application of legal thought to theology and vice versa; the project itself, however, was the product of an age in which the two spheres of learning were understood to be interwoven.[5]

Justinian styled himself as the ultimate interpretative authority in matters both human and divine. In section 1 of his *Novel* 131, issued in 543 to the Praetorian Prefect of the East, Justinian bestowed the 'force of law' on the canons enacted by the four 'ecumenical' church councils (Nicaea, Constantinople, Ephesus I, and Chalcedon) and accepted their dogmas as 'divine scriptures'. In theory at least, however, the task of enquiring into the 'sacred canons and divine laws' and supervising their correct observance was left to the ecclesiastics of the orthodox and catholic church. As the drafter of the preamble to Justinian's *Novel* 137 (given at Constantinople, 565) carefully phrased it:

> If we are anxious that the civil laws, the power of which God in his concern for mankind has entrusted to us, should be kept strong in all things to ensure the safety or our subjects, how much more zeal ought we to invest in the observation of the sacred canons and divine laws, which have been established for the salvation of our souls? Those who observe the sacred canons are deemed to be worthy of the aid of the Lord God, whereas those who violate them subject themselves to His condemnation. The most holy bishops are subject to a greater condemnation, for to them is entrusted the task of enquiring into the canons and taking heed lest violations of them go unpunished. We have learned that diverse suits have been brought against not a few clerics and monks and

Bildungswesen im spätantiken Konstantinopel (Stuttgart: F. Steiner, 1995) and compare also, for the West, Cassiodorus, *Institutes* 1, pr. 1 (*PL* 70. 1105), discussed by G. Fiaccadori, 'Cassiodorus and the School of Nisibis', *Dumbarton Oaks Papers*, 39 (1985), 135–7.

[4] Zacharius Scholasticus, *Life of Severus*, ed. M. A Kugener, *PO* 2 (1907), 46–92.

[5] On the recovery of Justinianic legal texts in the late 11th/12th cents see H. Lange, *Römisches Recht im Mittelalter* (Munich: Beck, 1997), 1–34, and E. Cortese, 'Alle origini della scuola di Bologna', in I. Birocchi and U. Petronio (eds.), *Cortese Scritti*, ii (Spoleto: Centro italiano di studi sull'alto medioevo, 1999), 1095–1137, and A. Winroth, *The Making of Gratian's* Decretum (Cambridge: CUP, 2000), 146–74.

bishops for failing to observe the sacred canons, in that they are not living in accordance with them. Some too have been discovered who do not even know the prayer for the sacred offering or the holy baptism.[6]

According to this legislative rhetoric, the general observance of 'the sacred canons and the divine laws' was an obligation owed to the Christian God by society as a whole; on the other hand, 'the sacred canons' also provided a particular set of precepts that Christian ecclesiastics and monks had to both observe and oversee. It was apparently the failure of certain individuals in this respect that provoked the issuing of *Novel* 137. Thirty years earlier, *Novel* 6. 1, addressed to the patriarch of Constantinople, had already spelt out this duty with reference to would-be bishops: even if a candidate had been prepared for episcopal office after having already spent a period of time as a monk or cleric, he must nonetheless 'read the canons that are sacred and universally accepted', which 'the Catholic and Apostolic church have accepted and handed down'. The constitution continues:

And while he who is approaching ordination is occupied in reading into them with all diligence, he who will administer the ordination is to enquire of the candidate whether he can observe and put into practice those things that the divine canons have decreed. And if he says he cannot, and that he is not equal to preserving the precepts of the divine canons, then ordination should by no means be imposed on him. If however he does undertake to affirm that he will carry out the injunctions contained in the canons, as far as he can do so as a man, then he is to be warned and advised that if he should fail to carry out the injunctions, he will be at odds with God and will be deprived of the standing that has been bestowed upon him. Furthermore, the civil laws will not leave any offence that he commits unavenged, since it has been justly pronounced, both by those who have ruled before us, and by us ourselves, that the sacred canons should have the force of law.[7]

The use of the term 'canon' to refer to conciliar enactments may not have become normative until the sixth century.[8] However, the idea of sacred decisions with 'the force of law', or indeed the broader concept of a 'legal system' internal to the Christian church (or even individual Christian communities), was by no means a Justinianic innovation.[9]

[6] Justinian, *Novel* 137 pr.

[7] Justinian, *Novel* 6. 1.8 (535).

[8] H. Hess, *The Early Development of Canon Law and the Council of Serdica* (Oxford: OUP, 2002), 78.

[9] See e.g. E. Dovere, *'Ius Principale' e 'Catholica Lex': Dal Teodosiano agli Editti su Calcedonia* (Naples: Jovene, 1995).

The question of how 'ecclesiastical law' itself developed in late antiquity, however, is a complex subject and a full answer lies beyond the scope of this monograph.[10] The present chapter, then, is primarily limited to suggesting the following line of argument: the fact that some key late Roman ecclesiastics were trained as forensic practitioners is crucial to explaining how it was that early 'canon law' was elaborated using specific techniques and procedures 'borrowed' from Roman law. Before we turn to early canon law and the development of conciliar and papal authority, however, we first need to consider the various foundational strands of early Judaeo-Christian 'internal' ideas and practices.

The terms *lex* and *nomos* did not necessarily point towards a textual law or a formal legal system; they were also normatively understood within Greco-Roman contexts as referring to a general 'way of life', in the sense of an individual's means of disciplining his or her self by following ethical precepts for 'living well', or indeed in terms of a disciplined way of life for a religious or philosophical community governed by a particular moral code.[11] The earliest Judaeo-Christian uses of the terms *lex* or *nomos* should perhaps be understood in these terms; the Gospels contained a *lex Christiana* in the sense that they provided guides on how to live as a follower of Christ, either as an individual or within a community group. In the first three centuries AD individual Judaeo-Christian communities elaborated their own body of regulatory customs and norms—in some points different from and antithetical to both Judaic and Graeco-Roman traditions, but touching more or less radically upon all institutions. Whilst acknowledging the diversity of early Judaeo-Christian communities, these sets of socio-ethical practices had a certain general coherence, partly as a result of the circulation of shared (Gospel) texts and/or oral traditions. We can perhaps speak of an increasing 'textualization' of Judaeo-Christian socio-ethical practices as copies of (pseudo-)apostolic writings (and later *Apostolic Constitutions*), Christian apologetics, and other examples of 'normative' literature circulated within and between

[10] For general discussion see A. Steinwenter, 'Der antike kirchliche Rechtsgang und seine Quellen', *ZRG, Kan. Abt.* 54 (1934), 1–116; L. Buisson, 'Die Entstellung des Kirchenrechts', *ZRG, Kan. Abt.* 83 (1966), 1–175; P. G. Caron, *I poteri guiridici del laicato nella chiesa primitiva*, 2nd edn. (Milan: A. Guiffrè, 1975); and O. Bucci, 'La genesi della struttura del diritto della Chiesa latina e del diritto delle Chiese Cristiane Orientali in rapporto allo svolgimento storico del diritto romano e del diritto bizantino', *Apollinaris*, 65 (1992), 93–135.

[11] Compare Seneca, *Ep.* 94. which speaks of the *praecepta*, *decreta*, and *leges* of philosophy. I owe this comparison, with thanks, to Professor David Sedley.

communities.[12] In any event, early 'Christians' were familiar with the idea of a *lex* or way of life specific to them—in addition, perhaps, to the Apostle Paul's understanding of Christ's law.[13] Individual communities also took internal steps to reinforce their 'way of life' by punishing infringements of it through sentences of public penance and excommunication.[14]

We should also note, in this context, the question of how (Judaeo-Christian) communities understood the *lex Judaica*, in particular the five Mosaic books of the *lex dei* (the *Pentateuch*).[15] Jewish communities and communities of gentile 'God-fearers' (*theosebeis*), of course, had their own 'way of life', framed by Jewish law and precepts of observance.[16] The discovery of a marriage-contract (*ketuba*), written in Aramaic and dated to 417, 'attests to the existence of a Jewish community at Antinoopolis' (about 400 kilometres south of Alexandria in Egypt) where two individuals, Samuel and Metra, were married 'according to the law [of all the daughters] of Israel'.[17] As Fergus Millar comments: 'The composition of a Jewish marriage contract in Aramaic suggests, against what would surely have been the general expectation, namely the use of Greek, that it was possible for there to be Diaspora communities where the knowledge of Aramaic (or Hebrew) had not been lost, and where Jewish law was consciously observed.'[18] The so-called *Collatio Legum Mosaicarum et Romanarum*, on the other hand, probably composed at Rome in the late fourth century, asserts a harmony between the 'opinions' of Moses taken from the Pentateuch and the opinions of various Roman classical jurists. Moses is framed throughout the text as a

[12] See Hess, *Early Development of Canon Law*, 35–7.

[13] For wide-ranging discussion see the collection of papers in J. D. G. Dunn (ed.), *Paul and the Mosaic Law* (Tübingen: J. C. B. Mohr (Paul Siebeck), 1996).

[14] See G. Rauschen, *Eucharistie und Busssakrament in den ersten sechs Jahrhunderten der Kirche* (Freiburg, Germany: Herder, 1908) and J. Gaudemet, 'Note sur les formes anciennes de l'excommunication', *Rev. SR* 23 (1944), 64–77.

[15] On various early theological attempts to relate the Old Testament to the New see M. Wiles, *The Divine Apostle* (Cambridge: CUP, 1967), 49–68. For comparison see J. W. Martens, *One God. One Law. Philo of Alexandria on the Mosaic and Greco-Roman Law* (Boston: Brill Academic Publishers, 2003).

[16] See A. Linder, *The Jews in Roman Imperial Legislation* (Detroit: Wayne State University Press, 1987) and B. S. Bachrach, 'The Jewish Community of the Later Roman Empire as Seen in the *Codex Theodosianus*', in J. Neusner and E. S. Frerichs (eds.), *'To See Ourselves as Others See Us': Christians, Jews and 'Others' in Late Antiquity* (Chico, Calif.: Scholars Press, 1985).

[17] F. Millar, 'Christian Emperors, Christian Church and the Jews of the Diaspora in the Greek East, CE 379–450', *Journal of Jewish Studies*, 55/1 (2004), 1–24, at 12.

[18] Ibid. 12.

iurisconsultus.[19] The Decalogue, in particular, received special treatment across a wide cross-section of late antique 'religious' communities. In the mid-fourth century the Emperor Julian argued in his treatise *Against the Galileans*: 'That is an admirable law of Moses, I mean the famous decalogue; "you shall not steal", "you shall not kill", "you shall not bear false witness".' Julian copied out 'word for word', as he himself puts it, 'every one of the commandments which [Moses] says were written by God himself', concluding that the commandments of the Decalogue are in fact obeyed by every nation (*ethnos*) anyway, excepting the two on worshipping no other gods and the Sabbath.[20] Julian thus differentiated the Decalogue from the whole package of 'Jewish' law, and thereby revealed his Christian background. At its most basic level the Decalogue, the *vetus lex*, could be understood as 'law' in a sense that Christians, Jews, and even a mid-fourth-century apostate emperor could agree upon.

Heresiological rhetoric from the second century onwards is, of course, full of 'judaizing' Christians; to the extent that modern scholars have argued that, by the time we reach the fifth century, the category of 'Judaizer' has simply become a convenient rhetorical label for social and sacramental exclusion.[21] There is late Roman evidence, however, that Christians across different levels of society were pondering how best to read (and act upon) the thousands of literal and specific Mosaic laws in the books of Genesis, Exodus, Leviticus, Numbers, and Deuteronomy.[22] For example, a letter written by Siricius, bishop of Rome, in reply to some queries from Himerius, bishop of Tarragona, shows that exegetical principles were being developed in response to concrete situations in the late fourth century.[23] Amongst other issues, it had come to Siricius'

[19] See esp *Collatio Legum Mosaicarum et Romanarum* 7. 1. Possible provenances for this work are discussed by G. Barone Adesi, *L'Età della Lex Dei* (Naples: Jovene Editore, 1992).

[20] Julian, *Against the Galileans* 152B–D, quoting Exodus 20: 2–4 and 13–17.

[21] On the rhetoric of 'anti-judaizing' heresiology in general see D. Boyarin, *Border Lines: The Partition of Judaeo-Christianity* (Philadelphia: University of Pennsylvania Press, 2004) and for broader discussion, A. H. Becker and A. Y. Reed (eds.), *The Ways that Never Parted: Jews and Christians in Late Antiquity and the Early Middles Ages* (Tübingen: Mohr Siebeck, 2003).

[22] For a 4th-cent. Syriac context see A. Lehto, 'Moral, Ascetic, and Ritual Dimensions to Law-Observance in Aphrahat's Demonstrations', *Journal of Early Christian Studies*, 14/2 (2006), 157–81.

[23] *Epistulae Romanorum Pontificum*, ed. Coustant, 623–38. The letter was written in the first year of Siricius' pontificate (384–99) in response to queries that Himerius had originally addressed to Pope Damasus.

attention that priests and deacons in Himerius' diocese were having children long after their ordination: 'and defending their sin with the excuse that it is read in the *vetus lex* that the chance to procreate was given to priests and ministers' (sections 8–10). In response, Siricius first demonstrates that these Christian clerics have interpreted the Mosaic law (Leviticus 20: 7) incorrectly: procreation is forbidden to priests in the *vetus lex*. Then Siricius argues on the authority of the Gospel and the Pauline epistles that as Jesus came to fulfil the *vetus lex* not to destroy it, so procreation is also forbidden in the 'unbreakable law of those [i.e. Christ's] sanctions'. Siricius concludes by informing Himerius that if any other attempt to plead an 'illicit privilege' from the *vetus lex* is made 'let them know that they have been expelled from every ecclesiastical office by the authority of the apostolic see'. Siricius' letter not only highlights the growing power of the papacy as privileged interpreters of sacred scripture, but also reveals the argumentative acumen of the Spanish priests and deacons who pleaded the *vetus lex* as their defence in the first place.

Finally, if we return to the various processes referred to by the umbrella-term *episcopalis audientia*, we can ask what kind of socio-ethical and/or socio-legal parameters governed the bishop's judgment of particular cases. In his treatise *De Sacerdotio*, John Chrysostom stated that a bishop faced a more complex task when acting as a judge than a secular magistrate did: as it is difficult for a bishop to discover which law ought to be applied, and more difficult again actually to apply that law after it has been found.[24] The *auctoritas* of Christian bishops may well have depended 'on tried and tested rules laid down, not by emperors, but by the Gospels and St Paul',[25] however we can reasonably assume that disputants would also have expected bishops to consider a *basic* framework of Roman law in delivering their judgments, as and when relevant. Ecclesiastics who were ignorant of the civil law could in fact be criticized for making 'mistakes'. Augustine's *Ep.* 8* is addressed to a certain cleric, possibly a bishop, named Victor, who (as Augustine styles it) is in legal difficulties *per ignorantiam iuris*. Augustine takes it upon himself to spell out the basic principles of Roman legal possession and ownership and admonishes Victor to act quickly upon them, lest the

[24] John Chrysostom, *De Sacerdotio* 3. 17 (*PG* 48. 658). Compare Augustine's statement at *De Opere Mon.* 29 that the civil cases he judged were not only numerous but also difficult to resolve.

[25] Harries, *Law and Empire*, 211.

case 'come before the bishop's court'.[26] The implication here, then, is that if a bishop did hear the case it would be with the basic Roman legal principles in mind.

In fact the post-Constantinian establishment of a 'legal system' internal to the institutional church was partly achieved by individual bishops acting in response to particular events. A case study of this activity is provided by Augustine's piecemeal elaboration of new ecclesiastical principles concerning succession to clerical and monastic goods. In the early fifth century a number of specific cases forced Augustine to formulate some general principles to cover situations where the bequests of clerics and monks involved a conflict of interests.[27] In his *Ep.* 83 (addressed from Augustine and the brothers of his community to Alypius), Augustine responds to the case of a certain Honoratus, who had been a monk at Thagaste (Augustine's home town) before his ordination as a priest in the neighbouring town of Thiava. Honoratus had died intestate *c.*405, without any family that could claim the right of legal succession to his goods.[28] An 'equitable' solution to the problem had been proposed by Alypius (the bishop of Thagaste): part of Honoratus' goods would be granted to the church at Thiava and the other part would be re-vindicated to his former monastery. The citizens of Thiava, however, had objected to this split and Alypius had thus appealed to Augustine to decide upon the case. The conflict of interests between the church at Thiava and the monastery at Thagaste was (eventually) resolved in favour of the former, through Augustine's formulation of three general principles. First Augustine laid down the rule that the goods of clerics should devolve to the church in which they had been ordained. The tenet of this principle was in accordance with a canonical ruling made by the 393 Council of Hippo (and apparently restated at a council in 397):

Likewise it is resolved that bishops, presbyters, deacons and all clerics, who are ordained with no property and in the time of their holding the office of bishop or priest should take possession of fields or estates of any kind, should be held

[26] See Vismara, *La giurisdizione civile*, 108–12, and compare Augustine, *Sermon* 355. 2: an account of a case concerning inheritance law, discussed by Roberti, 'Contributo allo studio delle relazioni fra diritto romano e patristica', 315.

[27] F. Martroye, 'Saint Augustin et le droit d'héritage des églises et des monastères: étude sur les origines du droit des communautés religieuses à la succession des clercs et des moines', *MSNAF* 68 (1908), 97–129, at 101–2.

[28] Augustine, *Ep.* 83. 4 (new edn. *CCSL* 21A. 124–5).

by the charge of usurpation, as if imperial property were at issue, unless having been admonished they give up their property to the church.[29]

In the absence of any direct canonical directives specifically concerning conflicts of interest between monasteries and churches, this canon probably provided Augustine with the general principle that the property of a cleric belonged to his church. Accordingly, in the case of Honoratus his ordination as a priest determined that the right of succession to his goods belonged with the church of Thiava, not the monastery of Thagaste. Augustine creatively stretched the norm of the 393 conciliar canon by applying it in new contexts.

The second principle enunciated in Augustine's *Ep.* 83 specifies that, in a case concerning clerics or monks, where legal claimants to the succession exist the goods should devolve to them in accordance with the rules of Roman civil law; this had been established by Augustine in an earlier dispute relating to a monk at Hippo named Privatus—the latter had been in possession of thirty *solidi* at his death which had been duly given to his brother. Augustine's third principle suggested a general 'internal' guideline with respect to the succession of monastic establishments: the right of a monastery's succession to the goods of one of its monks should be allowed only in the case of express testamentary stipulations to that effect.[30] Hence in resolving the question of who should succeed to Honoratus' goods, Augustine proposed an ensemble of rules that he then applied in later analogous disputes; he was thus engaged in reasoning out new ecclesiastical norms in response to practical situations. We find the principles that Augustine first elaborated in 405 repeated in an Eastern imperial constitution dated 434 (*C.Th.* 5. 3. 1, to Taurus PP and patrician). This imperial constitution formally recognized legal norms and practices that had already been elaborated through the piecemeal efforts of individual bishops, reacting to particular situations on the ground.[31]

[29] *CCSL* 149. 110, ll. 306–11: 'Item placuit, ut episcopi, presbyteri, diaconi, vel quicumque clerici qui nihil habentes ordinantur et tempore episcopatus vel clericatus sui agros vel quaecumque praedia nomine suo comparant, tamquam rerum dominicarum invasionis crimine teneantur; nisi admoniti in ecclesiam eadem ipsa contulerint.'

[30] Martroye, 'Saint Augustin et le droit d'héritage', 109, notes that any strings attached to bequests and legacies left to churches or monasteries were transferred along with the goods; that Augustine was well aware of this fact can be seen in his refusal of a legacy made to the church of Hippo by a *navicularius* (Augustine, *Sermon* 355. 4, *PL* 39. 1572).

[31] E. Dovere, 'Diritto romano e prassi conciliare ecclesiastica (secc. III–V)', *SDHI* 69 (2003), 149–64, at 161–2 suggests that until *c.*430–50, individual bishops were more important than church councils and their *decreta.*

Augustine, of course, cannot be taken for a typical late Roman bishop; his own writings were acknowledged within the later medieval tradition as a source of canon law in their own right. The texts of a limited number of other forensically trained late Roman bishops were also accepted as formal sources for 'medieval' canon law. For example, in the mid-sixth century a *scholastikos* named John (later patriarch of Constantinople) assembled a collection known as the *Synagoge* (or *Collection of the Fifty Titles*): alongside eighty-five 'apostolic' canons and material taken from the first four 'ecumenical' councils (amongst other synodal decisions), John included more than sixty 'canons' excerpted from letters originally written by Basil of Caesarea to Amphilocius of Iconium in the later fourth century.[32] Basil's stretching of existing definitions of apostasy to cover the practice of magic, as well as his distinction between 'voluntary' and 'involuntary' apostasy, were thus formally incorporated within the Eastern canonical tradition.[33] The transformation of individual forensically trained ecclesiastics and monks into 'patristic' sources of canon law thus dates back to at least the mid-sixth century in the East.

FORENSIC PRACTICE AND CHURCH COUNCILS

The church lives by the Roman law.[34]

The late Roman church councils and their 'decision-making' activity cannot be properly understood apart from the history of the early medieval 'canon law' collections: much of the material survives only as excerpted compilations, each composed and ordered at a given moment in time, by individuals acting in particular circumstances.[35] Modern scholars have attempted to reconstruct the history of the transmission

[32] Hess, *Early Development of Canon Law*, 54–5.

[33] On the definition of 'apostasy' compare *C.Th.* 16. 7 (seven constitutions dated 381–426) and *CI* 1. 7 (six constitutions dated 357–455).

[34] *Law of the Ripuarian Franks* 61 (58) 1, quoted from P. Stein, 'The Medieval Rediscovery of the Roman Civil Law', in D. L. Carey Miller and R. Zimmermann (eds.), *The Civilian Tradition and Scots Law: Aberdeen Quincentenary Essays* (Berlin: Ducker & Humblot, 1997), 75–86, at 76.

[35] See e.g. C. Munier, 'La Tradition littéraire des canons africains', *Rech. Aug.* 10 (1975), 1–22, and R. Mathisen, 'The "Second Council of Arles" and the Spirit of Compilation and Codification in Late Roman Gaul', *Journal of Early Christian Studies*, 5 (1997), 511–54.

of the 'foundational collections' of East and West: including the *corpus Antiochenum*, the various East Syrian and West Syrian collections, the Coptic tradition, the early recensions of the 'Isidoriana', the 'Prisca', the collections produced in North Africa and Gaul, and the various compilations of Dionysius Exiguus.[36] Behind these collections, however, lies a much broader context of late Roman 'canon' excerpting and copying—highlighted, for example, by the fifth-century church historian Socrates' use of a collection of 'synodal transactions', put together by a certain Sabinus, the fourth-century bishop of the 'Macedonian sect' at Heracleia in Thrace.[37] Churches belonging to different 'communions', what we might term 'heretical' or 'schismatic' sects, may well have copied and circulated different collections. Fergus Millar has found 'no systematic evidence, in the case of any of these Councils, as to who was responsible for preserving and then disseminating copies of the proceedings'.[38] Nonetheless, such records seem to have been widely available (with internal variations), especially from the early–mid-fifth century onwards. With these caveats in mind, let us now turn to the evidence for the application of forensic expertise in late Roman conciliar contexts.

Montgomery's 1995 study of the statutes of the *concilium Iliberitanum* tentatively suggested a relationship between late Roman forensic rhetoric and bishops deliberating in council.[39] The Council of Iliberis (Granada) apparently met in the early fourth century; according to its *acta*, attendance was comprised of nineteen bishops together with twenty-four presbyters and deacons, who agreed on eighty-one 'statutes'. Most of these eighty-one decisions concerned the classification of ecclesiastical offences and their corresponding penances. Montgomery suggests that the bishops' classification of these offences may have been influenced by the teaching that they had received in the 'ancient schools of rhetoric': 'When learning the art of pleading, students had to develop the capability of classifying and defining an offence and considering the character of the alleged perpetrator. Some of the Spanish bishops

[36] As summarized by Hess, *Early Development of Canon Law*, 53–9 and 82–9, and J. Gaudemet, 'Collections canoniques et codifications', *Revue de droit canonique*, 33 (1983), 81–109. See also in general, J. Gaudemet, *Les Sources du droit de l'église en occident du IIe au VIIe siècle* (Paris: Éditions du Cerf, 1985).

[37] On Socrates' use of Sabinus' collection see Urbainczyk, *Socrates of Constantinople*, 28 and 43–4.

[38] Millar, *Greek Roman Empire*, 237.

[39] H. Montgomery, 'Crime and Punishment in the Statutes of the Concilium Iliberitanum', *Studia Patristica*, 24 (1993), 169–74.

who were assembled at Iliberis must have had experience of this kind of education.'[40] Montgomery thus proposes that the systematic way of classifying the character of a crime taught by late Roman forensic rhetoric may have been used in the early fourth-century conciliar elaboration of penitential 'law'.[41]

The application of forensic techniques of reasoning can be seen more clearly in the councils of the late fourth- and early fifth-century North African 'Catholic' church. Augustine himself conceived the plan of regular assemblies in 392.[42] A council subsequently met at Hippo on 8 October 393 and an abbreviated form of its decisions was put into shape at a further council held at Carthage four years later. This redrafting of the original 393 record was part of an attempt to draw up, at least in outline, a complete body of 'institutional' norms for the North African 'Catholic' church. The redaction of the 397 text was entrusted to bishops from Byzacena, whose specific instruction was 'not to reproduce exactly the Hippo decisions, but to give certain matters greater precision'.[43] The resulting epitome (known under the title of the *Breviarium Hipponense*) was presented to the 397 Council of Carthage, prefaced by a joint letter (*ecclesiasticae utilitatis causa*) from Aurelius, the primate of Carthage, and the Byzacene bishops. The 397 assembly duly ratified the *Breviarium* and made its contents formally binding. These representatives of the North African church were thus employed in a self-conscious attempt to create a system of authoritative, ecclesiastical, collective decision-making. Moreover, the methods of reasoning adopted within individual decisions of subsequent North African councils shed an interesting light on how normative regulations were elaborated case-by-case.

The Council of Carthage held on 25 May 419 agreed to prohibit clerics from the practice of usury, but the primate Aurelius also took

[40] Ibid. 173.

[41] Compare E. J. Jonkers, 'Application of Roman Law by Councils in the Sixth Century', *RHD* 20 (1952), 340–3, discussing the appeals made to Roman legal principles at the Council of Orléans in 533 (that Roman law does not accept the dissolution of a marriage on account of illness); at the Council of Orléans, 541 (that Roman law exempted pagan priests from the obligation of *tutela* and that this privilege should be extended to Christian clerics); and at the Council of Mâcon 585 (which defends the church's right of asylum through an appeal to the analogous right of asylum granted by imperial legislation to the pagan imperial cult).

[42] F. L. Cross, 'History and Fiction in the African Canons', *JTS* NS 12 (1961), 227–47, at 229, with reference to Augustine *Ep.* 22. 2.

[43] *CCSL* 149. 28–9, ll. 14–18.

the opportunity to establish a method of reasoning that ought to be followed in defining such principles: where new propositions are needed with reference to matters that are not already defined, the council can act, 'but in those matters where Scripture has most openly ruled, the judgment is not something to be created, but to be followed'.[44] In other words, where scriptural meaning was clear, the bishops had to follow it; where scripture gave a less certain directive, it was up to the bishops to draw out the meaning and give it a 'form'. Once a decision had been formulated, it was open to the council to appeal to the Emperors to promulgate a relevant constitution. This process is referred to in a canon from a Council of Carthage which apparently met on 13 June 407:

It is resolved that, following gospel and apostolic teaching, a husband who has been dismissed by his wife, or a wife who has been dismissed by her husband, should in neither case be joined to another person, but rather should remain as they are, or be reconciled to each other. If they reject this, they should be brought to penitence. In this cause the promulgation of an imperial law should be sought.[45]

By this mechanism, the decisions of *provincial* church councils could receive executive force through imperial constitutions.[46] One of the factors that determined the success of such petitions was, of course, the persuasive expertise of the individual bishops who were mandated to plead at the imperial court.[47]

The influence of late Roman law is particularly evident in the procedural rules and regulations that were developed with reference to synodal tribunals. Steinwenter, writing in 1934, argued that the procedural law of the *Codex Iuris Canonici* was one of the strongest

[44] *CCSL* 149. 102, ll. 32–41: 'Quamquam novellae suggestiones, quae vel obscura sunt vel sub genere latent, inspectam a nobis formam accipient. Ceterum de quibus apertissime scriptura sanxit, non ferenda sententia est sed sequenda.'

[45] *CCSL* 149. 218, ll. 1230–4: 'Placuit ut, secundum evangelicam et apostolicam disciplinam, neque dimissus ab uxore, neque dimissa a marito, alteri coniungatur, sed ita maneant, aut sibimet reconcilientur; quod si contempserint, ad paenitentiam redigantur. In qua causa legem imperialem petendam promulgari.'

[46] Conversely, Jerome, *Apol. Contra Rufinum* 3. 18 implies that an imperial rescript could reverse the decision of a synod.

[47] For discussion of specific examples see E. T. Hermanowicz, 'Catholic Bishops and Appeals to the Imperial Court: A Legal Study of the Calama Riots in 408', *Journal of Early Christian Studies*, 12/4 (2004), 481–521. Compare, on the 451 Council of Chalcedon, D. Feissel, 'Pétitions aux empereurs et formes du rescrit', in D. Feissel and J. Gascou (eds.), *La Pétition à Byzance* (Paris: Centre de Recherche d'Histoire et Civilisation de Byzance, 2004), 33–52, at 46–7, and Millar, *Greek Roman Empire*, 34–5.

indications of the 'living power' of Roman law; however, he also noted that whilst the question of the influence of Roman law on canonical processes in the Middle Ages had been 'researched, clarified and confirmed' by Canonists and Romanists alike, the same question had not been fully answered for the 'Antique period'.[48] Steinwenter's own contribution focused on late Roman conciliar procedures for handling cases concerning internal church discipline. For example, he noted that a synodal disciplinary hearing usually opened with a personally presented *libellus* of complaint from the plaintiff, through which a demand was made that the defendant be summoned—the granting of the summons by the synod was thus to be understood as an official act, analogous to the same procedure in a civil *cognitio*.[49] He also suggested a number of textual correspondences between imperial legislation on procedural law and conciliar regulations: *C.Th.* 9. 2. 3, given at Constantinople in December 380, for instance, specified that an accuser must furnish security *in poenam reciproci* in the initial phases of a case—the same measure is found in a 'canon' from a Council of Constantinople, held in 382.[50] The 419 Council of Carthage, on the other hand, adopted a more general ruling that anyone who was excluded from making an accusation according to Roman public law was equally prevented from doing so in a conciliar process.[51] The same North African council elaborated on ecclesiastical procedural regulations by appealing to Roman juristic texts: a canon concerning the capacity to give evidence is framed using a passage from the *Pauli Sententiae*.[52] Meyer has suggested recently that the same standards of proof applied in

[48] A. Steinwenter, 'Der Einfluss des römischen Rechts auf den antiken Kanonischen Prozess', *Atti del congresso internazionale di diritto romano, Roma*, I (1934), 227–41, at 227. See also Steinwenter, 'Die Rechtsstellung der Kirchen und Klöster nach den Papyri', *ZSS, Kan. Abt.* 19 (1930), 1–50; P. Legendre, 'Le Droit romain, modèle et langage: De la signification de l'Utrumque ius', in *Études d'histoire du droit canonique dédiées à Gabriel Le Bras*, ii (Paris: Sirey, 1965), 913–30; and L. Buisson, 'Die Entstellung des Kirchenrechts', *ZRG, Kan. Abt.* 83 (1966), 1–175.

[49] Steinwenter, 'Der Einfluss des römischen Rechts', 228.

[50] Ibid., 232. See now also S. Pietrini, *Sull' Iniziativa del processo criminale romano (IV–V secolo)* (Milan: A. Guiffè, 1996).

[51] *CCSL* 149. 231, ll. 1599–1601: 'Item placuit ut omnes servi vel proprii liberti ad accusationem non admittantur, vel omnes quos ad accusanda publica crimina leges publicae non admittunt.'

[52] Ibid., ll. 1613–15: 'Testes autem ad testimonium non admittendos, qui nec ad accusationem admitti praecepti sunt, vel etiam quos ipse accusator de sua domo produxerit', and *Pauli Sententiae* 5. 15. 1: 'Suspectos gratiae testes, et eos vel maxime, quos accusator de domo produxerit vel vitae humilitas infamarit, interrogari non placuit'. Compare also *D.* 22. 5. 24 and *Collatio Legum Mosaicarum et Romanarum* 9. 3. 1.

church courts as in secular courts.[53] The significance of these examples and others (discussed by Steinwenter in particular) does not, however, lie in the fact that the church councils on occasion 'adopted' Roman procedural regulations, but rather that new ecclesiastical norms and principles were *developed* from them. In other words, late Roman ecclesiastics utilized and expanded specific Roman norms beyond their original sphere of application, in response to particular circumstances. It is perhaps thus misleading to speak of a general 'modelling' of one legal system on another; bishops, acting in council, reacted to specific situations by identifying aspects of Roman procedural law as 'raw material' to be adapted and elaborated as necessary. In the later Roman Empire canon law 'received' Roman law via the technical forensic skill of individual ecclesiastics acting in council.

The practical working out of ecclesiastical procedures with reference to internal church discipline—including the determination of qualification for clerical offices based on 'orthodox' or 'heretical' belief—also prompted the development of a complex internal structure of appeals from one ecclesiastical tribunal to another. The formal elaboration of the church's own legal and jurisdictional hierarchy evolved piecemeal from the early fourth century onwards. The bishop of Rome's status as a final appellate judge (in analogy with the imperial court) likewise only emerged gradually and certainly not without the provincial churches' defence of their 'canonical' right to judge ecclesiastical cases without interference from Rome.[54] In 378 a council at Rome appealed to the Emperor Gratian for clarification of the church's appellate structure, and the resulting rescript (cited in the *Collectio Avellana* 13. 11–16) outlined a hierarchy of ecclesiastical jurisdiction: a regional bishop was subject to his metropolitan bishop but could appeal directly to the papal tribunal (composed of the Pope himself and five or six other bishops) or to a regional council of at least fifteen bishops. The metropolitan bishop was subject to the jurisdiction of the papacy, or to a judge delegated by Rome. Once again, the detailed practices governing this appellate structure were determined by the case-by-case application of regulations taken from Roman law.

[53] Meyer, *Legitimacy and Law*, 243. Rules governing the evidentiary value of witnesses, rather than 'texts', differed.

[54] On the 'appeal canons' of the Council of Serdica see Hess, *Early Development of Canon Law*, 179–200, with further bibliography. The appeal structure of the civil bureaucracy is discussed in Ch. 2 above.

Augustine, *Ep.* 9*, provides a specific example of this process at work. The letter describes the case of a prominent layman who had appealed to the Roman see in a case concerning the criminal prosecution of certain ecclesiastics. Augustine objects that the layman's petition had not contained a full disclosure as to the facts of the case, hence the 'pragmatic' judgment of the Pope in favour of the appellant should not stand when the case comes to be re-examined in Alypius' episcopal tribunal. In the final paragraph of the letter (addressed to Alypius himself) Augustine explicitly argues from what is customary in Roman procedure to what ought to be customary in analogous ecclesiastical situations (*Ep.* 9*. 4). It was individuals such as Alypius and Augustine who possessed the necessary forensic techniques to create a procedural 'system' internal to the church itself.

FORENSIC PRACTICE AND THE PAPAL ELABORATION OF 'ECCLESIASTICAL' LAW

From the fourth century onwards the Roman papacy was self-consciously employed in adapting both the procedural structures of late Roman law and its substantive principles in order to form the basis of a new system of 'ecclesiastical law'; moreover, it has become almost a commonplace of modern scholarship that the model for the elaboration of papal authority was provided by the juridical traditions of Roman law.[55] The papal court, as Pietri has argued, functioned along lines already laid down for Roman civil procedures: this included the public nature of the tribunal, the reading of all juridical instruments before the assembly and the examination of witnesses.[56] The papal *scrinium* was in fact organized as the mirror image of the relevant imperial bureaux and there is some evidence to suggest that, from the late fourth century onwards, the church at Rome attempted to maintain a 'central archive', collecting and cataloguing the judicial acts of the individual churches with which it was in communion.[57] The papal *scrinium* also developed

[55] See Gaudemet, *Les Sources du droit de l'église*, 58–60.

[56] Pietri, *Roma Christiana*, 670.

[57] Ibid. 675. See also Bucci, 'La genesi della struttura del diritto della Chiesa latina', 131: 'Gli Archivi del Vescovo di Roma sono a immagine di quelli imperiali e i vescovi in comunione con il Vescovo di Roma si costituiscono i propri archivi come i governatori di provincia si costituivano gli archivi con i documenti ricevuti.'

its own style of epistolary communication, using arguments developed from scripture, from the writings of key ecclesiastics, and from Roman jurisprudence.[58] This type of activity suggests that at least some of the personnel who staffed the papal offices were capable of appropriating the bureaucratic rhetoric of the imperial chancellery, whilst at the same time conserving 'the original traditions of Christian epistolography'.[59]

Individual bishops of Rome, from at least the mid–late fourth century onwards, also made a paradigmatic use of civil law techniques in order to justify their pontifical sentences.[60] In this context, Pietri describes the legislative technique of late Roman popes as 'la méthode des juristes ecclésiastiques'. The techniques of the first papal decretalists were, of course, exactly the same as those employed in the drafting of imperial rescripts. The Pope, by means of his decretals, responded to the questions of bishops who found themselves in difficulties concerning either the judicial organization of the church or the application of substantive principles of *ius ecclesiasticum*.[61] In this context, the elaboration of a law specific to the church was achieved through the same mechanisms as the elaboration of late Roman law itself.

Forensically trained ecclesiastics played a highly significant role in the creation of a complex ecclesiastical juridical structure in the later Roman Empire. Moreover, they also applied their forensic expertise to the casuistic elaboration of substantive 'canon law' principles and procedural regulations alike. Put simply, early 'canon' and 'ecclesiastical' law assimilated procedures and principles from Roman law because some of the individuals who elaborated the former had been trained as practitioners of the latter. We should thus think in terms of a constant late Roman *case-specific* interaction between legal practitioners within the church and legal practice outside it.

In Part III we shall move on to explore the role of forensic practitioners in the development of 'heresy law'; this subject provides a case-study for the creative expansion of Christian doctrine through its entry into

[58] See, for instance, S. Pietrini, *Religio e Ius Romanum nell'epistolario di Leone Magno* (Milan: A. Guiffrè, 2002).

[59] Pietri, *Roma Christiana*, 676 and also 1470–1.

[60] Ibid. 1482–90.

[61] J. Gaudemet, 'Elementi giuridici romani nella formazione del diritto ecclesiastico dei primi secoli', in M. Pavan and U. Cozzoli (eds.), *Mondo Classico e Cristianesimo* (Rome: Istituto della Enciclopedia Italiana, 1983), 171–82. W. Ullmann, *Gelasius I (492–496): Das Papsttum an der Wende der Spätantike zum Mittelalter* (Stuttgart: A. Hiersemann, 1981) discusses the 'decretals' of Innocent I (at 35–44); Zosimus (at 44–8); Boniface I (at 48–56); Leo the Great (at 61–70); and Gelasius (esp. 135–41).

the legal arena, as well as a case-study on how forensic practitioners could contribute to the development of late Roman law in general. As room was made within Roman law for the criminal offence of heresy, so new theological arguments were developed to distinguish heresy and orthodoxy. These definitions were individually tested, stretched, and redefined through actual prosecutions in both civil and ecclesiastical contexts. As we have seen in Part II, leading late Roman ecclesiastics had the necessary forensic expertise to exploit that dialectic.

III

ORTHODOXY, HERESY, AND THE COURTS

8

Defining Heresy and Orthodoxy

DEFINING HERESY

> Thus to capture in a strict definition what it is that makes a man a heretic is, in my opinion, either impossible or very difficult.[1]

When Augustine died in 430 his *De Haeresibus* (*On Heresies*) lay unfinished: the treatise had been intended as a manual for the use of both 'Catholic' clerics and laity, enabling them to detect heretical error and defend the faith.[2] It had originally been requested by a deacon of the church at Carthage, Quodvultdeus, who was apparently experiencing problems in detecting heretics within his own congregation. Quodvultdeus had repeatedly asked Augustine to produce a brief, concise, and summary handbook of heresies (a *commonitorium*) for practical use. Augustine, however, wanted to do more. He mentions two potential models for his treatise: the six-volume work on the errors of the philosophers written by the second-century Platonist Celsus and the *Anakephalaiosis*, a summary of Bishop Epiphanius of Salamis' 'medicine chest' (*Panarion*) of antidotes to the 'snakebites' of heretical sects.[3] Augustine used the categories of the eighty heretical sects named by the Christian Epiphanius in his own classifications, but he wished a specific comparison to be made between his own project and that undertaken by the (pagan) philosopher. What was the point of this comparison with Celsus?

[1] Augustine, *De Haeresibus*, pr. 7 (*CCSL* 46. 289, ll. 100–2): 'Quid ergo faciat haereticum regulari quadam definitione comprehendi, sicut ego existimo, aut omnino non potest aut difficillime potest.'

[2] See Augustine *Eps*. 221–4 (*CSEL* 57. 442–54).

[3] On these and other possible sources for Augustine's *De Haeresibus* see G. Bardy, 'Le "De haeresibus" et ses sources', in G. Morin and A. Casamassa (eds.), *Miscellanea Agostiniana: Testi e Studi*, ii (Rome: Tipografia Poliglotta Vaticana, 1931), 397–416.

Augustine explains that Celsus had laid out the opinions of all the philosophers who had founded 'schools' up to his own times, 'for he could do no more than that'.[4] Augustine had higher ambitions: 'As for myself, I want to do more than this: I want to furnish a means, if it is also God's will, of avoiding every heresy, be it known or unknown; and likewise the means of judging each one as it makes its appearance.'[5] Augustine's own plan for the *De Haeresibus* thus divided his treatise into two parts: the first was to classify existing heretical sects and the second was theoretically to define what makes a heretic 'heretical'.[6] In this second part of his treatise Augustine wanted to lay down abstract rules for detecting and judging heretical error, rules which would encompass the future, as well as the present and the past.

The gulf separating philosophy from Christian theology, the project of Celsus from that of Augustine, is symbolized in their different understandings of the word *hairesis*. *Hairesis* for Celsus, as in everyday usage, would have implied a neutral choice to follow one path (or school of thought) rather than another, and for the Christian Augustine, on the other hand, it implied a bad personal choice, a deviation from the single right path that led to God.[7] The best that Celsus could do, in Augustine's eyes, was thus to provide a list of the (mistaken) doctrines of past philosophers, whereas Augustine could set himself the task of laying down ground rules for the detection of errors that did not yet exist, precisely because he was certain that there was a set of timeless and universal Christian beliefs that future heretics would deviate from. However, as Karen King has noted in her brilliant and challenging *What is Gnosticism?* (2003) 'There was no predetermined orthodoxy that was simply there, waiting to be more carefully defined. Constructing a heretical other simultaneously and reciprocally exposes

[4] Augustine, *De Haeresibus*, pr. 7 (*CCSL* 46. 288, ll. 71–3): 'Opiniones omnium philosophorum qui sectas varias condiderunt usque ad tempora sua—neque enim plus poterat—sex non parvulis voluminibus quidam Celsus absoluit.'

[5] Ibid. pr. 7 (*CCSL* 46. 289, ll. 96–8): 'Ego vero magis hoc volo facere, si et deus velit, unde possit omnis haeresis, et quae nota est et quae ignota, vitari, et unde recte possit quaecumque innotuerit iudicari.'

[6] Ibid. pr. 7 (*CCSL* 46. 289, ll. 108–10): '(Erunt ergo primae partes operas huius de haeresibus quae post Christi adventum et ascensum adversus doctrinam ipsius existerunt, et utcumque nobis innotescere potuerunt.) In posterioribus autem partibus, quod faciat haereticum disputabitur.'

[7] For further discussion see S. Marcel, 'From Greek *Hairesis* to Christian Heresy', in W. R. Schoedel, and R. L. Wilken (eds.), *Early Christian Literature and the Classical Intellectual Tradition: In Honorem Robert M. Grant* (Paris: Éditions Beauchesne, 1979), 101–16.

the partial, mutable, and irregular character of orthodoxy.'[8] That Augustine failed, after numerous attempts, to write the second section of his *De Haeresibus* perhaps illustrates King's point. However, the fact that he attempted to write the second section at all is testimony to Augustine's own conviction that a timeless and universal orthodoxy did in fact exist.

Recent historical scholarship on late antique heresy has taken a significant rhetorical turn, as noted by Virginia Burrus:

> Patristic scholars have continued to be drawn to revisionist interpretations of ancient theological controversies. From one perspective, the recent fascination with controversy merely echoes the polemical preoccupations of the ancient texts, which inhabit a rhetorical universe shaped by the pressures of an intensely competitive society. But with the waves of postmodernist cultural theory beginning to lap at the edges even of the highly conservative fields of ancient history and historical theology, other answers to the question of the current lure of the heretical also suggest themselves. A heightened interest in the subaltern and the subversive flourishes in pockets of inquiry dispersed throughout the academy, as scholars seek to uncover the strategies by which men and women have historically resisted the social and discursive disciplines, the 'regimes of truth,' of which orthodoxies are formed. As the clarity of the monologic becomes suspect, a new appreciation emerges for the complexity of the dialogic, the many-voiced speech of the historical texts.'[9]

The 'current lure of the heretical' is thus politically motivated. According to King it fosters an 'ethical, self-reflective critique', founded on an 'ethos of critical reflexivity, democratic debate, intellectual, multilingual, and multidisciplinary competence'.[10] The historical deconstruction of

[8] K. King, *What is Gnosticism?* (Cambridge, Mass. and London: Harvard University Press, 2003), 25.

[9] V. Burrus, *The Making of a Heretic: Gender, Authority and the Priscillianist Controversy* (Berkeley, Los Angeles, and London: University of California Press, 1995), 1. See also A. Cameron, 'How to Read Heresiology', *Journal of Medieval and Early Modern Studies*, 33/3 (2003), 471–92; R. Lyman, 'Historical Methodologies and Ancient Theological Conflicts', in M. Zyniewicz, *The Papers of the Henry Luce III Fellows in Theology*, iii (Atlanta, Ga.: Scholars Press, 1999), 75–96; and T. M. Shaw, 'Ascetic Practice and the Genealogy of Heresy: Problems in Modern Scholarship and Ancient Textual Representation', in D. B. Martin and P. Cox Miller, *The Cultural Turn in Late Ancient Studies: Gender, Asceticism, and Historiography* (Durham, NC: Duke University Press, 2005), 213–36. Compare P. Athanassiadi, 'The Creation of Orthodoxy in Neoplatonism', in G. Clark and T. Rajak (eds.), *Philosophy and Power in the Graeco-Roman World* (Oxford: OUP, 2002), 271–91.

[10] King, *What is Gnosticism?*, 245, quoting the words of Elisabeth Schüssler Fiorenza. Also ibid. 243, 'I am actually doing what I am critiquing: writing the origins and history

'monologic' discourse, however, does not necessarily reveal 'dialogic' perspectives.

As Burrus herself has argued, the 'heretical' and the 'orthodox' should be understood by the historian as 'performative' concepts, involving the scripting of social roles that were then played out on the level of textual strategies: crucially, Burrus argues, the orthodox themselves were expected to act a part.[11] In the fourth century, performing the socially scripted role for being recognizably orthodox included being in possession of the 'correct' or 'straight' belief, being unanimous with (or 'in') Christ, and believing a simple and artless truth. The social script for the 'heretic', on the other hand, required having the 'wrong' or 'deviant' belief, being splintered into many sects (separated from Christ), and being mendacious and fraudulent. Needless to say, the social script for being heretical was not produced by the 'heretic'. Hence no matter how much we deconstruct 'the heretic', the discursive space that we are left with remains, in this context, monologic. Burrus is undoubtedly correct that 'Late ancient Christian orthodoxy involved a bit of shamming', however a crucial part of the 'orthodox' social script involved believing precisely that there was no sham: that orthodoxy and heresy were 'real' concepts, that could *potentially* be given a definite historical content.

The second- and third-century polemicists Justin, Irenaeus, and Tertullian each claimed that the demand for a right path (understood as both orthodoxy and *orthopraxis*) had been built into the earliest Christianity through the pivotal idea of the Last Judgment[12]—a claim undoubtedly influenced by so-called Gnostic texts that argued for the almost universal salvation of humanity (*The Apocryphon of John*) or discarded the concept of a final judgment at all (*The Gospel of Truth*).[13] The very concept of a universal tribunal, the Last Judgment, on the other

of Gnosticism in order to "Subvert the game" ' and 246, 'My objective has been, not to replace "orthodoxy" with "heresy" as a new normative foundation, but to further critical reflexivity with regard to the discourses and methods of historiographical scholarship.'

11 V. Burrus, ' "In the Theater of this Life": The Performance of Orthodoxy in Late Antiquity', in W. Klingshirn and M. Vessey, *The Limits of Ancient Christianity: Essays on Late Antique Thought and Culture in Honor of R. A. Markus* (Ann Arbor: University of Michigan Press, 1999), 80–96.

12 For instance, Matt. 25: 31–46, Christ seated on a throne, judging between sheep and goats, sending the former into life eternal and the latter into everlasting punishment; Acts 17: 31, a future day has been set aside for Christ's judgment; and James 4: 12, there is one lawgiver who is able to save and destroy. Also 2 Cor. 5. 10 and John 12: 48–50.

13 King, *What is Gnosticism?*, 27.

hand, implies some expectation of a universal legal order. According to Tertullian it also implied universal theological belief:

These testimonies of a strict discipline existing among us are an additional proof of truth, from which no one can safely turn away, who keeps in mind that future judgement, when we must all stand before the tribunal of Christ, to render an account of our faith itself. What then will they say, those who shall have defiled the virgin [i.e. faith], which Christ committed to them, by the adultery of heresy?[14]

For Tertullian all Christians shall be judged according to their faith as well as their actions. The revealed doctrines of Christ's divine mysteries do not themselves admit of rational interpretation; hence the mysteries contained in scripture are also 'the testimonies of a strict discipline', they are the *regula fidei* (the 'rule of faith'). The baptized Christian is bound by the rule of faith, and the 'heretic' will have no defence before the tribunal of Christ. The demand for a prescribed orthodoxy could thus be represented as having been built into the theology of Christianity from its inception. The central place of the Last Judgment suggested a set of 'Christian' ethical practices and beliefs that could be applied universally, and the fulfilment of the promises of the revelation implied that all individuals would be judged according to the same criteria. 'Orthodoxy may be as much a metamorphosis (or pseudo-metamorphosis) of the foundational religious idea as heresy.'[15] Nonetheless in the second and third centuries, in certain circles at least, we can speak of a 'pre-Nicene orthodoxy': the concept existed, even if the content was (always) under construction.

The rhetorical classification and naming of the 'heretic' thus performed a crucial function in ancient theological polemic and discourse. According to the Gospel of Luke Christ appointed seventy-two apostles and sent them out ahead of him; they returned rejoicing:

'Lord', they said, 'even the devils submit to us when we use your name'. He said to them, 'I watched Satan fall like lightning from heaven. Truly, I have given you the power to tread underfoot serpents and scorpions and the whole

[14] Tertullian, *De Praescriptione Haereticorum* 44 (*CSEL* 70. 56, ll. 1–7): 'Proinde haec pressioris apud nos testimonia disciplinae ad probationem ueritatis accedunt, a qua diuertere nemini expedit qui meminerit futuri iudicii, quo omnes nos necesse est apud Christi tribunal adstare, reddentes rationem in primis fidei ipsius. Quid ergo dicent, qui illam stuprauerint adulterio haeretico uirginem traditam a Christo?'

[15] R. Williams, 'Does it Make Sense to Speak of Pre-Nicene Orthodoxy?', in R. Williams (ed.), *The Making of Orthodoxy: Essays in Honour of Henry Chadwick* (Cambridge: CUP, 1989), 1–23, at 3.

strength of the enemy; nothing shall ever hurt you. Yet do not rejoice that the spirits submit to you; rejoice rather that your names are written in heaven.'[16]

In this Lukan narrative, the power of the seventy-two apostles to cast out serpents, scorpions (both later understood to refer to heretics), and devils was confirmed by Christ himself, but was founded on the fact that their names had already been 'written in heaven'. By the second century the possession of Christ's name was used as a title to orthodoxy: Justin refused to apply the name of Christ to divergent sects, despite his theological position that all the baptized remain at least externally bound together as a unity.[17] In effect, an individual who exercised choice over Christ's deposit of faith committed the same sin as Adam over the tree of knowledge: both turned away from God to self. The pride of the heretic could therefore be 'fittingly' symbolized by the application of his own name to doctrines that he had interpreted for himself, as opposed to trusting in the apostolic authorities confirmed by Christ.

In the fourth-century dialogue known as the *Consultationes Zacchei christiani et Apollonii philosophi*, the Christian character Zaccheus provides a typology of heretics and their errors, ostensibly for the benefit of his non-Christian interlocutor, a philosopher named Apollonius: heretics abandon the apostolic tradition, they follow their leaders into a perversion of the faith, and 'they change the name of their religion at the same time as they change what they think'.[18] Rhetorical strategies of naming and classifying were widespread amongst fourth- and fifth-century Christians.[19] According to Augustine, the Arians called Catholics (here understood as the 'true' Christians) Athanasians or Homoousians, whilst the Pelagians named them Traducians, the Donatists referred to them as Macharians, and the Manichaeans branded them Pharisees.[20] Of course, every Christian polemicist (with the singular exception of the Manichaean) claimed the title of 'true Christian' for himself.

[16] Luke 10: 17–20.

[17] Justin, *Dialogus cum Tryphone* 35. 4. 6. The most recent critical edn. of this text is M. Marcovich, *Iustini Martyris. Apologiae pro Christianis, Dialogus cum Tryphone* (Berlin and New York: Walter de Gruyter, 2005).

[18] *Consultationes Zacchei christiani et Apollonii philosophi* 2. 11. 3 (*SC* 402. 78–82). Ibid. 2. 11. 6 names Mani, Marcion, Photinus, Sabellius, and Arius as founders of heresies, with the qualification that Patripassians got 'their name from their error'.

[19] For general discussion see H. Inglebert, 'L'Histoire des hérésies chez les hérésiologues', in B. Pouderon and Y.-M. Duval (eds.), *L'Historiographie de l'Église des premiers siècles* (Paris: Beauchesne, 2001), 105–25.

[20] Augustine, *Contra Julianum Opus Imperfectum* 1. 71 (*CSEL* 85/1. 91–2, ll. 36–43).

As Ayers has argued with reference to fourth-century Trinitarian theology: 'Such heresiological labels enabled early theologians and ecclesiastical historians to portray theologians to whom they were opposed as distinct and coherent groups, and they enabled writers to tar enemies with the name of a figure already in dispute.'[21] 'Heresiological labelling', Ayers comments astutely, thus has the effect of covering up 'the complexity of theological development'. With respect to the definition of Arianism, for example: 'No clear party sought to preserve Arius' theology. Many who are termed Arian justly protested their ignorance of his teaching or works; their theologies often have significantly different concerns and preoccupations.'[22] The term 'Arian' was a polemical rhetorical label; nonetheless, as I shall argue below, this does not mean that we should approach 'Arianism' solely as a rhetorical construct.

PHILOSOPHY, LAW, AND ORTHODOXY

From at least the second century the application of philosophical techniques to scriptural exegesis encouraged the categorization of theological belief, despite the Pauline scriptural warnings against 'pointless philosophical discussions'.[23] Le Boulluec has studied the relationship between discursive strategies in ancient philosophical and theological contexts, focusing primarily on the application of philosophical methods of reasoning to the construction of heresiological categories in the second and third centuries.[24] In fact whether a 'proper use of philosophy' had been applied to the 'true faith', or not, became itself a normative discursive strategy.[25] By its very nature, however, philosophical debate could not provide the criteria from which an 'authoritative' content of

21 L. Ayers, *Nicaea and its Legacy: An Approach to Fourth-Century Trinitarian Theology* (Oxford: OUP, 2004), 2.

22 Ibid. 13.

23 2 Tim. 2: 14–19 and 1 Tim. 6: 20–1. For a carefully nuanced discussion see R. Lyman, 'Hellenism and Heresy', *Journal of Early Christian Studies*, 11/2 (2003), 209–22.

24 A. Le Boulluec, *Le Notion d'hérésie dans la literature grecque IIe–IIIe siècles* (Paris: Études Augustiniennes, 1985). See also E. G. Weltin, *Athens and Jerusalem: An Interpretative Essay on Christianity and Classical Culture* (Atlanta, Ga.: Scholar's Press, 1987).

25 See M. Williams, *Rethinking 'Gnosticism': An Argument for Dismantling a Dubious Category* (Princeton: Princeton University Press, 1996) and E. F. Osborn, 'Reason and the Rule of Faith in the Second Century AD', in R. Williams (ed.), *The Making of Orthodoxy: Essays in Honour of Henry Chadwick* (Cambridge: CUP, 1989), 40–61.

orthodox beliefs could be derived and maintained; after the conversion of Constantine, on the other hand, Roman law held out the possibility that it could. The logic of the late Roman courtroom demanded an arguable case, and then it declared a winner and a loser.

Eusebius of Caesarea's account of the case of Paul of Samosata (bishop of Antioch *c*.261 until his synodal deposition *c*.268/9) is revealing in this context.[26] Eusebius devotes four chapters of his *Ecclesiastical History* to Paul, in which he cites evidence including excerpts taken from the synodal deposition letter itself, addressed to the then bishops of Rome and Alexandria and sent some forty years or so before Eusebius himself was writing.[27] According to Eusebius' narrative, then, Paul had already been condemned for heterodox belief, alongside innovations in liturgy and practice, by a synod at Antioch *c*.264—but to no effect. A second synod was thus assembled about five years later. At this second synod the bishops subjected Paul to a dialectical inquiry, but the 'person foremost in calling him to account and in utterly refuting his attempts at concealment was Malchion', who was 'a learned man' and head of an Antiochene school of rhetoric.[28] Eusebius thus styles Malchion as a rhetorically skilled interrogator, who was also renowned for 'the extraordinary authenticity of his Faith in Christ' and had been appointed a presbyter; it was the combination of Malchion's forensic acumen and his Christian faith that resulted in Paul's excommunication from the Antiochene church.[29] The synodal sanction, however, apparently lacked executive force. Paul refused to give up possession of the church house to his successor, Domnus. The bishops thus petitioned the Emperor Aurelian (270–5), who issued a rescript ruling that the building should be given to the bishop in communion with the bishops of Italy and Rome.[30]

The heresy of Paul had of course been identified during the synodal proceedings and Eusebius is careful to stress that Malchion (whom

[26] On the geographical, political, and cultural background to the Paul of Samosata affair see F. Millar, 'Paul of Samosata, Zenobia and Aurelian: The Church, Local Culture and Political Allegiance in Third-Century Syria', *Journal of Roman Studies*, 61 (1971), 1–17.

[27] H. de Riedmatten, *Les Actes du procès de Paul de Samosate: Étude sur la Christologie du IIIe au IVe siècle* (Fribourg, Switzerland: Éditions St-Paul, 1952), 15.

[28] Eusebius, *HE* 7. 29. 1–2, on which see de Riedmatten, *Les Actes*, 20. For the *rhetor* Malchion see also Heath, *Menander: A Rhetor in Context*, 260, and Kaster, *Guardians of Language*, 73.

[29] De Riedmatten, *Les Actes*, 136–58 gives extant fragments from the acts of the Synodal depositional hearing against Paul.

[30] Eusebius, *HE* 7. 30. 19, see Millar, 'Paul of Samosata', 14–16.

he portrayed, remember, as the authentic Christian skilled in forensic rhetoric) had deliberately employed stenographers to take notes as he conducted his disputation with Paul—notes that Eusebius states he knows to be still extant.[31] If these stenographic records stating that Paul had been judged a heretic really did exist, then they almost certainly would have been used as part of the legal dossier on Paul presented, in the form of a petition, to the imperial court of Aurelian. The fact that an emperor resolved the dispute over Paul's possession of a church house and (incidentally) confirmed his heresy, may well tell us more about the age of Eusebius than the age of Paul of Samosata. With his portrayal of Malchion however, Eusebius is very careful to represent the forensic skills needed to invoke imperial authority as being provided from within the Christian community itself.

In his attempts to urge the formation of a 'Catholic' and universal body of belief for an imperial church, the Emperor Constantine resorted to the sanctions of law in an attempt to enforce the anathemas against Arius and those 'of his opinions', pronounced at the Council of Nicaea (325). In a letter of 324, addressed to 'Arius and those of his name', Constantine had suggested a philosophical model for handling doctrinal disagreement:

> But so that I may bring to the attention of your Wisdoms a slight comparison, you surely know how philosophers themselves all agree in one set of principles, and often when they disagree in some part of their statements, although they are separated by their learned skill, yet they agree together again in unity when it comes to basic principle. If this is so, surely it is far more right that we, who are the appointed servants of the great god should in a religious commitment of this kind, be of one mind with each other?[32]

Less than a year after exhorting them to be more like philosophers, however, Constantine apparently condemned Arius (and his followers) with a sentence taken from Roman law: *infamia*.[33] *Infamia* involved the diminution of the esteem in which a person was held in Roman society (*existimatio*)—those declared *infames* could be excluded from the right of making applications in civil and criminal trials or from holding certain offices, as well as more specific disqualifications.[34] According to the

[31] Eusebius, *HE* 7. 29. 2.

[32] Eusebius, *Vita Con.* 2. 71. 2–3, tr. A. Cameron and S. Hall, *Eusebius, Life of Constantine* (Oxford: OUP, 1999), 182. See Ayers, *Nicaea and its Legacy*, 18.

[33] See *D.* 3. 2, *De his qui notantur infamia.* Also *CI* 2. 11 and 10. 59.

[34] Berger, *Encyclopedic Dictionary*, art. 'Infamia', 500. For the application of *infamia* as a punishment for crimes against the Christian faith see A. H. J. Greenidge, *Infamia:*

Constantinian text as given by the fifth-century ecclesiastical historian Socrates, the precedent cited for the condemnation of Arius and those who 'hold his opinions' was, ironically in the light of the 324 letter, a prior sentence issued against the Neoplatonic philosopher Porphyry:

Victor Constantine Maximus Augustus to the bishops and people. Since Arius has imitated wicked and impious persons, it is just that he should undergo the like *infamia*. Since Porphyry that enemy of piety, having composed licentious treatises against religion, found a suitable recompense and such as from that time forward branded him with *infamia*, overwhelming him with deserved reproach, his impious writings also having been destroyed; so now it seems fit that both Arius and such as hold his opinions should be denominated Porphyrians, that they may take their name from those whose conduct they have imitated.[35]

Arius, and any who supported him, were to be branded with the name of Porphyrians; with a rhetorical flourish, the *legal* censure of divergent theological belief was achieved by defining a new group (Arius and his supporters) and branding it with an old name. The concept of 'Arianism' thus entered the Roman legislative arena.

Over one hundred years later, a constitution issued in the name of the Emperor Theodosius II looked back to this Constantinian measure to justify the condemnation of the theological 'innovations' of Nestorius.[36] This 435 condemnation, as Millar notes, is

known to us from three different sources: a Latin version, found in the *Codex Theodosianus* which is in the form of a letter addressed to Leontius, Prefect of Constantinople; an (apparently) complete text in Greek, with no addressee or date or place of issue, and headed simply 'Copy of an Imperial Law,' known from the Greek *Acta* [*ACO* 1. 1. 3, para. 111]; and a brief note in Rusticus's version of the *Tragoedia* [of Irenaeus], summarizing the content of the law.[37]

Its Place in Roman Public and Private Law (Oxford: Clarendon Press, 1894), 144–53 and 209–13 (without discussion of Constantine's constitution against Arius).

35 The only extant version of this text is at Socrates, *HE* 1. 9 (tr. in *NPNF* 2 2. 14). On the date of Porphyry's *Against the Christians* see T. D. Barnes, 'Scholarship and Propaganda? Porphyry Against the Christians and its Historical Setting', *BICS* 39 (1994), 53–65; both Eusebius of Caesarea and Methodius of Olympus (Lycia) produced direct refutations (non-extant). Eusebius also included a polemic against Porphyry in the preface to the 2nd edn. of his *Chronicle*, probably composed 325/6 (see Barnes, *Constantine and Eusebius*, 113).

36 On the theological and historical background to the controversy see S. Wessel, *Cyril of Alexandria and the Nestorian Controversy: The Making of a Saint and a Heretic* (New York and Oxford: OUP, 2004).

37 Millar, *Greek Roman Empire*, 176. The version at *C.Th.* 16. 5. 66 is also excerpted at *CI* 1. 5. 6.

Millar's translation of this Theodosian constitution combines the extant Latin and Greek versions: the preface (cut from the Theodosian Code) begins by stating that 'those who behave impiously towards the divinity should be punished with appropriate penalties and *be addressed with names suitable to their baseness*'.[38] The constitution continues:

> Since Nestorius, the leader of a monstrous teaching [Latin *superstitio*], has been condemned, it remains to apply to those who share his opinions and participate in his impiety a condemnatory name, so that they may not, by abusing the appellation of Christians, be adorned by the name of those from whose doctrines they have impiously separated themselves. Therefore we decree that those everywhere who share in the unlawful doctrines of Nestorius are to be called 'Simonians'. For it is appropriate that those who, in turning away from the divine, imitate his impiety should inherit the same appellation as he, just as the Arians, by a law of the deceased Constantine are called, because of the similarity of their impiety, 'Porphyrians' after Porphyry, who, having attempted to battle against the true religion by the power of reason, left behind books, but not records of (true) learning.[39]

Appealing to a series of documents from Schwartz's *Acta Conciliorum Oecumenicorum* and the mid-fifth-century text of Irenaeus' *Tragoedia*, Millar has brilliantly traced the subsequent diffusion of this constitution through bureaucratic and ecclesiastical channels alike: culminating in a letter addressed back to the Emperors Theodosius and Valentinian by certain bishops (including the then metropolitan bishop of the province of Cilicia Prima, as well as the bishops of Rome, Constantinople, and Antioch), who state that they are 'co-anathematizing, along with Nestorius himself, also those who assert the same impious doctrines as he, that is the "Simoniani", as your order justly named them'.[40] A new legal classification, albeit one grafted onto the scriptural figure of Simon Magus, was thus laid down, and this measure provoked concrete action

[38] Tr. Millar, *Greek Roman Empire*, 176 (italics mine).

[39] Ibid. 176–7. 'Simonians' refers to Simon Magus—represented in late antique heresiology as the original heresiarch who founded the heretics' counterfeit genealogical line (in opposition, of course, to the true authority conveyed by apostolic succession). For discussion of Simon Magus see A. Tuzlak, 'The Magician and the Heretic: The Case of Simon Magus', in P. Mirecki and M. Meyer (eds.), *Magic and Ritual in the Ancient World* (Leiden: Brill, 2002), 416–26. Augustine's list of heresies in the *De Haeresibus* begins with 'Simonians'.

[40] Millar, *Greek Roman Empire*, 178; ibid. 179–91 on the various fates of Nestorius and those associated with him.

from the ecclesiastical hierarchy. This fact stands, whether the threat to anathematize the 'Simonians' remained on a symbolic level, or whether it was actually enforced against individuals for whom the name could be made to stick. In fact, through a process of naming, classifying, and reasoning out from existing precedents, any alleged 'deviation' from Christian doctrine could potentially become the focus of a legal case, subject to imperial constitutions, as well as ecclesiastical sanctions.

The use of private creeds and anathemas in the fourth and fifth centuries also underscores the fluidity of Christian doctrine, and the taxonomical processes at work in the formation of an agreed set of 'orthodox' beliefs in any given context, at any particular time. For example, at the 'dedication Council of Antioch' (341), Theophronius of Tyana apparently read out a private creed, in which he condemned Marcellus of Ancyra and 'those who taught as he did'.[41] The wording of private creeds could, of course, be altered and anathemas revoked: within two or three years Arius and certain others who had been exiled in the wake of the Council of Nicaea (325) were readmitted to communion.[42] The wording of the anathemas originally pronounced against them, however, continued to have a lasting effect—in fact, as Lienhard has suggested, the anathemas issued at Nicaea in 325 were possibly more important than the Creed itself, in terms of the development of doctrinal controversies between the 320s and 350s/360s.[43] The wording of private creeds and the issuing of anathemas against named individuals established concrete networks of ecclesiastical communication (i.e. 'communion'), as well as mapping out the 'acceptable' boundaries of a spiritual community.

At *Ecclesiastical History* 4. 24 Eusebius gives a highly rhetorical description of the bishop as shepherd of his flock, in the context of the pre-Nicene Eastern churches:

> Since the heretics no less at that time were like tares despoiling the pure seed of apostolic teaching, the shepherds of the churches everywhere, as though frightening away wild beasts from Christ's sheep, sought to hold them back; so that at one time they would resort to persuasions and exhortations to the brethren, at another they would oppose them openly and partly through oral

[41] J. T. Lienhard, *Contra Marcellum: Marcellus of Ancyra and Fourth-Century Theology* (Washington DC: Catholic University of America Press, 1999), 5. Marcellus of Ancyra was a vocal opponent of the 'heterousians' (adopting Lewis Ayer's term, intended to replace the traditional label of 'Arians').

[42] Ayers, *Nicaea and its Legacy*, 19.

[43] As argued by Lienhard, *Contra Marcellum*, 'Introduction'.

discussions and refutations, partly through written efforts, expose their opinions as false by means of the most solid demonstrations.[44]

Writing in the early fourth century, Eusebius clearly places a duty of separating wrong belief from right doctrine on the bishops themselves, as the leaders of their own individual communities. However, notwithstanding Eusebius' 'description' of episcopal engagement in oral and written controversies, 'control over the Eucharist and the liturgy was a bishop's main weapon against disorder in the Church'.[45] Disorder could, of course, include acts of violence against church property and clerics, alongside 'moral failings' by clergy and laity alike, as much as any accusation of suspect doctrine—as shown, for example, by petitions from penitents seeking to be readmitted to the Eucharist, after a period of exclusion, in Apa Abraham's communities (in and around the city of Hermonthis in Upper Egypt, late sixth- to early seventh-century).[46] An awareness of individuals or groups who had been excluded from a given community operated on the micro-level: hence the late fourth-century Council of Laodicea (Phyrgia) laid down that the blessings (*eulogiae*) of heretics could not be received 'lawfully' as they were absurdities (*alogiai*); the sharing in blessings and prayers was a sign of communion—the implication being that the 'heretic' is always, potentially, 'one of us'.[47]

In the charged atmosphere of mid to late fourth-century North Africa, on the other hand, Optatus berates the (schismatic) 'Donatists' for shirking on the duty of greeting other baptized Christians with the customary 'kiss in the Holy Spirit':

For there are some of you who themselves deny the usual kisses in a conventional greeting, and there are many who are taught not to say 'Hello' to any of us. And it seems to them that this is commanded by a lesson, which, however, they do not understand, not knowing of whom the Apostle said this: 'Do not even

[44] Eusebius, *HE* 4. 24, tr J. E. L. Oulton, *Eusebius Ecclesiastical History*, i (Cambridge Mass.: Harvard University Press, 1932), 384.

[45] A. Papaconstantinou, review of G. Schmelz, *Kirchliche Amtsträger im spätantiken Aëgypten nach den Aussagen der griechischen und koptischen Papyri und Ostraka*, Archiv für Papyrusforschung und verwandte Gebiete, 13 (Munich and Leipzig: K.G. Saur, 2002).

[46] Ch. 4 of Schmelz, *Kirchliche Amtsträger,* discusses the Apa Abraham archive in this context.

[47] Council of Laodicea, canon 32. Also canon 6: heretics cannot enter the church whilst they persist in heresy; canons 7 and 8: procedures for readmission of catechumens, communicants, and clergy who had abjured their heresy, including renewed catechetical instruction; canons 10 and 31, church members are not to marry their children to heretics, without certain measures having been taken first.

take meals with these people, do not say hello to them, for their speech creeps like a cancer'.[48]

Whether we should read this remark as part of Optatus' textual strategy of portraying the 'Donatists' as the party that persisted *in separating itself* from the 'True' church, or whether we approach it as a spotlight on the everyday life of late fourth-century North African Christians (and their exegetical practices), it nonetheless highlights the potential for ecclesiological and doctrinal conflict to be played out on the level of concrete social interaction. A further possible day-to-day context is catechetical instruction: Gregory of Nyssa, Augustine, and Cyril of Jerusalem each imply that catechetical instruction had to vary according to the 'starting point' of the catechumen: the instruction suitable for a 'manichee' will not work for an 'Arian', for example. Some catechumens were also instructed in how to spot a 'heretic'—if you are entering an unfamiliar city and need to ask for directions to the 'church', as Cyril of Alexandria and Augustine both argued, how otherwise will you be able to identify which 'church' you are being directed to?[49]

The late fourth- to sixth-century 'handbooks against heresy', which circulated in both the Eastern and Western Empires, were clearly assembled with practical as well as ideological contexts in mind. Extant examples include Epiphanius of Salamis' *Panarion*, itself excerpted in a much shorter, more manageable form known as the *Anakephalaiosis* (probably not compiled by Epiphanius himself, but nonetheless circulating under his name) and Theodoret of Cyrrhus' *Compendium of Heretical Fables*, alongside diverse taxonomic works by Philastrius of Brescia, Augustine of Hippo, and Gennadius of Marseilles and an anonymous *Indiculus de haeresibus*, produced some time before 428.[50] The 'Donatists' in North Africa apparently circulated their own catalogues of heresies (no longer extant) and we should reckon on other

[48] Optatus 4. 5 (*CSEL* 26. 108): 'nam et vos ipsi aliqui in perfunctoria salutatione oscula denegatis solita et docentur multi, ne ave dicant cuiquam nostrum, et videntur sibi hoc de lectione, sed non intellecta mandari ignorantes, de quibus apostolus hoc dixerit; cum his nec cibum capere; ave illi ne dixeritis; serpit enim eorum sermo velut cancer'. Tr. M. Edwards, *Optatus: Against the Donatists* (Liverpool: Liverpool University Press, 1997), 88.

[49] See Humfress, 'Citizens and Heretics: Late Roman Lawyers on Christian Heresy', in E. Iricinschi and H. Zellentin (eds.), *Heresy and Identity in Late Antiquity* (Tübingen: Mohr Siebeck, 2007), for further discussion.

[50] Discussed by Cameron, 'How to Read Heresiology', and J. McClure, 'Handbooks Against Heresy in the West, from the Late Fourth to the Late Sixth Centuries', *Journal of Theological Studies*, 30 (1979), 186–97.

'distinct' communities of Christians doing likewise.[51] Anti-heretical *Florilegia*, which claimed to do nothing more than 'cut and paste' existing texts were also in circulation: for example, the pseudo-Augustinian *Solutiones Diversarum Quaestionum ab Haereticis Obiectarum*, probably put together between 470 and 490 in North Africa, opens with the statement, 'In this corpus are contained the answers of Aurelius Augustinus to diverse questions thrown up by the heretics'.[52] It is perhaps no coincidence that these handbooks circulated widely at the same time as imperial legislation against named heretical groups and individuals began to intensify.

A striking claim for the practical use of anti-heretical polemic is made in the anonymous work known as the *Contra Varimadum*, composed between 439 and 484 (perhaps *c*.445–50), by an African author, possibly writing in exile in Naples. The preface gives an account of how the text itself came into existence: a work by a certain Varimadus, a 'deacon of the Arian sect', was passed on by a 'learned and extremely pious man' to the present author, who decided that Varimadus' work demanded refutation not just in a 'private report', but rather in 'a full scale attack on his propositions which draws on weighty evidence'. Thus, the preface continues, everyone who reads the present work will be able to rebut the heretics' objections 'not, as they are usually met, with mere words, but with legal documents'—the aim being that, having been refuted in all respects 'those who endeavour to construct such fictions on the basis of the teachings of the prophets and the apostles shall be thrown into confusion, and reduced to nought'. The 'legal documents' that the reader of the *Contra Varimadum* is provided with are in fact extracts from sacred scripture.[53] Furthermore, the author styles himself as a *defensor* of the Catholic faith—from book 1, section 2 onwards the text takes the form of 'Arian' claims, followed by 'Catholic' refutations (in the form of 'if they say x, you should say y'). The fact that there is a broader context here than scriptural exegesis

[51] As stated by Augustine at *Contra Cresconium* 2. 3. 4 (*BA* 31. 156).

[52] *Solutiones diversarum quaestionum ab haereticis obiectarum*, pr. (*CCSL* 90. 141).

[53] *Contra Varimadum*, pr., *CCSL* 90. 9, ll. 3–11. 'Sed quia nunc conperimus eos nihil velle sibi privatis verbis opponi, sed magis propositiones suas desiderent testimoniorum virtutibus oppugnari, mediocribus et ingenii tardioribus consulentes, ita sancto nos spiritu adivvante responsionem mostram universes eorum obiectionibus testmonialiter coaptauimus, ut is qui legerit, non nudis, ut solent obicere, verbis sed legalibus valeat refellere documentis: ut omni ex parte convicti confundantur, et ad nihilum redigantur, qui super fundamentum prophetarum apostolorumque doctorum talia figmenta construere moliuntur.'

alone is noted in the mention of 'Arians' having been constrained by imperial law.[54] The forensic style of the *Contra Varimadum* thus interwines scriptural exegesis and legal process on a number of different levels.

At the Last Judgment, according to Paul's First Epistle to the Corinthians, each of 'Christ's ministers' and the 'stewards of the mysteries of God' (later understood to refer to the episcopal office) would have to render an account of the trust placed in them—just as individuals in formal positions of trust were required to do by Roman law, at the end of their period of office. The trust placed in Christ's 'stewards', however, included the care of the souls of those for whom the bishop was responsible: hence the salvation of the bishop's own soul could be said to depend on his salvation of others. From Constantine onwards, the involvement of bishops in the prosecution of heresy cases could be justified within this soteriological context. In 396 or 397 Augustine wrote a letter to the Donatist Bishop Eusebius justifying the prosecution of Donatists under Roman law. Augustine first made a general argument based on citizenship rights: 'no one can blame me if I have brought them [certain Donatists] to public notice in the public records—a privilege which cannot be refused to me, I think, in a city which enjoys Roman citizenship'.[55] Entering an event into the public records validated its use as evidential proof in any future legal case.[56] Moreover, Augustine continues, he is instructed by scriptural authority not to remain silent before the public records—he must refute and legally condemn 'those who teach the things they ought not, as I can prove by the words of the Lord and the Apostles. Let no man think that I can be enjoined to silence in these matters.'[57] Thus Augustine could present the legal prosecution of 'schismatics' and 'heretics' as a logical outcome of scriptural commands.

[54] *Contra Varimadum*, 9, ll. 26–7.

[55] Augustine, *Ep.* 35. 3 (new edn. *CCSL* 31. 128, ll. 55–8): 'Aut si male facio, per tuam benivolentiam ista corrigenda curare, de me nullus queratur si haec illi perferri in notitiam per codices publicos fecero, qui mihi negari, ut arbitror, in Romana civitate non possunt.'

[56] Compare *CCSL* 149. 199–200, ll. 590–600: the 401 Council of Carthage (advised perhaps by Augustine himself) orders that letters should be sent from the council to the African judges so that they could aid 'the common mother, the Catholic Church' by recording events in public acts and thus enabling prosecutions.

[57] Augustine, *Ep.* 35. 3 (new edn. *CCSL* 31. 128–9, ll. 58–62): 'Nam cum Deus imperet ut loquamur et praedicemus verbum, et docentes quae non oportat refellamus, et instemus *opportune atque importune*, sicut dominicis in apostolicis Litteris probo, nullus hominum mihi silentium de his rebus persuadendum arbitretur.'

HERETICS AND ROMAN LAW

'Cast out the edict! Nobody believes by an edict!'[58] These formulaic phrases were chanted by a congregation assembled in the main church at Antioch, around 438, in reaction to the reading of an imperial edict that condemned Nestorius. Even if we agree with the Antiochene crowd that law cannot compel belief, anti-heretical legislation was an enduring feature of the late antique landscape. The remainder of this chapter will approach the late Roman anti-heretical 'laws' from the perspective of the legislator. Chapter 9 will attempt to contextualize the same material by viewing it from the angle of forensic practice.

It is worth stressing at the outset, however, that the concept of an autonomous, authoritative, 'law' that strove to enforce 'right belief', by outlawing 'criminal' deviations from it, may be an accurate portrayal of legislative intentions (or rather imperial bureaucratic rhetoric), but it is nonetheless a flawed paradigm for the late Roman historian to adopt. As the sociologists Goffman and Giddens have argued, 'social control should be viewed from the perspective of interaction, not of behaviour determined by institutional or other mechanisms'.[59] Thus rather than asking whether anti-heretical 'laws' were 'applied', or how successfully they were enforced, we should raise a series of questions like those posed by David Cohen with reference to ancient Athenian law. What legal norms regulated heresy? In what ways were these norms interpreted? What were 'the normative expectations of the community, or different parts of the community' with regard to heresy and anti-heresy legislation? Finally, how were these normative expectations 'translated into patterns of social control and definitions of deviance and normality'? As I have argued in Part I, a focus on forensic rhetoric stresses the 'practical knowledge' associated with legal processes—thus revealing the strategies that particular actors could use to manipulate a given system or structure. I shall return to this point with particular reference to late Roman heresy cases below.

[58] S. G. F. Perry, *The Second Synod of Ephesus* (Dartford: Orient Press, 1881), 129, quoted from Millar, *Greek Roman Empire*, 189.

[59] Quoted from D. J. Cohen, *Law, Sexuality and Society: The Enforcement of Morals in Classical Athens* (Cambridge: CUP, 1991), 7.

The potential to define wrong religious belief, or actions resulting from wrong religious belief, as a crime under Roman law only existed after Constantine had incorporated Christianity into the legal framework of the Empire.[60] Between the fourth and sixth centuries a significant body of imperial texts were issued against 'heretical' and 'schismatic' beliefs and practices, far outnumbering the surviving laws against 'paganism'. Attempting to define explicitly what was 'orthodox', rather than stating what was not, was also a strategy open to the drafters of late Roman constitutions; although, again, we should approach these definitions as specific reactions to concrete situations, rather than as 'general' definitions.[61] Strictly speaking, legislation against Christian heretics (as well as other constructed groups such as 'apostates') was an innovation after Constantine—but there was nonetheless a pre-existing context within which that legislation was developed.

What we today might classify as an offence or crime against religion was understood under the Late Republic and Early Empire as a crime against the social fabric itself, and as an attack on public order, as it threatened the entire community's relationship with the gods.[62] The juristic development of the *ius sacrum*, the branch of Roman law that had traditionally 'embraced the legal principles and institutions which are connected with the right relations of men to gods, with questions of cult, sacrifices, temples, consecrations, games and sacerdotal functions, wherever they may occur'[63], had undoubtedly come to a halt by at least the third century. However, ensuring right relations between the Empire and God(s) remained a focus of Roman law throughout the post-classical age.[64] What changed in the later Roman period was not

60 See T. D. Barnes 'Legislation Against the Christians', *JRS* 58 (1968), 32–50, on Eusebius, *Vita Const.* 3. 66, which apparently reports a Constantinian 'edict', probably issued before Sept. 325, addressed to 'Novatians, Valentinians, Marcionites, Paulians, you who are called Cataphrygians and all you who devise and support heresies by means of your private assemblies'. These 'groups' are forbidden to assemble, their meeting houses are confiscated and they are 'encouraged' to join the Catholic church.

61 Discussion in C. Humfress, 'Roman Law, Forensic Argument and the Formation of Christian Orthodoxy (III–VI Centuries)', in S. Elm, E. Rebillard, and A. Romano (eds.), *Orthodoxie, christianisme, histoire—Orthodoxy, Christianity, History: Travaux du groupe de recherches 'Definir, maintenir et remettre en cause l'orthodoxie dans l'histoire du christianisme'* (Rome: École Française de Rome, 2001), 125–47 and Bianchini, *Caso concreto*, esp. 92–8 with specific reference to *Sirm. Const.* 6 and *C.Th.* 16. 5. 62.

62 Humfress, 'Citizens and Heretics'.

63 Berger, art. 'Ius Sacrum', *Encyclopedic Dictionary*, 532.

64 It is worth noting in this context that the text chosen by the compilers to head *C.Th.* 16. 1 (under the rubric *de fide catholica*) reads in its entirety: 'If any *iudex* or

the overall framework for maintaining men and God(s) in their proper relationship, but rather the legal definition of which cultic acts were to count as *religio* (i.e as licit and thus promoting the health and welfare of the Empire).

For those late antique bishops whose voices we hear most frequently, Christianity alone could ensure right relations between men and a single (Christian) God—an argument that Roman Emperors from at least Theodosius I onwards seem to have accepted.[65] Not all 'Christian' acts, however, could be defined as *religio*. From a normative Christian perspective, maintaining right relations between the human and the divine demanded the establishment and maintenance of right doctrinal belief. For instance, according to an imperial letter addressed to Proclus, proconsul of Asia, and read out by a secretary of the divine consistory, Veronicianus, at the first session of the Council of Chalcedon (451), the Second Council of Ephesus was convened in order 'to completely excise the root of evil, so that by suppressing everywhere the unsettling of doctrine we may preserve in its purity proper prayer in men's minds and thereby secure the protection of the state and of human blessings'.[66] Late fourth- to sixth-century imperial legislators held that 'orthodoxy' had to be defined and enforced, and heresy identified and excluded, if the fabric of Empire was not to suffer. Moreover, a number of constitutions from the early fifth century onwards are orientated towards the 'conversion' of repentant heretics, rather than their punishment.[67]

In the imperial constitutions collected in the Theodosian Code at 16. 5, under the rubric *de haeretics,* and in the Justinianic Code at 1. 5 under the rubric *de haeretics et manichaeis et samaritis*, the defence of

apparitor should appoint men of the Christian religion *as custodians of temples*, he shall know that neither his life nor his fortunes will be spared' (Valentinian to Symmachus PU, 365/4).

[65] On the relevant legislation of Theodosius I see J. Rougé, 'La Législation de Théodose contre les hérétiques: Traduction de *CTh*. XVI. 5. 6–24', in J. Fontaine and C. Kannengiesser (eds.), *Épektasis: Mélanges patristiques offerts au Cardinal Jean Daniélou* (Paris: Beauchesne, 1972), 635–49; L. De Giovanni, 'Ortodossia, eresia, funzione dei chierici: Aspetti e problemi della legislazione religiosa tra Teodosio e Teodosio II', *AARC* 6 (1986), 59–73; Aiello, 'Costantino "eretico". Difesa della "ortodossia" e anticostantinianesimo in età teodosiana', *AARC* 10 (1995), 55–83; and R. M. Errington, 'Christian Accounts of the Religious Legislation of Theodosius I', *Klio,* 79/2 (1997), 398–443.

[66] Tr. Price and Gaddis, *The Acts of the Council of Chalcedon*, i. 138–9.

[67] See in general F. De Saint-Palais d'Aussac, *La Réconciliation des hérétiques dans l'église latine* (Paris: Éditions franciscaines, 1943). Also Ch. 9 below.

the 'Catholic' church is identified with the defence of the Empire itself: in the words of the drafter of a 409 constitution, legislation is issued 'for the health of all, that is in the interests of the sacrosanct Catholic church'.[68] Or, as the drafter of a 407 constitution specified, with particular reference to 'Manichaeans', 'Phyrgians', and 'Priscillianists': 'In the first place we want such heresy to be understood as a public crime, because that which is committed against divine religion works to the injury of all.'[69] Given this framework, the prosecution of 'illicit' Christian behaviour could be developed using a variety of 'criminal' classifications and categories already in existence.[70] In the late Roman Imperial constitutions heresy is referred to variously as a *sacrilegium*;[71] a *criminosa religio*;[72] a *perfidia*;[73] and a *nefaria superstitio*.[74] Heretics were thus potentially punishable under already defined Roman law penalties.[75] This ideological framework could also, of course, be justified by events on the ground: such as the occasions in 366, 372, and 418–19 when the Prefect of the City of Rome was called upon to intervene in

[68] *C.Th.* 16. 5. 47 (issued at Ravenna and addressed to Jovius PP):'pro salute communi, hoc est pro utilitatibus catholicae sacrosanctae ecclesiae'. Compare *Nov.Th.* 3 pr. (438).

[69] *C.Th.* 16. 5. 40. 1 (issued at Rome, 407, addressed to Senator, Prefect of the City): 'ac primum quidem volumus esse publicum crimen, quia quod in religionem divinam conmittitur, in omnium fertur iniuriam'. For different perspectives on heresy as a 'crime' see H. H. Anton, 'Kaiserliches Selbstverständnis in der Religionsgesetzgebung der Spätantike und päpstliche Herrschaftsinterpretation im 5. Jahrhundert', *Zeitschrift für Kirchengeschichte*, 88 (1977), 38–84, and L. Barnard, 'The Criminalization of Heresy in the Later Roman Empire: A Sociopolitical Device?', *Journal of Legal History*, 121 (1995), 121–46.

[70] For discussion see Humfress, 'Roman Law, Forensic Argument and the Formation of Christian Orthodoxy'.

[71] e.g. *C.Th.* 16. 2. 25 (issued at Thessalonica, 380) and *C.Th.* 16. 5. 8 (issued at Constantinople, 381, addressed to Glycerius, Count of the Orient), with reference to 'Eunomians' and 'Arians' or 'adherents of the dogma of Aetius'.

[72] *C.Th.* 16. 5. 13 (issued at Constantinople, 384, addressed to Cynegius PP).

[73] e.g. *C.Th.* 16. 5. 63 (issued at Aquileia, 425, addressed to Georgius, Proconsul of Africa).

[74] *C.Th.* 16. 5. 48 (given at Constantinople, 410, addressed to Anthemius PP). Compare *C.Th.* 16. 5. 5 (given at Milan, 379, addressed to Hesperius PP); *C.Th.* 16. 5. 10 (given at Constantinople, 383, addressed to Constantianus, vicar of the diocese of Pontus), with specific reference to 'Tascodrogitae'; *C.Th.* 16. 5. 34 (given at Constantinople, 398, addressed to Eutychianus PP), with reference to 'Eunomian' and 'Montanist' clerics; and *C.Th.* 16. 5. 39 (given at Ravenna, 405, addressed to Diotimus), with reference to 'Donatists'.

[75] Discussed in detail by R. Maceratini, *Ricerche sullo status giuridico dell'eretico nel diritto romano-cristiano e nel diritto canonico classico (da Graziano ad Uguccione)* (Padua: Edizioni CEDAM, 1994), 74–81 ('Le pene') and 81–96 ('Le conseguenze civili', including *infamia*).

cases concerning the maintenance of public order, because of violent clashes between Christians.[76]

From the late Roman imperial legislators' (varied) perspectives, control over 'heretical' meeting places and assemblies was crucial on both practical and symbolic levels. The rhetoric in this respect, of course, meshes with ideas and concepts that we have already met: for example, a constitution issued at Constantinople in 381 and addressed to Eutropius PP, forbids the gathering of 'crowds' at the 'unlawful assemblies of all the heretics', and also orders that 'all persons' who do not subscribe to the stated Nicene credal formulation must be 'removed and completely excluded from the threshold of all churches'. The 'heretic' is here, once again, the 'other' who is already within the group—a fact underscored, in the same constitution, by the order that all inveterate heretics 'shall be driven away from the very walls of the cities'.[77] Three constitutions issued at Constantinople in 383 forbid the right of assembly, 'in any multitude', to 'Tascodrogitae', 'Eunomians', 'Arians', 'Macedonians', 'Pneumatomachi', 'Manichaeans', 'Encratites', 'Apoctactites', 'Saccophori', 'Hydroparastatae', and 'Apollinarians'; houses where such meetings take place are to be confiscated to the imperial fisc.[78] Of course, the taxonomic naming and grouping in these constitutions externalizes the threat of the heretic, classifying them into categories already known from heresiological rhetoric—thus the legislation also functions 'symbolically', in that it allows the Emperors to style themselves as active and vigilant protectors of the Empire against the dangerous heretics lurking within.[79]

[76] For discussion see Chastagnol, *La Préfecture Urbaine à Rome*, 87, and C. Pietri, 'L'Hérésie et l'hérétique selon l'église romaine (ive–vie s.)', *XIII Incontro di studiosi dell'antichità cristiana: Eresia ed eresiologia nella chiesa antica, Augustinianum*, 25 (1985), 867–87. Gaddis, *There is No Crime*, discusses violence and religious conflict in general.

[77] *C.Th.* 16. 5. 6. 1: 'Arceantur cunctorum haereticorum ab illicitis congregationibus turbae'; *C.Th.* 16. 5. 6. 3: 'Ab omnium submoti ecclesiarum limine penitus arceantur, cum omnes haereticos illicitas agere intra oppida congregationes vetemus ac, si quod eruptio factiosa temptaverit, ab ipsis etiam urbium moenibus exterminato furore propelli iubeamus ut cunctis orthodoxis episcopis, qui Nicaenam fidem tenent, catholicae ecclesiae toto orbe reddantur.'

[78] *C.Th.* 16. 5. 10 (addressed to Constantianus, vicar of the diocese of Pontus); *C.Th.* 16. 5. 11 and *C.Th.* 16. 5. 12 (both addressed to Postumianus, but with different dates).

[79] See also *C.Th.* 16. 5. 14 (given at Thessalonica, 388, to Cynegius PP), naming Apollinarians; *C.Th.* 16. 5. 15 (given at Stobi, 388, to Trifolius PP), 'no right of assembly, no discussions, no secret meetings, no altars, no ceremonies'; *C.Th.* 16. 7. 4 (given at Concordia, 391, to Flavianus PP), directed against the practice of second baptism; *C.Th.* 16. 5. 34 (given at Constantinople, 398, to Eutychianus PP), naming 'Eunomians' and 'Montanists'; *C.Th.* 16. 4. 6 (given at Constantinople, 404, to Eutychianus PP),

A number of constitutions target the teaching of 'heretical' doctrines directly: *C.Th.* 16. 6. 2 (issued at Constantinople in 377) instructs those who love their 'impious doctrine' to nurture their poison to their own detriment, 'in domestic secrecy and alone'. Two years later a constitution issued at Milan, and addressed to Hesperius PP, forbade the existence of all heresies(!), and in particular the practice of second baptism; the heretic must keep 'such noxious doctrines' to himself, and 'shall not reveal them to others to their hurt'.[80] Imperial constitutions that ban the teaching of 'heretical opinions' appeal to a traditional Graeco-Roman vocabulary concerning the polluting and contagious effect of *superstitiones*.[81] On a practical level, however, these teaching bans were part of a wider targeting of the structure of 'heretical' congregations. The text excerpted at *C.Th.* 16. 5. 22 (given at Constantinople in 394, addressed to Victorius, proconsul of Asia) reads in its entirety: 'Heretics shall have no authority to create or legally to confirm bishops'.[82] As we shall see in Chapter 9, however, defining who was, and who was not, 'heretical' or 'orthodox' was no easy matter, for imperial officials and ecclesiastics alike.

The following example of the mid–late fourth-century so-called 'Luciferians' will serve to illustrate the potential fluidity and interdependence of theological and legal contexts. In 356 (under the Emperor Constantius, a supporter of the 'party of Arius') Bishop Hilary of Poitiers was indicted at the ecclesiastical Council of Béziers for his 'anti-Arian' views.[83] However, in 359 Hilary wrote the treatise *De Synodis*,

instructing governors that schismatic assemblies are also to be understood as illicit. On the later Justinianic material see A. Berger, 'La concezione di eretico nelle fonti giustinianee', *Rend. Accademia Nazionale dei Lincei, serie 8 Classe di scienze morali, storiche e filologiche*, 10 (1955), 353–68, and, in general, M. P. Baccari, 'Communione e cittadinanza (a proposito della posizione giuridica di eretici, apostati, giudei e pagani secondo i codici di Teodosio II e Justiniano)', *SDHI* 57 (1991), 264–80.

[80] *C.Th.* 16. 5. 5: 'Quisquis opinionem plectibili ausu dei profanus inminuit, sibi tantummodo nocitura sentiat, aliis obfutura non pandat.' On 'heretical teachers', see also *C.Th.* 16. 5. 13 (384), 16. 5. 31–2 (396), and 16. 5. 33.

[81] See also H. Maier, ' "Manichee!" Leo the Great and the Orthodox Panopticon', *Journal of Early Christian Studies*, 4/4 (1996), 441–60, at 443, on the vocabulary used by Pope Leo with reference to Manichaeism. See in general, F. Zuccotti, *'Furor Haereticorum': Studi sul trattamento giuridico della follia e sulla persecuzione della eterodossia religiosa nella legislazione del tardo impero romano* (Milan: Guiffrè, 1992).

[82] *C.Th.* 16. 5. 22: 'Haeretici neque episcopi faciendi potestatem neque episcoporum confirmationes licitas habeant.' Compare *C.Th.* 16. 5. 45 (given at Ravenna, 408, to Theodorus PP).

[83] For discussion see C. L. Beckwith, 'The Condemnation and Exile of Hilary of Poitiers at the Synod of Béziers (356 C.E.)', *Journal of Early Christian Studies*,

intended as an attempt at contributing to the rapprochement between 'Arian' (heterousian) and 'anti-Arian' (homousian) views, before the coming ecclesiastical Councils of Rimini and Seleucia—on whose outcome the various parties in the dispute placed a decisive importance. In the second part of the *De Synodis* (chs. 66–92) Hilary compared the *homoousion* (i.e. the Nicene) formulation and the *homoiousion* (i.e. the Eastern formulation of the Nicene Creed, regarded as 'Arian' by the West), and interpreted the concept *like in substance* as equivalent to *equal in substance.* Hilary thus attempted to prove how either one or other of the terms could be interpreted in an orthodox and in a heterodox fashion, so that the one term was equivalent to the other, in the end. This conciliatory interpretation was criticized by Lucifer, bishop of Caralis (Sardinia), as 'heretical' and contrary to the Nicene faith.

In an appendix to the *De Synodis* Hilary attempted to vindicate himself against Lucifer's accusation, but admitted to having defended the *homoiousion* above all for tactical reasons. Thus between 356 and 361 it was Lucifer of Caralis, rather than Hilary of Poitiers, who claimed to be the title-bearer of Western 'anti-Arian orthodoxy'. In the pamphlet *Moriendum Esse Pro Dei Filio*, addressed to the Emperor Constantius himself, Lucifer insisted repeatedly that he was ready to die in defence of the Nicene faith.[84] Less than twenty years later (notwithstanding Theodosius I's defence of the 'Nicene faith' in the East) the category of 'Luciferian' was being used as a term of abuse.

In the *Collectio Avellana*, a collection of 'papal' letters addressed to the Emperors, the writer complains that his (homousian) party has been falsely classified as 'Luciferians':

> But we have to discuss this matter of the odium that comes from the false name, that of Luciferians, which they throw against us. Who does not know that a name is attributed to acolytes of a man whose new doctrine of some kind has been handed down to his disciples on the authority of the master? But our master is Christ, we follow his doctrine, we are marked with the sacred appellation of his name, we should not be called rightly anything other than Christians because we follow nothing else than what Christ taught through the apostles. Heretics are marked by the names of men, because they hand down

13/1 (2005), 21–38. My account follows the outline given by Barnes, *Athanasius and Constantius*, 141–3 and 152–64.

[84] Lucifer had previously addressed the Emperor Constantius in his pamphlets *De Non Conveniendo cum Haereticis* and *De Regibus Apostaticis*.

the doctrines of men. He deprives himself of the name of Christian who does not follow the discipline of Christ.[85]

The writer then challenges his opponents to prove that Lucifer himself was a heretic:

Let them now say what Lucifer taught that was new, not handed down from the teaching of Christ, not transmitted to posterity by the apostles, disciples of the saviour. Lucifer wrote books to Constantius not, like most people, courting intellectual fame, but collecting Scriptural evidence in the most skilful way against the heretics and against the patron of heretics himself [Arius]. Let them mark down what he wrote contrary to the Scriptures, what he wrote that was new as a heretic.[86]

The author of this letter certainly does not repudiate the writings of Lucifer of Caralis, nor does he accept the charge that Lucifer was a heretic. The author—and the group on whose behalf he writes to the Emperor—is happy to be placed within the same theological camp as Lucifer, the objection is that this does not make them 'Luciferians': 'our master is Christ, we follow his doctrine, we are marked with the sacred appellation of his name, we should not be called rightly anything other than Christians because we follow nothing else than what Christ taught through the apostles'. The only name personally acceptable to a late Roman Christian was Christ's.

In 395 an imperial constitution issued at Constantinople instructed Aurelianus, the proconsul of Asia, to judge a bishop named Heuresius as a 'Luciferian' apparently because: 'Those persons who may be discovered to deviate, even in a minor point of doctrine, from the tenets and the path of the Catholic religion are included under the

[85] *Collectio Avellana*, *Ep*. 2. 86 (*CSEL* 35. 30, ll. 27–31, l. 10): 'name et hoc ipsum necessarium est, ut falsi cognomenti discutiamus invidiam, qua nos iactant esse Luciferianos. Quis nesciat illus cognomentum tribui sectatoribus, cuius et nova aliqua doctrina transmissa est ad discipulos ex auctoritate magisterii ? Sed nobis Christus magister est, illius doctrinam sequimur atque ideo cognomenti illius sacra appellatione censemur, ut non aliud iure dici debeamus quam Christiani, quia nec aliud sequimur quam quod Christus per apostolos docuit. Haereses autem ideo hominum appellationibus denotatae sunt, quia et hominum commenta tradiderunt. Perdit enim in se Christiani nominis appellationem, qui Christi non sequitur disciplinam.'

[86] *Collectio Avellana*, *Ep*. 2. 87 (*CSEL* 35. 31, ll. 10–17): 'dicant nunc, quid Lucifer novum docverit, quod non ex Christi magisterio traditum est, quod non ab apostolis discipulis Salvatoris transmissum est in posteros. Et bene, quod libros scripsit ad Constantium, non, ut plerique, gloriam captans ingenii sed divina testimonia aptissime congerens contra haereticos et contra ipsum patronum haereticorum, ad divinam aemulationem pro filii dei amore succensus. Denotent, quod illic contrarium scripturis, quid novum quasi haereticus scripsit.'

designation of heretics and must be subject to the sanctions which have been issued against them.'[87] Despite the complexity of the internal theological arguments, 'Luciferianism' had entered the legislative sphere as a proscribed heretical sect. Moreover, according to letters transmitted within the *Collectio Avellana*, prosecutions were undertaken by 'heterousian' parties against 'the orthodox' (in this context 'pro-Nicene' or 'homousian') bishops using the legal category of Luciferianism.[88] The ability to make a theological name stick like mud became an important tool in the prosecution of heresy cases under the later Empire.

In conclusion, the 'other', as King has noted, 'is a rhetorical tool to think with'—but by the mid to late fourth century virtually all Christian polemicists were rifling through the toolbox.[89] Tempting as it might be to view 'the orthodox' and 'the heretical' in terms of 'the monologic' pitted against 'the dialogic', the 'heretic' could in fact be just as monologic as the 'orthodox'—precisely because they believed themselves to be *the* orthodox. Late Roman heresiology, then, was not simply a discourse controlled by the 'orthodox' at the expense of the 'heretic'—all Christians were inscribed within it whether they wanted to be or not. Nor was the late Roman discourse of heresiology a 'rhetorical construct'; rather it 'produced its own field'. In other words, it created the very objects that previously it 'had been thought merely to explain or describe'.[90] For example, an individual accused of being a 'Priscillianist' had to defend him or herself from this charge by engaging with a normative expectation of what a 'Priscillianist' was, regardless of what the defendant 'actually' was, or at least understood themselves to be.

[87] *C. Th.* 16. 5. 28. Jerome wrote a 'dialogue against the Luciferians', *c.*379, styled as a public debate, recorded by stenographers, between a 'Luciferian' named Helladius and one of the 'Orthodox'—the dialogue begins by questioning whether Arians and heretics in general are 'Christians'.

[88] *Collectio Avellana*, *Ep.* 2. 91 (*CSEL* 35. 32): 'Those impious scoundrels . . . tried to blacken supporters of the true faith by calling them *Luciferi*, unaware in their pitiable state that they were committing the grossest sacrilege . . . But this fraud, this atrocity, was done against the faithful in Spain and among the Triveri and in Rome and in various regions of Italy.' At *Ep.* 2. 92 it is specified that Luciferians were persecuted *per iudices* and *per manum militarem* (*CSEL* 35. 33, ll. 1–4).

[89] King, *What is Gnosticism?*, 24. For wide-ranging discussion see J. Neusner and E. S. Frerichs (eds.), *'To See Ourselves as Others See Us': Christians, Jews and 'Others' in Late Antiquity* (Chico, Calif.: Scholars Press, 1985).

[90] A. McHoul and W. Grace, *A Foucault Primer: Discourse, Power and the Subject* (Melbourne, Australia: Melbourne University Publishing, 1997), 10.

Heresiological categories and classifications were thus part of late Roman lived experience. What was to be defined as 'right' and 'wrong' belief, was constructed through argument; moreover, the very processes of theological and legal definition threw up new matters to be defined and categorized. Individuals, however, are not passive subjects of a given structure (such as 'law' or 'orthodoxy', for example), but rather active participants—constituting and reconstituting the structure itself by their constant negotiation of its rules and expectations.[91] In Chapter 9 I shall apply this perspective to analysing concrete legal processes involving accusations of heresy in late antiquity.

[91] For a rather different, thought-provoking, theory (perhaps with limited application to late Roman law as opposed to developed modern legal systems), see G. Teubner, 'How the Law Thinks: Toward a Constructivist Epistemology of Law', *Law and Society Review*, 23 (1989), 727–57.

9

Heresy and the Courts

HERETICS BEFORE THE COURTS

> And the definition of a crime and delict is what? The proof of it in a court of law.[1]

The introduction of the Christian concepts of 'heresy' and 'orthodoxy' into the Roman legislative sphere necessitated the categorization and systematization of religious belief in legal contexts. As we saw in Chapter 8, imperial constitutions grouped and named 'heretics', opening the way for legal processes to take place against them. But did these legal processes actually occur? Was there, in fact, a 'persistent short-fall in the application of intolerant laws' in the later Roman Empire? A short-fall that may have been caused, as Peter Brown memorably phrases it, by an 'unavoidable hiatus between theory and practice, brought about by the merciful, systemic incompetence of the imperial administration in enforcing its own laws'.[2] Whilst not wishing to argue for the smooth efficiency of the imperial bureaucracy(!), there is, nonetheless, an alternative to this 'intolerant yet ineffective laws' scenario (as suggested in Chapter 8). If we view the imperial constitutions as, for the most part, responsive texts that reacted to concrete situations and to cases thrown up by the functioning of the bureaucratic courts, alongside other venues, then the question of 'application' versus 'non-application' necessarily has to be rethought.[3]

As Brown himself has argued, there is firm evidence outside the legal Codes for the prosecution of late Roman Manichees (evidence that we shall return to below).[4] There is also the celebrated case of the execution

[1] Libanius, *Oration* 45. 2 (composed *c.*386) tr. Norman, Loeb II, 163.

[2] Brown, *Authority and the Sacred*, 38–9.

[3] See Ch. 8 above.

[4] P. Brown, 'The Diffusion of Manichaeism in the Roman Empire', *JRS* 59 (1969), 92–103, esp. 97–8.

of Priscillian and a number of his associates in 386 or 387, by the Emperor Maximus, most probably on a formal charge of *maleficium* but with various accompanying accusations of subversive doctrines and practices.[5] Finally there is sporadic evidence for localized targeting of particular groups, such as Constantine's instruction addressed, as he puts it, 'to men of mine', to search out 'Donatists' and bring them to the imperial court—alongside later rough handling and 'persecution' of 'Donatists' by imperial military authorities.[6] None of this adds up to a (systematic) 'persecuting society'.[7] This chapter will also argue, however, that accusations concerning 'heresy' were part of a much broader socio-legal context than simply prosecuting individuals *for being heretics*. For example, by the late fourth century a number of laws had cut down the civil rights of certain heretical groups to own or transmit property.[8] An accusation of 'heresy' levelled against an opponent could thus be used strategically by individuals involved in inheritance, property, and family law cases. In addition I will also examine the use of heresy accusations by Christian clerics in particular, in both bureaucratic and ecclesiastical forensic contexts. First, though, I shall turn to individual prosecutions against 'heretics', and in particular to the tricky taxonomic challenges posed by 'Manichees'.

Mani himself had been born into a Southern Mesopotamian Jewish-Christian community, known as the Elchasites; he claimed to be an

[5] On Priscillian see H. Chadwick, *Priscillian of Avila: The Occult and the Charismatic in the Early Church* (Oxford: Clarendon Press, 1976) and Burrus, *Making of a Heretic*. On the trial and execution of Priscillian and his associates see K. M. Girardet, 'Trier 385: Der Prozess gegen die Priszillianer', *Chiron*, 4 (1974), 577–608; A. R. Birley, 'Magnus Maximus and the Persecution of Heresy', *Bulletin of the John Rylands University Library*, 66 (1983–4), 29–33; G. Puglisi, 'Giustizia criminale e persecuzioni antieretiche (Priscilliano e Ursino, Ambrogio e Damaso)', *Siculorum Gymnasium*, 43 (1990), 91–137; and Honoré, *Law in Crisis*, 188.

[6] Constantine's order: Optatus, appendix 5, 'Letter of Constantine to the Catholic bishops'. In a series of incisive articles Brent Shaw has sounded a salutary note of caution concerning our understanding of 'Donatism' itself, and its relationship with violence: B. Shaw, 'African Christianity: Disputes, Definitions, and "Donatists"', in M. R. Greenshields and T. A. Robinson (eds.), *Orthodoxy and Heresy in Religious Movements: Discipline and Dissent* (Lewiston: Edwin Mellen Press, 1992), 4–34, and B. Shaw, 'Who were the Circumcellions?', in A. H. Merrills (ed.), *Vandals, Romans and Berbers: New Perspectives on Late Antique Africa* (London: Variorum, 2004), 227–58.

[7] Cameron, 'How to Read Heresiology', 482, with further relevant literature at n. 79.

[8] Also noted by P. Brown, 'Religious Coercion in the Later Roman Empire: The Case of North Africa', in P. Brown, *Religion and Society in the Age of St Augustine* (London: Faber & Faber, 1972), 301–31, at 312, with particular reference to the 'Donatists'.

'Apostle of Jesus Christ', whose mission and writings fulfilled the Christian Gospel (just as some Christians claimed to have fulfilled the promise given to Abraham).[9] The followers of Mani's missionary religion thus took the name of *both* Christ and Mani—the use of the latter as a term of self-designation is clearly revealed in the newly discovered documents relating to the (probably mid-fourth-century) Manichaean community at Kellis, in the Dakhleh Oasis.[10] However, self-designation as a community of Manichees in a village within an Egyptian oasis did not have the same potential effects as declaring oneself a 'Manichee' in the goldfish-bowl environments of late Roman cities and towns, particularly, it seems, in the West.[11]

In AD 302—though some scholars favour 297—the Emperors Diocletian and Maximianus issued the first (extant) Roman legal prohibition against 'Manichees', addressed to Julian, proconsul of Africa, and apparently incorporated within book 7 of the Gregorian Code under the title 'de maleficis et Manichaeis'.[12] This text was issued in response to a report (*relatio*) sent from the office of the proconsul of Africa: Julian, like a latter-day Pliny confronted with the prospect of judging 'Christians', was apparently at a loss as to how to proceed concerning certain 'Manichaeans'. The drafters of the imperial reply, having

[9] On Mani himself see now L. Koenen and C. Römer, *Der Kölner Mani-Kodex: Über das weden seines Leibes* (Opladen: Westdeutscher Verlag, 1988); on accounts of Mani's origins before the discovery of the Cologne-Mani Codex see M. Scopello, 'Hégémonius, les Acta Archelai et l'histoire de la controverse anti-Manichéene', in R. E. Emmerick, W. Sundermann, and P. Zieme, *Studia Manichaica: IV Internationaler Kongreß zum Manichäismus, Berlin, 14–18. Juli 1997* (Berlin: Akademie Verlag, 2000), 528–45; and on 'Manichaeism as a Christian *Gnosis*', see N. A. Pedersen, *Demonstrative Proof in Defence of God: A Study of Titus of Bostra's Contra Manichaeos—The Work's Sources, Aims and Relation to Contemporary Theology* (Leiden and Boston: Brill, 2004), 6–12.

[10] See the references to the *Topos Mani* throughout the texts edited by R. S. Bagnall, *The Kellis Agricultural Account Book*, Dakhleh Oasis Project, 7 (Oxford and Oakville, Conn.: Oxbow Books, 1997). On late Roman Manichaean 'community texts' in general see now I. Gardner and S. N. C. Lieu, *Manichaean Texts from the Roman Empire* (Cambridge: Cambridge University Press, 2004), 259–81.

[11] On Manichaeism and the rise of the bishop in the late Roman city see Brown, 'Diffusion of Manichaeism', 101. *C.Th.* 16. 5. 7. 3 (given at Constantinople, 381, addressed to Eutropius PP) forbids Manichees from establishing meeting places in both small urban settlements and 'renowned cities'.

[12] *Collatio Legum Mosaicarum et Romanarum* 15. 3 (*FIRA* 2. 581). For detailed discussion of the text and its transmission see E. Volterra, 'La costituzione di Diocleziano e Massimiano contro I Manichei', in *Atti del Convegno sul Tema: La Persia e il mondo Greco-Romano (Roma 11–14 Aprile 1965)* (Rome: Accademia Nazionale dei Lincei, 1966), 27–50. On *maleficia* see *D.* 47. 1. 3 and also J. B. Rives, 'Magic in Roman Law: The Reconstruction of a Crime', *Classical Antiquity*, 22 (2003), 313–39.

railed against the 'Manichees' as a treacherous and barbaric threat from Persia, instructed the proconsul that their practices should be classed as *maleficia*.[13] 'Manichees' were thus subsumed, for the purposes of sentencing, under an existing category of Roman criminal law, with correspondingly harsh (potential) penalties. Polemic against the Manichees caught on quickly—predominately, but not exclusively, within Christian contexts.[14] The judgement of Cyril, bishop of Jerusalem, that the Manichees are 'to be especially despised' echoes through late antique imperial legislative rhetoric and Christian invective alike.

According to Augustine, a group of Catholic Christians denounced a member of the Manichaean elect, Faustus, before the proconsul of Africa in 383—Faustus was duly tried and convicted.[15] A number of other Manichees were apparently condemned before the African Proconsul Messianus sometime after January 385: their cases were known to Augustine because the 'Donatist' bishop Petilianus had attached the relevant proconsular records to an open letter, in an attempt to implicate Augustine himself in the affair.[16] Furthermore, if we can trust Augustine's evidence on this point, then public trials against Manichees also occurred in late fourth-century Paphlagonia (Asia Minor) and Gaul; the source of Augustine's knowledge here, however, was the gossip of a 'Catholic Christian' at Rome.[17] An imperial constitution, issued at Milan in May 399 and addressed to Dominator, vicar of Africa, states that Manichees are to be sought out and brought to public trial; however, as we have seen from Augustine, this may indicate a shift in legislative gear in the Western Empire, rather than a change in forensic practice.[18] We should also note in this context that a public

[13] *Collatio Legum Mosaicarum et Romanarum* 15. 3. 5: 'Et quia omnia, quae pandit prudentia tua in relatione religionis illorum, genera maleficiorum statutis evidentissime sunt exquisita et inventa commenta, ideo aerumnas atque poenas debitas et condignas illis statuimus.'

[14] A Neoplatonist philosopher, Alexander of Lycopolis produced a text *Against the Doctrines of Mani* (ed. A. Brinkmann, 1895; repr. Stuttgart: Teubner, 1989), as did the Christian Marius Victorinus (not extant, but noted at *PL* 8. 1008) and Titus, bishop of Bostra (*Contra Manichaeos*, written between 363 and 377), amongst others.

[15] Augustine, *Contra Faustum Manichaeum* 5. 8 (*CSEL* 25^1. 280).

[16] Augustine, *Contra Litteras Petiliani*, 3. 25.30 (*BA* 30. 644).

[17] Augustine, *De Natura Boni Contra Manichaeos* 47 (*CSEL* 25. 886–8): during the trial the accused apparently confessed to eating semen, and cited the *Thesaurus* (Manichaean scripture) as their written authority for doing this. For this particular claim in another legal process see Augustine, *De Haeresibus* 46, ll. 75–81, in relation to the 'confessions' of Margaret and Eusebia.

[18] *C.Th.* 16. 5. 35. Compare *C.Th.* 16. 5. 15 (issued at Stobi, 388, addressed to Trifolius PP), which does not refer to Manichees explicitly: the PP is to appoint 'as

criminal accusation suspended any procedural defences that the accused otherwise might have been entitled to—no claim for *praescriptio fori*, for example, or for *praescriptiones* based on time or person, could be (legally) pleaded by an individual suspected of Manichaeism.[19]

In a constitution given at Constantinople in May 381, addressed to Eutropius PP, the Emperor Theodosius I laid down a number of regulations concerning the civil disabilities that were to be enforced, as punishments, on convicted Manichees.[20] Section 3 of the constitution, however, also implies that some Manichees had developed a singular defence strategy:

> We further add to this sanction that the Manichaeans shall not establish in the conventicles of the small towns or in renowned cities their accustomed tombs of feral mysteries; they shall be kept completely from sight of the throngs of the municipalities. Nor shall they defend themselves with dishonest fraud under the pretence of those deceptive names by which many, as We have learned, wish to be called and signified as of approved faith and chaste character; especially since some of the aforesaid persons wish to be called the Encratites, the Apoctactites, the Hydroparastatae, or the Saccophori, and by a variety of diverse names falsify, as it were, the ceremonies of their religious professions. For none of the aforesaid persons shall be protected by a profession of names but shall be held infamous and execrable because of the crimes of their sects.[21]

The fact that certain individuals were attempting to deny the name of 'Manichee' in order to escape the criminal charge had apparently been reported to the Palatine legal officials ('as We have learned', quoted above). The practice was thus occurring on the ground. A letter written by Basil of Cappadocia to Amphilocius of Iconium

watchmen' certain 'very faithful persons' to arrest members of perfidious sects and 'bring them before the courts'. Also Valentinian III, *Nov.* 18. 2 (445). For the East see *C. Th.* 16. 5. 9. 1 (issued at Constantinople, Mar. 382, addressed to Florus PP).

[19] On *praescriptiones* and their use in court see Chs. 4 and 6 above.

[20] See in general P. Beskow, 'The Theodosian Laws against Manichaeism', in P. Bryder (ed.), *Manichaean Studies I: Proceedings of the First International Conference on Manichaeism, August 5–9, 1987* (Lund: Plus Ultra, 1988), 1–17, and G. Barone-Adesi, 'Eresie sociali ed inquisizione Teodosiana', *AARC* 6 (1986), 119–66.

[21] *C. Th.* 16. 5. 7: 'Illud etiam huic adicimus sanctioni, ne in conventiculis oppidorum, ne in urbibus claris consueta feralium mysteriorum sepulcra constituant; a conspectu celebri civitate penitus coherceantur. Nec se sub simulatione fallaci eorum scilicet nominum, quibus plerique, ut cognovimus, probatae fidei et propositi castioris dici ac signari volent, maligna fraude defendant; cum praesertim nonnulli ex his Encratitas, Apotactitas, Hydroparastatas, vel Saccoforos nominari se velint et varietate nominum diversorum velut religiosae professionis officia mentiantur. Eos enim omnes convenit non professione defendi nominum, sed notabiles atque execrandos haberi scelere sectarum.' See below for discussion of the earlier sections of the text.

(both forensically trained), sometime in the 370s, gives detailed instructions for dealing with 'Apoctactites', 'Saccophori', 'Encratites', and 'Cathari'—mentioning three out of the five labels (including Manichaeans) given in the 381 imperial constitution quoted above.[22] Whether any of the accused individuals were 'really' Manichees or not is irrelevant in this context: they had entered the heresiological name-game by virtue of being hauled before an imperial magistrate or a bishop. What is important here is that, by at least *c*.381, some of these individuals had attempted to play the system by making the labelling work in their defence.[23] Presumably this forensic strategy was successful enough to have provoked its referral to the Emperor's judgment.

Augustine's *De Haeresibus* gives further examples of specific trials held against Manichees.[24] A number of hearings apparently took place 'in the Church at Carthage', under the direction of Ursus the Tribune, when Quodvultdeus was a deacon there (possibly *c*.421).[25] Ursus interrogated a girl, Margaret, and a woman, Eusebia, on allegations that they had been involved in 'Manichee' practices—including sprinkling flour underneath a couple having sex, in order to capture the semen so that it could be eaten by the elect (thereby, reasons Augustine, releasing the trapped divine light particles from their material prison, in accordance with 'Manichaean' cosmological principles). Augustine is careful to explain that Ursus' cross-examinations took place at different times: the testimony of Eusebia was not influenced by the testimony of Margaret, thus ensuring two independent confessions of Manichaean 'depravity'. The magistrate, however, apparently obtained Eusebia's confession 'with difficulty'.[26] As a result of these hearings, Augustine implies, Manichees in general will no longer be able to defend themselves with the plea that 'some others' practise this rite, 'using the name of the Manichaeans'.[27]

22 Basil, *Ep*. 188. 1 and 199. 47, as noted by S. Mitchell, *A History of the Later Roman Empire* (Oxford: Blackwell Publishing, 2007), 234. See also S. Mitchell, *Anatolia: Land, Men and Gods in Asia Minor*, ii (Oxford: Clarendon Press, 1993), 96–108.

23 Compare the argument of F. Decret, 'Du bon usage du mensonge et du parjure: Manichéens et Priscillianistes face à la persécution dans l'empire chrétien (IVe–Ve siècles)', in M.-M. Mactoux and E. Geny, *Mélanges P. Lévêque*, iv (Paris: Belles Lettres, 1990), 140–58.

24 Augustine, *De Haeresibus* 46. 9 (ll. 66–9). For discussion of the 'Manichee' section as a whole, see J. van Oort, 'Mani and Manichaeism in Augustine's *De haeresibus*. An Analysis of *haer*. 46, 1', in Emmerick *et al*., *Studia Manichaica* 451–63.

25 Frakes, *Contra Potentium Iniurias*, 189, suggests that Ursus the Tribune was probably also the recipient of Augustine's *Ep*. 22*.

26 Augustine, *De Haeresibus* 46. 9 (*CCSL* 46. 314–15, ll. 69–88).

27 Ibid. 46. 9 (*CCSL* 46. 314, ll. 64–6).

Having given an account of these proceedings, Augustine goes on to state that some other Manichees have been 'led to the Church' in more recent times, as episcopal *acta* sent by Quodvultdeus prove. Under careful examination these 'Manichees' had also confessed to the 'Eucharistic' practice outlined above—thus suggesting that the prosecuting bishop had perhaps learnt from Ursus' tactics.[28] One of the accused, a certain Viator, had attempted to argue that the Manichaean sect was in fact divided into three groups: Catharists, Mattarii, and Manichees proper; he then claimed that the only ones who committed the proscribed acts were the Catharists, of whom he was not one. The episcopal prosecutor, however, countered with a nice display of forensic acumen: each of the three is a species of the same *genus*, 'Manichaeism', hence the charge against Viator was proven.[29] Taking his cue from the episcopal *acta*, Augustine takes up this proof in his *De Haeresibus* and shows by logical demonstration how each of the aforementioned three sects (Manichees, Mattarians, and Catharists) drew their doctrines from general Manichaean principles—moreover, Augustine claims that it is a logical consequence of their fundamental beliefs that Manichees should also be known as 'purifiers' (Catharists). Both concrete trials and anti-Manichaean polemic, then, were informed by forensic expertise from within the church.[30]

The two public 'debates' held at Hippo between Augustine and a 'Manichee' named Fortunatus in August 392, and between Augustine and a famed member of the Manichaean elect, Felix, in December 404, were in fact the first stages of two criminal hearings.[31] Augustine's texts are redrafted versions of stenographic records, originally taken as part

[28] Ibid. 46. 9 (*CCSL* 46. 315, ll. 80–3): 'Et recenti tempore nonnulli eorum reperti et ad ecclesiam ducti, sicut gesta episcopalia quae nobis misisti ostendunt, hoc non sacramentum sed exsecramentum sub diligenti interrogatione confessi sunt.'

[29] Ibid. 46. 10 (*CCSL* 46. 315, ll. 84–9): 'Quorum unus nomine Viator eos qui ista faciunt proprie Catharistas vocari dicens, cum alias eiusdem Manichaeae sectae partes in Mattarios et specialiter Manichaeos distribui perhiberet, omnes tamen has tres formas ab uno auctore propagatas, et omnes generaliter Manichaeos esse negare non potuit.'

[30] Compare M. Scopello, 'Julie, manichéenne d'Antioche: (d'après la "Vie de Porphyre" de Marc le Diacre, ch. 85–91)', *Ant. Tard.* 5 (1997), 187–209.

[31] As also argued by F. Decret, 'Objectif premier vise par Augustin dans ses controverses orales avec les responsables Manichéens d'Hippone', in J. van Oort, O. Wermerlinger, and G. Wurst, *Augustine and Manichaeism in the Latin West* (Leiden: Brill, 2001), 57–66, at 57–8: 'Dans les deux cas, il ne s'agissait pas en effet d'une invitation pour un discussion doctrinale, mais bien d'une convocation, sous peine de dénonciation aux autorités et donc d'arrestation come "hérétiques" condamnés par la legislation en vigueur.'

of the legal *acta* for each case.[32] At the beginning of Augustine's *Contra Felicem Manichaeum* we are told that Felix had already handed over his *codices* to public officials, where they now awaited the bonfire.[33] He was then sent before Augustine, the bishop. Felix's defence tactic, at least as represented by Augustine, was to prove that the Manichaean beliefs he professed and taught did not subvert the Catholic faith, but in themselves faithfully followed sacred scripture. According to Felix, the Manichees are the true Christians, and he seeks to prove his argument with reference to the New Testament and the works of Mani himself. As already noted, however, his books had been confiscated and are never released, although Felix demands them with the argument that no litigant can be expected to plead his case without his documents. Felix was not getting a 'fair' trial. Of course, the whole setting for the hearing was theatrically staged as public entertainment, as indeed were all late Roman public trials.[34]

Augustine commences by reading aloud the beginning of Mani's *Epistola Fundamenti*, before demanding that Felix prove in what way Mani could be an apostle of Christ, when there is no mention of him in the Acts of the Apostles.[35] Augustine then attempts to prove that the content of Mani's *Epistola Fundamenti* is completely diverse from the Acts of the Apostles and is thus deviant from the rule of faith, through citations from each. After a long discussion during which Augustine attempts to counter Felix's claim that Manichees have as much right to interpret scripture as the Catholics do, Felix finally asks Augustine to clearly state what his errors are.[36] Augustine ignores Felix's question and in turn demands that Felix must declare himself for either Christ or Mani. Felix responds that he cannot, as he fears the application of the imperial laws. Augustine, in turn, accepts this as proof of Felix's

32 On the *Acta Contra Fortunatum Manichaeum* and the *Contra Felicem Manichaeum* see E. Volterra, 'Appunti intorno all'intervento del vescovo nei processi contro gli eretici', *BIDR* 42 (1934), 453–68. On Felix as a member of the Manichaean 'elect', see also Possidius, *Vita Augustini* 16.

33 Augustine, *Contra Felicem*, *CSEL* 25^2. 815, ll. 17–19: 'nunc vero cum hesterno die libellum curatori dederis et publice clamitaveris, cum codicibus tuis te paratum esse incendi, si quid mali in ipsis fuerit inventum'. Compare *C.Th.* 9. 16. 12 (409).

34 Maier, '"Manichee!": Leo the Great', n. 36, notes 'evidence that trials of Manichees had by late antiquity become ritualized': namely the 'Commonitorium quomodo sit agendum cum Manichaeis qui convertuntur' (*PL* 42. 1153–6), and the 'Forma epistolae quam dat episcopus conversis' (*PL* 65. 28–30).

35 Augustine, *Contra Felicem* (*CSEL* 25^2. 802, ll. 1–8).

36 Ibid. (*CSEL* 25^2. 814).

falsehood; if Felix fears the application of the imperial laws than he is not a true martyr, but a false martyr, and this proves that the inspired speech of the Holy Spirit has not come to Felix's aid.

At this point in the hearing Felix requests a *dilatio* (postponement) of the proceedings for five days, so that he can prepare the answers for his defence. Augustine grants this, with the proviso that Felix remain in the custody of a predetermined person. By the close of their next session, Felix had abjured Mani and his 'blasphemies', and had signed the acts as Felix *Christianus*.[37] The legal process aimed at 'conversion' rather than punishment; however, denouncing other Manichees was a non-negotiable clause in the plea bargain.[38] There are a number of other late Roman texts that describe bishops disputing with 'Manichees', some of which (at least) should be understood in the context of legal trials, rather than simply as theological debates.[39]

In fact, the prosecution of Manichees and other 'heretical' groups that fell under the rubric of public criminal processes, must have given rise to at least some of the occasions, analysed in Chapter 6 above, where imperial magistrates and bishops were both involved in the same legal cases. A prosecution against a 'Manichee', or anyone accused of adherence to any other 'sect' under a public criminal process, had to be lodged before a magistrate, because of the requirement of formally entering a criminal accusation into the public records (the *inscriptio*).[40] The accused could then be handed over to a bishop for interrogation,

[37] The abjuration formulae of a Manichee named Felix is given at the end of Augustine's *Contra Felicem* in some manuscripts (*CSEL* 25^2. 852): 'Ego Felix, qui Manichaeo credideram, nunc anathemo eum et doctrinam ipsius et spiritum seductorem, qui in illo fuit, qui dixit deum partem suam genti tenebrarum miscuisse et eam tam turpiter liberare, ut virtutes suas transfiguraret in feminas contra masculina et ipsas iterum in masculos contra feminea daemonia, ita ut postea reliquias ipsius suae partis configat in aeternum globo tenebrarum. has omnes et ceteras blasphemias Manichaei anathemo.' For discussion see J. M. and S. N. C. Lieu, '"Felix Conversus ex Manichaeis": A Case of Mistaken Identity', *JTS* NS 231 (1981), 173–6.

[38] Conversion not punishment: *C.Th.* 16. 5. 41 (given at Rome, 407, addressed to Porphyrius, proconsul of Africa), naming Donatists and Manichees. On denunciations see e.g. Augustine, *Ep.* 221, addressed to Quodvultdeus, on the former Manichee Theodorus, who had denounced a number of Manichees when he 'converted'. This Theodorus may well be connected with the events described at *De Haeresibus* 46. 9–10. For the charge that Augustine himself had been denounced in such a context see Augustine, *Contra Litteras Petiliani* 3. 16. 19 and (*BA* 30. 622) and 3. 25. 30 (*BA* 30. 644).

[39] e.g. Apthonius disputing with Aetius of Antioch (Philostorgius, *HE* 3. 15) and Elpidius disputing unnamed Manichees (Augustine, *Confessions* 5. 11. 21); see also Rufinus, *Historia Monachorum* 9 (*PL* 21. 426–7) and Leo, *Sermon* 16. 4 (*PL* 54. 178).

[40] *N. Val.* 18. 1. 2 (issued at Rome, 445, addressed to Albinus PP) formally abolishes this requirement with specific reference to Manichees: 'Sitque publicum crimen et omni

as outlined in the North African examples above.[41] If an accusation was proved then a public attestation of the relevant sentence was made, and the documents relating to the decided case were entered into the public *acta*. However, in November 407, under the regime of Stilicho, a constitution was issued at Rome, addressed to Porphyrius, proconsul of Africa: this text stated that if a heretic, whether a 'Manichee', 'Donatist', or any kind of 'sect' professed the 'Catholic faith and rites' the criminal charge against them was to be annulled.[42] In practice, however, the magistrates seem to have suspended the enforcement of the judicial penalties rather than simply abandoning the suit altogether; this suspension could itself be revoked in the event of the former 'heretic' relapsing into 'error', and the full penalties of the law would (theoretically) apply immediately.[43]

This procedure for the suspension of legal penalties in the event of 'conversion' can be seen clearly from a set of twenty-one separate 'abjuration' formulae from Philadelphia (Lydia), dating from between 428 and 431, and recorded in a medieval manuscript of the *acta* of the 431 Council of Ephesus.[44] These confessions, made by twenty-four individuals (with some abjuring jointly) were apparently the result of a concerted campaign by a certain James, acting on the instructions of Nestorius (subsequently himself to be declared 'heretical') and a number of those associated with him. Eleven of the formulae begin with the 'self'-identification of the individual as either a *Tessareskaidekatitês* or a 'Novatian', usually in the manner of 'I, [insert name] son of [insert name], Philadelphian, a [insert heretical name being abjured],

volenti sine accusationis periculo tales arguere sit facultas.' This constitution was itself prompted by the activities of Pope Leo.

41 Compare the transcript of an interrogation by Germinius, 'Arian' bishop of Sirmium, on 13 Jan. 366, of three 'Catholics', Heraclianus, Firmianus, and Aurelianus, who had been arrested and brought before the bishop, who himself was sat on an episcopal chair in public, surrounded by clergy. During the interrogation the crowd apparently demanded that the three 'Catholics' be taken before the secular authorities to be executed as 'disturbers of the peace'. See 'Altercatio Heracliani laici cum Germinio episcopo sirmiensi', ed. C. P. Caspari, *Kirchenhistorische anecdota: Nebst neuen Ausgaben patristischer und kirchlich-mittelalterlicher Schriften*, i (Oslo: Christiania Malling, 1883), 133–47.

42 *C.Th.* 16. 5. 41. The validity of constitutions issued under Stilicho was thrown into doubt after his downfall—prompting North African ('Catholic') church councils to seek reconfirmation, possibly granted by *C.Th.* 16. 5. 43 (Dec. 408?).

43 See Volterra, 'Appunti intorno all'intervento del vescovo', for further discussion. On the prosecution of 'Donatists' in North Africa see below.

44 See F. Millar, 'Repentant Heretics in Fifth-Century Lydia: Identity and Literacy', *Scripta Classica Israelica*, 23 (2004), and Millar, *Greek Roman Empire*, 154–5.

having acknowledged the true belief of orthodoxy . . .'.[45] The other formulae abjure particular 'heresies' or 'heretical' beliefs within the body of the text itself. Every one of these twenty-one separate texts, with the singular exception of one signed by a *scholasticus* (advocate) named Flavius Nymphidius, swear a formal oath to abide by their confession of heretical error and their conversion to the 'true faith of orthodoxy'; in seventeen of the records the following formulaic phrase is used, with some minor variations: 'swearing by the holy and consubstantial Trinity and by the piety and victory of the masters of the oikoumenê, Flavius Theodosius and Flavius Valentinianus, the eternal Augusti, that *if I ever contravene any of these, I am subject to the rigour of the laws*'.[46]

These twenty-one abjuration formulae should thus be seen as formal legal documents, witnessing the fact that the legal penalties which should have been applied to these 'repentant heretics' are to be suspended, as a result of their having converted to the 'orthodox faith'—as defined for them, of course, by their interrogator, a certain Bishop Theophanius of Philadelphia, with the assistance of various members of his clergy. Having entreated the 'God-beloved' bishop, and having signed and witnessed the formula itself, the penitent may then have undergone some additional ritual of 'readmission' to Theophanius' 'orthodox' (or with the benefit of hindsight, 'Nestorian') communion—such as the imposition of hands or anointing with chrism.[47] In other contexts this readmission to Christian communion may have included a ceremony of rebaptism—a practice which itself entered into the Roman legal arena in the later fourth century, with specific reference to the 'criminal acts' of 'Donatists', 'Montanists', 'Novatians', and 'Eunomians'.[48]

From a late Roman bishop's perspective, 'enabling' the conversion of heretics (i.e. the 'others' of any given local ecclesiastical community) was an obvious means of bolstering and advertising episcopal power and authority, in both practical and symbolic terms; we should not, however, assume that it was the only means, nor that all bishops agreed with the practice of securing 'heretical' abjurations using the threat of Roman legal penalties. Nonetheless, as we have seen, the involvement

[45] Following Millar, 'Repentant Heretics', 124, in using his formula no.12 as the main type of model within the set.

[46] Ibid., formula no. 12 (tr. Millar), my italics.

[47] As noted by Gregory the Great, *Ep.* 57 (*PL* 77. 1204–8), allegedly looking back to 4th- and 5th-cent. practices.

[48] See the constitutions collected under *C.Th.* 16. 6 and *CI* 1. 6, under the same title 'Ne sanctum baptisma iteretur'.

of the bishop in such processes was certainly not confined to securing confessions from Manichees alone.[49]

We also have to reckon with the 'secular' bureaucratic officials and their willingness, or otherwise, to become involved in the prosecution of 'heretics': the relevant late Roman constitutions establish penalties for magistrates and their office staff who are not cooperating, perhaps as a result of their personal beliefs, their patronage networks, their laziness, their receipt of bribes or other corrupt practices, or a combination of all four. In one particularly stark case, the *magister memoriae*, Benivolus, apparently resigned his office in 386 'rather than draft a law permitting the assembly of Arian heretic congregations'.[50] A letter of Basil of Caesarea, addressed to Eusebius of Samosata, paints a vivid picture of his relations with the then *vicarius* of Thrace, a high-ranking bureaucratic official:

> The first and greatest of my troubles was the visit of the Vicar. As to whether he is a man really heretically minded I do not know, for I think he is quite unversed in doctrine, and has not the slightest interest or experience in such things, for I see him day and night busy, both in body and soul, in other things. But he is certainly a friend of heretics.[51]

Basil then claims that the same *vicarius* had summoned an ecclesiastical synod in Galatia (Ancyra), deposed a bishop at Parnassus and replaced him with another, ordered the removal of Gregory on the accusation of one man, and made Basil's congregation at Caesarea liable to public liturgical burdens—at the same time as 'he advanced the adherents of Eustathius'.[52] Thus for Eustathius, bishop of Sebaste, and his supporters, this imperial magistrate was far from 'uncooperative'.

49 Contra Brown, 'Diffusion of Manichaeism', 100, speaking of the 'exceptional role of the Catholic bishop' in the suppression of Manichaeism: 'The only studies of the role of the bishop in the trial of heretics in the later Roman Empire—because the only evidence—concern the trials of Manichees', with a footnote to Volterra, 'Appunti intorno all'intervento del vescovo' and W. Ensslin, 'Valentinians II Novellen xvi u xviii von 445', *ZSS, Röm. Abt.* 57 (1937), 367–78.

50 Matthews, *Laying Down the Law*, 179 and 247–8. On uncooperative local officials, in the context of 'anti-pagan' legislation', see S. Bradbury, 'Constantine and the Problem of Anti-Pagan Legislation in the Fourth Century', Classical Philology 89 (1994), 120–39 at 133. Augustine, *Contra Litteras Petiliani* 2. 84. 186 (*BA* 30. 450–2) discusses the non-enforcement of pecuniary fines, the laws against 'Donatists', and the politics of bread-making.

51 Basil, *Ep.* 237 (written in 376), tr. R. J. Deferrari, *St Basil: The Letters*, iii (Cambridge, Mass.: Loeb Classical Library, 1930), 406–7.

52 On Basil's changing relations with Eustathius, bishop of Sebaste, see P. Rousseau, *Basil of Caesarea* (Berkeley, Calif.: University of California Press, 1994), 233–69.

On the other hand, an imperial bureaucrat who was respected (or at least feared) by the local population could play an ameliorating role in Christian conflict: in the wake of the famous pitched battle between the supporters of Pope Damasus and Pope Ursinus at Rome, the Emperor Valentinian sent a rescript to the urban prefect (which was in fact an imperial reply to a petition that had been lodged by *defensores ecclesiae* acting on Damasus' behalf). The closing section of this imperial rescript states, perhaps with too much optimism, that the urban prefect 'alone is said now to be held in obedience by dissenters out of the churches of the Catholic religion'.[53] It was, of course, the urban prefect's duty to re-establish civic order. In all of the cases discussed above, the interdependence of the Roman 'legal' and ecclesiastical spheres is clear.

THE USE OF HERESY ACCUSATIONS BY PRIVATE INDIVIDUALS

> Those who are caught posting scandalous written accusations (*libelli famosi*) in church shall be anathematized.[54]

Fourth-century church councils and emperors alike agreed that if an individual had a social reputation worth losing, they had to be able to defend it at all costs.[55] A story told by Libanius underscores the point: an informer launched a character assassination on 'an important man' who was connected by birth to the city where he had served consecutively in high-ranking municipal posts. The distinguished individual in question decided to meet the attack with silence, but the civic elite judged this 'a poor defence'. The case was duly contested in the courts, where the informer's accusations were unmasked as slanderous, and

[53] *Collectio Avellana* 6 (*CSEL* 35. 49, ll. 1–17). Incidentally, *Collectio Avellana* 2. 83 (*CSEL* 35. 30, ll. 4–10) claims that Damasus had previously employed *scholastici* to persecute 'catholic' presbyters and laymen.

[54] Transmitted in later collections as canon 52 of the early 4th-cent. (possibly pre-Constantinian) Council of Elvira (Spain). See in general M. Meigne, 'Concile ou collection d'Elvire', *Revue d'histoire ecclésiastique*, 70 (1975), 361–87 and Hess, *Early Development of Canon Law*, 40–2.

[55] On the Emperor Licinius' early 4th-cent. edict *De Accusationibus* see S. Corcoran, 'A Tetrarchic Inscription from Corcyra and the Edictum de Accusationibus', *ZPE* 141 (2002), 221–30. See also *C.Th.* 9. 34 and *CI* 9. 36, under the title 'de famosis libellis'.

justice *was seen* to have been done.[56] As Maud Gleason has astutely noted: 'The management of reputations required articulation of the community's standards and ideals; it required both individual and audience.'[57] In the face-to-face Christian communities of late antiquity, an accusation of 'heresy', whether made formally or simply spread by gossip and rumour, likewise demanded public action. When the monk and sometime 'undercover Priscillianist', Fronto, apparently laid charges of heresy against a certain Severus and Severa, before an ecclesiastical tribunal at Tarragona, Severus' relation by marriage, the Christian *comes Hispaniarum* Asterius, defended the family honour by mobilizing a small military force. As a result of his initial accusations, Fronto now found himself convicted in the court of local public opinion of having insulted 'an entire household of noble men', of having injured Asterius himself, and of having defamed his daughter.[58] Whatever we are to make of Fronto's (woolly) tale of Priscillianist wolves in sheep's clothing,[59] tainting an individual with an accusation of heresy could be a powerful, if unpredictable, strategy.

Heresy accusations could also be used strategically in legal cases concerning property, inheritance, and family law. Petitioning for 'ownerless' property, or disputing wills and legacies, was a time-honoured Roman pastime.[60] From Theodosius I onwards, however, a series of imperial constitutions specify that individuals convicted of being 'Manichees', 'Eunomians', 'Phyrgians', 'Priscillianists', and 'Donatists' have no rights (varyingly) to transmit their own property 'by execution of a testament, legacy or gift' or to receive any inheritance, legacy, or gift.[61] 'Apostates'

[56] Libanius, *Oration* 22. 34–5 (*c*.385), 'To Ellebichus', who was in fact the advocate who had pleaded the legal case on behalf of the distinguished civic official. On reputations in court see Chs. 2 and 4 above.

[57] M. Gleason, 'Visiting and News: Gossip and Reputation-Management in the Desert', *Journal of Early Christian Studies*, 6/3 (1998), 501–21.

[58] Augustine, *Ep.* 11*. 9. M. Kulikowski, 'Fronto, the Bishops, and the Crowd: Episcopal Justice and Communal Violence in Fifth-Century Tarraconensis', *Early Medieval Europe*, 11 (2002), 295–320, at 306 notes Fronto's 'affront to the honour of Asterius and his family', but also claims that 'theology was irrelevant' in provoking Asterius' intervention in the affair. I would suggest instead that, for Asterius, a Christian, being seen to hold the 'correct' theological beliefs (as defined by context) was an integral part of maintaining social reputation.

[59] For discussion see R. Van Dam, 'Sheep in Wolves' Clothing: The Letters of Consentius to Augustine', *JEH* 37 (1985), 515–35.

[60] See *C.Th.* 10. 10 and *CI* 10. 11–12

[61] Imperial constitutions which specify civil disabilities against 'Manichees' include: *C.Th.* 16. 5. 7 (given at Constantinople, May 381, to Eutropius PP); *C.Th.* 16. 5. 9 (given at Constantinople, Mar. 382, to Florus PP); and *C.Th.* 16. 5. 18 (given at Rome,

from Christianity to 'the sacrileges of the temples' or 'to the rites of the Jews' also have analogous civil disabilities applied to them from the early 380s onwards.[62] As Honoré states: 'Once it becomes possible to oppose say, one's father's will or undo a gift made during his lifetime by arguing that the beneficiary was or is a Eunomian, Manichee or Donatist, title to property becomes much less secure.'[63] Late Roman *delatores* (informers) and *accusatores* thus had a new 'Christian' context to work within.[64]

Under certain (varying) conditions dead people could also be accused of having been a 'Manichee' or an 'apostate'; if the charge was proved, it thus became possible to contest the inheritance of any property that the deceased had planned to transmit to his or her chosen heirs.[65] Complicated rules were also laid down in an attempt to govern the transmission of paternal or maternal goods, where the father or mother were 'heretics' and the children were either 'heretics' (no inheritance) or 'Catholics' (inheritance rights intact); or for entering into an inheritance, where the children were heretics but the parents were orthodox (no inheritance). These measures undoubtedly had a symbolic value, in that, once again, the Emperors were claiming, or rather advertising, their 'control' over the 'heretics' concerned. However, there is also evidence that these rules were being used, or at least subverted, in forensic contexts.

Fifth- and sixth-century drafters of imperial constitutions attempted to close a series of legal loopholes that were being developed and exploited in the courts, whereby property was transmitted to or from a

June 389, to Albinus, prefect of the City); against 'Eunomians': *C.Th.* 16. 5. 17 (given at Milan, May 389, to Tatianus PP): revoked by *C.Th.* 16. 5. 23 (given at Adrianople, March 395, to Rufinus PP), *C.Th.* 16. 5. 27 (given at Constantinople, Dec. 395, to Caesarius PP), and *C.Th.* 16. 5. 36 (given at Constantinople, July 399, to Eutychianus PP); revocation revoked(!) by *C.Th.* 16. 5. 58 (given at Constantinople, Nov. 415, to Aurelianus PP); against 'Manichees', 'Phyrgians', and 'Priscillianists' collectively: *C.Th.* 16. 5. 40. 1 (given at Rome, Feb. 407, to Senator, prefect of the City); against 'Donatists' and 'heretics' in general: *C.Th.* 16. 5. 54, pr. (given at Ravenna, June 414, to Julianus proconsul of Africa). See also Justinian, *Novel* 45.

[62] Civil disabilities against 'apostates' from Christianity: *C.Th.* 16. 7. 3 (given at Padua, May 383, to Postumianus, PP) and *C.Th.* 16. 7. 7 (given at Ravenna, Apr. 426, to Bassus PP).

[63] Honoré, *Law in Crisis*, 9.

[64] On the activities and social backgrounds of *delatores* and *accusatores* under the Late Republic and Early Empire see S. H. Rutledge, *Imperial Inquisitions: Prosecutors and Informants from Tiberius to Domitian* (London: Routledge, 2001).

[65] *C.Th.* 16. 7. 3 (383) and *C.Th.* 16. 5. 40. 5 (407).

member of a proscribed 'sect' through the use of a third ('non-heretical') party, or via a pretended sale.[66] In the early fifth century 'Donatists' also had civil disabilities applied to them in imperial legislation; although we should note in this context that the canons of African church councils had already specified that property was not to be left by certain Christians to pagans and heretics, even if they were relatives.[67] Augustine (again) gives us a glimpse of these civil disabilities in action, in a sermon most probably preached after 414. Augustine addresses the 'Donatists':

> Wake up, you heretics, listen to the shepherd's testament of peace [i.e. Christ's 'New' testament], come to the peace. You are angry with the Christian emperors because they have decreed that your testaments have no validity in your families . . . How many clever *iurisperiti* you consult, how many loopholes you look for so that your testament may stand against the emperor's law![68]

Individuals accused of being 'Donatists' were thus apparently employing legal experts (*iurisperiti*) to develop forensic dodges for them.

Other strategies for the defence included petitioning the emperors for case-specific exemptions to the rules. For example, sometime around 415 some 'Eunomians' had apparently petitioned the Emperors for the right to make testaments, donate property, and receive gifts, and had duly obtained private rescripts to that effect.[69] The 415 constitution orders, perhaps rather feebly, that any 'Eunomian' who has benefited from such a rescript must be deprived of what they have gained. The application of all these rules, of course, depended on a number of variables, including whether the individual accused of being a particular 'heretic' had sufficient property to merit attention, and whether other individuals were interested in denouncing them to the authorities, thus creating the potential to claim a share of any subsequently confiscated property.

The property that was confiscated as a result of these civil disabilities against 'heretics' and apostates from Christianity was apparently

[66] *CI* 1. 5. 10 (466–72?). See Humfress, 'Citizens and Heretics', for further discussion and earlier 4th-cent. examples.

[67] See e.g. the decisions of the council of Hippo in 393 (Mansi ii. 917). Other regional church councils in both the East and West had issued similar judgments. Honoré, *Law in Crisis*, 232, notes the imposition of civil disabilities against 'Donatists' in the imperial constitutions.

[68] Augustine, *Sermon* 47. 13. 22 (*PL* 38. 310–11): 'Vigilate haeretici, audite a pastore testamentum pacis, venite ad pacem. Irascimini christianis Imperatoribus, quia testamenta vestra valere noluerunt in domibus vestris . . . Quot iurisperitos consulis, quantas fraudes, ut stet testamentum tuum contra ipsam legem Imperatoris inquiris?' See also Augustine, *Tractates on the Gospel of John* 6. 25.

[69] *C.Th.* 16. 5. 58. 4 (given at Constantinople, Nov. 415, to Aurelianus PP).

viewed as a money-spinner by the imperial fisc—it was also seen as a potential source of income by the *delatores* (informers) who brought such property to the authorities' notice.[70] An imperial constitution issued at Constantinople in 444, however, forbids any private petitions for 'ownerless property': it also tellingly states that no person shall henceforth petition for the property of a deceased man or woman, whatever 'sect' such a deceased person belonged to, thereby implying that such petitions had been received from informers in the past.[71]

If we turn briefly to the Justinianic material we find, predictably, that the legal situation became even more complicated. For example, *CI* 1. 5. 19 (addressed to Demosthenes PP, 529) refers to a number of scenarios in which 'heretical' parents were apparently seeking to defraud their 'orthodox' children, by not providing for their upkeep and their dowries, amongst other things. A number of Justinianic constitutions also lay down rules on the use of 'heretics' as formal witnesses, to a variety of different effects. Much of this material is scattered throughout the Justinianic corpus, including Justinian's *Novels*, which were never officially promulgated as a collection. Hence we find the *iurisperitus* Julianus, a late sixth-century law teacher at the Beirut school, instructing his pupils that:

> If you are looking for information about the production of witnesses, read *Code* Book 4, ch. 20, *Digest* book 22 ch. 5 'On Witnesses', and in the *Novels*, that same constitution, which is under the same heading, 'On Witnesses'. But if a question is brought before you about heretical witnesses, then read the last constitution in *Code* Book 1 ch. 5. Read too, however, the constitution in the *Novels* around 60, in which you will find that heretics of curial status can give testimony in every way. If the issues of religion and of heretics arise before you, you should read those chapters that occur in *Code* Book 1 ch. 5 and the several other chapters that follow.

Julianus thus fully expected that his students would have to give responses to late sixth-century litigants on a variety of topics concerning 'heretics'.

[70] e.g. *C.Th.* 16. 5. 7. 1 ('Manichees') and *C.Th.* 16. 5. 17 ('Eunomians').

[71] *N. Th.* 17. 2. 3 (= *CI* 10. 12. 2, given at Constantinople, 444, to Zoilus): 'Nemo igitur audeat ad petitionem rerum defuncti defunctaeve, cuiuscumque fortunae *vel sectae* sit, etsi fisco nostro locus pateat, aspirare, cum ne illis quidem, quorum actu atque officio petitionum procedebat effectus, impune liceat nostris sanctionibus adversari.' More detailed regulations are given in s. 4 of the constitution.

ECCLESIASTICS AND ACCUSATIONS OF HERESY

'Each of us was afraid that, if expelled as a heretic, he would ruin those he had baptized; the danger affected not so much him, as those who had been baptized after professing their faith in Christ'.[72] These words, spoken by Theodore, bishop of Claudiopolis (Isauria) during the first session of the 451 Council of Chalcedon, serve as a reminder of what some late antique bishops, at least, believed was at stake in clerical accusations of heresy. A deposed bishop not only lost his authority, his civic power-base, and his various exemptions from taxation and compulsory public burdens—he also damned his congregation's souls. The sheer number and variety of late antique processes initiated by ecclesiastics, against other ecclesiastics, is bewildering; as is the constant intertwining of 'secular' and ecclesiastical venues, despite repeated attempts to establish a working system of *privilegium fori* for bishops (if not for Christian clerics as a whole).

A charge of heresy against a cleric could be handled as a local and internal disciplinary matter, as in the case of the subdeacon Victorius, convicted of Manichaeism and expelled from the city of Hippo by his bishop.[73] Or else a case could be heard 'opportunely' by a synod of bishops who had been initially called together for a different purpose; as in the case of Marcellus of Ancyra, who was asked to anathematize his views by the bishops who met at Jerusalem to witness the dedication of a new church of the Holy Sepulchre.[74] A 'heresy' charge could also be handled internally by a number of bishops assembled explicitly for that purpose, as was apparently the case when Bosporius, bishop of Colonia (Cappadocia), was tried for heresy. When he had been accused as a heretic by Helladius, bishop of Caesarea, a council was convened at Parnassas to try Bosporius—who apparently had the forensically skilled Amphilocius, bishop of Iconium, to help him with his defence.[75] Bosporius' case did not end before a conciliar tribunal,

72 *ACO* 2. 1. 1, *Actio* 1. 62 (tr. Price and Gaddis, *The Acts of the Council of Chalcedon*, 1. 142).

73 Augustine, *Ep*. 236 (written after 395), addressed to Bishop Deuterius.

74 See Lienhard, *Contra Marcellum* 3, for a brief synopsis of Marcellus' ecclesiastical career: deposed 336, reinstated by the (Eastern) Council of Serdica, deposed again *c*.338/9.

75 Gregory Nazianzen, *Ep*. 184, addressed to Amphilocius of Iconium.

however, as his accuser appealed against the decision to the imperial courts at Constantinople, provoking an outraged protest from Gregory of Nazianzus to Nectarius, the patriarch of Constantinople.[76] Despite Gregory's professed belief that bishops should not be dragged before 'civil tribunals', we nonetheless find him seeking the application of imperial laws against the 'Apollinarian's' consecration of another bishop at Nazianzus, in a letter addressed to Olympias the governor of Cappadocia Secunda.[77]

The *Acta* of the Council of Chalcedon, alongside the documents relating to the Council of Ephesus, 431, and various intervening synods, provide a wealth of evidence on fifth-century conciliar procedures in relation to ecclesiastical disciplinary hearings—as well as some stark claims concerning episcopal strategies and tactics. For example, in a petition read out at the council known as 'Ephesus II' (449), the archimandrite Eutyches claimed that Bishop Flavian of Constantinople had unilaterally excluded him from communion, deposed him from his position within his monastery and then had given him over to the mob, 'to be manhandled as a heretic, a blasphemer and a Manichee'.[78] Note here the recurring heresiological rhetoric. Eutyches, a skilled rhetorician, also claims that the original plea submitted against him to Flavian, by Eusebius of Dorylaeum (another consummate forensic player), had 'insolently called me a heretic without specifying in his plea any particular heresy, in the hope that in the testing conditions of a trial I would make some slip of the tongue as a result of the uproar, as was to be expected, and fall of a sudden into the error of uttering some novelty'.[79] In fact Eusebius of Dorylaeum's first formal indictment against Eutyches, read out at the first session of the Home Synod of Constantinople (8 Nov. 448), carefully attacks Eutyches' orthodoxy: 'I am ready to prove that his being called orthodox is a sham and that he has no part in the orthodox faith.'[80] This charge was repeated by Eusebius in the second session of Constantinople, 12 November 448, with Flavian presiding: 'I recently came to your Holiness and presented an indictment accusing Eutyches, presbyter and archimandrite of this

[76] Ibid. 185, addressed to Nectarius, patriarch of Constantinople. [77] Ibid. 125.

[78] *ACO* 2. 1. 1, *Actio* 1. 185 (tr. Price and Gaddis, *Acts of the Council of Chalcedon*, i. 163).

[79] Ibid. (tr. Price and Gaddis, *Acts of the Council of Chalcedon*, i. 162).

[80] Ibid. 230 (tr. Price and Gaddis, *Acts of the Council of Chalcedon*, i. 170). On the 448 'Home synod' and its impact on subsequent events see Gaddis, *There is No Crime*, 288–322.

city, of corrupting the orthodox doctrines of the church, both in private discussions and in the course of instructing those who come to him.'[81] Eusebius' initial strategy against Eutyches was thus to nail him on a charge of 'corrupting' orthodox belief.

Although the imperial authorities could be expected to enforce conciliar acts of deposition, in the great majority of cases, the situation on the ground remained volatile. As argued in Part II, many individual clerics either knew how to work the system themselves, or else could call in expert forensic assistance on their behalf. For instance, attempts by deposed bishops to seek imperial rescripts granting their reinstatement, or some other related privilege, were explicitly forbidden—but continued to occur in practice.[82] In 386 imperial rescripts granting rights of assembly to 'Arian' ecclesiastics and their congregations were apparently circulating in the West, but according to the Palatine officials of Valentinian II the documents had never been authorized by the imperial chancery.[83] In early fifth-century North Africa, Augustine claims that he holds in his hands a copy of the petition that the 'Donatists' had presented to the Emperor Julian, alongside the records of where exactly they made their representation; around 405 copies of this Julianic rescript were still being pleaded in the courts, as proof that the 'Donatists' were in fact 'Catholics'.[84]

In 404 Possidius, the bishop of Calama (North Africa), had occasion to institute a *defensor ecclesiae* as his personal legal representative in a case against his counterpart Donatist bishop, Crispinus. The circumstances surrounding the case are complex, but Possidius claimed to have been the victim of a violent personal assault carried out by members of the 'Donatist' party within the diocese of Calama:

Therefore, in order that the progress of the Church's peace might not be further impeded the *defensor ecclesiae* did not remain silent before the law. A warning was consequently issued to Crispinus, the Donatist bishop in the city and region of Calama, who had long been recognised as a *scholasticus*. According to the civil laws that were directed against the heretics, he became liable to a

[81] *ACO* 2. 1. 1, 238 (tr. Price and Gaddis, *Acts of the Council of Chalcedon*, i. 172).

[82] See *C.Th.* 16. 2. 35 (= *Sirm* 2, issued at Ravenna, Feb. 405/400, addressed to Hadrianus PP).

[83] *C.Th.* 16. 5. 16, on the identification of this constitution with the Western court of Valentinian II see Honoré, *Law in Crisis*, 37.

[84] Augustine, *Contra Litteras Petiliani* 2. 97. 224 (*BA* 30. 514–18) and *C.Th.* 16. 5. 37 (issued at Ravenna, Feb. 405, under the consulship of Stilicho. addressed to Hadrianus PP).

fine of gold. When he protested against the regulations Crispinus was brought before the Proconsul, where he denied that he was a heretic. It then became necessary that the *defensor ecclesiae* withdraw and a Catholic bishop oppose and convict Crispinus of being a heretic. For if the heretic had succeeded in his dissimulation, ignorant people might have considered him a Catholic bishop. Thus, due to neglect, an obstacle might have arisen in the path of weak people.[85]

From Possidius' account we can surmise that the individuals who were actually responsible for the assault against him could not themselves be prosecuted for the crime. A *defensor ecclesiae* was thus appointed, in order to pin the ultimate responsibility on the 'Donatist' Bishop Crispinus.[86] Crispinus could not be prosecuted for personal assault, as he himself was not guilty of that crime; however, he could be prosecuted on another basis. In this way the 'Donatist' party could be made to pay, indirectly, for the violence against Possidius. The *defensor* appealed to a law already in existence (probably *C.Th.* 16. 5. 21, issued in 392), which established that any person ordaining a heretical cleric would be liable to a fine of ten pounds of gold. Crispinus, however, had a defence: he denied before the proconsul that he was a heretic.

At this point the *defensor* retired from the case, presumably as he did not have the necessary theological skill to oppose Crispinus' defence plea. Only a Catholic bishop could prove that the charge should stick. According to Possidius, Augustine at this point insisted that both bishops of Calama met face to face, resulting in Crispinus being pronounced a 'heretic' by a proconsular sentence.[87] At this point Crispinus appealed to the Emperor at Ravenna, who judged against him and imposed a fine on the accused and the proconsul, together with his office staff—as a punishment for having allowed the appeal. The fact, however, that the forensic *defensor* had withdrawn to enable a bishop to take over the case highlights the potential for theological and ecclesiological argument within late Roman courtrooms.

[85] Possidius, *Vita Augustini* 12. The incident is also mentioned by Augustine at *Contra Cresconium grammaticum Donatistam* 3. 47. 51 (where it is characterized as an 'easy conviction' of a 'Donatist' bishop on a charge of heresy); also Augustine, *Ep.* 105. 2. 4 and *Ep.* 88. 7.

[86] For a slightly different reading of the incident see Gaddis, *There is No Crime*, 126: 'Possidius was ambushed and severely beaten at the behest of his Donatist rival, Crispinus of Calama. The Catholics, it could be argued, were asking for it: this new wave of violence followed directly upon the Catholics' decision in 401 to send missionaries into areas such as Southern Numidia formerly conceded to the Donatists.'

[87] Possidius, *Vita Augustini* 12. Possidius claims that he interceded for Crispinus, 'as an act of charity', and requested that the penalty of the fine of gold be withdrawn.

As a final example of forensic argumentation in a late Roman 'ecclesiastical' context I shall now turn, briefly, to the North African 'Donatist schism' itself. The fact that both Felix and Caecilian had been the subject of judicial proceedings in the 310s set the legal framework for the 'Donatist' controversy.[88] From the beginning of the schism both 'Catholics' and 'Donatists' employed professional advocates to argue their case. The dossiers that resulted from these legal processes were duly entered into the legal *acta* and henceforth set out precedents that could later be claimed by each side in the dispute. These forensic dossiers comprised verbatim extracts from the courtroom proceedings that dated all the way back almost to the origin of the schism, as well as imperial letters and the acts of ecclesiastical councils. Between 330 and 347 the 'Catholics' apparently extracted material from the original dossiers in order to produce their own 'anti-Donatist' *florilegia*, and we should certainly reckon on 'Donatists' undertaking similar practises with respect to court *acta* (also producing various martyr texts). In the context of Augustine's polemic with the Donatist bishop, Petilianus, the deployment of these legal dossiers took on a new dimension. Augustine, the former teacher of forensic rhetoric, disputed against Petilianus, a former professional *advocatus*, and legal texts were part of the raw material for their arguments. At the 411 so-called 'Council of Carthage' both 'Catholic' and Donatist *defensores* reworked the relevant legal material, once again showcasing forensic techniques of argument.[89] The complex reworking of the original dossiers, however, was not confined to the hands of forensically skilled bishops. The original dossiers themselves formed the basis for the activities of practising advocates, all members of professional corporations, arguing up to a century later for the restitution of basilicas and moveable goods. Forensic expertise was essential to the dissident 'Donatist' church in establishing an ecclesiastical structure to rival that of the North African 'Catholics'.

The 'Donatists' even turned their own internal schisms to their advantage. During the 390s the 'Donatist' church was split into two parties, labelled 'Primianists' and 'Maximianists'. The first legal process

[88] For detailed accounts of the early history of the North African schism see P. Monceaux, *Histoire littéraire de l'Afrique chrétienne depuis les origines jusquà l'invasion arabe*, iv (Paris: E. Leroux, 1912), 8–25; F. Martroye, 'La Répression du Donatisme et la politique religieuse de Constantin et de ses successeurs en Afrique', *MSNAF* 73 (1913), 23–140 esp. 44–60; and K. M. Girardet, *Kaisergericht und Bischofsgericht: Studien zu den Anfängen des Donatistenstreites (313–315) und zum Prozeß des Athanasius von Alexandrien (328–346)* (Bonn: R. Habelt, 1975).

[89] See Ch. 6 above.

relating to this internal division was lodged before the African proconsul Herodes in May 394. The 'Primianist' bishop Restitutus hired the services of a professional advocate, Nummasius, in order to demand the expulsion of the 'Maximianist' bishop, Salvius, from the see of Membressa. Augustine summarizes the key aspects of this case in his *Commentary on the Psalms*:

They [sc. the Primianists] took on the appearance of being Catholic, so that they might exclude the heretics. For indeed a judge can do nothing else than judge according to the laws. They said they were the Catholics: they were admitted to plead. They said the others were heretics: the judge asked for the proof. The Council of Bagai was produced, it had been inserted into the proconsular acts, and the proconsul pronounced them orthodox according to the law.[90]

In his works *Contra Cresconium* and *Contra Litteras Petiliani* Augustine reproduced verbatim extracts from the proconsular records; by piecing these records together the forensic arguments employed in the 394 'Donatist' proceedings can be reconstructed. The case of the 'Primianist' Restitutus was admitted to court because his advocate Nummasius lodged his plea as one from a 'Catholic' bishop. Nummasius accused the opposing 'Maximianist' bishop of heresy, and the proconsul demanded proof of the allegation. Nummasius duly produced the condemnation of the 'Maximianist' sect pronounced at the ('Donatist') Council of Bagai on 24 April 394.[91] The proconsul accepted the proof and Nummasius then summed up his client's case, which he divided into four consequential arguments of fact. Nummasius carefully framed his conclusions in order to provide the proconsul with a clear model to follow in giving sentence. First, he noted that the 'Maximianist' bishop Salvius had been deposed by a council of the 'true Catholic Church'; second, he stated that Salvius was a heretic, or ought to be assimilated with other heretics, because he was outside that true Catholic Church; third, he argued that Salvius thus fell under the anti-heresy laws enacted by the Emperors; and finally he concluded by returning to the concrete case at hand, and requested that the basilica at Membressa, held by

[90] Augustine, *Enarratio in Psalmum* 57. 15, 'sermo ad plebem' (*CCSL* 39. 721, ll. 28–35); 'Modo catholicus es, ut valeas ad excludendum haereticum. Iudex enim non posset nisi legibus suis iudicare. Dixerunt se catholicos; admissi sunt agere: dixerunt illos haereticos; quaesivit unde probaretur: lectum est concilium Bagaitanum, ubi damnati sunt Maximianistae; insertum est Actis proconsularibus, probatum est quod illi damnati non deberent tenere basilicas, et pronuntiavit proconsul ex lege.'

[91] Augustine, *Contra Cresc.* 4. 5 (*BA* 31. 474–6): the Council of Bagai's condemnation of Maximianus, as extracted from the proconsular *Gesta* of Herodes.

Salvius for the 'Maximianists', be returned to the true Catholics (sc. to the Primianists and their bishop Restitutus). The proconsul accepted the advocate's framing of the case and delivered his sentence accordingly.

Thus the 'Maximianist' bishop was classified as heretical and the Primianists ('Donatists') were declared 'orthodox Catholic' by a judicial sentence—that Augusine claimed had been won by bribery. This sentence was invoked as a precedent in subsequent cases between 'Primianists' and 'Maximianists' (again pleaded by professional advocates) over the next two years.[92] A series of casuistic precedents thus built up in which a 'Donatist' sect was categorized as the Catholic party in North Africa. When the internal schism between the Primianists and Maximianists was resolved in 396, the reunited 'Donatist' party then attempted to use these precedents against the 'official Catholic' Church, in subsequent legal proceedings over the restitution of 'Catholic' basilicas.

Augustine's treatise 'On baptism, against the Donatists', written *c*.400, was devoted to proving that the 'Donatist' practice of rebaptizing Christians was a tenet of false doctrine. Theological arguments concerning the nature of the sacrament of baptism—and specifically whether the sacrament had an efficacy in itself or depended upon the sanctity of the minister bestowing it—had lain at the heart of the 'Donatist' controversy from its beginnings. Moreover, the 'Donatists' could claim no less a figure than Cyprian as their authority for the 'orthodox' practice of rebaptism. Optatus had also attempted to clarify Christian doctrine on this point.[93] It was left to Augustine, however, to disinherit the 'Donatists' from the theological patronage of Cyprian, and condemn second baptism as heretical. Part of Augustine's strategy in classifying the practice of rebaptism as a 'heretical' dogma involved a distinction between the lawful possession of the sacrament and its efficacy in salvation. As the 'Donatists' were schismatics, Augustine argued, they could properly institute the sacrament of baptism—but without love for Christ's unity it remained ineffectual for their ultimate salvation. The sacrament could only be rendered effectual by entering into communion with the true Catholic Church. By repeatedly refusing communion with that church, the 'Donatists' thus committed an error of doctrine.

[92] Augustine, *Contra Cresc.* 3. 56. 62 (*BA* 31 394–8): 2 Mar. 395 the advocate Titianus pleaded before the proconsul Herodes, for the priest Peregrinus and the *seniores* of the 'Primianist' church at Assuras against the 'Maximianist' bishops Felicianus and Praetextatus. See also *Contra Cresc.* 4. 5 (*BA* 31. 472–6).

[93] Optatus, *De Schism. Donatist.* 6. 1 (*CSEL* 26. 126).

In book 1 of the *Contra Litteras Petiliani* (written in the year following the completion of 'On baptism') Augustine deliberately equates the terms *schismaticus* and *haereticus*. The crime of the 'Donatists' is schism. However, their theological fault lies in the fact that they have persisted in separating themselves from the communion of the universal Catholic Church.[94] Thus the groundwork was already laid for Augustine's neat formula, asserted against the 'Donatist' Cresconius in 405, that inveterate schism should be classified as a heresy *per se*.[95]

The same theological arguments which Augustine developed in order to classify 'Donatism' as a heresy reappear in the Emperor Honorius' law of 12 February 405 which, for the first time, legally categorized 'Donatists' as heretics. The preamble to the edict opens with the words:

> We provide, by the authority of this decree, that adversaries of the Catholic faith shall be extirpated. By this new constitution, therefore, We especially decree the destruction of that sect which, in order not to be called a heresy, prefers the appellation of schism. For those who are called Donatists are said to have progressed so far in wickedness that with criminal lawlessness they repeat the sacrosanct baptism, thus trampling under foot the mysteries, and they have infected with the contagion of a profane repetition men who have been cleansed once and for all by the gift of divinity, in accordance with religious tradition. Thus it happened that a heresy was born from a schism.[96]

It should come as no surprise that this edict was enacted in response to the demands of the 404 Council of Carthage.

The imperial edict of 12 February 405 (eventually) opened the way for forced conversions from 'Donatism' to Catholicism. Modern scholars are thus accustomed to referring to 405 as the year in which the Catholic Church, and specifically Augustine himself, changed tactics against the 'Donatists' and began applying the rigour of imperial laws against them. However, as we have seen, the 405 constitution was the culmination of almost a century of complex interactions between theological and

[94] Augustine, *Contra Litteras Petiliani* 2. 94 217 (*BA* 30. 506–8).

[95] Augustine, *Contra Cresc.* 2. 7. 9 (*BA* 31. 168).

[96] *C.Th.* 16. 6. 4 (issued at Ravenna and addressed to the Praetorian Prefect Hadrianus): 'Adversarios catholicae fidei exstirpare huius decreti auctoritate prospeximus. Ideoque intercidendam specialiter eam sectam nova constitutione censuimus, quae, ne haeresis vocaretur, appellationem schismatis praeferebat. In tantum enim sceleris progressi dicuntur hi quos Donatistas vocant, ut baptisma sacrosanctum mysteriis recalcatis temeritate noxia iterarint et homines semel, ut traditum est, munere divinitatis ablutos contagione profanae repetitionis infecerint. Ita contigit, ut haeresis ex schismate nasceretur.' The edict itself is a complex and comprehensive piece of anti-heretical legislation. Further extracts are given at *C.Th.* 16. 5. 38, 16. 6. 3, and 16. 6. 5.

forensic arguments. As Monceaux eloquently concluded, 'The dissident church had need of advocates, She was born, she grew up where she could, she was to die, in the midst of forensic processes.'[97]

The introduction of the concepts of 'heresy' and 'orthodoxy' into the late Roman legislative sphere necessitated the legal categorization and systematization of religious belief itself. Within this context, litigants and forensic practitioners (both 'secular' and ecclesiastical) played an important role in developing new theological/legal classifications—in no small part due to the fact that the imperial constitutions themselves were (mainly) responses to arguments and strategies developed through forensic practice. Viewed from the angle of courtroom activity, we can also see how litigants and forensic practitioners attempted to develop defence strategies against 'heresy' prosecutions; applying the taxonomic techniques of late Roman forensic rhetoric to concrete cases, as in the case of the North African 'Manichee', Viator. Accusations involving 'heresy' were not just a 'legal' phenomenon, but were part of the fabric of late Roman life. The late antique church was dominated, at least as far as its disputes were concerned, by a culture of forensic argumentation.

[97] P. Monceaux, *Histoire littéraire de l'Afrique chrétienne depuis les origines jusquà l'invasion arabe*, vi (Paris: E. Leroux, 1922), 358.

10

Conclusion

> Because of this, it has always been my custom to tie myself down as little as possible to what the Greeks call 'Catholic' rules—that is (to translate as well as we can), 'universal' or 'perpetual' rules. Rules are rare indeed that cannot be weakened or subverted in some respect.[1]

As the late first-century teacher of rhetoric Quintilian was well aware, general rules have to be continually modified and negotiated in practice. This fact stands whether the rules in question are rhetorical, 'legal', or indeed theological. In late antiquity, practitioners of forensic rhetoric were trained in how to handle general legal principles and imperial constitutions persuasively and creatively. In other words, late Roman rhetorical schools, in both the East and the West, taught their pupils how to handle imperial legislation (when an instant case demanded it) pragmatically, as 'a resource for influencing the outcome of disputes', rather than 'a canon for deciding them'.[2] The duty of the late Roman advocate, and indeed the *iurisperitus* employed in private cases, lay in exploiting the dialectic between any relevant 'normative' rule and its concrete application, in favour of their client's case. Thus within the technical branch of ancient rhetoric, 'laws' were already held to exist within a domain of rhetorical argumentation. What emerges from this perspective is not the 'intellectual inferiority' of late Roman law, but the creativity and ingenuity of late Roman forensic practitioners.

From the perspective of the *practical* life of late Roman law, then, questions of interpretation, classification, and relevancy were endemic;

[1] Quintilian, *Inst*. 2. 13. 14: 'Propter quae mihi semper moris fuit, quam minime alligare me ad praecepta, quae kauolikå vocitant, id est (ut dicamus quomodo possumus) universalia vel perpetualia. Raro enim reperitur hoc genus, ut non labefactari parte aliqua et subrui possit' (tr. D. A. Russell, *Quintilian, The Orator's Education*, Loeb Classical Library (Cambridge, Mass., and London: Harvard University Press, 2001), 345.

[2] Heath, *Menander: A Rhetor in Context*, 294 at n. 33, quoted in Ch. 4 above.

they were not 'resolved' by the great legal codification projects of Theodosius and Justinian, notwithstanding the imperial legislative rhetoric of the compilers. Techniques of forensic argument either continued to be applied in the courts, or (as and when necessary) were applied to the texts of the Codes themselves. Moreover, the forensic arguments of advocates, *iurisperiti*, and *iudices*, particularly those acting in the higher bureaucratic courts, frequently provoked the need for new imperial constitutions to be drafted. Thus, if we wish to understand the development of late Roman law within its socio-legal context, we must move beyond the study of 'normative' legislation towards a detailed study of forensic activity within the lawcourts (Part I).

The age of Constantine certainly cannot be taken for the age of Justinian: the shifts in Roman social, economic, and political life across these three centuries were radical, and in some respects they should be taken as discontinuous. Constantine did not simply plant the acorns that became Justinian's oak trees. Nonetheless, for the most part, the story of late Roman forensic practice is one of remarkable continuity across periods of otherwise rapid change.

In setting out to rewrite the history of the practice of late Roman law, I have self-consciously used the surviving works of 'ecclesiastical' writers and 'Christian' theologians, alongside other literary and documentary evidence, including the later papyri and rhetorical handbooks. In general, and with some important exceptions noted in Part I, this 'ecclesiastical' material has not been exploited systematically by historians or legal scholars. Yet it has proved to be a significant source for late Roman forensic practice. The reason why it is such a significant source can be explained by a simple fact: many ecclesiastical writers had themselves received a traditional career-orientated education in forensic rhetoric, and some key ecclesiastics also went on to receive a technical 'legal' education in preparation for practice as *iurisperiti* or legal experts (Chapters 5 and 6). When these individuals joined the ecclesiastical 'bureaucracy', or entered into monastic environments, or even began simply writing 'Christian' polemic, the techniques that they had learnt at rhetorical school were applied in new contexts.

Despite the tensions felt and identified by some late Roman Christians and ecclesiastics, 'conversion' to Christianity did not erase the technical skills of persuasive eloquence already learnt in the 'secular' sphere. When Evagrius scholasticus set out on the daunting task of continuing the *Ecclesiastical History* of Eusebius up to his present day (the late sixth century), he explicitly put his trust in a Christian God 'who gave both wisdom to fishermen and changed an unreasoning tongue into articulate eloquence'.[3] Not all bishops or clerics, of course, had been trained in the skills of forensic rhetoric (whether they had actually practised as advocates or not). In the early fifth century, Augustine set aside a specific section of his treatise on catechism to instruct (North African) ecclesiastics who were either unlettered or 'rude' in speech, in how to handle those catechumens who came from the 'common' schools of rhetoric (and grammar), and were thus puffed up with pride and admiration for the eloquence of the forum.[4] Moreover, the fact that some leading ecclesiastics had received this educational (and indeed socio-cultural) formation, has important implications for how we view the development of early canon law and the advancement of the church, within both the late Roman and the early medieval world.

The gradual elaboration of ecclesiastical law was achieved through a constant case-specific interaction between legal practitioners within the church and legal practice outside the church. The fact that some key late Roman ecclesiastics were trained as forensic practitioners is crucial to explaining how it was that early 'canon law' was elaborated using specific techniques and procedures 'borrowed' from Roman law (Chapter 7). Of course, there is a much wider story to be told here in terms of the 'living law' of the early church, or more accurately churches. I am conscious of the fact, for example, that I have not tackled the 'Jewish' background, and continuing influences, adequately. On the other hand, I hope to have provided at least some comparative material—enough, for example, to contextualize the vexed question of the establishment and development of the so-called *episcopalis audientia*, as well as the synodal practices of various regional and 'oecumenical' church councils. The forensic training of ecclesiastics also allowed them, as individuals, to participate in the legal hierarchy of the imperial bureaucracy, pleading at the imperial court for privileges and exemptions, arguing for the extension of case-specific rescripts before praetors and proconsuls, seeking the promulgation of new imperial legislation, and then transforming its content by applying it to analogous cases.

One of the most innovative aspects of late Roman law was the creation and use of new legal categories in the prosecution of 'heretics' (Part III). By the late fourth century, the various procedural regulations

[3] Evagrius scholasticus, *HE* 1. 5 (tr. M. Whitby, *Ecclesiastical History of Evagrius Scholasticus* (Liverpool: Liverpool University Press, 2001), 5.

[4] Augustine, *On the Catechising of the Uninstructed* (*De Catechizandis Rudibus*) 13 (*CCSL* 46. 135–6).

concerning the prosecution of heresy were well instituted, as was the idea that heretics needed to be dealt with by imperial and 'canon' law alike (Chapter 8). The difficulties surrounding such prosecutions often lay in the fact that the church's doctrine itself was not crystallized. However, the constant ecclesiastical references to a canon of orthodox belief, alongside the 'rhetorical' practices of labelling and categorization, imparted a gloss of certainty, and it is this certainty that was transmitted into the Theodosian and Justinianic Codes. The structural or institutional vocabulary for orthodoxy was thus in place, but the ideas governing its content were still fluid. Litigants and forensic practitioners (both 'secular' and ecclesiastical) thus played an important role in developing new theological/legal classifications and then reifying them—in no small part due to the fact that the imperial constitutions themselves were (in the main) responses to arguments and strategies developed through forensic practice. Litigants and forensic practitioners also, moreover, attempted to develop defence strategies against heresy prosecutions (Chapter 9). In late antiquity, the ideas of 'orthodoxy' and 'heresy' alike were continually being renegotiated, within a culture heavily indebted to forensic argumentation.

Christian theology suggested that a 'Catholic' rule existed, and that 'universal' trial and judgment was possible through the eschatological fact of the Last Judgment. In the lawcourts of the Late Empire, however, prosecutions involving accusations of 'heresy' did not proceed from such a solid doctrinal or juristic basis. Earthly litigation for souls was a more complicated procedure than the heavenly one. Yet in the former culminated the transformation of bishops from the fishermen of an apostolic church to the forensic orators of an imperial one.

APPENDIX I

Appendix I. Advocates in the Eastern Empire (Fourth to Sixth Century)

Abureius, 388–92 (*PLRE* I, 5)
Rhetor/advocate, Arabia. Wrote a panegyric on Bonus (Lib. *Ep.* 1035).

Acacius, 357–65 (*PLRE* I, 6: no. 6)
Rhetor/advocate, at Antioch and in Palestine.

Acacius, 361–5 (*PLRE* I, 6: no. 7)
Rhetor/advocate, studied in Athens and lived in Cilicia.

Acontius, 365 (*PLRE* I, 11)
Rhetor/advocate (Lib. *Ep.* 226), became provincial governor (Lib. *Ep.* 1495).

Adamantius, 356 (*PLRE* I, 12: no. 1)
Advocate, according to Lib. *Ep.* 488 he was able but idle.

Adamantius, 360/390 (*PLRE* I, 12: no. 2)
Teacher of rhetoric, received Greg. Naz. *Ep.* 235.

Adelphius, late 4th cent. (*PLRE* I, 13: no. 2)
Advocate (*scholastikos*), had property at Vanota (Greg. Nyss. *Ep.* 20).

Aetius, 362 (*PLRE* I, 26: no. 2)
Advocate at Ancyra, but educated at Antioch (Lib. *Ep.* 733, 769).

Agathias, mid/late 6th cent.
Studied law, practised as an advocate at Constantinople, wrote histories (Agathias, *Histories*, pr. and 3. 1. 4).

Agroecius, 361
Advocate at court of Domitius Modestus *comes Orientis*, originally from Armenia and now being sought by the city council (Lib. *Ep.* 293).

Alcimus, 356 (*PLRE* I, 38)
Teacher of rhetoric at Nicomedia (Lib. *Ep.* 397), he moved to Rome leaving (St) Basil in charge of his school (Lib. *Ep.* 501).

Alexander, 364–5 (*PLRE* I, 41: no. 9)
Rhetor, advocate, and *agens in rebus* (Lib. *Ep.* 1193, 1197, 1199, 1505).

Fl. Arcadius Alexander, 487 (*PLRE* II, 58)
Advocate (*scholastikos*), who then possibly became governor of Arabia in 487.

Alexander, 538
Advocate at the court of the PPO (Justinian, *Novel* 82. 1 pr).

Alladius, 4th cent. (*PLRE* I, 45)
Advocate (*scholastikos*) in Egypt.

Ammonius, 4th cent.
Advocate (*P.Oxy.* LIV. 3758, ll. 39–77 and 156–80 (325) and *P.Oxy.* LIV. 3764 (326)).

Ammon, early/mid-4th cent.
Scholasticus/advocate (see *P. Ammon*).

Fl. Ampelius, mid-5th cent.
'Most eloquent *scholasticus* and *pater civitatis*' (Roueché, *Aphrodisias*, nos. 42–4).

Amphilochius, before 361 (*PLRE* I, 57: no. 2)
Advocate (Lib. *Ep.* 670), then teacher of rhetoric. Father of Amphilochius, bishop of Iconium and uncle of Gregory Nazianzus.

Amphilochius, late 4th cent.
Advocate, gave it up for a life of Christian contemplation (Basil, *Letter* 150). Became bishop of Iconium in 373.

Anastasios, 6th cent.
Advocate (*ekdikos*) of the city of Oxyrhynchus, who drafted a repudiation of a betrothal on behalf of a certain John, father of Euphemia (*P.Oxy.* 129).

Anatolius, 538
Vir spectabilis, mentioned as a retired advocate in Justinian's *Novel* 82. 1 pr.

Andragathius, 360 (*PLRE* I, 62)
Advocate of PP *Orientis*, before whom he proved his rhetorical skill. (Lib. *Ep.* 222–3).

Anticles, 362 (*PLRE* I, 70)
Rhetor/advocate from Cilicia, commended by Libanius to Celsus, *praeses Ciliciae* in 362.

Antonius, mid/late 5th cent. (*PLRE* II, 107: no. 3)
Rhetor and advocate. He entered public life to help his sister in a lawsuit, but acquired a name for excessive zeal.

Appio, 538
Vir spectabilis, advocate of the fisc and assessor (Justinian, *Novel* 82. 1. 1).

Apringius, 355–64 (*PLRE* I, 86)
Advocate. Summoned to Antioch in 355 to start his career (Lib. *Ep.* 422, which specifies that his father was also an advocate). Later studied law at Beirut.

Aquilinus, early/mid-5th cent. (*PLRE* II, 125: no. 2)

Advocate at Constantinople with (the historian) Sozomen (Sozomen, *HE* 2. 3. 10–11).

Arsenius, early/mid-5th cent. (*PLRE* I, 110: no. 2)
Advocate at Antioch and fellow student of Libanius (Lib. *Ep.* 37, 541, 1224, 1233, 1474).

Arsenius, d. 364 (*PLRE* I, 111: no. 3)
Advocate at Antioch, after having been a pupil of Libanius (Lib. *Ep.* 1260).

Asclepius, d. 511 (*PLRE* II, 163: no. 5)
Advocate, probably at Antioch. He amassed a fortune by his practice in the lawcourts.

Asterius, mid/late 4th cent.
Advocate at Constantinople? Bishop of Amasea, Pontus (see Chapter 6).

Athanasius, late 5th/early 6th cent.
Brother of a certain Paralios, studied the laws of the *politieia* (civil law) in Phoenicia, then became a monk at Alexandria (Zacharias Scholastikos, *Life of Severus,* ed. and tr. Marc-Antoine Kugener, *Patrologia Orientalis*, 2 (Paris, 1907), 14–15).

Auxentius, 357 (*PLRE* I, 142: no. 3)
Rhetor and advocate (Lib. *Ep.* 595, 596).

Auxentius, early/mid-5th cent. (*PLRE* II, 204: no. 3)
Defensor (*ekdikos*) and therefore advocate. Received *Ep.* 2. 309 of Nilus the Monk.

Besarion, 303 (*PLRE* I, 161)
Advocate (*scholastikos*) at Thebes (O.Tait II. 2086).

Fl. Bonus, late 4th cent. (*PLRE* I, 164)
Advocate (Lib. *Ep.* 1035).

Cardemeas (?), 507 (*PLRE* II, 260)
Advocate (*scholastikos*), possibly at Antinoopolis in the Thebaid (*P.Lond.* III. 253 n. 992 = Mitteis, *Chrest.* n. 365).

Calliopius, 388 (*PLRE* I, 175: no. 3, and Kaster, *Guardians of the Word*, 131)
Teacher of grammar before practising as an advocate (Lib. *Ep.* 18), then became *magister epistularum* of the East.

Carterius, 379/380 (*PLRE* I, 182: no. 3)
Advocate (*defensor*), judge (*cognitor*), *consularis* of Syria (Symm. *Ep.* 9. 31).

Cimon, Arabius, mid/late 4th cent. (*PLRE* I, 92)
Advocate, served at the court of *consularis Syriae* (Lib. *Or.* 28. 9, of 384; 54. 7–15, of 388). He was the son of Libanius, who wanted him to become a rhetorician, but he enrolled himself among the advocates (*sundikoi*) instead (Lib. *Ep.* 959).

Chrysogonus, 364 (*PLRE* I, 205: no. 2)
Rhetor and advocate in Phoenice. He first studied rhetoric under Libanius, then went to Antioch to study medicine but was not accepted on the course; he was then swindled out of his property by his guardians. Libanius appealed to two governors of Phoenice to enrol him as rhetor and advocate (Lib. *Ep.* 1208 and 1280).

Constantine, 533/534
Advocate at court of PPO. Member of commission that produced Justinian's *Digest* (*Const. Tanta* 9) and member of commission that produced the second edition of Justinian's *Codex* (*Const. Cordi* 2).

Cyris, 4th cent. (*PLRE* I, 238)
Advocate (*scholastikos*) at Hermopolis in the Thebaid (*P.Flor.* I. 71. 653 and 87. 8).

Demetrios, 390
Part of a team of three advocates, in a civil process before the *praeses* of Thebais (*P.Lips.*, no. 38).

Diodorus, late 5th/early 6th cent. (*PLRE* II, 359: no. 3)
Advocate at Caesarea.

Diognetus, 388 (*PLRE* I, 257)
Former pupil of Libanius (Lib. *Ep.* 358); Libanius wrote his letters of recommendation for the post of advocate in Constantinople (Lib. *Ep.* 847, 857, 858).

Dionysius, 363 (*PLRE* I, 258: no. 6)
Pupil of Libanius (Lib. *Ep.* 1168, 1204). Served as advocate under the governor of Isauria (Lib. *Ep.* 837), but shortly after retired to look after his family estates. Two years later he came out of retirement and conducted a successful defence (Lib. *Ep.* 1501).

Flavius Dionysius, 335 (*PLRE* I, 259: no. 11)
Advocate (Lib. *Or.* 1. 36). Then governor of Phoenice, appointed *consularis Syriae* and was in charge of the ecclesiastical Council of Tyre in 335.

Domninus, 364–5 (*PLRE* I, 265: no. 2)
Advocate before 364 (Lib. *Or.* 56. 11 and *Ep.* 952), then governor of Phoenice and senator of Constantinople before 390.

Domnio, 388 (*PLRE* I, 266: no. 2)
Advocatus fisci before 388 (Lib. *Ep.* 861), then *vicarius Asiae* in 388.

Elias, early/mid-5th cent. (*PLRE* II, 390: no. 2)
Advocate (*scholastikos*), received Theodoret of Cyrrhus, *Ep.* 10.

Eudaemon, mid-4th cent. (*PLRE* I, 289: no. 3 and Kaster, *Guardians of the Word*, 279: no. 55)

Advocate, trained in rhetoric and practising at Elusa in Palestine in 357 (Lib. *Ep*. 315). He was also a sophist and a poet, and in 360 Libanius requested an official stipend for him (*Ep*. 132). Author of grammatical treatises.

Eunapius, 367/368 (*PLRE* I, 295: no. 1)
Phyrgian *rhetor*, represented Lydians before Julian, who gave him a difficult legal case, which he won.

Eunomus, 357–60 (*PLRE* I, 29: no. 2)
Rhetor and advocate at Elusa in Palestine (Lib. *Ep*. 315 and 164).

Eusebius, 361
Advocate at court of Domitius Modestus, *comes Orientis*, originally from Armenia and now being sought by city council (Lib. *Ep*. 293).

Eusebius of Dorylaeum, early/mid-5th cent.
Advocate at Constantinople *c*.426–30, bishop of Dorylaeum (see Chapter 6).

Eustochius, 360–5 (*PLRE* I, 313)
Advocate (Lib. *Ep*. 240, 789, 1525), from Palestine, retired by 390 (Lib. *Ep*. 915).

Euthali(u)s, late 4th/5th cent. (*PLRE* I, 314: no. 1)
Advocate (*scholastikos*) at Apamea.

Euthymius, 390 (*PLRE* I, 315)
Advocate (*sundikos*, Lib. *Ep*. 974–5) and then *vicarius Asiae* in 396.

Eutolmius, 533
Advocate at court of PPO. Member of commission that produced Justinian's *Digest* (*Const. Tanta* 9).

Eutropius, 389 (*PLRE* I, 318: no. 3)
Attended rhetorical school, then studied law and became an advocate, then became assessor to the PP *Orientis*, and was appointed consular of Syria in 389. Libanius wrote his *Oration* 4 against him.

Evagrius, late 5th/early 6th cent. (*PLRE* II, 402–3)
Advocate.

Evagrius scholasticus, mid/late 6th cent.
Studied law at Constantinople in the late 550s, pursued a legal career at Antioch: 'Like his cousin and fellow lawyer John of Epiphania, he came to be attached to the service of Gregory, Patriarch of Antioch (570–92) and it is quite possible that he had always worked within the patriarchate as a legal advisor' (M. Whitby, *The Ecclesiastical History of Evagrius Scholasticus* (Liverpool: Liverpool University Press, 2000), p. xiv).

Evagrius, late 5th/early 6th cent.
Wanted to become a monk, but his father forced him to go to Beirut to study law, after which he 'shone in Constantinople, in the *Stoa*, amongst the

advocates' (Zacharias Scholastikos, *Life of Severus*, ed. and tr. Marc-Antoine Kugener, *Patrologia Orientalis*, 2 (Paris, 1907), 55–6).

Evangelius, early/mid-6th cent.
Lawyer at Caesarea.

Flavianus, 538
Advocate of the fisc (Justinian, *Novel*, 82. 1 pr.).

Gaianus (*PLRE* I, 378–9: no. 6)
Advocate, assessor to an Antiochene official pre-362, governor of Phoenicia between 362 and 363.

Gaudentius, 357–62 (*PLRE* I, 385: no. 2)
Advocate (*sunegoros*) in Arabia.

Glaucus, 4th cent. (*PLRE* I, 397)
Advocate (*scholastikos*) probably from Hermopolis in the Thebaid (*P.Lips.* I. 100, col. iv. 2).

Gregory of Nyssa, mid-4th cent.
Teacher of rhetoric, then bishop of Nyssa (see Chapter 6).

Heliodorus, mid-4th cent. (*PLRE* I, 411: no. 2)
Advocate (Lib. *Or*. 62. 46–9). Libanius alleges that he was originally a 'retailer of fish sauce' who was called to the bar of the proconsul of Achaea at Corinth. He ended up a rich man with vast estates in Macedonia, Aetolia, and Acarnania through the bequest of half of the property of a woman whose claims he had successfully defended.

Helpidius, 357–61 (*PLRE* I, 414: no. 3)
Rhetor and advocate. Educated in Athens (Lib. *Ep*. 546), then became a teacher of rhetoric in Palestine (Lib. *Ep*. 546 and 312). In 361 he went to Constantinople in order to seek a place as an advocate (Lib. *Ep*. 299–301).

Heraclidius, mid/late 4th cent.
Attempted to leave the practice of advocacy for a life of Christian contemplation but the magistrates sought him out 'like a deserter' (Basil, *Ep*. 150).

Heraclius, 391 (*PLRE* I, 419: no. 7)
Advocate in Antioch, 384–8 (Lib. *Or*. 28. 9. 13 and 54. 13. 76). Governor of Armenia in 391.

Hermias, 504
Scholastikos and *defensor* of Oxyrhynchus (*P.Oxy*. XVI. 1882 and 1883).

Herminus, late 4th/early 5th cent.
Defence advocate in a criminal case (*P. Lips*. 40).

Hermolaus, 360 (*PLRE* I, 426)
Advocate in Antioch in 360. He practised advocacy whilst attending Libanius' classes (Lib. *Ep*. 203).

Herodes, 395
Part of a team of three advocates in a civil process, before the *praeses* of Thebais (*P. Lips.*, no. 38).

Hesychius, ?4th/5th cent. (*PLRE* I, 429: no. 3)
Advocate at the court of the PPO.

Flavius Asclepiades Hesychius, *c.*391 (*PLRE* I, 429: no. 4)
Advocate at Antioch in 384 (Lib. *Or.* 28. 9), became an assessor (Lib. *Ep.* 854). He was appointed provincial governor and then *praeses Thebaidos* in 390–1.

Fl. Ant(onius) Hierocles, mid-4th cent. (*PLRE* I, 431: no. 3)
Advocate, who made money out of his profession but spent it whilst governor of Arabia and *consularis Syriae* in 348. He also taught as professor of rhetoric (Lib. *Ep.* 517).

Hilarius, *c.*360 (*PLRE* I, 434: no. 4)
Advocate.

Horion, *c.*325–50
Advocate, worked on a case on behalf of Sambathion of the village of Karanis (*P. Col.* VII. 174).

Hyperechius, 366 (*PLRE* I, 449)
Advocate (*sunegoros*) under the governor of Galatia.

Ioannes, late 5th cent.
Ecclesiae scholasticus at Amida (see Chapter 6).

Iohannes, 534
Advocate at court of PPO. Member of commission to produce the second edition of Justinian's *Codex* (*Const. Cordi* 2).

Flavius Isaac, 464
Scholastikos and *defensor* of Cynopolis (*P. Oxy,* VI. 902).

Ischyrion, 325
Defence advocate in *P. Oxy.* LIV. 3758.

Isidorus, 4th cent. (*PLRE* I, 465: no. 2)
Advocate (*scholastikos*) at Hermopolis in the Thebaid.

Jacobus, 533
Advocate at court of PPO. Member of commission that produced Justinian's *Digest* (*Const. Tanta* 9).

Johannes, 533
Advocate at court of PPO. Member of commission that produced Justinian's *Digest* (*Const. Tanta* 9).

Flavius Julianus, 336
Advocate in the Oxyrhynchite nome (*P. Oxy.* VI. 901).

Klearchos, mid/late 4th cent.
Advocate, then governor.

Laurentius, early/mid-5th cent. (*PLRE* II, 658: no. 3)
Advocatus fisci.

Laurentius, 475/476 (*PLRE* II, 658: no. 5)
A leading advocate at Constantinople, appointed as PP *Orientis* in 475/6.

Leonides, 533
Advocate at court of PPO. Member of commission that produced Justinian's *Digest* (*Const. Tanta* 9).

Leontius, 533
Advocate at court of PPO. Member of commission that produced Justinian's *Digest* (*Const. Tanta* 9).

Macarius, 481 (*PLRE* II, 696: no. 3)
Advocate (*sunegoros*) in the forum of the Thebaid (*P.Princ.* II. 82).

Macarius, mid-6th cent.
Advocate, a former pupil of Procopius of Gaza (Procopius, *Ep.* 153 and 97).

Marcarius, 583
Advocate (*scholastikos*), involved in a dispute between a mother and son (*P.Mon.* 6).

Macedonius, 363 (*PLRE* I, 526: no. 2)
Advocate who on retirement became *defensor* of Tarsus.

Vindaonius Magnus, 375–6 (*PLRE* I, 536)
Advocate in Phoenice in 364. In 373 he was *comes sacrarum largitionum* and by 375 *praefectus urbis Constantinopolitanae*.

Maximus, 378 (*PLRE* I, 585: no. 25)
Advocate (*scholastikos*) of noble birth (Basil, *Ep.* 277).

Megethius, 363 (*PLRE* I, 592: no. 2)
Advocate in Antioch in 363 (Lib. *Ep.* 1361).

Menas, 534
Advocate at court of PPO. Member of commission that produced Justinian's *Digest* (*Const. Tanta* 9). Member of commission to produce the second edition of Justinian's *Codex* (*Const. Cordi* 2). Possibly the same Menas mentioned in Justinian, *Novel* 82. 1 pr as an advocate at the court of the PPO in 538.

Miccalus 360
Advocate (or possibly assessor) under Priscianus, governor of Euphratensis and governor of Thrace in 362.

Naucratius, mid/late 4th cent. (*PLRE* I, 618)
Advocate, brother of Basil and Gregory of Nyssa, retired to become a monk (see Chapter 6).

Nemesios, 386/7 (*PLRE* I, 622)
Advocate (Greg. Naz. *Carm. hist.* 2. 7. 1–4), then governor of Cappadocia Secunda.

Nilammon, 390
Part of a team of three advocates in a civil process before the *praeses* of Thebais (*P.Lips.*, no. 38).

Optimus, late 4th cent.
Advocate, bishop of Agdamia (Phyrgia) and Antioch (see Chapter 6).

Orion, mid-6th cent.
Advocate, a former pupil of Procopius of Gaza who studied law in Constantinople (Procopius, *Ep.* 144 and 155).

Paeanius, 364 (*PLRE* I, 657)
Advocate practising in Palestine (Lib. *Ep.* 1306).

Palladius, 360 (*PLRE* I, 659: no. 5)
Advocate (*sunegoros*) under the *praeses Euphratensis* (Lib. *Ep.* 179).

Parnassius, early/mid-5th cent. (*PLRE* II, 832: no. 1)
Advocate (*sunegoros*).

Patalas, 363 (*PLRE* I, 669)
Advocate (*scholastikos*) at Jovian's court at Antioch.

Plato, 533
Advocate at court of PPO. Member of commission that produced Justinian's *Digest* (*Const. Tanta 9*).

Plenis, 338 (*PLRE* I, 706)
Advocate (*scholastikos*) in the Thebaid.

Poemenius, 325
Advocate and drafter of will in *P.Oxy.* LIV. 3758, ll. 181–213 and advocate for prosecution in *P.Oxy.* LIV. 3759.

Pylaemenes, 402/413 (*PLRE* II, 931)
Advocate (*sunegoros*) at Constantinople.

Priscianus, 364 (*PLRE* I, 727: no. 1)
Advocate at Beirut and Antioch before 360, governor of Euphratensis 360–1, of Cilicia 363–4, and of Palestina Prima, 364.

Procopius, early/mid-6th cent.
Received legal training, and then from 527 acted as assessor to the general Belisarius (A. Cameron, *Procopius and the Sixth Century* (Berkeley, Calif.: University of Berkeley Press, 1985), 8).

Prosdocius, 533
Advocate at court of PPO. Member of commission that produced Justinian's *Digest* (*Const. Tanta* 9).

Rufinus, early 6th cent.
Ecclesiae scholasticus of Ephraem, patriarch of Antioch.

Sabinus, 356
Advocate at the court of the Eastern Prefect, Strategius Musonianus, in 356, then governor of Syria in 358–9 (Lib. *Ep.* 545, 339).

Sarapion, 451/457 (*PLRE* II, 977: no. 2)
Advocate (*scholasticos*). He was 'the first of the advocates at Alexandria' in the time of the patriarch Proterius. A monophysite, he was arrested for his religious beliefs and sent to the Emperor Marcian at Constantinople; he was freed and permitted to enrol among the advocates (*scholastici*) at Constantinople, where he again rose to first position.

Saturninus, 365 (*PLRE* I, 805: no. 5)
A successful advocate, appointed to office by PPO Secundus Salutius (Lib. *Ep.* 1489–90).

Serapion of Thmuis, mid-4th cent.
Scholasticus, bishop of Thmuis (see Chapter 6).

Sergius, 517 (*PLRE* II, 994–5: no. 7)
Advocate (*rhetor*), practised in the court of the Praetorian Prefect. In 517 he was appointed PP *Orientis.*

Severinus, 398–9 (*PLRE* I, 830: no. 3)
Advocate, *comes rei privatae* of Theodosius 388–90, *comes sacrarum largitionum* of Theodosius 391, and *praefectus urbis Constantinopolitanae* 398–9.

Severus, 393/4 (*PLRE* I, 834: no. 14)
Advocate, he had been a pupil of Libanius but was withdrawn in his second year for misconduct (Lib. *Or.* 57. 3–6). By 393 he was governor of Syria.

Severus of Antioch, late 5th/early 6th cent.
Studied rhetoric at Constantinople with his two brothers, after the death of his father; began with the sophist John and then was taught by a certain Sopater, 'famed in the art of the rhetoric'. Apparently applied himself 'assidiously to the study of the precepts of the ancient rhetors and forced himself to imitate their style' (Zacharias Scholastikos, *Life of Severus,* ed. and tr. Marc-Antoine Kugener, *Patrologia Orientalis*, 2 (Paris, 1907), 11–12). Studied law at Beirut *c.*486, then bishop of Antioch, involved in controversy over Chalcedonian Christology (Evagrius, *HE* 3. 33).

Silvanus, 359 (*PLRE* I, 841: no. 3)
Studied law at Beirut and then became advocate of the *comes Orientis* in 359 (Lib. *Ep.* 87).

Silvanus, 363 (*PLRE* I, 841: no. 4)
Advocate (*causarum defensor*) at Nisibis in 363 (Amm. Marc. 25. 9. 4).

Sisinnius, d. 427
Orator at Constantinople, 'Novatian' bishop (see Chapter 6).

Sozomenus, early/mid-5th cent. (*PLRE* II, 1023–4: no. 2)
Advocate (*scholastikos*) at Constantinople *c.*440, historian (Sozomen, *HE* 2. 3. 10–11).

Stephanus, 538
Advocate at the court of the PPO (Justinian, *Novel* 82. 1 pr.). Possibly also one of the commissioners for Justinian's *Digest* (*Const. Tanta* 9).

Symbulus, 365 (*PLRE* I, 863)
Advocate in 365 (Lib. *Ep.* 1481).

Theon, 325
Advocate in the Thebaid (*P.Oxy.* LIV. 3758, ll. 39–77 and 98–131).

Theodosius, 349 (*PLRE* I, 902: no. 1)
Advocate (*advocatus*) in the court of Fl. Strategius at Hermopolis in the Thebaid.

Theodorus, 364–5 (*PLRE* I, 897: no. 11)
Advocate at Antioch from 358. He had studied law at Beirut and then rhetoric at Antioch. Acted as an assessor then became *vicarius* of Asia (363–6), provincial governor (364–5).

Aur. Theodorus, 398 (*PLRE* II, 1097: no. 6)
Grammarian and advocate at Hermopolis (*P.Lips.* 56).

Theodore of Mopsuestia, late 4th cent.
Advocate, monk, and bishop of Mopsuestia, Cilicia (see Chapter 6).

Theodorus of Cyzicus, 538
Advocate at the court of the PPO (Justinian, *Novel* 82. 1 pr.).

Timotheus, 533
Advocate at court of PPO. Member of commission that produced Justinian's *Digest* (*Const. Tanta* 9).

Victor, 538
Advocate at the court of the PPO (Justinian, *Novel* 82. 1 pr.).

Zacharias Scholastikos, late 5th/early 6th cent.
Studied grammar and rhetoric at Alexandria and then law at Beirut. Zacharias advised Severus to compare the discourses of the sophist Libanius, whom he admired as an equal of the ancient rhetors, to those of the bishops Basil and Gregory (Zacharias Scholastikos, *Life of Severus,* ed. and tr. Marc-Antoine Kugener, *Patrologia Orientalis*, 2 (Paris, 1907), 10–13). Wrote a *Life* of Severus of Antioch.

Zeno, early/mid-6th cent.
Professional *rhetor* (advocate) at Constantinople, renowned for both his legal skill and eloquence. Anthemius, the architect responsible for the building of

Hagia Sofia after Nika riot of 532, apparently played a trick on him (Agathias, *Histories* 5. 6. 7–8).

Zenodotus, 507 (*PLRE* II, 1198)
Advocate (*scholastikos*) in the Thebaid (*P.Lond.* III. 253 n.922 = Mitteis, *Chrest.* n. 365).

Zosimus, mid-6th cent.
Advocate, a former pupil of Procopius of Gaza (Procopius, *Ep.* 153).

Anonymous, early/mid-4th cent.
Advocate. Father of Apringius, above (Lib. *Ep.* 422).

APPENDIX II

Appendix II. Advocates in the Western Empire (Fourth to Early Sixth Century)

Acilius Glabrio, mid-4th cent. (*PLRE* I, 397: no. 2 and Kaster, *Guardians of the Word*, 287, no. 64)
Advocate and also teacher of grammar at Bordeaux (Aus., *Prof.* 24. 7).

Adelphius, mid-4th cent. (*PLRE* I, 14: no. 4)
Rhetor and advocate (Sid. Ap. *Ep.* 5. 10. 3).

Sextilius Agesilaus Aedesius, 355/376 (*PLRE* I, 15)
Advocate in Africa and at the imperial court.

Africanus, *c.*370 (*PLRE* I, 26: no. 3)
Advocate in Rome, then provincial governor (Amm. Marc. 29. 3. 6).

Latinus Alcimus Alethius, mid-4th cent. (*PLRE* I, 39: no. 2)
Advocate at Bordeaux, also a teacher of rhetoric (Aus. *Prof.* 2. 17).

Ambrosius, 526–33 (*PLRE* II, 69: no. 3)
'Distinguished advocate' (Cass. *Var.* 11. 4). He was a student at Rome in 511, and may have been previously a student at Milan. In 526 he was appointed *quaestor* and in 533 he appears as the *agens vices* of the Praetorian Prefect in Italy.

Fl. Ambrosius, 370/379 (*PLRE* I, 52–3: no. 5)
Advocate at the court of the *consularis Siciliae*.

Publius (A)elius Apollinaris, late 3rd/4th cent. (*PLRE* I, 84: no. 3)
Advocate (*actor causarum*), governor of Corsica, and *praefectus vigilum*.

Apronianus, 315 (*PLRE* I, 86: no. 2)
Advocate at Carthage. Acted in the inquiry into the case of Felix of Apthungi held before the proconsul of Africa in 315.

Aemilius Magnus Arborius, early/mid-4th cent. (*PLRE* I, 98: no. 4 and Kaster, *Guardians of the Word*, 105)
Teacher of rhetoric at Tolosa (Aus. *Prof.* 17), and practised as an advocate in the courts of the governors in Narbonensis, Novempopulana, and Tarraconensis.

Armentarius, 510/511 (*PLRE* II, 150: no. 2)
Advocate at Rome (Cass. *Var.* 3. 33).

Asterius, late 5th/early 6th cent. (*PLRE* II, 172: no. 9)
Advocate (*causidicus*) and senator.

Audentius, d. 443 (*PLRE* II, 185)
Advocate at the court of the *praeses Dalmatiae*: 'Depos(itio) b(onae) m(emoriae) Audenti adul(escentis) c(larissimi) tog(ati) fori Dalm(atiae)'.

Aurelius Augustinus, 354–430
Teacher of rhetoric, 'Catholic' bishop of Hippo (see Chapter 6).

Ausonius, 310–95
Teacher of rhetoric at Bordeaux, divided his time between teaching rhetoric and practising as an advocate in his early career (see Kaster, *Guardians of the Word*, 103).

Martianus Minneius Felix Capella, 5th cent. (*PLRE* II, 259)
Advocate (Mart. Cap. 6. 577). He was an African, from Carthage, and the author of a surviving work in nine books, prose and verse, on the seven liberal arts.

Ragonius Vincentius Celsus, *c.*389 (*PLRE* I, 195: no. 9)
Advocate (Symm. *Rel.* 23. 3, *CIL* vi. 1760 = xiv. 173 (Ostia), and *CIL* vi. 1759 = *ILS* 1272).

Constantius, 4th/6th cent. (*PLRE* II, 319: no. 8)
Advocate, possibly at Milan (*CIL* v. 618 n. 8 = Rossi ii. 164 n. 8 = *ILCV* 244 Milan).

Decoratus, 524 (*PLRE* II, 350: no. 1)
Advocate (*advocatus*) at Ravenna in 508; had a long and successful career (Cass. *Var.* 5. 4).

Attius Tiro Delphidius, mid-4th cent. (*PLRE* I, 246)
Taught rhetoric at Bordeaux and then practised as an advocate, appearing in the courts both of praetorian prefects and provincial governors (Aus. *Prof.* 6. 13–18). Obtained Palatine offices under Magnentius (Aus. *Prof.* 6. 23–4). Resumed his practice as a *rhetor* in Aquitania in 355, but appeared as an advocate in a case before Julian in 359 (Amm. Marc. 18. 1. 4).

Blossius Aemilius Dracontius, late 5th cent. (*PLRE* II, 379–80: no. 2)
Advocate (*togatus fori*) in the court of the proconsul at Carthage.

Dynamius, mid-4th cent. (*PLRE* I, 275, and Kaster, *Guardians of the Word*, 105)
Advocate (*causidicus*) of Bordeaux. He was accused of adultery and fled to Hilerda in Spain where he taught rhetoric under the assumed name Flavinus (Aus. *Prof.* 24).

Emeritus, early 5th cent.
Advocate in Numidia, 'Donatist' bishop (see Chapter 6).

Emporius, 5th/6th cent. (*PLRE* II, 392)
Orator and practising advocate. Author of a Latin treatise on rhetoric (*RLM* 561–74).

Epictetus, late 4th cent. (*PLRE* I, 279)
Advocate (*causidicus*). He was disbarred for slander and Symmachus wrote *Ep.* 9. 31 seeking his reinstatement.

Eubulus, 436 (*PLRE* II, 403)
Ex-*magister scrinii*, member of the first commission appointed to compile the Theodosian Code in 429. *Quaestor sacri palatii* (East) in 435. At the time of the second commission he was PPO Illyrici. Began his legal career as an advocate.

Euentius, 364–407 (*PLRE* II, 413: no. 1)
Advocate and *consularis Viennensis* before 407.

C. Marius Euentius, late 4th/early 5th cent. (*PLRE* II, 414: no. 2)
Advocate (*advocatus*), then appointed *defensor* of Fanum Fortunae and other towns by order of the Emperor for five years.

Eugenes, 506–7 (*PLRE* II, 414–16)
Advocate (*advocatus*). In 506 he was *quaestor palatii* and in 507 *magister officiorum.*

Exsuperius, 335 (*PLRE* I, 321: no. 1)
Advocate and teacher of rhetoric at Bordeaux (Aus. *Prof.* 18. 7–15). Became a *praeses* in Spain in 335.

Felix, late 4th cent. (*PLRE* II, 458: no. 1)
Practised advocacy. At his request Symmachus petitioned Limenius (*vicarius* in the West) to enrol Felix at his bar. Felix disliked the court of the urban prefect of Rome and wanted somewhere quieter (Symm. *Ep.* 5. 75).

Festus of Tridentum, 370s (*PLRE* I, 334: no. 3)
Advocate (*contogatus* with Maximinus) in the Western Empire, *consularis Syriae*, and then *proconsul Asiae*. Historian.

Fidelis, 527–8 (*PLRE* II, 469–70)
Advocate (*advocatus*), whose father had been also been an advocate at Milan (Cass. *Var.* 8. 18–19). In 527 he was appointed *quaestor palatii* and in 537 PPO Italiae.

Florus, 508–10 (*PLRE* II, 482: no. 4)
Advocate (*advocatus*) at Ravenna, mentioned in 508 and 510 by Ennod. *Ep.* 7. 10 and 8. 23. In 501, however, he was already noted as a powerful orator (Ennod., *Ep.* 1. 2.).

C. Chirius Fortunatianus, late 4th cent. (*PLRE*, I 369: no. 3)
Rhetor, author of an *Ars Rhetorica*, had also possibly practised as an advocate.

Gregorius, early 5th cent.
Advocate, mentioned by Pope Innocent I (*Ep.* 3. 7).

Helpidius, 400 (*PLRE* II, 536: no. 3)
Advocate or possibly assessor. In 400 Helpidius and Titianus ended their legal

training and were commended by Symmachus to the *comes sacrarum largitionum* Limenius as suitable for forensic posts (Symm. *Ep.* 5. 74).

Herculius, *c.*398 (*PLRE* II, 545: no. 1)
Advocate at Rome (Symm. *Ep.* 9. 43).

Fl. Honoratianus, 4th cent. (*PLRE* I, 438: no. 3)
Advocate in Numidia.

Honoratus, *c.*503 (*PLRE* II, 567–8: no. 2)
Advocate (*advocatus*) practising at Spoletium *c.*503.

A. Vitellius Felix Honoratus, 260 (*PLRE* I, 440: no. 10)
Advocatus fisci four times, in Italy, Noricum, Numidia, and Africa Proconsularis, and then *praepositus* in southern Italy.

Ianuarius, 384/402 (*PLRE* I, 454: no. 6)
Teacher of rhetoric at Rome in 384, possibly an advocate and later became a magistrate (Symm. *Ep.* 9. 32).

Innocentius, 388 (*PLRE* I, 458: no. 4)
Advocate, probably at the court of the *vicarius Africae* (Aug. *Civ. Dei* 22. 8). He lived at Carthage in 388, when he gave lodgings to Augustine and Alypius on their return from Italy.

Iulianus, 370/379 (*PLRE* i. 472)
Advocate in Rome, Symmachus commended him to Ausonius in Gaul (Symm. *Ep.* 1. 43). He returned to Rome around 379/80 with a letter of commendation from Ausonius to Symmachus (Aus. *Ep.* 2 = Symm. *Ep.* 1. 32).

Iustinianus, 408 (*PLRE* II, 645: no. 2)
Advocate (*sunegoros*) at Rome, then assessor to Stilicho in 408.

Lactantius, early 4th cent.
Teacher of rhetoric, Christian apologist (see Chapter 6).

Lampadius, *c.*380 (*PLRE* I, 493: no. 3)
Advocate (*causidicus*) at the court of a PPO.

Luciolus, 4th cent. (Kaster, *Guardians of the Word*, 105)
Rhetorican and advocate at Bordeaux (Aus. *Prof.* 3. 11).

Marcellinus, mid-5th cent. (*PLRE* II, 70: no. 5)
Advocate (*togatus*) at Narbo in Gaul.

Marcellus, 507/511 (*PLRE* II, 713: no. 4)
Advocate, promoted to *advocatus fisci* by Theodoric.

Marcianus, 506 (*PLRE* II, 716: no. 13)
Advocate (*causidicus*) in 506.

Marcomannus, 4th cent. (*PLRE* I, 557)
Rhetor and advocate. Source used by C. Iulius Victor in his *Ars rhetorica.* Teacher and source of Sulpicius Victor, *Institutiones Oratoriae* (*RLM* 311–52)

Marculus, 4th cent. (*PC* I, 696)
Rhetorician, bishop, 'Donatist' martyr.

Marinus, *c.*371 (*PLRE* I, 560: no. 3)
Advocate (*causarum defensor*) in Rome, put to death in 371/2 for having used magic arts to obtain a wife (Amm. Marc. 28. 1. 14).

Marius Victorinus, mid/late 4th cent.
Orator, teacher of rhetoric at Rome, and Christian polemicist (see Chapter 6).

Marsus, mid-5th cent. (*PLRE* II, 728)
Advocate of the *praefectura urbis Romae.*

Martyrius?, 398/400 (*PLRE* II, 731)
Advocate who undertook a case involving relatives of Symmachus and was commended by Symmachus to Patricius, *magister epistularum* (Symm. *Ep.* 7. 64).

Maximinus, last office 371–6 (*PLRE* I, 577: no. 7)
Advocate; *praeses Corsicae* (before 365); *praeses Sardiniae*; *corrector Tusciae* 366; *praefectus annonae* 368/70; *vicarius urbis Romae* 370–1; PPO *Galliarum* 371–6.

Nummasius 394 (*PLRE* I, 635; *PC* 788)
Advocate (*advocatus*), who appeared in the court of the African proconsul Herodes (Aug. *C. Cresc.* 4. 4.5); his *postulatio* constituted a precedent used by the advocate Titianus in a similar case. In Aug. *Ep.* 108. 4. 13 he is named as the advocate whose client was the Donatist bishop Restitutus.

Opilio, 527–8 (*PLRE* II, 808: no. 4)
Advocate at the court of the *magister officiorum*, who was also his brother (Cass. *Var.* 8. 16–17). In 527 he was appointed *comes sacrarum largitionum.*

Paulinus of Nola, d. 431
Advocate, *consularis* of Campania, bishop of Nola (see Chapter 6).

Petilianus, late 4th/early 5th cent.
Advocate, 'Donatist' bishop of Cirta (see Chapter 6).

Postumianus, 396 (*PLRE* I, 718: no. 3)
Advocate in 383 practising at Rome. Became a senator.

Prudentius, early 5th cent.
Advocate, Christian poet (see Chapter 6).

M. Aur. Restitutus, 412/414 (*PLRE* II, 940–1: no. 3)
Advocate (*togatus*) and then *curator rei publicae* of Membressa in Africa Proconsularis.

Rufinus, 396/398 (*PLRE* II, 952: no. 1)
Advocate. Lost a case but was retained by Symmachus (*Ep.* 8. 17).

Rufinus, early 5th cent.
Advocate, mentioned by Pope Innocent I (*Ep.* 3. 7).

Salvius, early 5th cent.
Recipient of letter included in *spuria* of Sulpicius Severus. Described as a practising *advocatus*, Salvius had often pleaded in the same tribunal as the author of the letter; now they were in legal dispute with each other. The letter itself provides a résumé of the dossier for the case (see Chapter 4).

C. Caelius Saturninus (*signo* Dogmatius), 334–5 (*PLRE* I, 806: no. 9)
Advocatus fisci per Italiam, then held posts at the Imperial court, followed by three financial offices and various palatine offices until he became Praetorian Prefect in Gaul, 334–5.

Uranius Satyrus, 375 (*PLRE* I, 809)
Advocate (*advocatus*) at the court of the Praetorian Prefect. Ambrose of Milan's brother. Rose to the office of governor in a Western province.

Fl. Severus, 373 (*PLRE* I, 835–6: no. 24)
Advocate, before he became *praeses* of a province in Africa, *c*.373 (Symm. *Or*. 6).

C. Iulius Rufinianus Ablabius Tatianus, 340 (*PLRE* I, 875–6: no. 4)
Advocatus fisci who rose to the position of *consularis Campaniae c*.340.

Flavius Mallius Theodorus, 397 (*PLRE* I, 900: no. 27)
Advocate in court of PPO (?of Italy) 376. After holding the governorship of an African province and a post in a province of Macedonia, he became *magister memoriae*. In 380 he was PPO *Galliarum* and from 397–9 PPO *Illyrici, Italiae et Africae*. Augustine dedicated his *De Beata vita* to him (*Retract*. 1. 2).

Titianus, 400 (*PLRE* II, 1122: no. 3)
Advocate or assessor, commended to the *comes sacrarum largitionum* Limenius together with Helpidius (Symm. *Ep*. 5. 74).

Titianus, 395 (*PLRE* I, 917: no. 4, and *PC* 1115–16)
Advocate in Africa, he appeared before the proconsul Herodes on 2 Mar. 395.

Gennadius Torquatus, 396/404 (*PLRE* ii. 1124)
Advocate at Rome. In 396 he was *praefectus augustalis* and, between 396 and 404, proconsul for Egypt and then Achaea.

Victor, 401–31 (*PLRE* II, 1158: no. 3)
Advocate (*advocatus*), possibly at Salona where he died aged 30.

Victor of Thabbora, early 5th cent.
Advocate, 'Donatist' bishop of Thabbora (see Chapter 6).

Anonymous 1, 390/394 (*PLRE* I, 1030: no. 172)
Advocate (*causidicus*) serving in the court of the PPO Flavianus at Milan (Symm. *Ep*. 11. 42).

Anonymous 2, mid/late 5th cent. (*PLRE* II, 1224: no. 27).

Distinguished advocate, became *comes sacrarum largitionum* and *magister officiorum*.

Anonymous 3, 399/400 (*PLRE* II, 1232: no. 84)
Advocate, commended by Symmachus for enrolment at the court of the Praetorian Prefect (Symm. *Ep*. 7. 88).

Anonymous 4, late 5th/early 6th cent. (*PLRE* II, 1236: no. 116)
Advocate at Milan and father of the advocate Fidelis (see above).

Anonymous 5, early 5th cent.
Author of Ps.-Sulpicius Severus, *Ep*. 1 (see Salvius, above). Described as a retired advocate (*ex togato*).

Bibliography

Aiello, V., 'Costantino "eretico": Difesa della "ortodossia" e anticostantinianesimo in età teodosiana', in *AARC* 10 (1995), 55–83.

Albertario, E., 'Di alcuni riferimenti al matrimonio e al possesso in Sant' Agostino', *Rivista di filosofia neoscolastica*, supplemento speciale at vol. 23 (1931), 367–76.

Allen, P., *Evagrius Scholasticus: The Church Historian* (Louvain: Spicilegium Sacrum Lovaniense, 1981).

Amarelli, F., 'Cristianesimo e istituzioni giuridiche romane: Contaminazioni influenze recuperi', *Bullettino dell'Istituto di diritto romano Vittorio Scialoja*, 39 (1997; publ. 2003), 445–56.

—— *Vetustas Innovatio*: *Un'antitesi apparente nella legislazione di Costantino* (Naples: Jovene, 1978).

Amato, E., Roduit, A., and Steinrück, M. (eds.), *Approches de la troisième sophistique: Hommages à Jacques Schamp* (Brussels, Latomus 296, 2006).

Amidon, P. R. (tr.), *The* Church History *of Rufinus of Aquileia Books 10 and 11* (New York and Oxford: Oxford University Press, 1997).

Anderson, G., *The Second Sophistic: A Cultural Phenomenon in the Roman Empire* (New York: Routledge, 1993).

Andreotti, R., 'Problemi della constitutio de postulando attribuita all'imperatore Giuliano e l'esercizio della professione forense nel tardo impero', *RIDA* 19 (1972), 181–218.

Anton, H. H., 'Kaiserliches Selbstverständnis in der Religionsgesetzgebung der Spätantike und päpstliche Herrschaftsinterpretation im 5. Jahrhundert', *Zeitschrift für Kirchengeschichte*, 88 (1977), 38–84.

Athanassiadi, P., 'The Creation of Orthodoxy in Neoplatonism', in G. Clark and T. Rajak (eds.), *Philosophy and Power in the Graeco-Roman World* (Oxford: Oxford University Press, 2002), 271–91.

Atkins, E. M., and Dodaro, R. J. (eds.), *Augustine, Political Writings* (Cambridge: Cambridge University Press, 2001).

Ayers, L., *Nicaea and its Legacy: An Approach to Fourth-Century Trinitarian Theology* (Oxford: Oxford University Press, 2004).

Baccari, M. P., 'Communione e cittadinanza (a proposito della posizione giuridica di eretici, apostati, giudei e pagani secondo i codici di Teodosio II e Justiniano)', *SDHI* 57 (1991), 264–80.

Bachrach, B. S., 'The Jewish Community of the Later Roman Empire as Seen in the *Codex Theodosianus*', in J. Neusner and E. S. Frerichs (eds.), *'To See Ourselves as Others See Us': Christians, Jews and 'Others' in Late Antiquity* (Chico, Calif.: Scholars Press, 1985).

Bagnall, R. S., *Egypt in Late Antiquity* (Princeton: Princeton University Press, 1993).

—— *The Kellis Agricultural Account Book*, Dakhleh Oasis Project, 7 (Oxford and Oakville, CT: Oxbow Books, 1997).

Baldwin, B., 'Dioscorus of Aphrodito: The Worst Poet of Antiquity?', *Atti del XVII Congresso Internazionale di Papirologia*, ii (1984), 327–31.

Baldwin, C. S., 'St Augustine and the Rhetoric of Cicero', *Proceedings of the Classical Association*, 22 (1925), 24–6.

Bardy, G., 'Le "De haeresibus" et ses sources', in G. Morin and A. Casamassa (eds.), *Miscellanea Agostiniana: Testi e Studi*, ii (Rome: Tipografia Poliglotta Vaticana, 1931), 397–416.

Barnard, L., 'The Criminalization of Heresy in the Later Roman Empire: A Sociopolitical Device?', *Journal of Legal History*, 121 (1995), 121–46.

Barnes, T. D., *Ammianus Marcellinus and the Representation of Historical Reality* (New York: Cornell University Press, 1998).

—— *Athanasius and Constantius: Theology and Politics in the Constantinian Empire* (Cambridge, Mass.: Harvard University Press, 1993).

—— *Constantine and Eusebius* (Cambridge, Mass.: Harvard University Press, 1981).

—— 'Foregrounding the Theodosian Code', *Journal of Roman Archaeology*, 14 (2001), 671–85.

—— 'Legislation Against the Christians', *JRS* 58 (1968), 32–50.

—— 'Scholarship and Propaganda? Porphyry Against the Christians and its Historical Setting', *BICS* 39 (1994), 53–65.

—— *Tertullian: A Historical and Literary Study* (Oxford: Oxford University Press, 1971).

Barone-Adesi, G., 'Eresie sociali ed inquisizione Teodosiana', *AARC* 6 (1986), 119–66.

—— *L'Età della Lex Dei* (Naples: Jovene Editore, 1992).

Barry, M. I., (1924) *St Augustine the Orator: A Study of the Rhetorical Qualities of St Augustine's Sermones Ad Populum* (Washington, DC: Catholic University of America, 1924).

Baxter, C., 'Notes on the Latin of Julian of Eclanum', *Bulletin du Cange*, 21 (1929), 5–54.

Beck, A., *Römisches Recht bei Tertullian und Cyprian: Eine Studie zur frühen Kirchenrechtgeschichte* (Halle, Max Niemeyer Verlag, 1930).

Becker, A. H., and Reed, A. Y. (eds.), *The Ways that Never Parted: Jews and Christians in Late Antiquity and the Early Middles Ages* (Tübingen: Mohr Siebeck, 2003).

Beckwith, C. L., 'The Condemnation and Exile of Hilary of Poitiers at the Synod of Béziers (356 C.E.)', *Journal of Early Christian Studies*, 13/1 (2005), 21–38.

Behrends, O., 'Der assessor zur Zeit der klassischen Rechtswissenschaft', *ZSS Rom. Abt.* 86 (1969), 192–226.

Bell, H. I., 'The Episcopalis Audientia in Byzantine Egypt', *Byzantion*, 1 (1924), 139–44.

Berger, A., *Encyclopaedic Dictionary of Roman Law* (Philadelphia: Transactions of the American Philological Society, 1953).

____ 'La concezione di eretico nelle fonti giustinianee', *Rend. Accademia Nazionale dei Lincei, Serie 8, Classe di Scienze morali, storiche e filologiche*, 10 (1955), 353–68.

Beskow, P., 'The Theodosian Laws against Manichaeism', in P. Bryder (ed.), *Manichaean Studies*, i. *Proceedings of the First International Conference on Manichaeism, August 5–9, 1987* (Lund: Plus Ultra, 1988), 1–17.

Betancourt Serna, F., *El libro anónimo* De Interdictis: *Codex Vaticanus Latinus No. 5766* (Seville: University of Seville, 1997).

Betz, H. D., 'The Problem of Rhetoric and Theology According to the Apostle Paul', in A. Vanhoye (ed.), *L'Apôtre Paul: Personnalité, style et conception du ministère* (Leuven: Leuven University Press, 1986), 16–48.

Bianchi Fossati Vanzetti, M. (ed.), *Pauli Sententiae: Testo e interpretatio* (Padua: Cedam, 1995).

Bianchini, M., *Caso concreto e 'lex generalis'* (Milan: Giuffrè, 1979).

____ 'Sulla giurisprudenza nell'Italia tardoantica', *Labeo*, 36/1 (1990), 85–115.

Biondi, B., *Giustiniano primo principe e legislatore cattolico* (Milan: Pubblicazioni della Università cattolica del Sacro Cuore, 1936).

____ *Il diritto romano cristiano*, i-iii (Milan: Guiffrè, 1952–4).

____ 'Religione e diritto canonico nella legislazione di Giustiniano', *Acta Congressus Iuridici Internationalis*, 1 (Rome: Pontificium Institutum Utriusque Iuris, 1935).

Birks, P., 'New Light on the Roman Legal System: The Appointment of Judges', *Cambridge Law Journal*, 47/1 (1998), 36–60.

Birley, A. R., 'Magnus Maximus and the Persecution of Heresy', *Bulletin of the John Rylands University Library*, 66 (1983–4), 29–33.

Bischoff, B., and Nörr, D.,'Eine unbekannte Konstitution Kaiser Julians', *Bayerische Akad. der Wiss.*, Phil.-Hist. Klasse, 58 (1963), 1–51.

Bohácek, M., 'Un esempio dell'insegnamento di Berito ai compilatori: *Cod.Just.*2,4,18', *Studi Riccobono*, 1 (1936), 337–96.

Bonini, R., ' "Interrogationes" forensi e attività legislativa giustinianica', *SDHI* 33 (1967), 279–319.

Bossowski, F., 'Quo modo usu forensi audientiae episcopalis suadente non nulla praecepta ad instar iuris Graeci aut Hebraici etc. in iure Romano recepta sint exponitur', *Acta Congressus Iuridici Internationalis*, 1 (Rome: Pontificium Institutum Utriusque Iuris, 1935), 361–410.

Bowen, A., and Garnsey, P. (tr.), Lactantius, *Divine Institutes* (Liverpool: Liverpool University Press, 2003).

Bowie, E., 'Literature and Sophistic', in A. Bowman, P. Garnsey, and D. Rathbone (eds.), *Cambridge Ancient History*, xi. The High . . . 70–192, 2nd edn. (Cambridge: Cambridge University Press, 2000), 898–921.

Bowman, A. K., and Rathbone, D., 'Cities and Administration in Roman Egypt', *JRS* 82 (1992), 107–27.

Boyarin, D., *Border Lines: The Partition of Judaeo-Christianity* (Philadelphia: University of Pennsylvania Press, 2004).

Bradbury, S. (tr.), *Selected Letters of Libanius from the Age of Constantius and Julian* (Liverpool: Liverpool University Press, 2004).

Brinkmann, A. (ed.), Alexander of Lycopolis *Against the Doctrines of Mani* (repr. Stuttgart: Teubner, 1989).

Brown, P., *Authority and the Sacred: Aspects of the Christianisation of the Roman World* (Cambridge: Cambridge University Press, 1995).

—— *Power and Persuasion in Late Antiquity: Towards a Christian Empire* (Madison: University of Wisconsin Press, 1992).

—— 'Religious Coercion in the Later Roman Empire: The Case of North Africa', in P. Brown, *Religion and Society in the Age of St Augustine* (London: Faber & Faber, 1972), 301–31.

—— 'The Diffusion of Manichaeism in the Roman Empire', *JRS* 59 (1969), 92–103.

Browning, R., 'Education in the Roman Empire', in A. Cameron, B. Ward-Perkins, and M. Whitby (eds.), *Cambridge Ancient History*, xiv. *Late Antiquity: Empire and Successors A.D. 425–600*, 2nd edn. (Cambridge: Cambridge University Press, 2001), 855–83.

Brunt, P. A., 'The Bubble of the Second Sophistic', *BICS* 39 (1994), 25–52.

Bucci, O., 'La genesi della struttura del diritto della Chiesa latina e del diritto delle Chiese Cristiane Orientali in rapporto allo svolgimento storico del diritto romano e del diritto bizantino', *Apollinaris*, 65 (1992), 93–135.

Buckland, W. W., 'The *interpretationes* to *Pauli Sententiae* and the *Codex Theodosianus*', *Law Quarterly Review*, 60 (1944), 361–5.

—— and McNair, A. B., *Roman Law and Common Law*, 2nd edn. (Cambridge: Cambridge University Press, 1965).

Buisson, L., 'Die Entstehung des Kirchenrechts', *ZRG, Kan. Abt.* 52 (1966), 1–175.

Burrus, V., ' "In the Theater of this Life": The Performance of Orthodoxy in Late Antiquity', in W. Klingshirn and M. Vessey, *The Limits of Ancient Christianity: Essays on Late Antique Thought and Culture in Honor of R. A. Markus* (Ann Arbor: University of Michigan Press, 1999), 80–96.

Burrus, V., *The Making of a Heretic: Gender, Authority and the Priscillianist Controversy* (Berkeley, Los Angeles and London: University of California Press, 1995).

Cameron, A., *Christianity and the Rhetoric of Empire: The Development of Christian Discourse* (Berkeley and Los Angeles: University of California Press, 1991).

——'How to Read Heresiology', *Journal of Medieval and Early Modern Studies*, 33/3 (2003), 471–92.

——and Hall, S. (tr.), *Eusebius, Life of Constantine* (Oxford: Oxford University Press, 1999).

Carcaterra, A., 'Le operazione dell' avvocato: Euristica e logica a fronte della "narratio" dell' interessato', *SDHI* 52 (1986), 73–105.

Caron, P. G., *I poteri guiridici del laicato nella chiesa primitiva*, 2nd edn. (Milan: A. Guiffrè, 1975).

——'I tribunali della Chiesa nel diritto del Tardo Impero', *AARC* 11 (1996), 245–63.

Carusi, Z. B., 'Diritto romano e patristica', *Studi giuridici in onore di Carlo Fadda*, ii (Naples: Pierro, 1906), 71–97.

Castelli, C., 'L'esemplarità retorica di Gregorio di Nazianzo: Spunti per una riflessione', in E. Amato, A. Roduit, and M. Steinrück (eds.), *Approches de la troisième sophistique: Hommages à Jacques Schamp* (Brussels: Latomus 296, 2006), 63–79.

Cavigioli, G., 'Impronte di diritto romano nel carteggio di s. Paolo e nella volgata del nuovo Testamento', *Acta Congressus Iuridici Internationalis*, ii (Rome: Pontifical Institute, 1935), 91–100.

Cerrato, J. A., *Hippolytus between East and West: The Commentaries and the Provenance of the Corpus* (Oxford: Oxford University Press, 2002).

Chadwick, H., *Heresy and Orthodoxy in the Early Church* (Aldershot: Variorum, 1991).

——*Priscillian of Avila: The Occult and the Charismatic in the Early Church* (Oxford: Clarendon Press, 1976).

——(tr.), *Saint Augustine Confessions* (Oxford: Oxford University Press, 1991).

——'The Role of the Christian Bishop in Ancient Society', in *Protocol of the 35th Colloquy* (Berkeley, Calif.: Centre for Hermeneutical Studies, 1980), 1–14.

Charles-Edwards, T., 'Law in the Western Kingdoms between the Fifth and the Seventh Century', in A. Cameron, B. Ward Perkins, and M. Whitby (eds.), *Cambridge Ancient History*, xiv. *Late Antiquity: Empire and Successors A. D. 425–600*, 2nd edn. (Cambridge: Cambridge University Press, 2001), 260–87.

Chastagnol, A., *La Préfecture Urbaine à Rome sous le Bas-Empire* (Paris: Presses Universitaires de France, 1960).

——'L'Empereur Julien et les avocats de Numidie', *Antiquités Africaines*, 14 (1979), 225–35.

Chorus, J. M. J., 'L'Enseignement du droit romain en occident de 250–500: Essai de tableau', *Tijdschrift voor Rechtgeschiedenis*, 61 (1993), 195–204.

Cimma, M. R., *L'episcopalis audientia nelle costituzioni imperiali da Costantino a Giustiniano* (Turin: Giappichelli, 1989).

Cipriani, N., 'Aspetti letterari dell'Ad Florum di Giuliano d'Eclano', *Augustinianum*, 15 (1975), 125–67.

——'L'Ad Florum di Giuliano', in *Opere di Sant' Agostino, Polemica con Giuliano*, Nuova Biblioteca Agostiniana, 19/1 (Rome: Citta nuova, 1993), pp. vii–xix.

——'La morale pelagiana e la retorica', *Augustinianum*, 31 (1991), 309–27.

Clark, G., ' "Spoiling the Egyptians": Roman Law and Christian Exegesis in Late Antiquity', in R. Mathisen, *Law, Authority and Society in Late Antiquity* (Oxford: Oxford University Press, 2001), 133–47.

Clarke, G. W., 'The Secular Profession of St Cyprian of Carthage', *Latomus*, 24 (1965), 633–63.

Clarke, M. L., *Rhetoric at Rome* (London: Cohen & West, 1953).

Cohen, D. J., *Law, Sexuality and Society. The Enforcement of Morals in Classical Athens* (Cambridge: Cambridge University Press, 1991).

Collinet, P., *Histoire de l'école de droit de Beyrouth. Études historiques sur le droit de Justinien*, ii (Paris: Sirey, 1925).

—— 'Le Rôle de la doctrine et de la pratique dans le développement de droit privé romain au bas-empire', *RHDFE* 7 (1928), 551–83 and 8: 5–35.

Comeau, M., *La Rhétorique de saint Augustin d'après les* Tractatus in Ioannem (Paris: Gabriel Beauchesne, 1930).

Connolly, R.H. (tr.), *Didascalia Apostolorum: The Syriac Version Translated and Accompanied by the Verona Latin Fragments* (Oxford: Clarendon Press, 1929).

Conrat, M., 'Zur Kultur des römischen Rechts im Westen', *Mélanges Fitting*, i (Montpellier: L'Imprimerie Générale du Midi, 1907), 287–320.

Conybeare, C., *Paulinus Noster: Self and Symbols in the Letters of Paulinus of Nola* (Oxford: Oxford University Press, 2000).

Corcoran, S., *The Empire of the Tetrarchs: Imperial Pronouncements and Government, AD 284–324*, 2nd edn. (Oxford: Clarendon Press, 2000).

——'The Publication of Law in the Era of the Tetrarchs: Diocletian, Galerius, Gregorius, Hermogenian', in A. Demandt, A. Goltz, and H. Schlange-Schöningen (eds.), *Diokletian und die Tetrarchie: Aspekte einer Zeitenwende.* (Berlin and New York: de Gruyter, 2004), 56–73.

——'The Tetrarchy: Policy and Image as Reflected in Imperial Pronouncements', in D. Boschung and W. Eck (eds.), *Die Tetrarchie: Ein neues*

Regierungssystem und seine mediale Präsentation (Wiesbaden: Reichert Verlag, 2006), 31–61.

Coriat, J.-P., *Le Prince législateur: La Technique législative des Sévères et les méthodes de création du droit impérial à la fin du Principat* (Rome and Paris: BEFAR 294, 1997).

Cortese, E., 'Alle origini della scuola di Bologna', in I. Birocchi and U. Petronio (eds.), *Cortese Scritti*, ii (Spoleto: Centro italiano di studi sull'alto medioevo, 1999), 1095–1137.

Courtonne, Y. (ed. and tr.), *Saint Basile Lettres*, i (Paris: Les Belles Lettres, 1957).

Crawford, M., 'Discovery, Autopsy and Progress: Diocletian's Jigsaw Puzzles', in T. P. Wiseman (ed.), *Classics in Progress: Essays on Ancient Greece and Rome* (Oxford: Oxford University Press, 2002), 145–64.

Crifò, G., 'A proposito di episcopalis audientia', in *Institutions, société et vie politique: Collection de l'École Française de Rome*, 159 (1992), 397–410.

____ 'Romanizzazione e cristianizzazione: Certezze e dubbi in tema di rapporto tra cristiani e istituzioni', in G. Bonamente and A. Nestori (eds.), *I cristiani e l'Impero nel IV secolo: Colloquio sul Cristianesimo nel mondo antico. Atti del convegno Macerata 17–18 dicembre 1987* (Macerata: Università degli studi di Macerata, 1988), 75–106.

Crook, J., *Legal Advocacy in the Roman World* (London: Duckworth, 1995).

____ 'Once Again the *Controversiae* and Roman Law', in K. Lee, C. Mackie, and H. Tarrant (eds.), *Multarum Artium Scientia: Festschrift for R. Godfrey Tanner*, *Prudentia* suppl. (Auckland: University of Auckland, 1993), 68–76.

Cross, F. L., 'History and Fiction in the African Canons', *JTS* NS 12 (1961), 227–47.

Cuena Boy, F. J., *La episcopalis audientia: La justicia episcopal en las causas civiles entre laicos* (Valladolid: University of Valladolid, 1985).

Cumont, F., 'Ambrosiaster et le droit romain', *Revue d'histoire et de littérature religieuse*, 8 (1903).

Daube, D., 'A Corrupt Judge Sets the Pace', in D. Nörr and D. Simon (eds.), *Gedächtnisschrift für Wolfgang Kunkel* (Frankfurt: Klostermann, 1984), 37–52.

____ 'The Compilers' Use of a Revised Paul and Ulpian', *ZSS, Rom. Abt.* 90 (1973), 359–60.

____ 'Ne quis fecisse velit', in D. Cohen and D. Simon (eds.), *Collected Studies in Roman Law*, ii (Frankfurt: Klostermann, 1991).

David, J. M., 'Le Tribunal dans la basilique: Évolution fonctionnelle et symbolique de la république à l'empire', in *Architecture et société de l'archaïsme grec à la fin de la république romaine* (Paris and Rome: Collection de l'École Française de Rome 66, 1983), 219–41.

Davidson, J. J. (ed.), *Ambrose De Officiis*, I: *Introduction, Text, and Translation* (Oxford: OUP, 2001).

De Churruca, J., 'Un rescrit de Caracalla utilisé par Ulpien et interprété par Saint Augustin', in R. Feenstra and A. S. Hartkamp (eds.), *Collatio iuris romani: Études dédiées à Hans Ankum* (Amsterdam: Gieben, 1995), 71–81.

Decret, F., 'Du bon usage du mensonge et du parjure: Manichéens et Priscillianistes face à la persécution dans l'empire chrétien (IVe–Ve siècles)', in M.-M. Mactoux and E. Geny, *Mélanges P. Lévêque*, iv (Paris: Belles Lettres, 1990), 140–58.

——'Objectif premier vise par Augustin dans ses controverses orales avec les responsables Manichéens d'Hippone', in J. van Oort, O. Wermerlinger, and G. Wurst, *Augustine and Manichaeism in the Latin West* (Leiden: Brill, 2001), 57–66.

De Durand, G.-M. (ed. and tr.), Traités. *Marc le Moine: Introduction, texte critique, traduction, notes et index, SC* 455 (Paris: Éditions du Cerf, 2000).

De Filippi, M., *Fragmenta Vaticana: Storia di un testo normative*, 2nd edn. (Bari: Cacucci, 1998).

De Francisci, P., 'Ancora dell'editto nel periodo postclassico', *BIDR* 11 (1960), 39–46.

De Giovanni, L., 'Ortodossia, eresia, funzione dei chierici: Aspetti e problemi della legislazione religiosa tra Teodosio e Teodosio II', *AARC* 6 (1986), 59–73.

De Labriolle, P., 'Tertullien jurisconsulte', *NRHDFE* 30 (1906), 5–27.

De Marini Avonzo, F., 'I libri di diritto a Constantinopli nell'età di Teodosio II', *Annali della Facoltà di giurisprudenza di Genova*, 24/1–2 (1991–2), 103–13.

——'I rescritti nel processo del IV e V secolo', *AARC* 11 (1996), 29–39.

De Riedmatten, H., *Les Actes du procès de Paul de Samosate: Étude sur la Christologie du IIIe au IVe siècle* (Fribourg, Switzerland: Éditions St-Paul, 1952).

Derrett, J. D. M., 'The Theban Scholasticus and Malabar in c.355–60', *Journal of the American Oriental Society*, 82/1 (1962), 21–31.

De Saint-Palais d'Aussac, F., *La Réconciliation des hérétiques dans l'église latine* (Paris: Éditions franciscaines, 1943).

Dilts, M. R., and Kennedy, G. A. (eds.), *Two Greek Rhetorical Treatises from the Roman Empire: Introduction, Text, and Translation of the Arts of Rhetoric, Attributed to Anonymous Seguerianus and to Apsines of Gadara* (Leiden: Brill, 1997).

Dimopoulou, A. A., *La Rémunération de l'assistance en justice* (Athens: Éditions ant. N. Sakkoulas, 1999).

Dionisotti, A. C., 'From Ausonius' Schooldays? A Schoolbook and its Relatives', *Journal of Roman Studies*, 72 (1982), 83–125.

D'Ippolito, F. M., and Nasti, F., 'Diritto e papiri: Nuovi pareri giurisprudenziali da Phaun. III 45', *AARC* 15 (2005), 239–42.

—— 'Frammenti papiracei di un'opera della giurisprudenza tardo imperiale', *SDHI* 69 (2003), 383–98.

Dolbeau, F., *Augustin d'Hippone: Vingt-six sermons au peuple d'Afrique* (Paris: Institut d'études Augustiniennes, 1996).

Dossey, L., 'Judicial Violence and the Ecclesiastical Courts in Late Antique North Africa', in R. W. Mathisen (ed.), *Law, Society and Authority in Late Antiquity* (Oxford: Oxford University Press, 2001), 98–114.

Dovere, E., *De iure: Studi sul titolo 1 delle Epitomi di Ermogeniano* (Turin: Giappichelli, 2001).

—— 'Diritto romano e prassi conciliare ecclesiastica (secc. III–V)', *SDHI* 69 (2003), 149–64.

—— *'Ius Principale' e 'Catholica Lex': Dal Teodosiano agli Editti su Calcedonia* (Naples: Jovene, 1995).

Dunn, J. D. G. (ed.), *Paul and the Mosaic Law* (Tübingen, J. C. B. Mohr (Paul Siebeck), 1996).

Duval, N., 'Une basilique chrétienne à deux absides à Sabratha?', *RE Aug.* 33 (1987), 269–301.

Eckert, G., *Orator Christianus: Untersuchungen zur Argumentationskunst in Tertullians Apologeticum* (Stuttgart: Franz Steiner Verlag, 1993).

Edwards, M. (tr.), *Optatus: Against the Donatists* (Liverpool: Liverpool University Press, 1997).

Eger, O., 'Rechtswörter und Rechtsbilder in den Paulinischen Briefen', *ZNW* 18 (1918), 84–108.

Elm, S., *'Virgins of God': The Making of Asceticism in Late Antiquity* (Oxford: Clarendon Press, 1994).

Eno, R. B. (tr.), *St Augustine Letters 1–29** (Washington, DC: Catholic University of America Press, 1989).

Errington, R. M., 'Christian Accounts of the Religious Legislation of Theodosius I', *Klio,* 79/2 (1997), 398–443.

Falchi, F. L., *Sulla codificazione del diritto romano nel v e vi secolo* (Rome: Pontificia universitas lateranensis, 1989).

Fantham, E., *The Roman World of Cicero's* De Oratore (Oxford: Oxford University Press, 2004).

Feissel, D., 'Pétitions aux empereurs et formes du rescrit', in D. Feissel and J. Gascou, *La Pétition à Byzance* (Paris: Centre de Recherche d'Histoire et Civilisation de Byzance, 2004), 33–52.

—— 'Une constitution de l'empereur Julien entre text épigraphique et codification (*CIL* III, 459 et *CTh* 1,16,8)', in E. Lévy (ed.), *La Codification des lois dans l'antiquité* (Paris: De Boccard, 2000), 315–37.

——'Un rescrit de Justinien découvert à Didymes (1er avril 533)', *Chiron*, 34 (2004), 285–365.

——and Gascou, J. (eds.), *La Pétition à Byzance* (Paris: Centre de Recherche d'Histoire et Civilisation de Byzance, 2004).

——and Worp, K. (1988) 'La Requête d'Appion, évêque de syene, à Theodose II: P. Leid. Z revisé', *Oudheidkundige mededelingen uit het Rijksmuseum van Oudheden te Leiden*, 68: 97–11.

Felice, F., 'Su le idee giuridiche contenute nei libri V e VI delle Istituzioni di Lattanzio', *Rivista internazionale di scienze sociali e discipline ausiliarie*, 5 (1894), 581–6.

Ferrini, C., 'Le cognizioni giuridiche di Lattanzio, Arnobio e Minucio Felice', *Memorie dell'Accademia delle Scienze di Modena*, 2nd ser. 10 (1894), 195–210.

Fiaccadori, G., 'Cassiodorus and the School of Nisibis', *Dumbarton Oaks Papers*, 39 (1985), 135–7.

Flusin, B., *Miracle et histoire dans l'oeuvre de Cyrille de Scythopolis* (Paris: Études Augustiniennes, 1983).

Fögen, M.-T., *Die Enteignang der Wahrsager: Studien Zum Kaiserlichen Wissensmonopol in der Spätantike* (Frankfurt/Main: Suhrkamp, 1993).

——'Gesetz und Gesetzgebung in Byzanz: Versuch einer Funktionsanalyse', *Ius Commune*, 14 (1987), 137–58.

Fogliani, T. G., *Contributo alla ricerca di riferimenti legali in testi extragiuridici del III sec. d.c.* (Modena: Bassi & Nipoti, 1928).

Fonrobert, C., 'The Didascalia Apostolorum: A Mishnah for the Disciples of Jesus', *Journal of Early Christian Studies*, 9/4 (2001), 438–509.

Foucault, M., *L'Ordre du discours* (Paris: Gallimard, 1971), tr. Ian McLeod in R. Young (ed.), *Untying the Text: A Post-Structuralist Reader* (Boston: Routledge & Kegan Paul, 1981), 48–78.

Fournet, J. L., 'Entre document et litterature: La Pétition dans l'antiquité tardive', in D. Feissel and J. Gascou (eds.), *La Pétition à Byzance* (Paris: Centre de Recherche d'Histoire et Civilisation de Byzance, 2004), 61–74.

Frakes, R. M., *Contra potentium iniurias: The Defensor Civitatis and Late Roman Justice* (Munich: Verlag C. H. Beck, 2001).

Frier, B., *The Rise of the Roman Jurists* (Princeton: Princeton University Press, 1985).

Gaddis, M., *There is No Crime for those who have Christ: Religious Violence in the Christian Roman Empire* (Berkeley and Los Angeles: University of California, 2005).

Gager, J., *Re-inventing Paul* (Oxford: Oxford University Press, 2002).

——'Where does Luke's Anti-Judaism Come from?', in H. Zellentin and E. Iricinschi (eds.), *Heresy and Identity in Late Antiquity* (Tubingen: Mohr Siebeck, 2007), 300–5.

Gager, J., and Sijpesteijn, P. J., 'Settling a Dispute in Fourth Century Small Oasis', *ZPE* 105 (1995), 245–52.

—— and Van Minnen, P., *Settling a Dispute: Toward a Legal Anthropology of Late Antique Egypt* (Ann Arbor: University of Michigan Press, 1994).

Gardner, I., and Lieu, S. N. C., *Manichaean Texts from the Roman Empire* (Cambridge: Cambridge University Press, 2004).

Garnsey, P., *Social Status and Legal Privilege in the Roman Empire* (Oxford: Oxford University Press, 1970).

Gascou, J., 'Décision de Caesarius, gouverneur militaire de Thébaïde', *Travaux et mémoires*, Centre de recherche d'histoire et civilisation de Byzance, 14 (2002), 269–77.

—— and Mac Coull, L. S. B., 'Le Cadastre d'Aphroditô', *Travaux et mémoires du Centre de recherche d'histoire et civilisation de Byzance*, 10 (1987), 103–58, with 10 plates.

Gaudemet, J., 'Collections canoniques et codifications', *Revue de droit canonique*, 33 (1983), 81–109.

—— 'Droit séculier et droit de l'église chez Ambroise', in G. Lazzati, (ed.), *Ambrosius Episcopus: Atti del Congresso internazionale di studi Ambrosiani nel XVI. centenario della elevazione di sant'Ambrogio alla cattedra episcopale*, i (Milan: Vita e pensiero, 1976), 286–315.

—— 'Elementi giuridici romani nella formazione del diritto ecclesiastico dei primi secoli', in M. Pavan and U. Cozzoli (eds.), *Mondo classico e cristianesimo* (Rome: Istituto della Enciclopedia Italiana, 1983), 171–82.

Gaudemet, *La Formation du droit séculier et du droit de l'église aux IV et V siècles*, 2nd edn (Paris: Sirey, 1979).

—— *Le Droit romain dans le littérature chrétienne occidentale du IIIe au Ve siècle* (Milan: Guiffrè, 1978).

—— *Les Institutions de l'antiquité*, 3rd edn. (Paris: Montchrestien, 1991).

—— *Les Sources du droit de l'église en occident du IIe au VIIe siècle* (Paris: Éditions du Cerf, 1985).

—— 'Note sur les formes anciennes de l'excommunication', *Rev. SR* 23 (1944), 64–77.

Gebbia, C., 'S. Agostino e l'episcopalis audientia', *L'Africa Romana*, 8 (1989), 683–99.

Gibson, C. A., *Interpreting a Classic: Demosthenes and his Ancient Commentators* (Berkeley, Calif.: University of California, 2002).

Giet, S., *Les Idées et l'action sociales de saint Basile* (Paris: Librairie Lecoffre, 1941).

Gilliam, J. F., 'A Student at Berytus in an Inscription from Pamphylia', *Zeitschrift für Papyrologie und Epigraphik*, 13 (1974), 147–50.

Girardet, K. M., 'Trier 385: Der Prozess gegen die Priszillianer', *Chiron*, 4 (1974), 577–608.

Gleason, M., *Making Men: Sophists and Self-Presentation in Ancient Rome* (Princeton: Princeton University Press, 1994).

Goodenough, E. R., *The Jurisprudence of the Jewish Courts in Egypt: Legal Administration by the Jews under the Early Roman Empire as Described by Philo Judaeus* (New Haven: Yale University Press, 1929).

Goria, F., 'Giudici civili e giudici militari nell'età giustinianea', *Studia et Documenta Historiae et Iuris*, 61 (1995), 447–61.

Goulet, R. (ed.), *Macarios de Magnésie: Le Monogénès* (Paris: Librairie Philosophique J. Vrin, 2003).

Graffin, R., and Nau, F., *Théodore de Mopsueste: Controverse avec les Macédoniens* (Paris: Patrologie Orientalis 9, 1913).

Greatrex, G., 'Lawyers and Historians in Late Antiquity', in R. Mathisen (ed.), *Law, Society and Authority in Late Antiquity* (Oxford: Oxford University Press, 2001), 148–61.

Greenidge, A. H. J., *Infamia: Its Place in Roman Public and Private Law* (Oxford: Clarendon Press, 1894).

Guarino, A., *Storia del diritto romano* (Naples: Jovene, 1975).

Gui, I., Duval, N., and Caillet, J.-P. (1992) *Basiliques chrétiennes d'Afrique du Nord*, i (Paris: Collection des Études Augustiniennes 129, 1992).

Hadot, P., *Arts libéraux et philosophie dans la pensée antique* (Paris: Études Augustiniennes, 1984).

—— '"De lectis non lecta conponere" (Marius Victorinus, Adversus Arium II 7): Raisonnement théologique et raisonnement juridique', *Studia Patristica*, 1 (1957), 209–20.

Handley, M. A., 'One Hundred and Fifty-Two Addenda to PLRE from Gaul, Spain and Britain', *Historia*, 54 (2005), 93–105.

Harries, J., *Law and Empire in Late Antiquity* (Cambridge: Cambridge University Press, 1999).

—— 'Resolving Disputes: The Frontiers of Law in Late Antiquity', in R. E. Mathisen (ed.), *Law, Society and Authority in Late Antiquity* (Oxford: Oxford University Press, 2001), 68–82.

Harrison, S. J., Hilton, J. L., and Hunink, V. J. C., *Apuleius: Rhetorical Works* (Oxford: Oxford University Press, 2001).

Hauken, T., *Petition and Response: An Epigraphic Study of Petitions to Roman Emperors A.D. 181–249*, ii (Bergen: Norwegian Institute at Athens, 1998).

Heath, M., *Menander: A Rhetor in Context* (Oxford: Oxford University Press, 2004).

—— 'Practical Advocacy in Roman Egypt', in M. J. Edwards and C. Reid (eds.), *Oratory in Action* (Manchester: Manchester University Press, 2004), 62–82.

—— 'The Substructure of *Stasis*-Theory from Hermagoras to Hermogenes', *Classical Quarterly*, 44 (1994), 114–29.

Hebein, B., 'St Ambrose and Roman Law' (St Louis University, Ph.D. thesis, 1970).

Heggelbacher, O., *Vom römischen zum christlichen Recht: Iuristische Elemente in den Schriften des sogenanntes Ambrosiaster* (Freiburg, Switzerland: Universitätsverlag, 1959).
Hermanowicz, E. T., 'Catholic Bishops and Appeals to the Imperial Court: A Legal Study of the Calama Riots in 408', *Journal of Early Christian Studies*, 12/4 (2004), 481–521.
Herrmann, E., *Ecclesia in Re Publica* (Frankfurt: Lang, 1980).
Hess, H., *The Early Development of Canon Law and the Council of Serdica*, 2nd edn. (Oxford: Oxford University Press, 2002).
Hill, E. (tr.), *Augustine, Sermons*, ii *(20–50) on the Old Testament* (Brooklyn, NY: New City Press, 1990).
Hitzig, H. F., *Die Assessoren der römischen Magistrate und Richter* (Munich: Ackermann, 1893).
Hock, R. F., 'The Rhetoric of Romance', in S. Porter, *Handbook of Classical Rhetoric* (Leiden: Brill, 1997).
Hoffmann, A., *Kirchliche Strukturen und römisches Recht bei Cyprian Karthago* (Paderborn: Schöningh, 2000).
Honoré, T., *Emperors and Lawyers*, 2nd edn. (Oxford: Oxford University Press, 1994).
——'Eutropius' Lawyer (396–9) and Other Quaestors of Arcadius (394–408)', *ZSS, Rom. Abt.* 112 (1995), 172–94
——*Law in the Crisis of Empire, 379–455 AD: The Theodosian Dynasty and its Quaestors* (Oxford: Clarendon Press, 1998).
——Honoré, T., 'Roman Law AD 200–400: From Cosmopolis to Rechstaat?', in S. Swain and M. Edwards (eds.), *Approaching Late Antiquity* (Oxford: Oxford University Press, 2004), 109–32.
——'The Making of the Theodosian Code', *ZSS, Rom. Abt.* 103 (1986), 174.
——*Ulpian: Pioneer of Human Rights*, 2nd edn. (Oxford: Oxford University Press, 2002).
Huck, O., 'A propos de *CTh* 1,27,1 et *C. Sirm* 1. Sur deux textes controversés relatifs à l'episcopalis audientia constantinienne', *ZSS, Rom. Abt.* 120 (2003), 78–105.
Humfress, C., 'Advocates', in G. W. Bowersock, P. Brown, and O. Grabar (eds.), *Late Antiquity: A Guide to the Postclassical World* (Cambridge, Mass.: Harvard University Press, 1999), 277–8.
——'A New Legal Cosmos: Late Roman Lawyers and the Early Medieval Church', in P. Linehan and J. Nelson (eds.), *The Medieval World (*London: Routledge, 2001), 557–73.
——'Citizens and Heretics: Late Roman Lawyers on Christian Heresy', in E. Iricinschi and H. Zellentin (eds.), *Heresy and Identity in Late Antiquity* (Tübingen: Mohr Siebeck, 2007).
——'Cracking the *Codex*: Late Roman Legal Practice in Context', *BICS* 49 (2007), 251–64.

——'Judging by the Book: Christian Codices and Late Antique Legal Culture', in W. Klingshirn and L. Safran (eds.), *The Early Christian Book* (Washington, DC: Catholic University of America Press, 2007), 141–58.

——'Law and Legal Practice in the Age of Justinian', in Michael Maas (ed.), *Cambridge Companion to the Age of Justinian* (Cambridge and New York: Cambridge University Press, 2005), 161–84.

——'Law in Practice', in P. Rousseau (ed.), *The Blackwell Guide to Late Antiquity* (Oxford: Blackwell, forthcoming).

——'Poverty and Roman Law', in M. Atkins and R. Osborne (eds.), *Poverty in the Roman World* (Cambridge: Cambridge University Press, 2006), 183–203.

——'Roman Law, Forensic Argument and the Formation of Christian Orthodoxy (III–VI Centuries)', in S. Elm, E. Rebillard, and A. Romano (eds.), *Orthodoxie, christianisme, histoire—Orthodoxy, Christianity, History: Travaux du groupe de recherches 'Definir, maintenir et remettre en cause l'orthodoxie dans l'histoire du christianisme'* (Rome: École Française de Rome, 2001), 125–47.

Hunter, D. G., 'Libanius and John Chrysostom: New Thoughts on an Old Problem', *Studi Patristica*, 22 (1989), 129–35.

Ibbetson, D., 'High Classical Law', in A. Bowman, P. Garnsey, and D. Rathbone (eds.), *Cambridge Ancient History*, xi. *The High Empire A.D. 70–192*, 2nd edn. (Cambridge: Cambridge University Press, 2000), 184–99.

Inglebert, H., 'L'Histoire des hérésies chez les hérésiologues', in B. Pouderon and Y.-M. Duval (eds.), *L'Historiographie de l'Église des premiers siècles* (Paris: Beauchesne, 2001), 105–25.

Jackson, B., *Law, Fact and Narrative Coherence* (Liverpoool: Deborah Charles Publications, 1988).

Jaeger, H., 'Justinien et l'episcopalis audientia', *RHDFE* 38 (1960), 214–62.

Johnston, D., 'Epiclassical Law', in A. Bowman, P. Garnsey, and D. Rathbone, *The Cambridge Ancient History*, xi. *The High Empire A.D. 70–192*, 2nd edn. (Cambridge: Cambridge University Press, 2006), 200–7.

Johnston, D., *Roman Law in Context* (Cambridge: Cambridge University Press, 1999).

Jolowicz, H. F., *Historical Introduction to the Study of Roman Law* (Cambridge: Cambridge University Press, 1952).

Jones, A. H. M., 'St John Chrysostom's Parentage and Education', *Harvard Theological Review*, 46/3 (1953), 171–3.

—— *The Later Roman Empire: A Social, Economic and Administrative Survey* (Oxford: Blackwells, 1964).

Jones Hall, L., *Roman Berytus: Beirut in Late Antiquity* (London: Routledge, 2004).

Jonkers, E. J., 'Application of Roman Law by Councils in the Sixth Century', *TR* 20 (1952), 340–3.

Kaser, M., and Hackl, K., *Das römische Zivilprozessrecht*, 2nd edn. (Munich: C. H. Beck, 1996), 163–71.

Kaster, R., *Guardians of Language: The Grammarian and Society in Late Antiquity* (Berkeley, Calif.: University of California Press, 1988).

Katzoff, R., 'Precedents in the Courts of Roman Egypt', *ZSS* 89 (1972), 256–82.

Katzoff, R., 'Sources of Law in Roman Egypt: The Role of the Prefect', *ANRW* ii/13 (1980), 808–44.

Keenan, J. G., 'Egypt', in A. Cameron, B. Ward Perkins, and M. Whitby (eds.), *Cambridge Ancient History*, xiv (Cambridge: Cambridge University Press, 2001), 612–37.

——'Roman Criminal Law in a Berlin Papyrus Codex', *Archiv*, 35 (1989), 15–23.

Kelly, C., *Ruling the Later Roman Empire* (Cambridge, Mass., and London: Harvard University Press, 2004).

King, K., *What is Gnosticism?* (Cambridge, Mass., and London: Harvard University Press, 2003).

Kinzig, W., *Asterius, Psalmenhomilien* (Stuttgart: Anton Hiersemann, 2002).

Klein, R., *Tertullian und das römische Reich* (Heidelberg: C. Winter, 1968).

Koenen, L., and Römer, C., *Der Kölner Mani-Kodex: Über das weden seines Leibes* (Opladen: Westdeutscher Verlag, 1988).

Kovelman, A. B., 'From Logos to Myth: Egyptian Petitions of the 5th–7th Centuries', *Bulletin of the American Society of Papyrologists*, 28 (1991), 135–52.

Kramer, B., and Hagedorn, D., 'Zum Verhandlungsprotokoll P. Columbia VII 175', *ZPE* 45 (1982), 229–41.

Kreuter, N., *Römisches Privatrecht im 5. Jh. N. Chr.: Die Interpretatio zum westgotischen Gregorianus und Hermogenianus* (Berlin: Duncker & Humboldt, 1993).

Krüger, P., Mommsen, T., and Studemund, W., *Collectio Librorum Iuris Anteiustiniani*, iii (Berlin: Weidmann, 1878/90; repr. Hildesheim: Weidmann, 1999).

Kuehn, C. A., 'A New Papyrus of a Dioscorian Poem and Marriage Contract', *ZPE* 97 (1993), 103–15.

Kunkel, W., *Herkunft und soziale Stellung der römischen Juristen*, 2nd edn. (Graz: Böhlan, 1967).

Kustas, G., 'Saint Basil and the Rhetorical Tradition', in P. J. Fedwick, *Basil of Caesarea: Christian, Humanist, Ascetic*, i (Toronto: Pontifical Institute of Medieval Studies, 1981), 221–79.

Lammeyer, J., 'Die "audientia episcopalis" in Zivilsachen der Laien im römischen Kaiserrecht und in den Papyri', *Aegyptus*, 13 (1933), 200–1.

Lamoreaux, J., 'Episcopal Courts in Late Antiquity', *Journal of Early Christian Studies*, 3 (1995), 143–67.

Lancel, S., *Actes de la Conférence de Carthage en 411*, i, *SC* 194 (Paris: Éditions de Cerf, 1972).

Lanfranchi, F., *Il diritto nei retori romani* (Milan: Guiffrè, 1938).

Lange, H., *Römisches Recht im Mittelalter* (Munich: Beck, 1997)

Lardone, F. G., 'Roman Law in the Works of St Augustine', *Georgetown Law Journal* (1956), 435–56.

Lavan, L., 'The Political Topography of the Late Antique City: Activity Spaces in Practice', in L. Lavan and W. Bowden (eds.), *Theory and Practice in Late Antique Archaeology* (Leiden and Boston: Brill, 2003), 314 –37.

Le Boulluec, A., *Le Notion d'hérésie dans la literature grecque IIe-IIIe siècles* (Paris: Études augustiniennes, 1985).

Leclercq, H., 'Chaire episcopale', in F. Cabrol (ed.), *Dictionnaire d'archéologie chrétienne et de liturgie*, i (Paris: Letaizey et Ané, 1913), 19–75.

Lécrivain, C., 'Note sur le recrutement des avocats dans la période du bas empire', *MEFR* 5 (1885), 276–83.

Lee, A. D., 'Decoding Late Roman Law', *Journal of Roman Studies*, 92 (2002), 187.

Leff, M. C., 'The Material of the Art in the Latin Handbooks of the Fourth Century AD', in B. Vickers (ed.), *Rhetoric Revalued: Papers from the International Society for the History of Rhetoric* (New York: Center for Medieval and Early Renaissance Studies, 1982), 71–8.

Legendre, P., 'Le Droit romain, modèle et langage: De la signification de l'Utrumque ius', in *Études d'histoire du droit canonique dédiées à Gabriel Le Bras*, ii (Paris: Sirey, 1965), 913–30.

Lehto, A., 'Moral, Ascetic, and Ritual Dimensions to Law-Observance in Aphrahat's Demonstrations', *Journal of Early Christian Studies*, 14/2 (2006), 157–81.

Lenel, O., *Das Edictum Perpetuum*, 3rd edn. (Leipzig: Tauchnitz, 1927).

—— *Palingenesia Iuris Civilis*, 2 vols. (Leipzig: Tauchnitz, 1889), ii.

Lenox-Conyngham, A., 'The Judgement of Ambrose the Bishop on Ambrose the Roman Governor', *Studia Patristica*, 17/1 (1982), 63–5.

Lenski, N., 'Evidence for the Audientia Episcopalis in the New Letters of Augustine', in R. Mathisen (ed.), *Law, Society and Authority in Late Antiquity* (Oxford: Oxford University Press, 2001), 83–97.

Lepelley, C., *Les Cités de l'Afrique romaine au Bas-Empire*, ii. *Notices d'histoire municipale* (Paris: Études Augustiniennes, 1981).

—— 'Trois documents méconnus sur l'histoire sociale et religieuse de l'Afrique romaine tardive, retrouvés parmi les *spuria* de Sulpice Sévère', *Antiquités africaines*, 25 (1989), 235–62.

Lepelley, C., 'Un aspect de la conversion d'Augustin: La Rupture avec ses ambitions sociales et politiques', *BLE* 88 (1987), 229–46.

Levy, E., Review of Stroux's 'Summum ius', in *ZSS, Rom. Abt.* 48 (1928), 668–78.

Lewis, A., 'The Autonomy of Roman Law', in P. Coss (ed.), *The Moral World of the Law* (Cambridge: Cambridge University Press, 2000), 37–47.

Lewis, N., and Schiller, A. A., 'Another "Narratio" Document', in A. Watson (ed.), *Daube Noster* (Edinburgh: Edinburgh University Press, 1974), 187–200.

Lieberman, S., 'Roman Legal Institutions in Early Rabbinics and in the Acta Martyrum', *Jewish Quarterly Review*, 35 (1944), 1–57.

Liebeschuetz, J. H. W. G., *Antioch: City and Imperial Administration in the Later Roman Empire* (Oxford: Oxford University Press, 1971).

Liebs, D., *Die Jurisprudenz im spätantiken Italien (260–640 n. Chr)* (Berlin: Duncker & Humblot, 1987).

—— 'Die pseudopaulinischen Sentenzen', *ZSS, Rom. Abt.* 112 (1995), 151–171 and 113 (1996), 132–242.

—— 'Römische Jurisprudenz in Africa im 4. Jh. n. chr', *ZSS, Rom. Abt.* 106 (1989), 201–17.

Liebs, D., *Römische Jurisprudenz in Gallien (2 bis 8 Jahrhundert)* (Berlin: Duncker & Humblot, 2002).

—— 'Römische Provinzialjurisprudenz', *ANRW* ii/15 (1976), 288–362.

Lienhard, J. T., *Contra Marcellum. Marcellus of Ancyra and Fourth-Century Theology* (Washington, DC: Catholic University of America Press, 1999).

Lieu, J. M, and S. N. C., '"Felix Conversus ex Manichaeis": A Case of Mistaken Identity', *JTS* NS 23/1 (1981), 173–6.

Lim, R., *Public Disputation, Power, and Social Order* (Berkeley and Los Angeles: University of California Press, 1995).

Linder, A., *The Jews in Roman Imperial Legislation* (Detroit: Wayne State University Press, 1987).

Loerke, W., 'The Miniatures of the Trial in the Rossano Gospels', *Art History Bulletin*, 43/3 (1961), 171–95.

Lowther Clarke, W. K. (tr.), *St Gregory of Nyssa, The life of St Macrina* (London: SPCK, 1916).

Lucrezi, F., 'Sulla data di redazione della Collatio alla luce di due costituzioni costantiniane', *AARC* 14 (2003), 599–613.

Lyman, R., 'Historical Methodologies and Ancient Theological Conflicts', in M. Zyniewicz, *The Papers of the Henry Luce III Fellows in Theology*, iii (Atlanta, Ga.: Scholars Press, 1999), 75–96.

—— 'Hellenism and Heresy', *Journal of Early Christian Studies*, 11/2 (2003), 209–22.

Lyon, E., 'Le Droit chez Isidore de Péluse', *Études d'histoire juridique offertes à Paul Girard*, ii (Paris: Librairie Paul Geuthner, 1913), 209–220.

Maas, M. (tr.), *Exegesis and Empire in the Early Byzantine Mediterranean: Junillus Africanus and the* Instituta regularia divinae legis (Tübingen: Siebeck, 2003).

McClure, J., 'Handbooks against Heresy in the West, from the Late Fourth to the Late Sixth Centuries', *JTS*, 30 (1979), 186–97.

MacCormick, N., *Legal Reasoning and Legal Theory* (Oxford: Clarendon Press, 1994).

—— *Rhetoric and the Rule of Law: A Theory of Legal Reasoning* (Oxford: Oxford University Press, 2005).

Mac Coull, L. S. B., *Dioscorus of Aphrodito: His Work and his World* (Berkeley, Los Angeles and London: University of California Press, 1988).

Maceratini, R., *Ricerche sullo status giuridico dell'eretico nel diritto romano-cristiano e nel diritto canonico classico (da Graziano ad Uguccione)* (Padua: Edizioni CEDAM, 1994).

Maggio, L., 'Note critiche sui rescritti postclassici, I. Il c.d. processo "*per rescriptum*"', *SDHI* 61 (1995), 285–312.

—— 'Note critiche sui rescritti postclassici II. L'Efficacia normativa dei rescritti *ad consultationes* e dei rescritti *ad preces emissa*', *AARC* 14 (2003), 359–80.

McHoul, A., and Grace, W., *A Foucault Primer: Discourse, Power and the Subject* (Melbourne: Melbourne University Publishing 1997).

Maier, H., '"Manichee!": Leo the Great and the Orthodox Panopticon', *Journal of Early Christian Studies*, 4/4 (1996), 441–60.

Maine, H. J. S., *Ancient Law: Its Connection with the Early History of Society and its Relation to Modern Ideas*, 16th edn. (London: Murray, 1897).

Marcel, S., 'From Greek *Hairesis* to Christian Heresy', in W. R. Schoedel and R. L. Wilken (eds.), *Early Christian Literature and the Classical Intellectual Tradition: In Honorem Robert M. Grant* (Paris: Èditions Beauchesne, 1979), 101–16.

Marcovich, M., *Iustini Martyris: Apologiae pro Christianis, Dialogus cum Tryphone* (Berlin and New York: Walter de Gruyter, 2005).

Marrou, H. I., *Histoire de l'éducation dans l'antiquité* (Paris: Éditions du Seuil, 1948), tr. G. Lamb, *A History of Education in Antiquity* (London: Sheed & Ward, 1956), 311.

Martens, J. W., *One God. One Law. Philo of Alexandria on the Mosaic and Greco-Roman Law* (Boston: Brill Academic Publishers, 2003).

Martini, R., 'Ancora a proposito di Tertulliano', *Bullettino dell'Istituto di diritto romano Vittorio Scialoja*, 39 (2003), 117–26.

—— 'Sui pretesi modelli giuridici delle Div. Inst. di Lattanzio', *Atti del Seminario Romanistico Gardesano III* (Milan: Guiffrè, 1988), 423–32.

—— 'Tertulliano giurista e Tertulliano padre della chiesa', *SDHI* 41 (1975), 79–124.

Martroye, F., 'Les Plaidoiries devant la jurisdiction episcopale au IVe siècle', *BSNAF* (1918), 136–9.

Martroye, F., 'Saint Augustin et la compétence de la jurisdiction ecclésiastique au Ve siècle', *MSNAF* 70 (1910), 1–78.

——'Saint Augustin et la jurisprudence romaine', *BSNAF* (1916), 210–14.

——'Saint Augustin et le droit d'héritage des églises et des monastères: Étude sur les origines du droit des communautés religieuses à la succession des clercs et des moines', *MSNAF* 68 (1908), 97–129.

Marx, F. (1894) *Incerti auctoris de ratione dicendi ad C. Herennium lib iv iterum* (Leipzig: Teubner, 1894).

Mathisen, R., 'The "Second Council of Arles" and the Spirit of Compilation and Codification in Late Roman Gaul', *Journal of Early Christian Studies*, 5 (1997), 511–54.

Matthews, J., 'Ammianus on Roman Law and Lawyers', in J. den Boeft, D. den Hengst, and H. C. Teitler, *Cognitio Gestorum: The Historiographical Art of Ammianus Marcellinus* (Amsterdam: Royal Netherlands Academy of Arts and Sciences, 1992).

——*Laying Down the Law: A Study of the Theodosian Code* (New Haven: Yale University Press, 2000).

Maxwell, J. L., *Christianization and Communication in Late Antiquity: John Chrysostom and his Congregation in Antioch* (Cambridge: Cambridge University Press, 2006).

May, J. M., and Wisse, J. (tr.), Cicero *On the Ideal Orator* (New York and Oxford: Oxford University Press, 2001).

Méhész, K. Z., *Advocatus Romanus* (Buenos Aires: Zavalia, 1971).

Mélèze-Modrzejewski, J. M., 'Grégoire Le Thaumaturge et le droit romain: A propos d'une édition récente', *RHDFE* 49 (1971), 312–24.

Menzies, R. P., *The Development of Early Christian Pneumatology with Special Reference to Luke–Acts* (Sheffield: JSOT Press, 1991).

Mercogliano, F., *Tituli ex corpore ulpiano: Storia di un testo* (Naples: Pubblicazioni della Facoltà di Giurisprudenza dell'Università di Camerino 44, 1997).

Merdinger, J. E., *Rome and the African Church in the Time of Augustine* (New Haven and London: Yale University Press, 1997).

Metzger, E., *Litigation in Roman Law* (Oxford: Oxford University Press, 2005).

——'Roman Judges, Case Law, and Principles of Procedure', *Law and History Review*, 22 (2004), 243–75.

Meyer, E. A., *Legitimacy and Law in the Roman World:* Tabulae *in Roman Belief and Practice* (Cambridge: Cambridge University Press, 2004).

Michel, J.-H., 'La Satire 2, 1 à Trébatius ou la consultation du juriste', *RIDA* 46 (1999), 369–91.

——*A Greek Roman Empire: Power and Belief under Theodosius II 408–450* (Berkeley, Los Angeles, and London: University of California Press, 2006).

——'Christian Emperors, Christian Church and the Jews of the Diaspora in the Greek East, CE 379–450', *Journal of Jewish Studies*, 55/1 (2004), 1–24.

——'Paul of Samosata, Zenobia and Aurelian: The Church, Local Culture and Political Allegiance in Third-Century Syria', *Journal of Roman Studies*, 61 (1971), 1–17.

Mitchell, M. M., 'Reading Rhetoric with Patristic Exegetes: John Chrysostom on Galatians', in A. Y. Collins and M. M. Mitchell, *Antiquity and Humanity: Essays on Ancient Religion and Philosophy Presented to Hans Dieter Betz on his 70th Birthday* (Tubingen: Mohr Siebeck, 2001), 333–55.

Mommsen, T., 'Die Rechtsverhältnisse des apostel Paulus', *ZNW* 2 (1901), 81–96.

Monceaux, P., *St Jerome: The Early Years*, tr. F. J. Sheed (London: Sheed & Ward, 1933).

Montgomery, H., 'Crime and Punishment in the Statutes of the Concilium Iliberitanum', *Studia Patristica*, 24 (1993), 169–74.

Moretti, G., 'Il manuale e l'allegoria. La personificazione allegorica delle arti liberali come tradizione del genere manualistico', in M. S. Celentano (ed.), *Ars—Techne: Il manuale tecnico nelle civiltà greca e romana* (Chieti: Edizioni dell'Orso, 2003), 159–86.

Morgan, T., *Literate Education in the Hellenistic and Roman Worlds* (Cambridge: Cambridge University Press, 1998).

Munier, C., 'La Tradition littéraire des canons africains', *Rech. Aug.* 10 (1975), 1–22.

Nasrallah, L., *An Ecstasy of Folly: Prophecy and Authority in Early Christianity* (Cambridge, Mass.: Harvard University Press, 2004).

Nellen, D., *Viri litterati: Gebildetes Beamtentum und spätrömisches Reich im Westen zwischen 284 und 395 nach Christus*, 2nd edn. (Bochum: Brockmeyer, 1981).

Nelson, H. L. W. (1981) *Überlieferung, Aufbau und Stil von Gai*, Institutiones (Leiden: Brill, 1981).

Neri, C., 'Ci sono testimonianze giuridiche nelle fonti monastiche?', *AARC* 15 (2005), 107–17.

Neusner, J., and Frerichs, E. S. (eds.), *'To See Ourselves as Others See Us': Christians, Jews and 'Others' in Late Antiquity* (Chico, Calif.: Scholars Press, 1985).

Nonnoi, D., 'Sant' Agostino e il diritto romano', *Rivista Italiana per le Scienze Giuridiche*, 12 (1934), 531–622.

Norman, A. F. (tr.), *Antioch as a Centre of Hellenic Culture as Observed by Libanius* (Liverpool: Liverpool University Press, 2000).

Nörr, D., 'Pomponius oder "Zum Geschichtsverständnis der römischen Juristen"', *ANRW* ii/15 (1976), 497–604.

——'Zu den geistigen und sozialen Grundlagen der spätantiken Kodifikationsbewegung (Anon. *de rebus bellicis* xxi)', *ZSS, Rom. Abt.* 80 (1963), 109–40.

——'Zur Reskriptenpraxis in der Hohen Prinzipatzeit', *ZSS, Röm. Abt.* 98 (1981), 1–46.

Oberhelman, S. M., *Rhetoric and Homiletics in Fourth-Century Christian Literature* (Atlanta, Ga.: American Philological Association, 1991).

Ombretta Cuneo, P., *La Legislazione di Costantino II, Costanzo II e Costante (337–361)* (Milan: Guiffré, 1997).

Osborn, E. F., 'Reason and the Rule of Faith in the Second Century AD', in R. Williams (ed.), *The Making of Orthodoxy: Essays in Honour of Henry Chadwick* (Cambridge: Cambridge University Press, 1989), 40–61.

Oulton, J. E. L. (tr.), *Eusebius Ecclesiastical History* I (Cambridge, Mass.: Harvard University Press, 1932).

Papaconstantinou, A., review of G. Schmelz, *Kirchliche Amtsträger im spätantiken Aëgypten nach den Aussagen der griechischen und koptischen Papyri und Ostraka*, Archiv für Papyrusforschung und verwandte Gebiete, 13 (Munich and Leipzig: K. G. Saur, 2002), in *BMCR* 2003.09.47.

Parássoglou, G. M. (tr.), *The Archive of Aurelius Sakaon: Papers of an Egyptian Farmer in the Last Century of Theadelphia* (Bonn: Habelt, 1978).

Parks, E. P., *The Roman Rhetorical Schools as a Preparation for the Courts under the Early Empire* (Baltimore: Johns Hopkins University Press, 1945).

Patillon, M., *Anonyme de Séguier: Art du discours politique* (Paris: Les Belles Lettres, 2005).

Pedersen, N. A., *Demonstrative Proof in Defence of God: A Study of Titus of Bostra's Contra Manichaeos—The Work's Sources, Aims and Relation to Contemporary Theology* (Leiden and Boston: Brill, 2004).

Pergami, F., *La Legislazione di Valentiniano e Valente (364–375)*, *AARC* 2/4 (Milan: Guiffrè editore, 1993).

——*L'appello nella legislazione del tardo impero*, *AARC*, *Materiali per una palingenesi delle costituzioni tardo-imperiali*, serie terza 2 (Milan: Guiffré, 2000).

Perry, S. G. F., *The Second Synod of Ephesus* (Dartford: Orient Press, 1881).

Petit, P., *Les Étudiants de Libanius* (Paris: CNRS, 1957).

——*Les Fonctionnaires dans l'œuvre de Libanius: Analyse prosopographique* (Paris: Centre de recherches d'histoire ancienne, 1994).

Pickman, E. M., *The Mind of Latin Christendom*, i. *375–496* (Oxford: Clarendon Press, 1937).

Pierantoni, A., *Gli avvocati di Roma antica* (Bologna: N. Zanichelli, 1900).

Pietri, C., 'L'Hérésie et l'hérétique selon l'église romaine (ive–vie s.)', *XIII Incontro di studiosi dell'antichità cristiana: Eresia ed eresiologia nella chiesa antica*, *Augustinianum*, 25 (1985), 867–87.

——*Roma Christiana: Recherches sur l'Église de Rome, son organization, sa politique, son idéologie de Miltiade à Sixte III (311–440)* (Rome: Bibliothèque des Écoles Françaises d'Athènes et de Rome, 1976).

Pietrini, S., *Religio e Ius Romanum nell'epistolario di Leone Magno* (Milan: A. Guiffrè, 2002).

——*Sull' Iniziativa del processo criminale romano (IV–V secolo)* (Milan: A. Guiffrè, 1996).

Piras, M., and Piras, F., *Les Écoles de droit dans l'Occident postclassique et dans la Gaule romaine* (Caen: Impr. Ozanne, 1971).

Potter, D., *Prophets and Emperors: Human and Divine Authority from Augustus to Theodosius* (Cambridge, Mass.: Harvard University Press, 1994).

Price, R., and Gaddis, M. (ed. and tr.), *The Acts of the Council of Chalcedon* (Liverpool: Liverpool University Press, 2005).

Puglisi, G., 'Giustizia criminale e persecuzioni antiereticche (Priscilliano e Ursino, Ambrogio e Damaso)', *Siculorum Gymnasium*, 43 (1990), 91–137.

Pulitanò, F., *Ricerche sulla 'bonorum possessio ab intestato' nell'età tardo-romana*, (Turin: Giappichelli, 1999).

Purpura, G., 'Dalle raccolte di precedenti alle prime codificazioni postclassiche: Alcune testimonianze papiracee', *Ann. Sem. Giur. Univ. Palermo*, 42 (1992), 675–93.

Rankin, D. I., 'Was Tertullian a Jurist?', *Studia Patristica*, 31 (1997), 335–42.

Rapp, C., *Holy Bishops in Late Antiquity: The Nature of Christian Leadership in an Age of Transition* (Berkeley, Los Angeles: University of California Press, 2005).

Rauschen, G., *Eucharistie und Bußsakrament in den ersten sechs Jahrhunderten der Kirche* (Freiburg, Germany: Herder, 1908).

Rheinfelder, H., *Kultsprache und Profansprache in den romanischen Ländern* (Florence: Genf, 1933).

Riccobono, S. 'Fasi e fattori dell'evoluzione del diritto romano' *Mélanges de droit Romain dédiés George Cornil*, ii (Vanderpoorten, Gand, and Paris: Sirey, 1926), 238–381.

——'Il valore delle collezioni giuridiche bizantine per lo studio critico del *Corpus Iuris Civilis*', *Mélanges Fitting*, ii (Montpellier: L'Imprimerie General du Midi, 1908), 460–75.

——'La prassi nel periodo post-classico', *Atti del Congresso internazionale di diritto romano*, 1 (1934), 317–50.

Riché, P., *Education and Culture in the Barbarian West, Sixth through Eighth Centuries*, tr. J. J. Contreni (Columbia, SC: University of South Carolina Press, 1976).

Rives, J. B., 'Magic in Roman Law: The Reconstruction of a Crime', *Classical Antiquity*, 22 (2003), 313–39.

Roberti, M., 'Contributo allo studio delle relazioni fra diritto romano e patristica tratto dall'esame delle fonti Agostiniane', *Rivista di filosofia neoscolastica*, supplemento speciale al vol. 23 (1931), 305–66.

Robinson, O., *The Sources of Roman Law: Problems and Methods for Ancient Historians* (London: Routledge, 1997).

Rotondi, G., *Scritti Giuridici*, i (Milan: Ulrico Hoepli, 1922).

Rouché, C., 'The Functions of the Governor in Late Antiquity: Some Observations', *Antiquité Tardive*, 6 (1998), 31–6.

Rougé, J., 'La Législation de Théodose contre les hérétiques: Traduction de *CTh.* XVI.5.6–24', in J. Fontaine and C. Kannengiesser (eds.), *Épektasis: Mélanges patristiques offerts au Cardinal Jean Daniélou* (Paris: Beauchesne, 1972), 635–49.

Rubenson, S., 'Philosophy and Simplicity: The Problem of Classical Education in Early Christian Biography', in T. Hägg and P. Rousseau, *Greek Biography and Panegyric in Late Antiquity* (Berkeley, Los Angeles, and London: University of California Press, 2000), 110–39.

Russell, D. A., 'The Panegyrists and their Teachers', in M. Whitby (ed.), *The Propaganda of Power: The Role of Panegyric in Late Antiquity* (Leiden: Brill, 1998), 18–49.

Sabbah, G. (ed.), *Ammianus Marcellinus* (Paris: Budé, 1999).

Sampley, P., ' "Before God I do Not Lie" (*Gal.* 1. 20): Paul's Self-Defence in the Light of Roman Legal Praxis', *NTS* NS 23 (1977), 477–82.

Sarat, A., Constable, M., Engel, D., Hans, V., and Lawrence, S. (eds.), *Crossing Boundaries: Traditions and Transformations in Law and Society Research* (Evanston, Ill.: Northwestern University Press, 1998).

Schamp, J., 'Sophistes à l'ambon: Esquisses pour la Troisième Sophistique comme paysage littéraire', in E. Amato, A. Roduit, and M. Steinrück (eds.), *Approches de la troisième sophistique: Hommages à Jacques Schamp* (Brussels: Latomus 296, 2006) 286–338.

Schlange-Schöningen, H., *Kaisertum und Bildungswesen im spätantiken Konstantinopel* (Stuttgart: F. Steiner, 1995).

Schlossmann, H., 'Tertullian im Lichte der Jurisprudenz', *ZSS, Kan. Abt.* 27 (1906), 251–75 and 407–30.

Schmelz, G., *Kirchliche Amtsträger im spätantiken Aëgypten nach den Aussagen der griechischen und koptischen Papyri und Ostraka*, Archiv für Papyrusforschung und verwandte Gebiete, 13 (Munich and Leipzig: K. G. Saur, 2002).

Schöllgen, G., *Die Anfänge der Professionalisierung des Klerus und das Kirchliche Amt in der Syrischen Didaskalie* (Münster Westfalen: Aschendorffsche Verlagsbuchhandling, 1998).

Schulz, F., *History of Roman Legal Science*, 2nd corrected edn. (Oxford: Oxford Clarendon Press, 1953).

Schwartz, S., *Imperialism and Jewish Society* (Princeton: Princeton University Press, 2001).

Scopello, M., 'Hégémonius, les Acta Archelai et l'histoire de la controverse anti-Manichéene', in R. E. Emmerick, W. Sundermann, and P. Zieme, *Studia Manichaica, IV Internationaler Kongreß zum Manichäismus, Berlin, 14–18. Juli 1997* (Berlin: Akademie Verlag, 2000), 528–45.

Selb, W., 'Episcopalis audientia von der Zeit Konstantins bis zur Novelle XXXV Valentinians III', *ZSS, Rom. Abt.* 84 (1967), 162–217.

—— and Kaufhold, H., *Das syrisch-römische Rechtsbuch* (Vienna: Verlag der österreichischen Akademie der Wissenschaften, 2002).

Sellert, W. (ed.), *Das Gesetz in Spätantike und frühem Mittelalter* (Göttingen, Abhandlungen der Academie der Wissenschaften, 1992).

Sergène, A. 'Tertullien "de praescriptione hereticorum" XXXVII, 4 et la "longi temporis praescriptio" ', in *Études offertes à Jean Macqueron* (Aix-en-Provence: University of Aix-en-Provence, 1970), 605–12.

Shaw, B., 'African Christianity: Disputes, Definitions, and "Donatists" ', in M. R. Greenshields and T. A. Robinson (eds.), *Orthodoxy and Heresy in Religious Movements: Discipline and Dissent* (Lewiston: Edwin Mellen Press, 1992), 4–34.

—— 'Judicial Nightmares and Christian Memory', *Journal of Early Christian Studies*, 11/4 (2003), 533–63.

—— 'Who were the Circumcellions?', in A. H. Merrills (ed.), *Vandals, Romans and Berbers: New Perspectives on Late Antique Africa* (London: Variorum, 2004), 227–58.

Shaw, T. M., 'Ascetic Practice and the Genealogy of Heresy: Problems in Modern Scholarship and Ancient Textual Representation', in D. B. Martin and P. Cox Miller (eds.), *The Cultural Turn in Late Ancient Studies: Gender, Asceticism, and Historiography* (Durham, NC: Duke University Press, 2005), 213–36.

Sherwin-White, A. N., *Roman Society and Roman Law in the New Testament* (Oxford: Clarendon Press, 1963).

Sider, R. D., *Ancient Rhetoric and the Art of Tertullian* (Oxford: Oxford University Press, 1972).

Simon, D., 'Aus dem Kodexunterricht des Thalelaios, B. Die Heroen', *ZSS, Rom. Abt.* 87 (1970), 315–94.

—— 'Marginalien zur Vulgarismusdiskussion', in O. Behrends, M. Dießelhorst, H. Lange, D. Liebs, J. G. Wolf, and C. Wollschläger (eds.), *Festschrift für Franz Wieacker zum 70. Geburtstag* (Gottingen: Vandenhoeck & Ruprecht, 1978), 154–74.

Simon, D. V., *Konstantinisches Kaiserrecht: Studien anhand der Reskriptenpraxis und der Schenkungsrecht* (Frankfurt/Main: Forschungen zur Byzantinische Rechtsgeschichte 2, 1977).

Sirks, A. J. B., 'Late Roman Law: The Case of *Dotis Nomen* and the *Praedia Pistoria*', *ZSS, Rom. Abt.* 108 (1991), 187–212.

—— 'Instruction in Late Antiquity, the Law and Theology', *AARC* 15 (2005), 493–513.

Sivan, H., *Ausonius of Bordeaux: Genesis of a Gallic Aristocracy* (London and New York: Routledge, 1993).

Skard, E., 'Eine Bemerkung über spätrömisches Strafrecht in einer Homilie des "Sophisten" Asterios', *Symbolae Osloenses*, 25 (1947), 80–2.

Smith, R., *Julian's Gods: Religion and Philosophy in the Thought and Action of Julian the Apostate* (London and New York: Routledge, 1995).

Stein, P., 'Roman Law', in J. H. Burns (ed.), *The Cambridge History of Medieval Political Thought c.350–c.1450* (Cambridge: Cambridge University Press, 1988), 37–47.

____'The Medieval Rediscovery of the Roman Civil Law', in D. L. Carey Miller and R. Zimmermann (eds.), *The Civilian Tradition and Scots Law: Aberdeen Quincentenary Essays* (Berlin: Ducker & Humblot, 1997), 75–86.

Steinwenter, A., 'Der antike kirchliche Rechtsgang und seine Quellen', *ZRG, Kan. Abt.* 54 (1934), 1–116.

____'Der Einfluss des römischen Rechts auf den antiken Kanonischen Prozess', *Atti del congresso internazionale di diritto romano, Roma,* 1 (1934), 227–41.

____'Die Briefe des Q. Aurelius Symmachus als Rechtsquellen', *ZSS, Rom. Abt.* 74 (1957), 1–25.

____'Die Rechtsstellung der Kirchen und Klöster nach den Papyri', *ZSS, Kan. Abt.* 19 (1930), 1–50.

____'Rhetorik und römische Zivilprozess', *ZSS, Rom. Abt.* 64 (1947), 69–120.

Stirnimann, J. K., *Die praescriptio Tertullians im Lichte des römisches Rechtes und der Theologie* (Freiburg, Switzerland: Paulusverlag, 1949).

Stroux, J., *Summum ius summa iniuria: Ein Kapitel aus der Geschichte der 'Interpretatio Iuris'* (Freiburg: Himmelschein Symb. Friburgenses, 1926).

Studer, B., *La riflessione teologica nella chiesa imperiale (sec. iv e v)*, Sussidi Patristici dello Istituto Patristico Augustinianum, 4 (Rome: Istituto Patristico Augustinianum, 1989).

Taubenschlag, R., *The Law of Greco-Roman Egypt in the Light of the Papyri 322BC–640AD* (New York: Herald Square Press, 1944).

Teitler, H. C., *Notarii and Exceptores: An Inquiry into the Role and Significance of Shorthand Writers in the Imperial and Ecclesiastical Bureaucracy of the Roman Empire. From the Early Principate to c. 450 A.D.* (Amsterdam: J. C. Gieben, 1985).

Tellegen-Couperus, O. E., 'The Role of the Judge in the Formulary Procedure', *Journal of Legal History*, 22/2 (2001), 1–13.

Teubner, G., 'How the Law Thinks: Toward a Constructivist Epistemology of Law', *Law and Society Review*, 23 (1989), 727–57.

Todd, S. C., 'The Language of Law in Classical Athens', in P. Coss (ed.), *The Moral World of the Law* (Cambridge: Cambridge University Press, 2000), 17–36.

Tomulescu, C. S., 'Les Avocats dans l'édit du Maximum', *AARC* 2 (1976), 293–8.

Toscano, S., 'Casi di ordinaria giustizia nelle epistole Divjak di Agostino', *AARC* 11 (1996), 541–63.

Travers, M., *Les Corporations d'avocats sous l'empire romain* (Paris: Thèse, 1894).

Turpin, W., 'Formula, *Cognitio*, and Proceedings *Extra Ordinem*', *RIDA* 46 (1999), 499–574.

—— 'The Law-Codes and Late Roman Law', *Revue Internationale des droits de l'antiquité*, 3rd ser., 32 (1985), 339–53.

Tuzlak, A., 'The Magician and the Heretic: The Case of Simon Magus', in P. Mirecki and M. Meyer (eds.), *Magic and Ritual in the Ancient World* (Leiden: Brill, 2002), 416–26.

Ullmann, W., *A History of Political Thought: The Middle Ages* (London: Penguin, 1965).

—— *Gelasius I (492–496): Das Papsttum an der Wende der Spätantike zum Mittelalter* (Stuttgart: A. Hiersemann, 1981).

Urbainczyk, T., *Socrates of Constantinople, Historian of Church and State* (Ann Arbor: University of Michigan Press, 1997).

Vaggione, R. P., *Eunomius of Cyzicus and the Nicene Revolution* (Oxford: Oxford University Press, 2000).

Valentino, M., 'Il precedente giudiziale: esigenza di certezza e problema sistematico', *Labeo*, 44/2 (1998), 292–7.

van Oort, J., 'Mani and Manichaeism in Augustine's *De haeresibus*: An Analysis of *haer.* 46, 1', in R. E. Emmerick, W. Sundermann, and P. Zieme, *Studia Manichaica, IV Internationaler Kongreß zum Manichäismus, Berlin, 14–18. Juli 1997* (Berlin: Akademie Verlag, 2000), 451–63.

Velázquez Soriano, I., *Documentos de época visigoda escritos en pizarra (siglos VI–VIII)*, 2 vols. (Turnhout: Monumenta Palaeographica Medii Aevi series hispanica, 2000).

Vera, D., *Commento Storico alle Relationes di Quinto Aurelio Simmaco* (Pisa: Giardini editori, 1984).

Vessey, M., 'The Forging of Orthodoxy in Latin Christian Literature: A Case Study', *Journal of Early Christian Studies*, 4 (1996), 495–513.

—— 'The Origins of the Collectio Sirmondiana: A New Look at the Evidence', in J. Harries and M. Wood, *The Theodosian Code* (London: Duckworth, 1993), 178–99.

—— and Pollmann, K. (eds.), *Augustine and the Disciplines: From Cassiciacum to Confessions* (Oxford: Oxford University Press, 2005).

Veyne, P., 'Clientèle et corruption au service de l'état: La Vénalité des offices dans le Bas-Empire romain', *Annales (ESC)*, 36 (1981), 339–60.

Vincenti, U., *Il valore dei precedenti giudiziali nella compilazione giustinianea*, 2nd edn. (Padua: Cedam, 1995).

Vinzent, M., *Die theologischen Fragmente, Asterius von Kappadokien; Einleitung, kritischer Text* (Leiden: Brill, 1993).

Violardo, G., *Il pensiero giuridico di San Girolamo* (Milan: Società Editrice 'Vita e pensiero', 1937).

Vismara, G., *La giurisdizione civile dei vescovi* (Milan: A. Guiffré, 1995).
Vitton, I., *Concetti giuridici nelle opere di Tertulliano* (Rome: L'Erma di Bretschneider, 1924 reissued 1972).
Volterra, E., 'Appunti intorno all'intervento del vescovo nei processi contro gli eretici', *BIDR* 42 (1934), 453–68.
—— 'Appunti sulle scuole postclassiche occidentali', *Annali di Storia del Diritto*, 1 (1957), 51–65.
—— 'Collatio Legum Mosaicarum et Romanarum', *Memorie della classe di scienze morali, storiche e filologiche, Accademia Nazionale dei Lincei*, 6th ser. 3 (1930), 3–123.
Volterra, E., 'Considerazioni teologico-giuridiche di Asterio di Amasea', *Rivista italiana per le scienze giuridiche*, NS 4 (1929), 3–10.
—— 'La costituzione di Diocleziano e Massimiano contro I Manichei', in *Atti del Convegno sul Tema: La Persia e il mondo Greco-Romano (Roma 11–14 Aprile 1965)* (Rome: Accademia Nazionale dei Lincei, 1966), 27–55.
—— 'Le sette constituzioni di Valentiniano e Valente contenute nella *Consultatio Cuiusdam Veteris Iurisconsulti*', *BIDR* 85 (1982), 171–204.
—— 'Sul contenuto del Codice Teodosiano', *BIDR* 84 (1981), 85–124.
Von Schwind, F., *Zur Frage der Publikation im römischen Recht: Mit Ausblicken in das altgriechische und ptolemäische Rechtsgebiet* (Munich: Beitr. zur Papyrusforsch. 31, 1940).
Voss, W. E., *Recht und Rhetorik in den Kaisergesetzen der Spätantike: Eine Untersuchung zum nachklassischen Kauf- und Übereignungsrecht* (Frankfurt/Main: Forschungen zur Byzantinischen Rechtsgeschichte 9, 1982).
Walker, J., *Rhetoric and Poetics in Antiquity* (Oxford: Oxford University Press, 2000).
Wallraff, M., *Der Kirchenhistoriker Sokrates: Untersuchungen zu Geschichtsdarstellung, Methode und Person* (Göttingen: Vandenhoeck & Ruprecht, 1997).
Ware, T., 'The Ascetic Writings of Mark the Hermit' (Oxford, D.Phil. thesis, 1965).
Watson, A., *The State, Law and Religion: Pagan Rome* (Athens, Ga.: University of Georgia Press, 1992).
Weltin, E. G., *Athens and Jerusalem: An Interpretative Essay on Christianity and Classical Culture* (Atlanta, Ga.: Scholar's Press, 1987).
Wenger, L., *Der heutige Stand der römischen Rechtwissenschaft* (Munich: Beck, 1927) [= Münch. Beitr], 105–20
Wessel, S., *Cyril of Alexandria and the Nestorian Controversy: The Making of a Saint and a Heretic* (New York and Oxford, Oxford University Press, 2004).
Wickham, C., 'Land Disputes and their Social Framework in Lombard–Carolingian Italy, 700–900', in W. Davies and P. Fouracre, *The*

Settlement of Disputes in Early Medieval Europe (Cambridge: Cambridge University Press, 1986), 105–24.
Wieacker, F., 'Die krisen des späten Imperiums: Bemerkungen zu einem historiographischen Modell', *AARC* 10 (1995), 33–9.
——*Recht und Gesellschaft in der Spätantike* (Stuttgart: Kohlhammer, 1964).
Wieling, H., 'Advokaten im spätantiken Rom', *AARC* 11 (1996), 419–63.
——'Rechtsstudium in der Spätantike', *Juristische Schulung*, 40/1 (2000), 10–15.
Wilcken, U., 'Zu den Kaiserreskripten', *Hermes*, 55 (1920), 1–42.
Wiles, M., *The Divine Apostle: The Interpretation of Paul's Epistles in the Early Church* (Cambridge: Cambridge University Press, 1967).
Wilkinson, J., *Jerusalem Pilgrims before the Crusades*, 2nd edn. (Warminster: Aris & Philips, 2002).
Williams, M., *Rethinking 'Gnosticism': An Argument for Dismantling a Dubious Category* (Princeton: Princeton University Press, 1996).
Williams, R., 'Does it Make Sense to Speak of Pre-Nicene Orthodoxy?', in R. Williams (ed.), *The Making of Orthodoxy: Essays in Honour of Henry Chadwick* (Cambridge: Cambridge University Press, 1989), 1–23.
Winroth, A., *The Making of Gratian's* Decretum (Cambridge: Cambridge University Press, 2000).
Winter, B. W. *Philo and Paul among the Sophists: Alexandrian and Corinthian Responses to a Julio-Claudian Movement*, 2nd edn. (Grand Rapids, Mich., and Cambridge: Eerdmans, 2002).
Winterbottom, M., 'Schoolroom and Courtroom', in B. Vickers (ed.), *Rhetoric Revalued* (New York: Center for Medieval and Early Renaissance Studies, 1982), 59–70.
Young, F., *Biblical Exegesis and the Formation of Christian Culture* (Cambridge: Cambridge University Press, 1989).
——'The Rhetorical Schools and their Influence on Patristic Exegesis', in R. Williams (ed.), *The Making of Orthodoxy: Essays in Honour of Henry Chadwick* (Cambridge: Cambridge University Press, 1989), 182–99.
——Ayres, L., and Louth, A. (eds.), *The Cambridge History of Early Christian Literature* (Cambridge: Cambridge University Press, 2004).
Zingale, L. M., 'Libri di dottrina romana e fonti papirologiche: Riflessioni in margine ad alcune recenti acquisizioni', *AARC* 15 (2005), 221–37.
Zuccotti, F., *'Furor Haereticorum': Studi sul trattamento giuridico della follia e sulla persecuzione della eterodossia religiosa nella legislazione del tardo impero romano* (Milan: Guiffrè, 1992).

Index

Index Locorum

Legal Sources

Literary Sources

The manufacturer's authorised representative in the EU for product safety is Oxford University Press España S.A. of el Parque Empresarial San Fernando de Henares, Avenida de Castilla, 2 – 28830 Madrid (www.oup.es/en or product.safety@oup.com). OUP España S.A. also acts as importer into Spain of products made by the manufacturer.

www.ingramcontent.com/pod-product-compliance
Ingram Content Group UK Ltd.
Pitfield, Milton Keynes, MK11 3LW, UK
UKHW041144170926
475595UK00029B/1

9780198208419